The Oxford Anthology of the
Modern Indian City

The Oxford Anthology of the
Modern Indian City

The City in its Plenitude

Edited, Compiled, and Introduced by
VINAY LAL

OXFORD
UNIVERSITY PRESS

OXFORD
UNIVERSITY PRESS

Oxford University Press is a department of the University of Oxford.
It furthers the University's objective of excellence in research, scholarship,
and education by publishing worldwide. Oxford is a registered trademark of
Oxford University Press in the UK and in certain other countries

Published in India by
Oxford University Press
22 Workspace, 2nd Floor, 1/22 Asaf Ali Road, New Delhi 110002

© Oxford University Press 2013

The moral rights of the authors have been asserted

First Edition published in 2013
Third impression 2025

ISBN-13: 978-0-19-809180-6
ISBN-10: 0-19-809180-X

Typeset in Centaur MT Std 11/13.4
by The Graphics Solution, New Delhi 110 092
Printed in India at Manipal Technologies Limited

Contents

Contents

The City in Colonial India

Spaces, Sights, Surroundings:
Architecture of the City and Its Streets

Preface and Acknowledgements

The idea for this anthology, initially conceived as a single volume work, was first broached to me by Oxford University Press some 7–8 years ago, just around the time when I was contemplating the possibility of designing a seminar at the University of California, Los Angeles (UCLA), where I have been teaching since 1993, on the city in India since about 1800. After several decades of work on urbanization and the changing demography of India, the scholarship on the Indian city was beginning to exhibit a new turn. My introduction to this two-volume anthology points to some of the questions that were beginning to emerge from a new-found intellectual interest in the city that now seemed informed by strands of scholarship ranging from postmodernism and postcolonial theory to psychoanalysis and what was termed self-reflexive ethnography. Disciplines such as film studies, which barely existed in India, and still have comparatively few scholarly practitioners, had just come to the fore and the nexus of cinema and the city, which for India seemed to be captured by Bombay, at once presented itself as a subject of inquiry to cinema studies scholars, sociologists, historians, and cultural critics at large. The city had always been a site of glaring inequality, but the immense wealth that began to be generated as a consequence of the neo-liberalization policies that had been so readily embraced by the elites sharpened the divide between the haves and have-nots even further. Today's Mumbai is simultaneously the home, as the cliché goes, of what is doubtless the most expensive private residence in the world and most likely the world's largest 'slum' population as well. To that question which seemingly insurrectionary historians have been asking, 'to whom does the nation belong', has been added another query, 'to whom does the city belong?'

Numerous factors thus conspired to bring about this anthology. It is around this time, too, that publishers in India began to express an interest in Indian cities, even if the route taken was predictable. Over the last decade, Penguin, by way of illustration, has collected together contemporary writings on Indian cities in nearly ten volumes. The accent in each volume is not only on memoirs, travellers' narratives, essays, and public commentary; it is also on Mumbai, Delhi, Lucknow, or whatever city the volume revolves around, rather than on those conceptual ideas or themes which make the city in modern India available to us from comparatively different perspectives. To all of this, however, I would add a personal touch as well. My own interest in the city stems, in part, from my experiences wandering around the world since my early childhood, and prolonged stays in many of the largest cities in the world, including Delhi, Tokyo, Jakarta, London, Chicago, New York, and Los Angeles. Size alone does not make for a city, and, yet, it matters—as became all too apparent to me in the late 1970s, when I commenced my undergraduate studies at Johns Hopkins. I had never lived in a city as small as Baltimore; my instinct remained throughout to flee it, and it was the first winter vacation of my freshman year that took me to New York; and I have since always moved between large cities, dividing my time in recent years between Los Angeles and Delhi.

Both of these monstrously large urban clusters are, some would argue, just that—not cities. Many of those who have strong attachments to city life say that it is difficult to be at home in either Delhi or Los Angeles. Though we know the numerous ways in which one might feel at home, my peripatetic existence has perhaps made me receptive to the insights of the twelfth-century monk, Hugh of St. Victor: 'The man who finds his homeland sweet is still a tender beginner; he to whom every soil is as his native one is already strong; but he is perfect to whom the entire world is a foreign land. The tender soul has fixed his love on one spot in the world; the strong man has extended his love to all places; the perfect man has extinguished his.' Among some city enthusiasts, it is common to speak of 'loved' and 'unloved' cities: if in India Bombay and Calcutta have always been placed in the former category, each staunchly defended by its denizens and fondly remembered by those who have had the misfortune of being displaced to another habitation, Delhi is often roundly abused as a city of babus and Jats, ruffians and Punjabis, *junglee* in its disposition and mercilessly hostile to women, a den of uncouth politicians and civil servants who, in emulation of the political regimes that over a millennium have governed from Delhi, have continued the

practice of feeding the centre by milking dry the provinces. Many have
wondered how what was in effect a large town, before partition brought
refugees streaming into Delhi, has mushroomed into one of the world's
largest metropolises, and some question, as I have suggested, whether
Delhi can ever exude the feelings that apparently real cities generate. For
quite different reasons, my other home, Los Angeles, is not reckoned to
be a city—certainly not in the manner of New York, Chicago, or San
Francisco. Arriving here nearly twenty years ago, it struck me that the city
was built for automobiles; humans strutted along in due course, almost
accidentally. For many serious readers of a certain political disposition,
Mike Davis's *City of Quartz* (1990) remains the indispensable reading on
Los Angeles; but it was the British architect Reynar Banham who offered,
in *Los Angeles: The Architecture of Four Ecologies* (1971), what still remains the
most scintillating characterization of Los Angeles, about which Banham
said that it 'makes nonsense of history and breaks all the rules'. Banham
did not count himself among those who regarded it as an 'unspeakable
sprawling mess'; rather, it was perhaps the only place where the ocean,
the desert, and the mountains met (and collided) with each other—and
with the freeways.

Living in Delhi and Los Angeles, then, has kept alive for me the
question of what makes for a city, though I could not say that I might
have been guided by different considerations in choosing the selections
for this anthology had my experience in recent years been shaped by
prolonged stays in other cities. The lay of the land is delineated in the
introduction, and for the present I have the pleasant task of acknowledging
the obligations that I have incurred in the execution of this enterprise.
There are far too many friends, acquaintances, scholars, writers, and artists,
among them some whose work appears in the pages of this anthology,
who have helped in one manner or the other. Many authors were gracious
in allowing me to publish or reprint their pieces, and others responded
to my call to offer fresh pieces or translations; and yet others prevailed
upon their publishers to waive or reduce copyright fees. There are some
friends who sent tips about readings, others who shared their photography
or artwork. Many people have been generous with their enthusiasm and
support, and I thank each and every one—with apologies to those who
have inadvertently been left out: A.R. Venkatachalpathy, Aditya Nigam,
Ákos Östör, Aloke Roy Chowdhury, Amar Farooqui, Amaresh Misra,
Amitav Ghosh, Amitava Kumar, Ananthamurthy, Anju Relan, Antara Dev
Sen, Anubhav Nath, Ashis Nandy, Chandrakanta, Christopher Pinney,
Clinton Seely, Diana L. Eck, Esha De, Garga Chatterjee, Gautam Bhatia,

Girish Karnad, Jai Sen, James Manor, Jeremy Seabrook, Kathryn Hansen, Lina Fruzzetti, M.J. Akbar, M.V. Ramana, Mangalesh Dabral, Manisha Chaudhary, Manoj Mitta, Martha Ann Selby, Mary Fox, Meena Menon, N. Manu Chakravarthy, Naveen Kishore, Neera Adarkar, Pritish Nandy, Priyanka Nandy, Ram Rahman, Ranjit Lal, Ratnakar Tripathy, Ruchir Joshi, Rukun Advani, Scarlett R. Huffman, Shankar Ramaswami, Shiv Visvanathan, Shivaprakash, Suketu Mehta, Sunil Gangopadhyay, Swarup Roy, Tanya Luhrmann, Thomas Blom Hansen, Timeri N. Murari, Urvashi Butalia, V. Sriram, Vicky Roy, Vivek Shanbhag, William Radice, and Ziauddin Sardar. I recall, with gratitude, wonderful visits, in the company of my friend Ashwani Kumar, with Gieve Patel and Sudhir Patwardhan. And, finally, my thanks to Nitasha Devasar (who did not stay long enough at Oxford University Press to see the anthology through publication) and Mitadru Basu, whose patience must have been sorely tested.

Los Angeles   VINAY LAL
June 2012

Preface and Acknowledgements

Introduction

Modern India and the Claims of the City

The city in India is everywhere. It hogs the limelight, dominates our imagination, and occupies centrespace in the narrative of a nation that, some believe, is once again coming into its own after a long interlude of colonial rule and economic stagnation. If Bollywood is the index to our dreams, then the oft-encountered observation that the village has almost entirely disappeared from the narrative of the popular Hindi film might portend something truly significant. Rural India is of little interest to middle class Indians, and generally finds its way into the pages of the English dailies as the source of unwelcome news—as the supposed site of the country's worst superstitions, repressive social customs, and norms of lifestyle that seem unimaginably distant, even if many in the city still have memories of the village. The hinterland is where farmers consume pesticide and commit suicide, or where something called the khap panchayat seems intent on defaming India's image by unaccountably obstructing, to the point of violent death, the young from choosing their life partners. The city dwellers barely recognize, and would be loathe to admit, that many of the worst social ills that afflict the country—the abortion of female foetuses and the phenomenon that goes by the name of bride-burning— are predominantly of urban origin: these are much too easily passed off as problems encountered among illiterate villagers. When the driver, cook, sweeping lady, 'the domestic help' in short, suddenly insists on returning home to the village, often on a promised trip of a week that is bound to turn into a stay of a month or longer, the middle class Indian is once again brought to the painful awareness of the village's simultaneous proximity to and distance from the city. That is the village, a gross reminder of everything that urban India is leaving behind in its quest to leapfrog decades, if not centuries, and become modern.

For the first time since 1921, the growth in India's urban population has outpaced the increase in the numbers in the rural countryside: judging from the Census of 2011, 91 million Indians became part of the country's urban population over the course of a decade and 90.6 million people were added to the rural population in that same period of time.[1] 'India's urban population,' one journalist writes, 'grew from 290 million in 2001 to 340 million in 2008 and is expected to reach 590 million by 2030. The country's urbanisation is probably one of the biggest migration stories in the history of civilisation.'[2] The momentum of history at this juncture, an expert on urbanization has written, favours 'the Great Migration' and the rise of 'Homo urbanis'.[3] The evidence before the eyes is enough for those who, watching the colossal land grabbing that is sweeping India as nothing else, are inclined to a more radical reading than could possibly be furnished by any census. It is not only the metropolis that has been transformed in India, whether by gated communities, large apartment complexes, shopping malls, growing signs of inequality, or (as is true of Delhi) a metro, but also the very idea of the 'urban'. Commentators point to the enormous urban corridors that are cropping up throughout India: the idea of an uninterrupted urban belt between Pune and Mumbai, or between Delhi and Manesar, seems dwarfed by the notion of an urban corridor stretching from Mumbai to Delhi.[4] It has become nearly a cliché to argue that what empires were to the sixteenth century, or the nation-state to the 200 years preceding our time, the city will be to the history of the twenty-first century.

If the city in India is emerging as the site of great ferment, certainly agitating the minds of the country's novelists, filmmakers, entrepreneurs, and policy planners, it is well to recall that the city

---

[1] P. Sainath, 'Census findings point to decade of rural distress', *The Hindu* (26 September 2011), p. 1.

[2] C.P. Sunrendran, 'City Excentric', *The Times of India—Crest Edition* (9 April 2011), p. 6. The rate of urbanization in China has, if anything, been faster; the urban population nearly doubled in twenty years, from 1990 to 2010, to account for half of China's 1.35 billion people. If 590 million people are expected to populate India's cities by 2030, in China that figure would be 1 billion, equivalent to the expected population of Africa.

[3] Jeb Brugmann, *Welcome to the Urban Revolution: How Cities are Changing the World* (London: Bloomsbury; New Delhi: HarperCollins, 2010), pp. 53–4.

[4] See Arati R. Jerath, 'Paving Prosperity', *The Times of India—Crest Edition* (15 January 2011), p. 1.

in India is as old as Indian civilization. This comes as a surprise to those unacquainted with Indian history, or who have otherwise been fed on the idea, which has only diminished in recent years as the city of the Indian novel in English, of Bollywood films, and of high-tech aspirations—captured, for example, by the rise of companies such as Infosys and Wipro, or the designation of a considerable segment of the city of Hyderabad as Cyberabad, 'Cyber City'—has come to the fore, that India has from the outset been a predominantly agricultural civilization. Bombay, Calcutta, and Madras would shed their humble origins as little villages to become the great cities of colonial India, but ironically it is under British colonial rule that India would become marked as a pre-eminently rural country. Who would think, for example, that Agra and even Fatehpur Sikri might each have been, if the English merchant Ralph Fitch who visited these cities is to be believed, 'much greater than London and very populous' in 1585, or that only two decades later, in the early years of the reign of Jahangir, by which time the culture of Persian was well established in Indian administration and intellectual life, Agra with about half a million people had grown to twice the size of Isfahan.[5]

The city developed in India before the advent of the Mughals, indeed well before the advent of all the migrants, including the Aryans whose arrival in India is often thought to have given India some of its most characteristic features, who have helped populate the Indian landscape. Great cities have flourished along the banks of rivers, and Istanbul, Cairo, London, Paris, Benares, Bangkok, Budapest, and Moscow swiftly stream to mind. It may be said of Benares that it fills the word 'antiquity' with meaning, and Mark Twain, who visited the city in 1897, appears

[5] J.C. Locke, *The First Englishmen in India: Letters and Narratives of Sundry Elizabethans* (London: G. Routledge and Sons, 1930); J. Horton Ryley, *Ralph Fitch, England's Pioneer to India and Burma; His Companions and Contemporaries, with His Remarkable Narrative Told in His Own Words* (London: T. Fisher Unwin, 1899), pp. 96–7. In Fitch's words, 'Agra is a very great citie and populous, built with stone, having faire and large streetes, with a fair river running by it'; as for Fatehpur, 'the towne is greater than Agra, but the houses and streetes be not so faire.' Fitch found credible the report that the Mughal Emperor maintained 1,000 elephants, 30,000 horses, and 800 concubines. Today's 'urban corridor' almost appears to be anticipated in Fitch's narrative; thus, though Fitch reported the distance between Agra and Fatehpur as 12 miles, he found the entire way to be 'a market of victuals & other things, as full as though a man were still in towne, and so many people as if a man were in a market.'

to have captured the sentiments of many when he wrote that 'Benares is older than history, older than tradition, older even than legend, and looks twice as old as all of them put together.'[6] The colonial writer E.B. Havell, whose name is inextricably linked with the study of Hindu art and architecture, found it not an unreasonable conjecture 'that even before the Aryan tribes established themselves in the Ganges valley, Benares may have been a great centre of primitive sun-worship'. The Brahmins who had invested the city with 'special sanctity' were only following a 'tradition of those primeval days, borrowed, with so many of their rites and symbols, from their Turanian predecessors.'[7]

It is likely that had Mark Twain travelled to India three decades later, after the commencement of the excavations at Harappa and Mohenjo-daro that would lead to a radical change in the understanding of the Indian past, he would still have found nothing to dispute the view of Benares as the oldest continuously inhabited city in India. And, yet, as is commonly known, however prevalent the preposterous conceit about India as an essentially Aryan civilization, the known history of India commences with the Indus Valley people and their indigenous evolution from around the seventh millennium BCE.[8] The Mature Harappan civilization in 2500 BCE was essentially urban in character, and the cities that developed around the Indus show, as the work of archaeologists and historians of ancient India unambiguously suggests, remarkable signs of civic design, town planning, and some form of an administrative system. Harappa and Mohenjo-daro were 'rigorously planned in regular rectangular blocks, each measuring about 400 by 200 yards, divided from one another by broad main streets, and containing methodically drained lanes and buildings'.[9] Anyone familiar with modern Indian cities and towns, with their ramshackle structures and open sewers, or with the ease with which they flood during the monsoon season, might marvel at the

---

[6] Mark Twain, *Following the Equator: A Journey Around the World* (Hartford, Conn: American Publishing Co., 1898), Ch. 50.

[7] E.B. Havell, *Benares, The Sacred City: Sketches of Hindu Life and Religion* (London: Blackie & Son, 1905; reprint ed., Varanasi: Vishwa Vidyalaya Prakashan, 1990), p. 2.

[8] Hermann Kulke and Dietmar Rothermund, *A History of India*, 3rd ed. (London: Routledge, 1998), pp. 16–17; Romila Thapar, *Early India from the Origins to AD 1300* (London: Allen Lane, 2002; Berkeley: University of California Press, 2004), pp. 77–88.

[9] Sir Mortimer Wheeler, *Early India and Pakistan to Ashoka* (New York: Frederick A. Praeger, 1959), p. 97.

resourcefulness of the ancients and wonder why we seemingly have not been able to improve greatly upon the sewage technology of the Indus Valley people. Jawaharlal Nehru, writing in the 1930s, had perhaps an analogous thought in mind when he wondered if ancient Pataliputra, with its palaces and urbanity, could be the forerunner of Patna.[10] Nehru had the advantage, at least, of writing at a time when Bihar had staked a claim as one of the epicentres of the nationalist movement, though he would have witnessed in his lifetime much to suggest how what was once the city of empire had gradually diminished to become a provincial capital for low-country politicians.

Even as the idea of the city in India has a venerable past, there is much to suggest that it constitutes a wholly new terrain of experience for the vast majority of Indians. This is notwithstanding the fact that, the cities of the Indus Valley and of Mughal north India aside, there is much else that hearkens to the prominent place of cities in the centuries that went into the making of India. Madurai, as an illustration, has a recorded past extending to over two millennia. The city was visited by Megasthenes in the third century BCE and subsequently finds mention in Kautilya's *Arthasastra*. It is in the Pandyan capital of Madurai, as described in Adigal's second century CE epic the *Silappadikaram*, that Kannagi and her husband Kovalan seek to repair their lives, and it is the same city that Kannagi's curse condemns to be reduced to ashes when the King's guards unjustly behead Kovalan on the false charge of theft. Madurai retained its importance as an administrative and cultural centre through long periods of Pandya and Chola rule, and the city's famous Meenakshi Amman Temple, which appears to date back to at least the seventh century CE though the present structures were built by Madurai's Nayak kings in the sixteenth and seventeeth centuries, has long attracted visitors and pilgrims. Not all precolonial Indian cities have been so well served, comparatively speaking, by literary references, historical records, architectural aretefacts, or archaeological remains; many others, such as Kanuaj, which once served as the capital of Harshvardhana, and then gave its name to the contest for supremacy (dubbed as 'the Kanauj Triangle') that raged between the eighth and tenth centuries among three formidable regional powers—Gurjara-Pratiharas, Palas, and Rashtrakutas—are now pale shadows of their former selves.[11]

---

[10] Jawaharlal Nehru, *Discovery of India* (Calcutta: The Signet Press, 1946; new ed., Delhi: Oxford University Press, 1989), p. 34.

[11] The contest between these three powers, Romila Thapar has written, 'focused on capturing the city of Kanauj' (*Early India*, p. 406). See also John Keay, *India: A History* (New York: Grove Press, 2000), pp. 192–200.

Introduction

The city was, then, everywhere in India; and, yet, there is no gainsaying the fact that the city remains an unknown terrain for the majority of Indians. The city was always in close proximity to the village, feeding off the produce of the land and the labour of its workers, but the peasant could no more enter into the imagination of the city than he could fathom the riches of the palace. In the Raj Kapoor classic, *Shri 420*, the tramp's introduction to the city, and subsequently, even when he is more seasoned, to the world of the gambling den and the nightclub, leaves him bewildered. Indeed, the annals of Indian literature and cinema are rich in testimonies of what might be described as the 'first gaze' of the city. The peasant Shambu (Balraj Sahni), newly arrived in Calcutta from his natal village in a desperate attempt to make a quick pot of money that would enable him to forestall the forfeiture of his land to the avaricious moneylender, appears overwhelmed: cars speed by, people move around without greeting each other, trams criss-cross the streets, and all this under the immense bulk of the Howrah Bridge.[12] The double-decker bus moving before his eyes appears to Shambu as a double-storied home. Before the night is over, Shambu and his son Kanhaiya have been stripped of their money and belongings by a common thief, and even the temptation to return to the comfort of the village cannot be entertained: that, too, is one of the more alarming features of the city, that it swallows up those who walk into its entrails. It is with similar wonder though less bewilderment that Ritwik Ghatak's young runaway Kanchan, seeking to flee the confines of the village and the oppressiveness of his father, confronts the din and dizzying pace of the big city—here again captured, not accidentally, through images of Howrah Bridge.[13] Roads, trains, bridges: the city augurs mobility, the possibility of transcending the limits that the village appears to impose equally on one's imagination and movements. Thus, in *Pather Panchali*, both the novel and the film by the same name, the city is, unknown to the viewer, looming on the horizon. Apu and his sister Durga, from their village of Nischindpur, a few kilometres from the railway tracks, hear the train's whistle in the stillness of the night and determine to catch sight of the train—a train that, in time, will take Apu to the city of Benares when he is ten years old, and some years later to Calcutta.

[12] The reference here is to Bimal Roy's 1953 Hindi film, *Do Bigha Zameen* ('Two Acres of Land').
[13] I have drawn on Ritwik Ghatak's acclaimed 1959 Bengali film, *Bari Theke Paliye* ('The Runaway').

The popular Hindi film, whatever the hazards of reading it as a reflection of the country's social realities, has been supreme in its representation of Bombay, the 'maximum city' in Suketu Mehta's memorable and now much imitated phrase,[14] as something which acts upon the new entrant into the city as a previously unencountered drug. A late-nineteenth-century colonial writer, alert to the fact that often nothing is as mesmerizing as the alleyways, byways, nooks, corners, and holes of a great city, sketched in dark tones the opium dens of Bombay; and yet he was unable to fathom that the city is itself the ultimate opiate.[15] The village is to day what the city is to night, one is tempted to say, but such a formulation is much too tidy. The village appears to live only by the day, but the city—or at least some of it—never sleeps; indeed, it has now become the self-imagination of every city to suppose that it (uniquely) never sleeps. There is, one would rather say, one city by the day, another by the night: the city at night has its own history, peculiar passions, and people to match.[16] Coming home on a suburban train in the very early morning hours before daybreak from an all-night concert of classical Indian music in 1983, I recall sharing the train with hundreds of milkmen carrying large canisters of fresh buffalo's milk for Bombaywallahs. I had barely been aware of their presence before this time. Much more than this happens at night: the criminal underworld comes to life, prostitutes work the street, the bars resonate with the clink of glasses and the clatter of voices: as one writer, reflecting upon another great metropolis, put it in the nineteenth century, 'London, London, our delight/Great flower that opens but at night/Great City of the midnight sun/Whose day begins when day is done.'[17]

The city is unforgiving, to be sure, a point amply on display in countless number of Hindi films, not merely from the 1940s and 1950s, but down to the present day. I have adverted already to the heroic and unavailing travails of Shambu in *Do Bigha Zameen* ('Two Acres of Land'), a farmer who, in one last desperate attempt to hold on to his land, turns to rickshaw-pulling in the great city. One searing scene follows another,

---

[14] Suketu Mehta, *Maximum City* (New York: Knopf, 2004).
[15] S.M. Edwardes, *By-Ways of Bombay*, with illustrations by M.V. Dhurandhar (2nd ed., Bombay: D.B. Taraporevala Sons, 1912), pp. 21–8.
[16] Joachim Schlor, *Nights in the Big City: Paris, Berlin, London 1840–1930* (London: Reaktion Books, 1998 [1991]).
[17] Cited by Raymond Williams, *The Country and the City* (New York, 1973), p. 228.

but as the film shifts from the village to the city, the inhumanity of man to man is magnified many times over. A young woman hops upon a rickshaw; her lover comes running by, seats himself in Shambu's rickshaw, and urges him to give chase. Faster, faster: it is not for the likes of Shambu to protest, but perhaps he, too, is enticed by his client's offer of a grand sum of Rs 6 if he can catch up with the other rickshaw. One after another the two rickshaws hurl down the wide boulevard. They pass by a horse carriage—the whip cracks down the horse's back. And, instinctively, the young man in Shambu's rickshaw moves his hand as if he were wielding a whip, urging Shambu on to victory and glory. For that is what Shambu is in the ontology of the oppressor, a beast of burden. Here is not principally a narrative of man versus animal; here is not a tale of man versus the machine, as in *Naya Daur*,[18] another notable film from around the same period which pits the village hero and protector of the hearth against the city-returned businessman who, keen on maximizing productivity and profits, introduces machinery which renders obsolete the labour of those who have served their employer faithfully. Here, etched boldly through the world of the rickshaw pullers, is the story of man versus man.[19] Such a world must eventually come tumbling down: the wheel spins faster and faster, the rickshaw collapses, and Shambu's world comes crashing down on him. Laid low by injuries, Shambu feels his grip on his village land receding; his son, Kanhaiya, whose shoebox breaks into pieces as he attempts to flee from a raid by policemen, has a moral lapse and is tempted into pickpocketing. Meanwhile, Shambu's wife, Parvati, who fears for the worse when letters from her husband cease to arrive at their village home, takes it upon herself to arrive in the big city and search for her husband. An attractive but illiterate village woman wandering about a metropolis is an easy target for tricksters, rogues, and sexual profligates. She escapes from the clutches of one such scoundrel, but is run over by a car; though she survives, the land for which Shambu fought with blood, sweat, and tears must be forfeited as Shambu's hard-earned money is used to buy blood for her. One could say that Bimal Roy was working in the mould of tragedy; one could also say that the city is relentlessly cruel.

Shambu's generosity and humanity are barely understood in an environment where one only fends for oneself: he represents the last

---

[18] *Naya Daur* (1957) was directed by B.R. Chopra and starred Dilip Kumar, Vyjayanthimala, Ajit, and Jeevan.

[19] *Do Bigha Zameen* anticipates by three decades the documentary filmmaker Shashi Anand's bold exploration, in *Man versus Man*, of the political economy and culture of the hand-pulled rickshaw industry in Calcutta.

vestiges of, to borrow E.P. Thompson's phrase from his great study of the English working-class, a 'moral economy'.[20] In one touching scene, having lost the patronage of a family whose two children he ferried to school on his hand rickshaw, Shambu nevertheless persists in taking the two little girls to school even though he is no longer recompensed for his labour— and in so doing he refuses a new customer and thereby relinquishes the opportunity to add to his meagre earnings. It may be argued that attachment to the land and ties to kinsmen, friends, and acquaintances define the poles of the villager's existence, and certainly Shambu does not permit the new moneyed economy to define the contours of the moral contracts to which he feels bound. Nor is it accidental that almost the only people in the city who display any humanity are recent migrants from the village: the *bustee* (slum) to which Shambu and Kanhaiya make their way upon their arrival in the city is presided over by a matriarch known as Chachiji (aunt), who quickly makes them feel comfortable. However much Bimal Roy may have been moved by the traditions of Italian neo-realist cinema, or his own awareness of the grim realities of Indian social existence, Do Bigha Zameen also displays a keen understanding of the fact that the homeless in the pre-industrialized world are seldom without a community, and their poverty has little in common with the poverty of the rich, most spectacularly the urban rich.

The narrative of the country bumpkin in Raj Kapoor's *Shri 420* who allows himself to be captured by the glitter of the big city and in the process loses his soul (and his girl) might appear to represent an uncomplicated moral vision that can no longer be sustained, but it is unarguably still very much palpable to Indian sensibilities. In a film such as *Satya*, which commences with something of a painful litany of the terrors of Mumbai, in whose streets arrives a man from nowhere, a man with no antecedents and no past, is writ large the story of the Indian's encounter with the modern city. What is Satya's caste? From where has he come? Who are his kith and kin? What brings him to the city? Just who is Satya? His entry into the city is something like the story of the Primeval Man. Many elements of the story of Satya, the man and the film alike,[21] are easily identified: the large-scale migrations, which continue unabated, from the hinterland to urban areas; the anonymity promised by

[20] E.P. Thompson, *The Making of the English Working Class* (New York: Vintage Books, 1966 [1963].

[21] J.D. Chakravarthy appears in the title role in *Satya* (1998), a film sometimes described as having inaugurated 'mumbai noir'. It is directed by Ram Gopal Varma, who went on to make the sequel *Company* (2002).

the city; and the city with its promise of release from history and the ties that bind. Neither cremation nor burial mark death in the city: Satya goes from the city as he came into it, anonymously and unmourned. 'Urban life,' wrote Lewis Mumford, 'spans the historic space between the earliest burial ground for dawn man and the final cemetery, the Necropolis, in which one civilization after another has met its end.'[22] *Satya* easily lends itself to interpretation as a film on gang warfare, on the nexus of crime and politics in Mumbai (as in most other Indian cities); but there are graver intimations in it, amidst the flaying bodies and the brutal executions, of the city as necropolis, as a strange kind of living graveyard.

Once the city has made its way into the pores of the skin, inserted itself into the sinews of the mind, its arterial highways mesh with the veins of the body. It has been said of the city in India that it provides no anchor, and large strands of Indian cultural traditions, from high literature to (as we have seen) the popular Hindi film, appear to echo this view. Rabindranath Tagore sought to strike a balance between 'city and village' in his essay by the same name, but the lyrical terms in which he described the village suggest why he, 'an urban creature, cityborn', who had felt little the touch of the village in his youth, eventually abandoned Calcutta for the rural countryside. 'Villages are like women', wrote Tagore, and 'in their keeping is the cradle of the race.' Writing at a time when the nation had very much been conceived as 'Bharat Mata', Tagore's formulation permits us to see how the nation and the village are both rendered as, in Goethe's phrase, 'the eternal feminine', the nation deriving her succour from her thousands of villages and the villages in turn furnishing the nation with the core elements of her identity. Villages are, Tagore continues, 'nearer to nature than towns', and though villagers were greatly constrained by their 'habit of dependence' and their reluctance to innovate, they were 'in closer touch with the fountain of life. They possess a natural power of healing.'[23] Modern cities, Tagore recognized, had fed upon the social organism of the village and appropriated 'the life stuff of the community', and a single village freed from the 'shackles of helplessness and ignorance' could serve to revive India. At the other end of the spectrum from Tagore, in the popular culture—jokes, ballads, and theatre—of Calcutta's lowbrow citizens, a similar cynicism about the city

[22] Lewis Mumford, *The City in History: Its Origins, Its Transformations, and Its Prospects* (New York and London: Harcourt Brace Jovanovich, 1961), p. 7.

[23] Rabindranath Tagore, 'City and Village', in idem, *Towards Universal Man* (London: Asia Publishing House, 1961), pp. 311–12, 319.

was routinely encountered. *'Jal, juochuri, mithye katha,'* ran a popular ditty, *'Ei tin niye Kolikata'* ['Forgery, swindling and falsehood. These three make up Calcutta'].[24]

I recall the well-known Indian environmentalist, Sunderlal Bahuguna, who had made his home in the Garhwal region for nearly his entire life, telling me more than two decades ago, 'India lives in its villages.'[25] This might, read unambiguously as a demographic fact, be somewhat less true now, though nearly two-thirds of India's population still derives its living from agriculture. But, as a staunch disciple of Mohandas Gandhi, Bahuguna had something rather different in mind. He meant to suggest not only that the Indian sensibility has been largely shaped by the village, but also that the village furnishes Indians with their spiritual and cultural home. In this, Bahuguna would appear to have been following the master himself, for had Gandhi not said that 'the true India is to be found not in its few cities, but in its seven hundred thousand villages. If the villages perish, India will perish too'?[26] That this was far from being a stray thought on Gandhi's part is amply clear: not only are invocations to 7,00,000 villages common in Gandhi's writings over a period of three decades, but on many an occasion he would describe villages, still 'wholly untouched' after two centuries of colonial rule, as 'the real India'.[27] Gandhi was quite certain that 'a

---

[24] Cited by Sumanta Banerjee, 'Laughter as Subversion in Nineteenth Century Calcutta', in *The Calcutta Psyche*, ed. Geeti Sen (Delhi: Rupa & Co. and India International Centre, 1990), p. 195.

[25] Private conversation at his ashram, Summer 1986.

[26] I myself have not encountered this quote, attributed to Gandhi on hundreds of websites, in the *Collected Works of Mahatma Gandhi* [hereafter *CWMG*]. It appears to me to have been stitched together from two of Gandhi's many pronouncements on the village. The *Harijan* of 29 August 1936 reported a discussion between Maurice Frydman and Gandhi that took place at Sevagram on or before 25 August, where Gandhi was recorded as having said that 'that if the village perishes India will perish too. India will be no more India. Her own mission in the world will get lost' (*CWMG*, 69: 321). Inaugurating the Khadi and Village Industries Exhibition at Ramgarh on 14 March 1940, Gandhi stated: 'The true Indian civilization is in the Indian villages. The modern city civilization you find in Europe and America, and in a handful of our cities which are copies of the Western cities and which were built for the foreigner, and by him. But they cannot last' (*CWMG*, 78: 57).

[27] See Gandhi's discussion, *c.* 7 April 1940, with a Chinese visitor to Sevagram: *CWMG*, 78: 118.

Bombay or a Calcutta did not represent true India, but it was the seven lakhs of villages that were spread throughout the country which were real India'.[28] Indians were 'inheritors of a rural civilization', and the vastness of the country and of its population, conjoined to the climate and patterns of social evolution, had 'destined it for a rural civilization. Its defects are well known but not one of them is irremediable. To uproot it and substitute for it an urban civilization seems to me an impossibility. . . .'[29]

Though Bahuguna is a more complex figure than most Gandhians, and has epitomized the Gandhian outlook in many distinct ways, one should recall that Gandhians have had a tendency to out-Gandhi Gandhi or, which is much the same thing, render Gandhi into a figure that requires little or no interpretation. There is no doubting the fact that Gandhi looked to the village as the site of India's regeneration, and one can surmise his dark view of the city from his characteristically wry observation, when asked to comment on the rapid decline of wildlife in Indian jungles, that wildlife in the towns was certainly increasing.[30] However, what is less recognized, doubtless because many of Gandhi's critics have effortlessly persuaded themselves that he was a 'romantic' whose vision of India did not extend beyond the bullock cart, is the fact that he was absolutely forthright about the horribly dilapidated state of Indian villages. 'If we approach any village,' he wrote, 'the very first thing we encounter is the dunghill. If a traveller who is unfamiliar with these parts comes across this state of affairs, he will not be able to differentiate between the dunghill and the residential part. As a matter of fact, there is not much of a difference between the two.' Ved Mehta avers that Gandhi, the non-resident Indian returned from England and South Africa, saw India with the eyes of a foreigner:[31] apparently most Indians do not see filth for what it is, and they in any case go about their business in full obliviousness of the assault on their senses. But perhaps we ought to consider that Gandhi was also shaped in the vortex of the city, from London, Johannesburg, and Durban to Ahmedabad

---

[28] Speech at Khadi and Village Industries Exhibition, Ramgarh (14 March 1940), *CWMG*, 78: 57.
[29] 'What May Youth Do?' *Young India*, 7 November 1929, *CWMG*, 47: 377.
[30] Cited by T.N. Khoshoo, *Mahatma Gandhi: An Apostle of Applied Human Ecology* (New Delhi: Tata Energy Research Institute, 1995), p. 18.
[31] Ved Mehta, *Mahatma Gandhi and His Apostles* (New York: Viking, 1976; new ed., New Haven: Yale University Press, 1993), p. 243.

is in Ahmedabad, a great centre for the textile industry where Gandhi
could also witness first hand the contours of Hindu-Muslim relations,
that he put down his roots when he returned from South Africa. When
one thinks of Gandhi, it is not only his ashrams—Phoenix Settlement,
Tolstoy Farm, Satyagraha Ashram, Sevagram—that come to mind,[32]
but also his 'do or die' speech at what is now August Kranti Maidan at
Bombay, his peacekeeping efforts in Calcutta, and his last fast in Delhi
shortly before his assassination. It is in Madurai, the city that got caught
in Kannagi's rage, that Gandhi wrote a new and decisive chapter in the
sartorial history that he had long been penning, embracing for the first
time the loin-cloth in public.[33] The Gandhians are likely to recall the
image of Gandhi trudging through the villages in Bihar and Noakhali,
but the city was inevitably his playing ground as well; moreover, unlike
men in the Indian tradition who have thought that tranquility, peace
of mind, and ultimately moksha are only to be obtained far from the
madding crowds, he was quite certain that saintliness can only be tested
in slums. Before one can be at home in the village or the city, one
must be anchored in the mind. Or so, one suspects, must have thought
Gandhi.

[32] Gandhi's ashrams were never merely places of retreat, or even only sites
of social experimentation: it is from these ashrams that Gandhi, so to speak,
ventured into the city and so transfused an ancient institution with a new set of
complex social meanings. Though Gandhi's deployment of tradition has been
the subject of much scholarly inquiry, the canvas of those studies can be extended
much further. Gandhi was deeply 'ecological' in more than the ordinary sense of
the term: his instinct was always to work with the available social practices and
institutions, rather than to abandon them wholesale, and his inventiveness with
ashrams is only one illustration of the ecological mindset that he brought to bear
upon all domains of life.
[33] S.S. Kavitha, 'Etched in Everybody's Memory', *The Hindu* (2 December 2006).
Gandhi's first appearance in a loin-cloth was on 22 September 1921; in a letter
published in *The Hindu* on the following day, urging people to give up foreign
clothing, Gandhi acknowledged that many of his poor countrymen and women
had barely enough to cover their modesty. But in a warm climate, Indian men
at least could learn to be 'satisfied with a mere loin-cloth. . . . Let there be no
prudery about dress. India has never insisted on full covering of the body of
the males as a test of culture.' Cited in the above article; see also 'Message on
Loin-Cloth, Madura', *CWMG*, 24: 303–4.

The 'Urban Turn' in Indian Studies

The city and the village, or the town and the country, have been contrasted in every civilization,[34] and in the scholarly literature on India this distinction always carried much weight. The Italian Giovanni Botero, in his treatise on 'The Causes of the Magnificence and Greatness of Cities', established the city as a subject of study in Europe in 1606, but it was not until the rise of sociology in the middle part of the nineteenth century that the city was enshrined as a subject in its own right.[35] Where a historian such as Fustel de Coulanges held that the practice of communal forms of worship was critical to the development of the city,[36] Marx was inclined to the view that the city was best explained through its economic institutions. Writing in the late nineteenth century, Max Weber effected a significant departure from myriad forms of the institutional theory of the city in proposing that the city was best understood as a form of urban community with a distinct if shifting set of social relations.[37] The 'rumble of the tremendous human mill', as Henry James put it in an essay on London, would henceforth be the inescapable subject of sociology.[38] Indeed, the maverick Indian thinker, Shiv Visvanathan, has gone so far as to suggest that 'sociology and social policy can be read as a series of elaborate footnotes on the modern city',

[34] A.K. Ramanujan, among the first Indian scholars to give some thought to the image of the city, made a rather interesting observation to the effect that there is no parallel in South Indian oral literature, or even in Indian folklore as a whole, to the European tale of the town mouse and the country mouse. He argues that the distinction between the country and city is not marked in early Sanskrit or Tamil literature, and became entrenched only at a later time, perhaps somewhere around the time of Vatsyayana, the author of the *Kama Sutra.* See 'Towards an Anthology of City Images' (1971), reprinted in Vinay Dharwadker, ed., *The Collected Essays of A.K. Ramanujan* (Delhi: Oxford University Press, 1999), p. 55. Alain Danielou describes Vatsyayana as a Brahmin man of letters residing in the city of Pataliputra around the fourth century AD: see the *Complete Kama Sutra,* trans. and introduction by Danielou (Rochester, Vermont: Park Street Press, 1994), p. 4.
[35] Cf. G.S. Ghurye, *Cities and Civilization* (Bombay: Popular Prakashan, 1962), pp. 1–44.
[36] Fustel de Coulanges, *The Ancient City* (New York: Anchor Books, 1956).
[37] Max Weber, *The City,* trans. and ed., Don Martindale and Gertrud Neuwirth (New York: The Free Press, 1958).
[38] Cited by Mark Girouard, *Cities and People: A Social and Architectural History* (New Haven: Yale University Press, 1985), p. v.

and that the city is preeminently both site and metaphor for the unfolding 'drama of modernity'.[39]

The 'urban turn', so vividly on display in European history and sociology, was late in coming in Indian studies. Some might imagine that Gandhi's emphasis on 'village India' and on village reconstruction had set the national priorities, and that even more than the rise of the BJP and other like political forces, it is the rise of urban culture which has rendered Gandhi obsolete. Jawaharlal Nehru's views on the village appear to be encapsulated in a letter he addressed to Gandhi in 1945, where he described a village, 'normally speaking', as 'backward intellectually and culturally', a 'backward environment' from where progress was not to be expected. Nehru would go on to state that 'the fundamental problem of India is not Delhi or Calcutta or Bombay but the villages of India', and this would appear to put Nehru on a course of thinking quite at odds with the views of his mentor.[40] But two decades of tutelage under Gandhi had, one suspects, filled Nehru with more ambivalence than those who are inclined to view him unambiguously as a proponent of modernity are willing to recognize. Howsoever palpable his reservations about 'village India', he had also imbibed the sentiment that the village was the repository of the oldest memories and unbroken social links from one generation to another. Nehru was too imbued with the historical sensibility to disown entirely the Indian village, and in this matter as in many others, he sought, to use a clichéd formulation, to blend the old and the new.

One might, of course, summon other factors in an effort to explain why the city in India was not, until very recently, the focus of intellectual inquiries except among demographers and scholars of urbanization. Though numerous considerations come to mind, three merit close attention. First, the legacy of several generations of commentators, all riveted on what colonial scholars termed the 'village community' and an 'eternal India', cannot be overlooked. Conquerors and rulers had come and gone, but, on the view which persisted with remarkable tenacity among observers of Indian society, the country's villages persevered in an unchanging form despite all the political upheavals. Bound together by ties of custom, economic dependence, and elaborate social rituals, the

[39] Shiv Visvanathan and Harsh Sethi, 'Bhopal: A Report from the Future', *Lokayan Bulletin*, 7, no. 3 (1989), p. 51.
[40] 'Nehru's Reply to Gandhi', in M.K. Gandhi, *Hind Swaraj and Other Writings*, ed., Anthony J. Parel (Cambridge: Cambridge University Press, 1997), p. 152.

inhabitants of India's deeply hierarchical village communities remained impervious to the changes taking place around them. In the twentieth century, the mantle of the colonial scholar and his Indian imitators was assumed by the professional Indologist and anthropologist, and the monograph on the Indian village became the prototype of Western (and much Indian) scholarship on India.[41] Scholars were intently focused on Indian village customs, religion, kinship ties, festivals, and caste relations, and the notion that the 'real' India was to be encountered in its villages was so deeply entrenched that even otherwise predominant social science paradigms, such as those juxtaposing tradition with modernization, were deployed largely to understand how the village was likely to cope with modernization.[42] The anthropologist would return to his or her village after three decades to find that the village had colour television sets or cable TV, or that its women were a bit more 'modern', or that the railways or a bus route had brought the village within proximity to a large town or city.

Second, the immense growth of Indian cities is a relatively recent phenomenon, and one has to recall that Delhi had a population of much less than a million before the partition of India, and that even Bombay had fewer than one million people in 1910, and only about 4 million in 1960. By the year 2020 at least six Indian cities—Bangalore, Calcutta, Chennai, Delhi, Hyderabad, and Mumbai—are expected to number among the forty greatest urban agglomerations in the world, and none would have made the list of the top ten in 1960.[43] Delhi and Mumbai are already

[41] See, for example, *Village India: Studies in the Little Community*, ed., McKim Marriott (Chicago: University of Chicago Press, 1955). Arvind N. Das, *Changel: The Biography of a Village* (Delhi: Penguin Books, 1996), is a contemporary example of a village study of a very different kind.

[42] There were notable exceptions in the scholarly literature of the 1950s to the mid-1970s, such as Milton Singer's *When a Great Tradition Modernizes: An Anthropological Approach to Indian Civilization* (Chicago: University of Chicago Press, 1972), a considerable portion of its ethnography revolving around Madras (now Chennai). The choice of Madras is interesting, since the contrast would have been more sharply drawn had Singer conducted his fieldwork in Bombay. No city among the 'big four' has changed as much in recent years as Chennai, which had a reputation as something of an extended Indian village, closed to cosmopolitan influences, a city with little to attract a following among those interested in culinary adventures, nightlife, and art and music beyond that of the Carnatic.

[43] See 'The World's Largest Cities and Urban Areas in 2020', online at: http://www.citymayors.com/statistics/urban_2020_1.html (accessed 1 April 2012),

ranked second and fourth worldwide, respectively. If, moreover, one were
to even tentatively accept the suggestion that the city has an inextricable
relationship to the middle class, then it is clear why the city has only
since the late 1980s come to occupy an increasingly prominent place in
scholarly worldviews. Though Indian villages have long had their own arts
and crafts, from pottery-making and puppetry to harvest dances and forms
of storytelling, certain elements of modern culture were precipitated by
the emergence of a middle class in the space of the city. Both consumerism
and advertising characterize the city as much as mass transit and print
journalism. Indeed, even traditional arts, such as dances associated with
the performance of religious plays or the harvest season, have acquired
a new life in the city as forms of 'folk dances' that get performed from
time to time in celebration of simpler ways of living and as a reminder
that India is invested with a 'traditional culture'. Urban India, unaware
as cities and towns generally are about how the food arrives at the table,
needs village India as the source of its nostalgia about a past less subject to
the tyranny of clock-time and more attuned to the natural rhythms of life.
In the meantime, the city continues with its feverish pace of consumption,
blanketed by television commercials, the din of radio advertising, text
messaging, and massive billboards exhorting people to join the world of
consumers. Where until recently the Atlas or Hero bicycle were the perfect
icons of the villager on the move, the contemporary advertisements for cell
phones and automobiles are targeted to an urban middle-class population
that has accepted 'connectivity' and 'consumption' as the watchwords of
modern life.

Even as anthropological studies of India continued through the 1970s
to be devoted largely to the Indian village, Indian society and politics were
registering seismic changes. A few landmarks can help us understand the
circumstances under which the modern Indian city was emerging. Delhi
grew immensely after the partition and refugee or settler colonies were
critical to its growth.[44] Nor can one ignore the obvious fact that however
extensive the bureaucratic apparatus of the colonial state, the government
would witness tremendous growth in the post-1947 period. The role of
the central government is most often remembered in certain phrases such

and 'The Principal Agglomerations of the World', online at: www.citypopulation.
de/World.html (accessed 1 April 2012).
[44] See, for example, V.N. Datta, 'Panjabi Refugees and the Urban Development
of Greater Delhi', in Mushirul Hasan, ed., *Inventing Boundaries: Gender, Politics and
the Partition of India* (Delhi: Oxford University Press, 2000), pp. 268–84.

as 'the license Raj', and it is indubitably true that many people gravitated towards Delhi as the National Capital Region—as the place where power-brokers congregated, from where jobs and favours were disbursed, and to which Tamilians, Bengalis, and others came in the quest to find their fortunes under the new political dispensation.[45] Elsewhere in India, the concentration of factory labour was leading to a rapid acceleration of populations in urban centres such as Bombay, Calcutta, Ahmedabad, and Kanpur. Nehru's government, as is well known, was also heavily committed to industrialization. When the colonial official G.W. Forrest published his *Cities of India: Past and Present* in 1903, he included chapters on Mount Abu and Ajmer, Cuddalore, and Pondicherry, but none, for obvious reasons, on the steel cities of Jamshedpur or Bhilai. Though neither Jamshedpur, known as Sakchi before J.N. Tata prospected in its region and turned it into a steel city in 1919, nor Bhilai, where the Steel Authority of India commenced production of steel in 1959, number among India's largest cities, today both have a population in excess of 1 million. Whatever one's position on the question of how far, if at all, industrialization had come along in the nineteenth century, it is quite clear that various sectors of the economy, such as banking and insurance, had been in a state of infancy during the colonial period. Even during the so-called 'Hindu rate of growth' period of the Indian economy, these sectors witnessed remarkable growth and gave rise to a large, mainly city-centered, white-collar working class.

The city had, of course, been a space of political mobilization and indeed turbulent political activity in the nineteenth century. The city has never been able to disown that history, even if the endeavour of city administrations is generally to suppress memories of dissent and induce veneration for law and order. Memories of the British occupation of Delhi in 1803, and the subsequent fortification of the city in 1814–15, would be eclipsed by the more dramatic confrontation with colonial rule that took place during the Rebellion of 1857–8.[46] Though there was also widespread insurgent activity in the countryside during the rebellion, the siege of Lucknow and the devastation of Delhi are among the more keenly remembered episodes from that time. Some cities appear to be built and rebuilt only so that they might be sacked, repeatedly and insistently,

[45] The book that does most justice to the history of Delhi in this respect is *Delhi: Urban Space and Human Destinies*, eds, Veronique Dupont, Emma Tarlo, and Denis Vidal (Delhi: Manohar, 2000).
[46] See H.K. Kaul, ed., *Historic Delhi: An Anthology* (Delhi: Oxford University Press, 1985), pp. 385–409.

and Delhi must number among them. In the 14th century, the mad king (as he is frequently dubbed) of Delhi, Muhammad bin Tughluq, took it upon himself to empty the city of all its inhabitants and shift the entire population to a new capital hundreds of miles away. The Moroccan traveller Ibn Battuta, who had entered into the Sultan's employment, recorded the house-to-house search that Tughluq's soldiers undertook to ensure that there was complete compliance with the Sultan's orders. Upon finding that two men, one a cripple and the other blind, had defied his orders, the King ordered that the cripple be flung to his death from a mangonel while the blind man was dragged from Delhi to Daulatabad, a distance then covered in forty days. Says Ibn Battuta, 'He fell to pieces on the road, and all of him that reached Daulatabad was his leg.'[47] Four hundred years later, Nadir Shah did what other conquerors have done to Delhi, pillaging and plundering the city, terrorizing its inhabitants, and inscribing his peculiar signature on events: a tower of the skulls of his victims. The contemporary chronicler, Mirza Zuman, reported that on Monday the 11th of March, 1739, the slaughter commenced at eight in the morning and was halted at three in the afternoon, and of the citizens '120,000 were slaughtered, others computed them 150,000.'[48] Much fewer than four decades would elapse before the Afghans and the Marathas, engaged in a war to the end, together reduced 'the imperial city of Delhi, which, in the days of its glory, extended itself seventeen crores in length, and was said to contain two millions of people, [to] almost a heap of rubbish.'[49] This is the voice of Alexander Dow, and the contemporary reader, all too aware of the Scotsman's Orientalist framework, which allowed for little else in the history of India except an unremitting history of despotism, may be inclined to some skepticism; but here is an account by Dow's contemporary, the poet and pride of Delhi, Mirza Muhammad Rafi Sauda: 'How can I describe the desolation of Delhi? There is no house from where the jackal's cry cannot be heard. The mosques at evening are unlit and deserted, and only in one house in a hundred will you see a light burning. . . . The villages are deserted, the trees themselves are gone, and the wells are full of corpses. Jahanabad,

---

[47] Ibid., pp. 315–16. For one of the more unusual insights into Muhammad bin Tuqhluq's reign, see Elias Canetti, *Crowds and Power* (New York: Farrar, Straus and Giroux, 1984), pp. 424–33; and Girish Karnad, *Tughlaq* (Delhi: Oxford University Press, 1975).

[48] Kaul, ed., *Historic Delhi: An Anthology*, p. 356.

[49] Ibid., p. 373.

you never deserved this terrible fate, you who were once vibrant with life and love and hope, like the heart of a young lover . . . Not even a lamp of clay now burns where once the chandelier blazed with light. Those who once lived in great mansions now eke out their lives among the ruins.'[50]

It is doubtful that anything more chilling has been written on the devastation of Delhi, unless it be Ghalib's narrative of the terrible events that overtook the city in 1857 when the British recovered possession of Delhi from the rebels. He wrote in the *Dastambu* ('A Posy of Flowers'), a record of what transpired in Delhi between May and September of that fateful year, of the British victors who crushed the rebellion with unexampled ferociousness that 'all whom they found in the streets they cut down'; 'they held it lawful to slaughter the helpless and burn the houses'.[51] A letter written later in the year to his friend and fellow poet Hargopal Tufta gives glimpses of the wasteland that Delhi had become: 'Do not think I am exaggerating: everyone, rich and poor alike, and those who did not leave of their own accord have been expelled. . . . As for anyone coming to see me, who is there left in the city? House after house lies deserted, and the punishment of offenders goes on. Martial law was introduced from 11 May, and today, Saturday 5 December 1857, is still in force. No one knows how life goes on in the city.'[52] Delhi was smouldering in ruins, and Ghalib was contemplating the life of loneliness and penury to which he had been reduced, utterly shorn of the gaiety, revelry, and artistic license which had given poets such as himself a revered place in the city's culture. It is unlikely that, in his state of mind, Ghalib would have been prepared to countenance the idea that, in retrospect, ruins uniquely add something to the character and charms of a city.[53] The novelist Jun'ichirō Tanazaki once remarked that the aesthetics of Japanese architecture demands that a building be assessed not only by its own intrinsic design, but even more so by the shadow it casts.[54] Might one say of cities that they derive their characteristics from

---

[50] Ralph Russell and Khurshidul Islam, *Three Mughal Poets: Mir, Sauda, Mir Hasan* (Cambridge, Mass.: Harvard University Press, 1968), pp. 67–8; cited also by Kaul, *Historic Delhi*, pp. 374–5.

[51] Ralph Russell, ed., *The Oxford India Ghalib: Life, Letters and Ghazals* (Delhi: Oxford University Press, 2003), pp. 120–1.

[52] Ibid., p. 131.

[53] Harris Stone, *Hands-on, Hands-off: Experiencing History through Architecture* (New York: Monthly Review Press, 1991).

[54] Jun'ichirō Tanizaki, *In Praise of Shadows*, trans., Thomas J. Harper and Edward G. Seidensticker (Sedgwick, Maine: Leete's Island Books, 1977).

their hospitality to their former selves and their premonition of the ruins to which they are likely to be reduced? If architecture preys upon the play between light and shadow, does the city acquire its majesty from the play between built form and a landscape of ruins?

Delhi, as much as Lucknow,[55] still bears palpable reminders of the brutal suppression of the 1857 rebellion: though many have written of the city of memories, evidently one can also invoke the city as a space of memorialization—not merely a space filled by monuments and memorials, testaments to the captains of industry, nationalist heroes, and men and women of science and arts, or to episodes in the city's history, but also more elementally as a space that, in the first instance, generates passions and thus permits the very exercise of memorialization. The mistrust of the city, a point to which I have already adverted, among colonial officials can certainly be traced to the nineteenth century, but in the present iteration of this argument it becomes necessary to lay stress on the city as the site of turbulent political activity. The hubs of nationalist activity—Calcutta, Pune, Bombay, Amritsar, Kanpur—filled colonial officials with grave misgivings. Lord Curzon, the Viceroy who engineered the first partition of India, was scarcely alone in writing with derision of Calcutta's 'baboos' as genteel folk who, incapable of fighting with the sword, had resorted to the seditious pen. 'Calcutta is the centre,' he wrote to the Secretary of State for India on 2 February 1905, 'from which the Congress party is manipulated throughout the whole of Bengal, and indeed the whole of India. Its best wire-pullers and its most frothy orators all reside here. . . . The whole of their activity is directed to creating an agency so powerful that they may one day be able to force a weak government to give them what they desire.'[56] Curzon was firmly

---

[55] As Veena Talwar Oldenburg has argued, one particular form of retribution for 'native intransigence' consisted in levelling the old city and transforming it into a safe enclave for the British. The Lucknow Residency, where a small population of Britishers, soon to be lionized as heroes of the British Empire, withstood the rebels over a period of several months was allowed by the colonial regime to stand as a testament to British resilience, bravery, and military intelligence. The Residency remains in independent India a tourist spot, furnishing nationalists with an opportunity to provide an alternative reading. Much the same can be said of the sites of battles between the British and the rebels in the Civil Lines and Kashmiri Gate areas of Delhi. See *The Making of Colonial Lucknow, 1856–1877* (Princeton: Princeton University Press, 1984).

[56] Curzon to St. John Brodrick, 2 February 1905: Curzon Papers, Mss Eur F 111/168, India Office Collections, The British Library, London.

persuaded that any measure that 'would dethrone Calcutta from its place as the centre of successful intrigue' would be hotly resented by the city's elites—but he did not hesitate in putting himself to the test when, with a flourish of the pen, he sought the vivisection of Bengal. On the other end of India, in the Punjab, Lieutenant-Governor Michael O'Dwyer expressed a strong conviction that the unrest in his province could be laid at the doors of treasonous politicians and educated lawyers from the city who shared nothing of the aspirations of the men of the soil. The yeoman farmer of the Punjab, O'Dwyer and other colonial officials noted, had no inclination towards politics.

The city had become, by the twentieth century, the site of 'monster meetings' at which 1,00,000 people or more would gather to hear the Mahatma. What is a city without crowds? Yet it may be more accurate to say that the city had become the site for a newer kind of mass gathering: crowds had always been there, at, for instance, Prayag's Maha Kumbh Mela, the origins of which are still shrouded in considerable uncertainty.[57] The Kumbh has been described as possibly 'the largest gathering in history, 'the greatest show on earth': in 2007, the Ardh Kumbh Mela may have brought 70 million people to Allahabad (Prayag) over a period of 45 days. Nehru recalled from his childhood 'hundreds of thousands of people' arriving at Allahabad or Hardwar 'to bathe in the Ganges', and his mind was taken back to similar descriptions of these extraordinary demonstrations of faith written by Chinese travellers and others over 1,300 years ago.[58] But this was not the only kind of crowd that was beginning to energize the city in the twentieth century. Shahid Amin's justly famous piece on 'Gandhi as Mahatma' begins with an account of one such meeting in Gorakhpur,[59] and there is a touching scene in Mulk Raj Anand's 1930s novel, *Untouchable* (now critiqued for various forms of political incorrectness), where Bakha, the scavenger boy, makes his way, as do tens of thousands of others, towards the town Oval where the Mahatma is scheduled to make an appearance.[60]

[57] Kama Maclean, 'Making the Colonial State Work for You: The Modern Beginnings of the Ancient Kumbh Mela in Allahabad', *Journal of Asian Studies*, 62, no. 3 (August 2003), pp. 873–905.

[58] Jawaharlal Nehru, *The Discovery of India* (Delhi: Oxford University Press, 1999 [1946]), p. 51.

[59] Shahid Amin, 'Gandhi as Mahatma', in *Subaltern Studies III: Writings on South Asian History and Society*, ed., Ranajit Guha (New Delhi: Oxford University Press, 1984).

[60] Mulk Raj Anand, *Untouchable* (Middlesex: Penguin Books, 1940 [1935]), pp. 134–8.

Much of the literature on this period helps to underscore the point that while political life is by no means confined to the city, *politics is the business of the city.* In the years after Independence, this might have been apparent only in the more obvious and trivial sense as Delhi and regional capitals became centres of political patronage. By the early 1970s, as deep disenchantment over party politics, the planned economy, economic stagnation, and the shrinking space for creativity set in, the Indian city was once again poised to reaffirm its identity as a conduit for the expression of political dissent. In the heady days leading to the Emergency, the old Gandhian socialist, Jayaprakash Narayan, was able to command meetings of as many as half a million people. The lawns of Delhi's Boat Club, designed to provide the inhabitants of the dusty and scorched capital of a colonial city with some semblance of bucolic leisure, would resonate with calls, from students, trade union leaders, political activists, and the working classes, for Indira Gandhi's resignation—a history that survives in the countless other congregations, whether of striking workers, Dalits, Tibetan refugees, hunger strikers, communists, abused women, anti-dowry and anti-Sati activists, to which the Boat Club has been until quite recently a grudgingly hospitable ground in their quest for social justice and political voice.[61] These are, of course, only chapters in an unwritten ethnography of protest and the city, an ethnography to which every Indian city would have much to contribute.

Cultures of the City: Consumption, Citizenship, and Modernity

The 'maximum city' is not just Bombay, but, arguably, every city. This will appear as a very unlikely proposition to the multitudes who, for

[61] Nearly two decades ago, the government passed orders prohibiting public meetings at Delhi's Boat Club lawns. The major venue of protest then shifted to the grounds near Jantar Mantar, from where Anna Hazare launched his campaign against corruption in 2011, though other venues, among them India Gate and the Ramlila Grounds, have served as important landmarks in people's right to protest. Official authorities have repeatedly sought to inhibit the ability of people to stage protests at Jantar Mantar, though in August 2010, in response to a petition filed in Delhi's High Court by Bano Bee, an activist working on behalf of the victims of the 1984 Bhopal Gas Leak who were refused permission to hold a protest march, the Delhi Police affirmed that it recognized the right to protest as fundamental and non-negotiable if subject to certain restrictions. Some activists have struggled to find recognition for the Boat Club lawns, and subsequently the Jantar Mantar, as equivalent to London's Hyde Park.

one reason or another, are likely to place Bombay and Calcutta at one end of the spectrum of the imagined city, and Delhi at the other end. As the editors of a volume on Delhi wrote a few years ago, it is a 'city that nobody loves'—barring the irascible or rather irrepressible Khushwant Singh, 'a few chasers of djinns',[62] and 'some descendants of long-established Delhi families'.[63] The Calcuttawallahs no doubt think of Delhi as a city for philistines, while people who have been linked to Bombay for generations bemoan the fact that Delhi has nothing like Bombay's neighbourhoods. A certain middle-class discourse on India's cities is now firmly anchored in some home truths: though everyone recognizes that Bombay has hired killers, and there is even a specialized vocabulary that has developed around the underworld, the city is described as one where taxi drivers ply their trade without attempting to cheat every customer, women go about their business without fear of molestation, and 'law and order' prevails. Bombay is in this respect said to provide a studied contrast with the reckless ways of Delhi and its uncouth residents. Delhi's growing stature as a city of culture and the arts leaves many other Indians unimpressed, even repulsed: all of Delhi's affect is purportedly derived from its status as the country's showpiece, attracting the patronage of the state, foreign governments, and corporate houses, and many people argue that the warmth, sheer talent, and buzz that may be experienced, to take one illustration, by music lovers in Chennai during its famous month-long music season, has not the remotest counterpart in the capital's cultural scene.

It is easy to forget, then, that Delhi, as the publisher Ravi Dayal has reminded us, is also the centre of India's publishing world, the country's largest book market (and not merely of textbooks, to anticipate the critics), even honoured by UNESCO as the world's book capital,[64] and increasingly the possessor of the country's best intellectual and educational infrastructure.[65] And, yet, as Dayal concedes, there is 'no such thing as

[62] William Dalrymple, *City of Djinns: A Year in Delhi* (Middlesex: Penguin Books, 1993).

[63] Denis Vidal, Emma Tarlo, and Veronique Dupont, 'The Alchemy of an Unloved City', in idem, eds, *Delhi: Urban Space and Human Destinies*, p. 15.

[64] Madhumita Chakraborty, 'Delhi Turns the Book Capital of the World', *Financial Express* (23 April 2004).

[65] Ravi Dayal, 'A Kayastha's View', *Seminar*, no. 515: *First City? A Symposium on Remembering Delhi* (July 2002), pp. 21–3.

a Dilliwallah any more', it is 'nobody's city';[66] or, in the very different formulation of the architect Charles Correa, reflecting on the flower-laden traffic islands of Lutyens' Delhi, 'a city can be beautiful as habitat—trees, uncrowded roads, open spaces—and yet fail to provide that particular ineffable quality of urbanity which we call: CITY.'[67] If a city has an inextricable relationship to its residents, and if there are no Dilliwallahs, then just what kind of city is Delhi? And who is likely to sing of it today with the same tone of affection and longing found in the poetry of those eighteenth-century poets of Delhi, Mir and Sauda?

The inhabitants of Calcutta, in contrast, are known to defend their city with unbridled enthusiasm. From time to time, it has been condemned as a dying city, but every such criticism only strengthens Calcuttans' resolve to hold forth on its merits. Every cliché about Calcutta has been answered with its opposite, and Lapierre's 'city of joy' meets Kipling's 'city of dreadful night'.[68] Ironically, the fearful city that Kipling was writing about was known to many of his countrymen as 'the city of palaces',[69] a tribute to the entrepreneurial spirit of those in Bengal who began to thrive under the colonial dispensation and built themselves ornate residences, while the 'city of joy' invokes a 'city of slums', the narrative revolving around a Calcutta slum whose inhabitants face life with grit, fortitude, and optimism. Even among those who are not swayed by ties of loyalty, Calcutta is spoken of fondly as the city of books, poetry, political activism, strikes—and perhaps, though with much less force today than at the time when Nirad C. Chaudhuri was describing a social institution that lent a unique colour to life in the metropolis, a city most eminently of the

[66] Ashley Tellis, 'Delhi: Nobody's City', *The Hindu Folio: Cities* (12 August 2001).
[67] Charles Correa, 'India Inc.', *Seminar*, no. 445: *The Other City: A Symposium on the Haphazard Growth of Our Urban Areas* (September 1996), p. 66.
[68] Dominique Lapierre, *The City of Joy*, trans., Kathryn Spink (1985); Kipling's 1884 short story, 'The City of Dreadful Night', is available in dozens of collections. Kipling took the phrase from a long poem by the same name by the Scottish poet James Thomson (1834–1882), who wrote under the pseudonym Bysshe Vanolis. As he struggled with depression, insomnia, alcoholism, and loneliness, Thomson came to take a grim view of life in London.
[69] Jeremiah P. Losty, *Calcutta, City of Palaces: A Survey of the City in the Days of the East India Company* (London: Arnold Publishers, 1990); for an even more recent study of, in Krishna Dutta's words, 'the decaying mansion of the Babus,' built in a style that V.S. Naipaul termed 'Calcutta Corinthian', see Joanne Taylor, *The Forgotten Palaces of Calcutta* (New Delhi: Niyogi Books, 2006; rev. ed., 2011).

adda,[70] the only end of which is to defy the notion of a targeted objective and to retain the conversation as an end in itself. The political passions of Calcutta were to be inferred from a host of other circumstances besides the adda, from the renaming during the Vietnam War of the street on which the American Consulate was located as Ho Chi Minh Sarani in honour of his defiance of Yankee imperialism to the peculiar fact that as the Soviet Union and the countries that had once been its satellites radically disengaged from communism and became willing captives of the free market economy, Calcutta gallantly offered to house the statues of Lenin that were now being discarded by the dozens.[71]

Calcutta, some may then argue, has been supremely iconoclastic and thereby loved. But who can doubt that Bombay, with all the critics that it draws, similarly still remains a loved city? Visitors to Bombay are known to express themselves in much the same way as visitors to New York, excited, energized, and baffled by its immense possibilities, and ready with the view that it is a city they love to visit but one they would not make their home. And yet close to 20 million people live in its high rises, chawls, streets, and even some vast bungalows. As an architect, Charles Correa is saddened by the deterioration of the city's physical environment, and yet the restless and often unregulated energy of its enterprising and ambitious people have intensified its qualities as a city. Bombay is scarcely unique in its frenetic pace, but how should one think of its slum dwellers who sit on property worth inestimable amounts, or of the fact, if fact it be, that among the vows a Jain monk must take is one which forbids him to visit Bombay lest his spiritual discipline gets shred to pieces? Suketu Mehta's *Maximum City* ends with a narrative about Sevantibhai Ladhani, a Jain diamond merchant who is about to take *diksha*, a vow of renunciation that will put him, and members of his family, on the road with a begging bowl. Ladhani and his family are poised to arrive at a small Gujarati town where, 'in the full noonday light of worldly success', they will gift away all their possessions, a few million dollars worth of them: 'It will be a dramatic rejection of Bombay, of the sole reason why anybody would

---

[70] Nirad C. Chaudhuri, *The Autobiography of an Unknown Indian* (Berkeley: University of California Press, 1968 [1951]), pp. 383–6.

[71] The zeal of the right and the left has, one might say, something in common. When mad cow disease struck England, and thousands of cows were being incinerated even as there was talk of nearly the entire cattle population being put to death, the advocates of Hindutva, grievously wounded by the injuries being perpetrated against the sacred cow, put forth a proposal to ship Britain's cows to India.

want to live here.'[72] Sevantibhai's wife, Rakshaben, has been instructed by the *sadhvin* (female monastic head) of the order that she is about to join that she may never proceed south of Virar, where the local Bombay trains terminate: beyond is the big city. Not all cities are forbidden to the renunciate, only Bombay; indeed, says Rakshaben, 'Delhi, Calcutta, and other cities are okay': 'Bombay is the Sodom and Gomorrah of the Jain religion, *"Paap ni bhoomi"* [Sin City]'.[73] An opposite vow points to another kind of folklore, this one surrounding the 'City of Light', Kashi: some view Kashi as so holy that they take a vow, *kshetra sannyasa*, never to leave the city, even to go to the hospital of the Banaras Hindu University which is 100 metres south of the limits of Kashi.[74] What could be more unfortunate than to have lived one's entire life in Kashi and yet have died on a chance trip outside the city? However, what everyone took to be the city of virtue, the very site of *moksha*, the iconoclast Kabir despised as so much humbug: 'Going on endless pilgrimages, the world died,/exhausted by so much bathing.' Though Kabir himself lived in Kashi, he chose to leave it precisely when others would have died to enter its precincts—at the door of death. The nearby town of Magahar was, 'according to Kashi brahmins', so 'impure and disreputable' that anyone who died there was believed to be reborn as an ass. Here Kabir took his last stand: 'My whole life, I have wasted in Kashi/But, at the time of death, I have risen and come to Magahar.'[75]

The city everywhere in India is now coming into its own. Over 40 cities each have a population of more than one million, and the ramshackle towns that litter the Indian landscape, particularly in north India, are teeming with people and emerging as trade centres. Shops overflowing with consumer goods do not make a city, someone may object, and it may well be argued that in the 15 years or more that have elapsed since a sensitive young writer ate butter chicken in Ludhiana,[76] the glorified villages which pass as towns have

---

[72] Suketu Mehta, *Maximum City: Bombay Lost and Found* (New York: Vintage Books, 2004), p. 499.

[73] Ibid., pp. 504–5; 'Bombay is the Sodom': this is Mehta speaking, rather than Rakshaben.

[74] Diana L. Eck, *Banaras: City of Light* (Princeton: Princeton University Press, 1983), p. 28.

[75] Ibid., pp. 86–7; Charlotte Vaudeville, *Kabir* (New York: Oxford University Press, 1974), p. 46.

[76] Pankaj Mishra, *Butter Chicken in Ludhiana: Travels in Small Town India* (New Delhi: Penguin, 1995).

scarcely graduated towards the mode of city life. If Anita Desai is to be believed, Ludhiana and the other redoubtable haunts of butter chicken, jalebi, and makhni dal are perhaps somewhat reminiscent of Delhi shortly after Independence. 'Delhi in the 1950s, even New Delhi,' she has written, 'was really nothing more than handful of villages clustering together on the sand and dust of the northern plain.'[77] One will, of course, find more than 'sand and dust' in the towns and cities in the Doab and along the Gangetic Plains. Internet cafes had sprung up everywhere around the time the new millennium of the Gregorian calendar was ushered in, and the aptly named mobile phone has helped to introduce a different business culture besides appearing to mitigate the effect of distances among people who might not have been very mobile; and even automobiles have made their way into towns and small cities that not long ago were serviced only by state transportation buses. The billboards advertise and sell, so to speak, the city's notion of feminine beauty, and other like signs of urban culture, from 'boutique' stores and beauty parlours to supermarkets and the rudiments of an hospitality industry are now visible in areas well beyond the metropolitan centres. Something of the new money that has flown into middle-class homes described by Pavan Varma can be seen in what were until recently only squalid towns and provincial cities.[78] Arjun Appadurai has a point when he describes Bombay—the city of trade, banking, and commerce, and also of innumerable numbers rackets—as the 'city of cash',[79] but one wonders if the metropolis does not always emerge, leaving the *nagar* behind, when money's lustre begins to alter social relations.

The nineteenth-century colonial city clustered around other develop-ments. Much that has been written about the 'Bengal Renaissance' is focused on the activities of elites and an emergent class of people from modest homes in and around Calcutta who, in the heroic mode in which this narrative is customarily encountered, hungered for new knowledge to combat old superstitions and the dead weight of oppressive customs. One does not have to accede to every part of the narrative to recognize that by the first half of the nineteenth century, Calcutta was already supporting a

[77] Foreword to Krishna Dutta, *Calcutta: A Cultural and Literary History* (New Delhi: Roli Books, 2003), p. viiii.
[78] Pavan K. Varma, *The Great Indian Middle Class* (New Delhi: Viking, 1998).
[79] Arjun Appadurai, 'Spectral Housing and Urban Cleansing: Notes on Millennial Mumbai', *Public Culture*, 12, no. 3 (2000), p. 630.

number of periodicals, among them *Calcutta Journal Hurukuru* and *The Friend of India*, both in English, as well as several in Bengali, such as *Sambad Chandrika, Sambad Kaumadi,* and *Timir Nausak.* A lively press sprung up in Bombay and Pune by the second half of the nineteenth century, and throughout the nationalist period the colonial authorities found it a bracing challenge to reign in the vernacular press. In the pages of the Bombay-based *Kesari,* associated with Bal Gangadhar Tilak, and subsequently in the pages of *Young India,* a newspaper controlled by Gandhi from Ahmedabad, the British found a tenacious and well-articulated opposition to their rule. The young C.F. Andrews thought he witnessed a similar efflorescence of learning, and a liveliness of intellectual culture, in Delhi early in the twentieth century. He even termed it, though to some ears, who have never associated Delhi with the life of the mind, it sounds like an oxymoron, the 'Delhi Renaissance'.[80] The city became the nodal point of activities for writers, publishers, newspaper reporters, educators, and lawyers, and even relatively more provincial cities, such as Nagpur, Benares, Lucknow, and Trivandrum, could in turn boast of a thriving newspaper culture and various classes of elites, such as lawyers, who had to prosper in the city before they could think of moving to the *mofussil* (provinces). Once the scribe alone had made a living from the written word, but now large parts of city life revolved around those who traded in it. In the emergence of print culture, a publishing industry, and—from Elphinstone, Presidency, and Delhi College to the universities in Bombay, Allahabad, Delhi, and elsewhere—institutions of higher education, alongside such social phenomena as the adda or the coffeehouse, one can see the public sphere taking shape. By the 1920s and 1930s, a cluster of bookstores had emerged in the metropolitan cities; in the early 1950s, Satyajit Ray and his friends in Calcutta pioneered the film society movement; and by the late 1960s, art galleries were not altogether a novelty in cities such as Bombay. The old coffeehouses have now largely disappeared, but their place has been taken by others—and some in the present generation of college students doubtless find the idea of the city inconceivable without Café Coffee Day, that increasingly pervasive icon of the trendy coffeehouse which has displayed a remarkable penetration into small towns.

The history of the Indian city can surely be written in various idioms, and few people would think of doing so through the coffeehouse, and

---

[80] See C.F. Andrews, *Zaka Ullah of Delhi,* with introductions by Mushirul Hasan and Margrit Pernau (reprint ed., Delhi: Oxford University Press, 2003), pp. xxii–xxiii, 47.

that too in a country where it is the chai stall that is ubiquitous. Yet in the emergence of cafés is writ large the story of the transformation of urban India, especially viewed in relation to contemporary debates on changing social relations, the global economy, and citizenship. The large coffeehouses in the Connaught Place area of New Delhi were without pretension, dished out a basic fare, and were not prominent in class markers, being hospitable to office workers, students, and intellectuals alike. Women, however, were only occasionally seen there, and then seldom without the accompaniment of men. One hears of Barista and Café Coffee Day what has been said of McDonalds in other contexts, namely that women feel welcome and safe. On the other hand, Barista betrays in every detail the middle-class Indian desire to appear modern, cool, and integrated into the world economy. With its tasteless cups of bagged tea for Rs 50 or more, it is not calculated to attract a working-class clientele: even as it has helped to enlargen the public sphere, promoting along with its coffee certain notions of culture, conversation, and conviviality, the complementary process of the contraction of the public sphere can be seen at work. The modern coffeehouse is thus as good a place as any for studying emerging notions of citizenship in India, and it is no accident that Barista-style shops appeared around the same time as India started to become a global player in the business of call centres. The uninitiated, as Safina Uberoi's recent documentary on Indian call centres and outsourcing suggests,[81] are even known to conflate call centres with call girls, a deplorable confusion that nonetheless points to the convergence of several disjunctive histories. The culture of the tawaifs or courtesans mirrored the rise of cities: initially working from mobile encampments, the *tawaifs* in time came to establish themselves in *kothas*. The men of leisure in the city supped at their feet, ate from their fingers, and were initiated into the pleasures of love-making from women who could weave the erotic into poetry, dance, and music. Not many professions were open to unattached or unmarried women working by night—and not many are open to them today, though work at call centres is the most obvious exception. One might say that call centres in Indian cities have opened up new possibilities for the present generation of young city women: not only are women finding themselves

---

[81] *Outsourced!* (2006), a film by Anna Carter and Safina Uberoi, delves into four lives each in India and Australia. *Nalini by Day, Nancy by Night*, a 2005 documentary directed by Sonali Gulati, looks at India's call centres from the point of view of an Indian settled in the US.

the principal breadwinners, but many claim that they are better able to resist the pressures placed on them to marry. But in the zero-sum logic of modern politics, the Baristas coffeehouses and call centres have, in facilitating the entry into the modern culture and economy of certain segments of the population, enlisted certain dominant conceptions of privilege, entitlement, and citizenship. One quite suspects that those opposed to the attempted transformation of Indian cities into gigantic call centres, service centres, and laboratories for the West will soon be treated as pariahs or refugees,[82] akin to the non-Hindus and non-Maharashtrians who have valiantly struggled to keep alive traditions of pluralism in the beleaguered city that now goes by the name of Mumbai.

From the standpoint of the critic of globalization, the Indian city can only hope to enter into the stream of the modern world by contracting a place in the newest phase of coolitude. Once before, as Mohandas Gandhi warned in *Hind Swaraj* (1909), we were seduced by the glitter of the West. Although much has been written on the city as the site of violence, crime, and organized terror—Jamshedpur, 1979; Delhi, 1984; Bombay, 1992; Ahmedabad, 2002—the city is always opening itself up to new forms of violence. Many commentators have described rioting as a predominantly urban phenomenon, but throughout the 1980s and 1990s this was also true of such phenomena as bride-burning. The city appears to furnish ample opportunities to remake oneself, but it can also become the vortex for the consolidation of partial, even xenophobic, political identities. The success of the Shiv Sena in Bombay is only the most vivid illustration of this tendency. Even as the idea of the public sphere has been vastly extended,

---

[82] It might be noted that the business process outsourcing (BPO) industry in India is changing rapidly. On the one hand, the Philippines has recently overtaken India as the largest employer of call centre workers in the world; on the other hand, owing partly to skyrocketing costs of land in Indian metropolises, BPOs have increasingly been shifting to the rural countryside, to smaller towns and what are called Tier-II and Tier-III cities. This is likely to raise the hackles of the critics even more, since the rural countryside and the small towns will now be viewed as gravely susceptible to the depredations of the city. It is one thing for young men and women from the backwaters to go to the city, but altogether another thing when the lifestyle and mentality of the city arrive at the doorstep of the countryside. Recent works on call centres, written predominantly from the standpoint of political economy, or focused on such matters as the safety of young women who work by night, have remained largely oblivious to what appears to be one of the most enduring aspects of the BPO industry in India, namely its role in establishing a rural-urban continuum.

the streets of Indian cities persist in exuding their own culture, defying those distinctions between private and public that have sometimes been thought to lie at the heart of Western modernity. What is, and what will remain, specifically Indian about the Indian city? Among other pertinent questions, this is certainly one that animates this anthology.

Selections in this anthology: Sociologists and demographers in India have long been writing on urbanization in India, but there is a newer kind of literature, as I have already suggested, that has been emerging on the subject of cities in India, though some cities—Bombay, Calcutta, and Delhi—have been much better served by this literature than other cities such as Jaipur, Allahabad, or even Hyderabad. When Oxford University Press and I settled upon the idea of doing this anthology, we were in agreement that the anthology would steer clear of much of the older scholarly literature which can be safely located within a rather narrow conception of the social sciences. Very little of the trajectories that are so amply on display in the best of Indian history, from postcolonial theory and poststructuralism to feminism, were to be witnessed in the scholarly and popular literature on Indian cities a decade ago, though now the intellectual landscape is considerably more diverse. Second, as a corollary it comes as no surprise to find that there is very little treatment in the literature on the city as metaphor, and on the city as a site of art, music, theatre, public performance, literature, popular culture, and street culture. No one is unaware of the fact, to take another example, that city spaces are gendered, and there are casual observations strewn about Indian cities, or at least some of them, as male enclaves. Some people have commented on how unsafe most Indian cities are for women, and if the safety of women were a litmus test on how far one might view public spaces as truly democratic, it is doubtful that any Indian city would pass the test. Embracing such a view does not preclude one from staking another equally important position, namely that some element of surprise, uncertainty, and even physical insecurity is critical to the idea of a city. Surprisingly, notwithstanding the increased proliferation of scholarly studies informed by feminist insights, no book-length study of 'the gendered city' in the Indian context has yet been attempted, and indeed one would be hard-pressed to find more than a handful of scholarly articles.

There is no gainsaying the fact that though studies—among them, Ravi Kalia's three books on Gandhinagar, Chandigarh, and Bhubaneswar—have been published in recent years of cities that serve more as provincial capitals than as cosmopolitan centres, the scholarly lens continues to be focused on the metropolises of Calcutta, Bombay, and Delhi. Notwithstanding the persistent hullabaloo over Bangalore and Hyderabad, each with a xlv population of over five million, as modernist icons of resurgent India, I found comparatively little on either city, whether of scholarly provenance or more literary in its sensibility, that struck me as comparable to the best literature on the country's three largest metropolises.[83] To be sure, a city such as Lucknow has been relatively well-served by both popular memory and historical inquiry, but the sheer paucity of scholarly literature on Kanpur, Allahabad, Mysore, and even Jaipur (a major tourist destination) and Ahmedabad (a city, we may say, of immense political and economic calculations) should be sufficient indication of the fact that Lucknow remains something of an exception among the next rung of Indian cities. A certain melancholia about Lucknow; the rich literary, musical, and culinary culture of the courts of the Nawabs of Awadh; the enigmatic figure of Awadh's deposed ruler, Wajid Ali Shah; the association of Lucknow with courtesans; the history of Lucknow as one of the decisive battlegrounds during the Indian Rebellion of 1857—all this and much else besides have driven the interest in Lucknow.[84] One might have thought that Ahmedabad would similarly have attracted much attention: its prime importance as a centre of the textile industry may be gauged by the fact that it was once dubbed the 'Manchester of the East', and it is from Ahmedabad that Gandhi launched his political career in India. Its formidable architectural legacy spans the period from the sixteenth century to the present, and some of the twentieth century's prominent architects, among them Le Corbusier (better known in India for designing the capital city of Chandigarh) and Balkrishna Doshi, are represented in Ahmedabad by a considerable body of work. However, more than four decades after it was published, Kenneth Gillion's *Ahmedabad: A Study in Urban Indian History* (1968) still remains the only work of its kind on a city that is now better known among some scholars as a 'laboratory' of Hindutva. Whatever the inclination to celebrate the 'urban turn' in Indian studies, it has borne too few fruits.

There is, at present, no anthology of the modern Indian city, and certainly none that even remotely focuses on the city as a site of imagination, as a nodal point for contestations over modernity, and

---

[83] See, however, Janaki Nair, *The Promise of the Metropolis: Bangalore's Twentieth Century* (Delhi: Oxford University Press, 2005).

[84] As an instance of the passionate writing on Lucknow, see Amaresh Misra, *Lucknow: Fire of Grace—The Story of its Renaissance, Revolution and the Aftermath* (Delhi: HarperCollins India, 1999).

as a location of specific cultural phenomena. In putting together this anthology, I was animated by several other considerations. Over the last few years, in responding to queries about the nature of this enterprise, I generally had to begin with the explanation that the anthology was not focused on a particular Indian city, nor has it been conceptualized from the standpoint of offering a chronological account of the development of the city in modern India. Though I teach in a department of history, it did not seem to me that insights into the city would necessarily be best served by historical narratives; and, as shall be apparent to readers, I have drawn liberally upon fiction, poetry, travelogues, memoirs, oral histories, public and social commentary, and Indian cinema, as well as scholarly work in disciplines, besides history, such as anthropology and sociology. In a few instances, I commissioned translations for this anthology, or called upon younger scholars whose work seems to me richly deserving of wide public approbation; but, for the most part, I have extracted from previously published work, whether originally appearing in English or, as is more common, translated into English from Indian languages.

There is no other way of putting it except to say that the selections are entirely mine, indeed exceedingly personal. I was, to take one example, very keen on the inclusion of a few pages from Rohinton Mistry's *Such a Long Journey*. But here I was constrained by onerous copyright fees. Some readers will be struck by other obvious omissions, while others might well wonder at the wisdom of my choices. My aim, in the first instance, has been that the reader should get a feel for the modern Indian city—whether the city be Bombay, Delhi, Calcutta, Lucknow, Benares, or, indeed, no city in particular. Just what is it that makes for the texture and sensibility of a city? What associations and feelings does the city evoke, and how does the newcomer to the city in India experience its chaos, din, and buzz of activity? The 'Mosaic of the City' introduces the reader to the city's infinite variety, to the people who inhabit its spaces—residents, students, sweepers, labourers, traders, businessmen, householders, hookers, artists, and poets, as much as Muslims, Hindus, Christians, Jews, women, men, and children. What are the lures of the city, the anxieties it provokes, and the satisfactions it alone offers? Whom does the city possess, disown, and embrace, and why are some drawn to it while others are repulsed by its hurried pace, indifference, and monstrous appetite? The selections offer a sweeping view of the city at night and by day, the roar of the city and its oases of reflection, its constraints and its freedoms. There is, I hope, something in the anthology for every reader.

Mark Twain

Following the Equator

January 20th. Bombay! A bewitching place, a bewildering place, an enchanting place—the Arabian Nights come again? It is a vast city; contains about a million inhabitants. Natives, they are, with a slight sprinkling of white people—not enough to have the slightest modifying effect upon the massed dark complexion of the public. It is winter here, yet the weather is the divine weather of June, and the foliage is the fresh and heavenly foliage of June. There is a rank of noble great shade trees across the way from the hotel, and under them sit groups of picturesque natives of both sexes; and the juggler in his turban is there with his snakes and his magic; and all day long the cabs and the multitudinous varieties of costumes flock by. It does not seem as if one could ever get tired of watching this moving show, this shining and shifting spectacle. . . . In the great bazar the pack and jam of natives was marvelous, the sea of rich-colored turbans and draperies an inspiring sight, and the quaint and showy Indian architecture was just the right setting for it. Toward sunset another show; this is the drive around the sea-shore to Malabar Point, where Lord Sandhurst, the Governor of the Bombay Presidency, lives. Parsee palaces all along the first part of the drive; and past them all the world is driving; the private carriages of wealthy Englishmen and natives of rank are manned by a driver and three footmen in stunning oriental liveries—two of these turbaned statues standing up behind, as fine as monuments. Sometimes even the public carriages have this superabundant crew, slightly modified—one to drive, one to sit by and see it done, and one to stand up behind and yell—yell when there is anybody in the way, and for practice when there isn't. It all helps to keep up the liveliness and augment the general sense of swiftness and energy and confusion and pow-wow.

In the region of Scandal Point—felicitous name—where there are handy rocks to sit on and a noble view of the sea on the one hand, and on the other the passing and repassing whirl and tumult of gay carriages, are great groups of comfortably-off Parsee women—perfect flower-beds of brilliant color, a fascinating spectacle. Tramp, tramp, tramping along the road, in singles, couples, groups, and gangs, you have the working-man and the working-woman—but not clothed like ours. Usually the man is a nobly-built great athlete, with not a rag on but his loin-handkerchief; his color a deep dark brown, his skin satin, his rounded muscles knobbing it as if it had eggs under it. Usually the woman is a slender and shapely creature, as erect as a lightning-rod, and she has but one thing on—a bright-colored piece of stuff which is wound about her head and her body down nearly half-way to her knees, and which clings like her own skin. Her legs and feet are bare, and so are her arms, except for her fanciful bunches of loose silver rings on her ankles and on her arms. She has jewelry bunched on the side of her nose also, and showy clusterings on her toes. When she undresses for bed she takes off her jewelry, I suppose. If she took off anything more she would catch cold. As a rule she has a large shiney brass water jar of graceful shape on her head, and one of her naked arms curves up and the hand holds it there. She is so straight, so erect, and she steps with such style, and such easy grace and dignity; and her curved arm and her brazen jar are such a help to the picture—indeed, our working-women cannot begin with her as a road-decoration.

It is all color, bewitching color, enchanting color—everywhere all around—all the way around the curving great opaline bay clear to Government House, where the turbaned big native 'chuprassies' stand grouped in state at the door in their robes of fiery red, and do most properly and stunningly finish up the splendid show and make it theatrically complete. I wish I were a 'chuprassy'.

This is indeed India! the land of dreams and romance, of fabulous wealth and fabulous poverty, of splendor and rags, of palaces and hovels, of famine and pestilence, of genii and giants and Aladdin lamps, of tigers and elephants, the cobra and the jungle, the country of a hundred nations and a hundred tongues, of a thousand religions and two million gods, cradle of the human race, birthplace of human speech, mother of history, grandmother of legend, great-grandmother of tradition, whose yesterdays bear date with the mouldering antiquities of the rest of the nations—the one sole country under the sun that is endowed with an imperishable interest for alien prince and alien peasant, for lettered and ignorant, wise and fool, rich and poor, bond and free, the one land that all men desire to see, and having seen once, by even a glimpse, would not give that glimpse for the shows of all the rest of the globe combined. Even now, after the lapse of a year, the delirium of those days in Bombay has not left me, and

I hope never will. It was all new, no detail of it hackneyed. And India did not wait for morning, it began at the hotel—straight away. The lobbies and halls were full of turbaned, and fez'd and embroidered, cap'd, and barefooted, and cotton-clad dark natives, some of them rushing about, others at rest squatting, or sitting on the ground; some of them chattering with energy, others still and dreamy; in the dining-room every man's own private native servant standing behind his chair, and dressed for a part in the Arabian Nights.

Our rooms were high up, on the front. A white man—he was a burly German—went up with us, and brought three natives along to see to arranging things. About fourteen others followed in procession, with the hand-baggage; each carried an article—and only one; a bag, in some cases, in other cases less. One strong native carried my overcoat, another a parasol, another a box of cigars, another a novel, and the last man in the procession had no load but a fan. It was all done with earnestness and sincerity, there was not a smile in the procession from the head of it to the tail of it. Each man waited patiently, tranquilly, in no sort of hurry, till one of us found time to give him a copper, then he bent his head reverently, touched his forehead with his fingers, and went his way. They seemed a soft and gentle race, and there was something both winning and touching about their demeanor.

There was a vast glazed door which opened upon the balcony. It needed closing, or cleaning, or something, and a native got down on his knees and went to work at it. He seemed to be doing it well enough, but perhaps he wasn't, for the burly German put on a look that betrayed dissatisfaction, then without explaining what was wrong, gave the native a brisk cuff on the jaw and then told him where the defect was. It seemed such a shame to do that before us all. The native took it with meekness, saying nothing, and not showing in his face or manner any resentment. I had not seen the like of this for fifty years. . . .

Chapter XLII

Each person is born to one possession which outvalues all his others—his last breath.

—Pudd'nhead Wilson's New Calendar.

Toward midnight, that night, there was another function. This was a Hindoo wedding—no, I think it was a betrothal ceremony. Always before, we had driven through streets that were multitudinous and tumultuous with picturesque native life, but now there was nothing of that. We seemed to move through a city of the dead. There was hardly a suggestion of life in those still and vacant streets. Even the crows were silent. But everywhere on the ground lay sleeping natives-hundreds and hundreds. They lay stretched at full length and tightly wrapped in blankets, heads and all. Their attitude and their rigidity counterfeited death. The plague was not in Bombay then, but it is devastating the city now. The shops are deserted, now, half of the people have fled, and of the remainder the smitten perish by shoals every day. No doubt the city looks now in the daytime as it looked then at night. When we had pierced deep into the native quarter and were threading its narrow dim lanes, we had to go carefully, for men were stretched asleep all about and there was hardly room to drive between them. And every now and then a swarm of rats would scamper across past the horses' feet in the vague light—the forbears of the rats that are carrying the plague from house to house in Bombay now. The shops were but sheds, little booths open to the street; and the goods had been removed, and on the counters families were sleeping, usually with an oil lamp present. Recurrent dead watches, it looked like.

But at last we turned a corner and saw a great glare of light ahead. It was the home of the bride, wrapped in a perfect conflagration of illuminations,—mainly gas-work designs, gotten up specially for the occasion. Within was abundance of brilliancy—flames, costumes, colors, decorations, mirrors—it was another Aladdin show.

The bride was a trim and comely little thing of twelve years, dressed as we would dress a boy, though more expensively than we should do it, of course. She moved about very much at her ease, and stopped and talked with the guests and allowed her wedding jewelry to be examined. It was very fine. Particularly a rope of great diamonds, a lovely thing to look at and handle. It had a great emerald hanging to it.

The bridegroom was not present. He was having betrothal festivities of his own at his father's house. As I understood it, he and the bride were to entertain company every night and nearly all night for a week or more, then get married, if alive. Both of the children were a little elderly, as brides and grooms go, in India—twelve; they ought to have been married a year or two sooner; still to a stranger twelve seems quite young enough.

A while after midnight a couple of celebrated and high-priced nautch-girls appeared in the gorgeous place, and danced and sang. With them were men who played upon strange instruments which made uncanny noises of a sort to make one's flesh creep. One of these instruments was a pipe,

and to its music the girls went through a performance which represented
snake charming. It seemed a doubtful sort of music to charm anything
with, but a native gentleman assured me that snakes like it and will come
out of their holes and listen to it with every evidence of refreshment and
gratitude. He said that at an entertainment in his grounds once, the pipe
brought out half a dozen snakes, and the music had to be stopped before
they would be persuaded to go. Nobody wanted their company, for they
were bold, familiar, and dangerous; but no one would kill them, of course,
for it is sinful for a Hindoo to kill any kind of a creature. . . .

Then again the deep silence, the skurrying rats, the dim forms
stretched everywhere on the ground; and on either hand those open
booths counterfeiting sepulchres, with counterfeit corpses sleeping
motionless in the flicker of the counterfeit death lamps. And now, a year
later, when I read the cablegrams I seem to be reading of what I myself
partly saw—saw before it happened—in a prophetic dream, as it were.
One cablegram says, 'Business in the native town is about suspended.
Except the wailing and the tramp of the funerals. There is but little life
or movement. The closed shops exceed in number those that remain
open.' Another says that 325,000 of the people have fled the city and are
carrying the plague to the country. Three days later comes the news, 'The
population is reduced by half.' The refugees have carried the disease to
Karachi; '220 cases, 214 deaths.' A day or two later, '52 fresh cases, all of
which proved fatal.'

The plague carries with it a terror which no other disease can excite;
for of all diseases known to men it is the deadliest—by far the deadliest.
'Fifty-two fresh cases—all fatal.' It is the Black Death alone that slays
like that. We can all imagine, after a fashion, the desolation of a plague-
stricken city, and the stupor of stillness broken at intervals by distant
bursts of wailing, marking the passing of funerals, here and there and
yonder, but I suppose it is not possible for us to realize to ourselves the
nightmare of dread and fear that possesses the living who are present in
such a place and cannot get away. That half million fled from Bombay
in a wild panic suggests to us something of what they were feeling, but
perhaps not even they could realize what the half million were feeling
whom they left stranded behind to face the stalking horror without chance
of escape. Kinglake was in Cairo many years ago during an epidemic of
the Black Death, and he has imagined the terrors that creep into a man's
heart at such a time and follow him until they themselves breed the fatal
sign in the armpit, and then the delirium with confused images, and home-
dreams, and reeling billiard-tables, and then the sudden blank of death . . .

Hunger is the handmaid of genius

—Pudd'nhead Wilson's New Calendar.

One day during our stay in Bombay there was a criminal trial of a most interesting sort, a terribly realistic chapter out of the 'Arabian Nights,' a strange mixture of simplicities and pieties and murderous practicalities, which brought back the forgotten days of Thuggee and made them live again; in fact, even made them believable. It was a case where a young girl had been assassinated for the sake of her trifling ornaments, things not worth a laborer's day's wages in America. This thing could have been done in many other countries, but hardly with the cold business-like depravity, absence of fear, absence of caution, destitution of the sense of horror, repentance, remorse, exhibited in this case. Elsewhere the murderer would have done his crime secretly, by night, and without witnesses; his fears would have allowed him no peace while the dead body was in his neighborhood; he would not have rested until he had gotten it safe out of the way and hidden as effectually as he could hide it. But this Indian murderer does his deed in the full light of day, cares nothing for the society of witnesses, is in no way incommoded by the presence of the corpse, takes his own time about disposing of it, and the whole party are so indifferent, so phlegmatic, that they take their regular sleep as if nothing was happening and no halters hanging over them; and these five bland people close the episode with a religious service. The thing reads like a Meadows-Taylor Thug-tale of half a century ago, as may be seen by the official report of the trial:

'At the Mazagon Police Court yesterday, Superintendent Nolan again charged Tookaram Suntoo Savat Baya, woman, her daughter Krishni, and Gopal Vithoo Bhanayker, before Mr. Phiroze Hoshang Dastur, Fourth Presidency Magistrate, under sections 302 and 109 of the Code, with having on the night of the 30th of December last murdered a Hindoo girl named Cassi, aged 12, by strangulation, in the room of a chawl at Jakaria Bunder, on the Sewriroad, and also with aiding and abetting each other in the commission of the offense.

'Mr. F.A. Little, Public Prosecutor, conducted the case on behalf of the Crown, the accused being undefended.

'Mr. Little applied under the provisions of the Criminal Procedure Code to tender pardon to one of the accused, Krishni, woman, aged 22, on her undertaking to make a true and full statement of facts under which the deceased girl Cassi was murdered.

'The Magistrate having granted the Public Prosecutor's application, the accused Krishni went into the witness-box, and, on being examined by Mr. Little, made the following confession:—I am a mill-hand employed at the Jubilee Mill. I recollect the day (Tuesday) on which the body of the deceased Cassi was found. Previous to that I attended the mill for half a day, and then returned home at 3 in the afternoon, when I saw five persons in the house, viz.: the first accused Tookaram, who is my paramour, my mother, the second accused Baya, the accused Gopal, and two guests named Ramji Daji and Annaji Gungaram. Tookaram rented the room of the chawl situated at Jakaria Bunder-road from its owner, Girdharilal Radhakishan, and in that room I, my paramour, Tookaram, and his younger brother, Yesso Mahadhoo, live. Since his arrival in Bombay from his native country Yesso came and lived with us. When I returned from the mill on the afternoon of that day, I saw the two guests seated on a cot in the veranda, and a few minutes after the accused Gopal came and took his seat by their side, while I and my mother were seated inside the room. Tookaram, who had gone out to fetch some 'pan' and betelnuts, on his return home had brought the two guests with him. After returning home he gave them 'pan supari'. While they were eating it my mother came out of the room and inquired of one of the guests, Ramji, what had happened to his foot, when he replied that he had tried many remedies, but they had done him no good. My mother then took some rice in her hand and prophesied that the disease which Ramji was suffering from would not be cured until he returned to his native country. In the meantime the deceased Casi came from the direction of an out-house, and stood in front on the threshold of our room with a 'lota' in her hand. Tookaram then told his two guests to leave the room, and they then went up the steps towards the quarry. After the guests had gone away, Tookaram seized the deceased, who had come into the room, and he afterwards put a waistband around her, and tied her to a post which supports a loft. After doing this, he pressed the girl's throat, and, having tied her mouth with the 'dhotur' (now shown in Court), fastened it to the post. Having killed the girl, Tookaram removed her gold head ornament and a gold 'putlee', and also took charge of her 'lota'. Besides these two ornaments Cassi had on her person ear-studs, a nose-ring, some silver toe-rings, two necklaces, a pair of silver anklets and bracelets. Tookaram afterwards tried to remove the silver amulets, the ear-studs, and the nose-ring; but he failed in his attempt. . . .

There is only one India! It is the only country that has a monopoly of grand and imposing specialties. When another country has a remarkable thing, it cannot have it all to itself—some other country has a duplicate. But India—that is different. Its marvels are its own; the patents cannot be infringed; imitations are not possible. And think of the size of them, the majesty of them, the weird and outlandish character of the most of them!

There is the Plague, the Black Death: India invented it; India is the cradle of that mighty birth.

The Car of Juggernaut was India's invention.

So was the Suttee; and within the time of men still living eight hundred widows willingly, and, in fact, rejoicingly, burned themselves to death on the bodies of their dead husbands in a single year. Eight hundred would do it this year if the British government would let them.

Famine is India's specialty. Elsewhere famines are inconsequential incidents—in India they are devastating cataclysms; in one case they annihilate hundreds; in the other, millions.

India has 2,000,000 gods, and worships them all. In religion all other countries are paupers; India is the only millionaire.

With her everything is on a giant scale—even her poverty; no other country can show anything to compare with it. And she has been used to wealth on so vast a scale that she has to shorten to single words the expressions describing great sums. She describes 100,000 with one word—a 'lahk[sic]'; she describes ten millions with one word—a 'crore'.

In the bowels of the granite mountains she has patiently carved out dozens of vast temples, and made them glorious with sculptured colonnades and stately groups of statuary, and has adorned the eternal walls with noble paintings. She has built fortresses of such magnitude that the show-strongholds of the rest of the world are but modest little things by comparison; palaces that are wonders for rarity of materials, delicacy and beauty of workmanship, and for cost; and one tomb which men go around the globe to see. It takes eighty nations, speaking eighty languages, to people her, and they number three hundred millions.

On top of all this she is the mother and home of that wonder of wonders—caste—and of that mystery of mysteries, the satanic brotherhood of the Thugs.

India had the start of the whole world in the beginning of things. She had the first civilization; she had the first accumulation of material wealth; she was populous with deep thinkers and subtle intellects; she had mines, and woods, and a fruitful soil. It would seem as if she should have kept the lead, and should be to-day not the meek dependent of an alien master, but mistress of the world, and delivering law and command to every tribe and nation in it. But, in truth, there was never any possibility of such supremacy for her. If there had been but one India and one language—but there were eighty of them! Where there are eighty nations and several hundred governments, fighting and quarreling must be the common business of life; unity of purpose and policy are impossible; out

of such elements supremacy in the world cannot come. Even caste itself
could have had the defeating effect of a multiplicity of tongues, no doubt;
for it separates a people into layers, and layers, and still other layers, that
have no community of feeling with each other; and in such a condition
of things as that, patriotism can have no healthy growth.

Chapter XLIV

FROM DIARY

January 30. What a spectacle the railway station was, at train-time! It
was a very large station, yet when we arrived it seemed as if the whole
world was present—half of it inside, the other half outside, and both
halves, bearing mountainous head-loads of bedding and other freight,
trying simultaneously to pass each other, in opposing floods, in one
narrow door. These opposing floods were patient, gentle, long-suffering
natives, with whites scattered among them at rare intervals; and wherever
a white man's native servant appeared, that native seemed to have put
aside his natural gentleness for the time and invested himself with the
white man's privilege of making a way for himself by promptly shoving
all intervening black things out of it. In these exhibitions of authority
Satan was scandalous. He was probably a Thug in one of his former
incarnations.

Inside the great station, tides upon tides of rainbow-costumed natives
swept along, this way and that, in massed and bewildering confusion,
eager, anxious, belated, distressed; and washed up to the long trains
and flowed into them with their packs and bundles, and disappeared,
followed at once by the next wash, the next wave. And here and there, in
the midst of this hurly-burly, and seemingly undisturbed by it, sat great
groups of natives on the bare stone floor,—young, slender brown women,
old, gray wrinkled women, little soft brown babies, old men, young men,
boys; all poor people, but all the females among them, both big and little,
bejeweled with cheap and showy nose-rings, toe-rings, leglets, and armlets,
these things constituting all their wealth, no doubt. These silent crowds
sat there with their humble bundles and baskets and small household
gear about them, and patiently waited—for what? A train that was to
start at some time or other during the day or night! They hadn't timed
themselves well, but that was no matter—the thing had been so ordered
from on high, therefore why worry? There was plenty of time, hours and
hours of it, and the thing that was to happen would happen—there was
no hurrying it.

The natives traveled third class, and at marvelously cheap rates. They were packed and crammed into cars that held each about fifty; and it was said that often a Brahmin of the highest caste was thus brought into personal touch, and consequent defilement, with persons of the lowest castes—no doubt a very shocking thing if a body could understand it and properly appreciate it. Yes, a Brahmin who didn't own a rupee and couldn't borrow one, might have to touch elbows with a rich hereditary lord of inferior caste, inheritor of an ancient title a couple of yards long, and he would just have to stand it; for if either of the two was allowed to go in the cars where the sacred white people were, it probably wouldn't be the august poor Brahmin. There was an immense string of those third-class cars, for the natives travel by hordes; and a weary hard night of it the occupants would have, no doubt.

When we reached our car, Satan and Barney had already arrived there with their train of porters carrying bedding and parasols and cigar boxes, and were at work. We named him Barney for short; we couldn't use his real name, there wasn't time.

It was a car that promised comfort; indeed, luxury. Yet the cost of it—well, economy could no further go; even in France; not even in Italy.

It was built of the plainest and cheapest partially-smoothed boards, with a coating of dull paint on them, and there was nowhere a thought of decoration. The floor was bare, but would not long remain so when the dust should begin to fly. Across one end of the compartment ran a netting for the accommodation of hand-baggage; at the other end was a door which would shut, upon compulsion, but wouldn't stay shut; it opened into a narrow little closet which had a wash-bowl in one end of it, and a place to put a towel, in case you had one with you—and you would be sure to have towels, because you buy them with the bedding, knowing that the railway doesn't furnish them. On each side of the car, and running fore and aft, was a broad leather-covered sofa to sit on in the day and sleep on at night. Over each sofa hung, by straps, a wide, flat, leather-covered shelf—to sleep on. In the daytime you can hitch it up against the wall, out of the way—and then you have a big unencumbered and most comfortable room to spread out in. No car in any country is quite its equal for comfort (and privacy) I think. For usually there are but two persons in it; and even when there are four there is but little sense of impaired privacy. Our own cars at home can surpass the railway world in all details but that one: they have no cosiness; there are too many people together. . . .

January 31. Barroda. Arrived at 7 this morning. The dawn was just beginning to show. It was forlorn to have to turn out in a strange place

still. But the gentlemen who had come to receive us were there with
their servants, and they make quick work; there was no lost time. We
were soon outside and moving swiftly through the soft gray light, and
presently were comfortably housed—with more servants to help than we
were used to, and with rather embarassingly important officials to direct
them. But it was custom; they spoke Ballarat English, their bearing was
charming and hospitable, and so all went well.

Breakfast was a satisfaction. Across the lawns was visible in the distance
through the open window an Indian well, with two oxen tramping
leisurely up and down long inclines, drawing water; and out of the
stillness came the suffering screech of the machinery—not quite musical,
and yet soothingly melancholy and dreamy and reposeful—a wail of
lost spirits, one might imagine. And commemorative and reminiscent,
perhaps; for of course the Thugs used to throw people down that well
when they were done with them.

After breakfast the day began, a sufficiently busy one. We were driven
by winding roads through a vast park, with noble forests of great trees,
and with tangles and jungles of lovely growths of a humbler sort; and at
one place three large gray apes came out and pranced across the road—a
good deal of a surprise and an unpleasant one, for such creatures belong
in the menagerie, and they look artificial and out of place in a wilderness.

We came to the city, by and by, and drove all through it. Intensely
Indian, it was, and crumbly, and mouldering, and immemorially old, to all
appearance. And the houses—oh, indescribably quaint and curious they
were, with their fronts an elaborate lace-work of intricate and beautiful
wood-carving, and now and then further adorned with rude pictures of
elephants and princes and gods done in shouting colors; and all the ground
floors along these cramped and narrow lanes occupied as shops—shops
unbelievably small and impossibly packed with merchantable rubbish,
and with nine-tenths-naked natives squatting at their work of hammering,
pounding, brazing, soldering, sewing, designing, cooking, measuring out
grain, grinding it, repairing idols—and then the swarm of ragged and
noisy humanity under the horses' feet and everywhere, and the pervading
reek and fume and smell! It was all wonderful and delightful.

Imagine a file of elephants marching through such a crevice of a street
and scraping the paint off both sides of it with their hides. How big they
must look, and how little they must make the houses look; and when
the elephants are in their glittering court costume, what a contrast they
must make with the humble and sordid surroundings. And when a mad

elephant goes raging through, belting right and left with his trunk, how do these swarms of people get out of the way? I suppose it is a thing which happens now and then in the mad season (for elephants have a mad season).

I wonder how old the town is. There are patches of building—massive structures, monuments, apparently—that are so battered and worn, and seemingly so tired and so burdened with the weight of age, and so dulled and stupefied with trying to remember things they forgot before history began, that they give one the feeling that they must have been a part of original Creation. This is indeed one of the oldest of the princedoms of India, and has always been celebrated for its barbaric pomps and splendors, and for the wealth of its princes.

Chapter XLV

It takes your enemy and your friend, working together, to hurt you to the heart; the one to slander you and the other to get the news to you.
—Pudd'nhead Wilson's New Calendar.

Out of the town again; a long drive through open country, by winding roads among secluded villages nestling in the inviting shade of tropic vegetation, a Sabbath stillness everywhere, sometimes a pervading sense of solitude, but always barefoot natives gliding by like spirits, without sound of footfall, and others in the distance dissolving away and vanishing like the creatures of dreams. Now and then a string of stately camels passed by—always interesting things to look at—and they were velvet-shod by nature, and made no noise. Indeed, there were no noises of any sort in this paradise. Yes, once there was one, for a moment: a file of native convicts passed along in charge of an officer, and we caught the soft clink of their chains. In a retired spot, resting himself under a tree, was a holy person—a naked black fakeer, thin and skinny, and whitey-gray all over with ashes. . . .

Allahabad means 'City of God.' I get this from the books. From a printed curiosity—a letter written by one of those brave and confident Hindoo strugglers with the English tongue, called a 'babu'—I got a more compressed translation: 'Godville.' It is perfectly correct, but that is the most that can be said for it.

We arrived in the forenoon, and short-handed; for Satan got left behind somewhere that morning, and did not overtake us until after nightfall. It seemed very peaceful without him. The world seemed asleep and dreaming.

I did not see the native town, I think. I do not remember why; for an
incident connects it with the Great Mutiny, and that is enough to make
any place interesting. But I saw the English part of the city. It is a town
of wide avenues and noble distances, and is comely and alluring, and full
of suggestions of comfort and leisure, and of the serenity which a good
conscience buttressed by a sufficient bank account gives. The bungalows
(dwellings) stand well back in the seclusion and privacy of large enclosed
compounds (private grounds, as we should say) and in the shade and
shelter of trees. Even the photographer and the prosperous merchant ply
their industries in the elegant reserve of big compounds, and the citizens
drive in there upon their business occasions. And not in cabs—no; in the
Indian cities cabs are for the drifting stranger; all the white citizens have
private carriages; and each carriage has a flock of white-turbaned black
footmen and drivers all over it. The vicinity of a lecture-hall looks like
a snowstorm,—and makes the lecturer feel like an opera. India has many
names, and they are correctly descriptive. It is the Land of Contradictions,
the Land of Subtlety and Superstition, the Land of Wealth and Poverty,
the Land of Splendor and Desolation, the Land of Plague and Famine, the
Land of the Thug and the Poisoner, and of the Meek and the Patient, the
Land of the Suttee, the Land of the Unreinstatable Widow, the Land where
All Life is Holy, the Land of Cremation, the Land where the Vulture is a
Grave and a Monument, the Land of the Multitudinous Gods; and if signs
go for anything, it is the Land of the Private Carriage.

In Bombay the forewoman of a millinery shop came to the hotel in
her private carriage to take the measure for a gown—not for me, but
for another. She had come out to India to make a temporary stay, but
was extending it indefinitely; indeed, she was purposing to end her days
there. In London, she said, her work had been hard, her hours long; for
economy's sake she had had to live in shabby rooms and far away from
the shop, watch the pennies, deny herself many of the common comforts
of life, restrict herself in effect to its bare necessities, eschew cabs, travel
third-class by underground train to and from her work, swallowing
coal-smoke and cinders all the way, and sometimes troubled with the
society of men and women who were less desirable than the smoke and
the cinders. But in Bombay, on almost any kind of wages, she could live
in comfort, and keep her carriage, and have six servants in place of the
woman-of-all-work she had had in her English home. Later, in Calcutta,
I found that the Standard Oil clerks had small one-horse vehicles, and
did no walking; and I was told that the clerks of the other large concerns
there had the like equipment. But to return to Allahabad.

I was up at dawn, the next morning. In India the tourist's servant does not sleep in a room in the hotel, but rolls himself up head and ears in his blanket and stretches himself on the veranda, across the front of his master's door, and spends the night there. I don't believe anybody's servant occupies a room. Apparently, the bungalow servants sleep on the veranda; it is roomy, and goes all around the house. I speak of menservants; I saw none of the other sex. I think there are none, except child-nurses. I was up at dawn, and walked around the veranda, past the rows of sleepers. In front of one door a Hindoo servant was squatting, waiting for his master to call him. He had polished the yellow shoes and placed them by the door, and now he had nothing to do but wait. It was freezing cold, but there he was, as motionless as a sculptured image, and as patient. It troubled me. I wanted to say to him, 'Don't crouch there like that and freeze; nobody requires it of you; stir around and get warm.' But I hadn't the words. I thought of saying 'jeldy jow', but I couldn't remember what it meant, so I didn't say it. I knew another phrase, but it wouldn't come to my mind. I moved on, purposing to dismiss him from my thoughts, but his bare legs and bare feet kept him there. They kept drawing me back from the sunny side to a point whence I could see him. At the end of an hour he had not changed his attitude in the least degree. It was a curious and impressive exhibition of meekness and patience, or fortitude or indifference, I did not know which. But it worried me, and it was spoiling my morning. In fact, it spoiled two hours of it quite thoroughly. I quitted this vicinity, then, and left him to punish himself as much as he might want to. But up to that time the man had not changed his attitude a hair. He will always remain with me, I suppose; his figure never grows vague in my memory. Whenever I read of Indian resignation, Indian patience under wrongs, hardships, and misfortunes, he comes before me. He becomes a personification, and stands for India in trouble. And for untold ages India in trouble has been pursued with the very remark which I was going to utter but didn't, because its meaning had slipped me: 'Jeldy jow!' ('Come, shove along!')

Why, it was the very thing.

In the early brightness we made a long drive out to the Fort. Part of the way was beautiful. It led under stately trees and through groups of native houses and by the usual village well, where the picturesque gangs are always flocking to and fro and laughing and chattering; and this time brawny men were deluging their bronze bodies with the limpid water, and making a refreshing and enticing show of it; enticing, for the sun was already transacting business, firing India up for the day. There was plenty of this early bathing going on, for it was getting toward breakfast time, and with an unpurified body the Hindoo must not eat.

Then we struck into the hot plain, and found the roads crowded with pilgrims of both sexes, for one of the great religious fairs of India was being held, just beyond the Fort, at the junction of the sacred rivers, the Ganges and the Jumna. Three sacred rivers, I should have said, for there is a subterranean one. Nobody has seen it, but that doesn't signify. The fact that it is there is enough. These pilgrims had come from all over India; some of them had been months on the way, plodding patiently along in the heat and dust, worn, poor, hungry, but supported and sustained by an unwavering faith and belief; they were supremely happy and content, now; their full and sufficient reward was at hand; they were going to be cleansed from every vestige of sin and corruption by these holy waters which make utterly pure whatsoever thing they touch, even the dead and rotten. It is wonderful, the power of a faith like that, that can make multitudes upon multitudes of the old and weak and the young and frail enter without hesitation or complaint upon such incredible journeys and endure the resultant miseries without repining. It is done in love, or it is done in fear; I do not know which it is. No matter what the impulse is, the act born of it is beyond imagination marvelous to our kind of people, the cold whites. There are choice great natures among us that could exhibit the equivalent of this prodigious self-sacrifice, but the rest of us know that we should not be equal to anything approaching it. Still, we all talk self-sacrifice, and this makes me hope that we are large enough to honor it in the Hindoo.

Two millions of natives arrive at this fair every year. How many start, and die on the road, from age and fatigue and disease and scanty nourishment, and how many die on the return, from the same causes, no one knows; but the tale is great, one may say enormous. Every twelfth year is held to be a year of peculiar grace; a greatly augmented volume of pilgrims results then. The twelfth year has held this distinction since the remotest times, it is said. It is said also that there is to be but one more twelfth year—for the Ganges. After that, that holiest of all sacred rivers will cease to be holy, and will be abandoned by the pilgrim for many centuries; how many, the wise men have not stated. At the end of that interval it will become holy again. Meantime, the data will be arranged by those people who have charge of all such matters, the great chief Brahmins. It will be like shutting down a mint. At a first glance it looks most unbrahminically uncommercial, but I am not disturbed, being soothed and tranquilized by their reputation. 'Brer fox he lay low,' as

Uncle Remus says; and at the judicious time he will spring something on the Indian public which will show that he was not financially asleep when he took the Ganges out of the market.

Great numbers of the natives along the roads were bringing away holy water from the rivers. They would carry it far and wide in India and sell it. Tavernier, the French traveler (17th century), notes that Ganges water is often given at weddings, 'each guest receiving a cup or two, according to the liberality of the host; sometimes 2,000 or 3,000 rupees' worth of it is consumed at a wedding.'

The Fort is a huge old structure, and has had a large experience in religions. In its great court stands a monolith which was placed there more than 2,000 years ago to preach (Budhism) by its pious inscription; the Fort was built three centuries ago by a Mohammedan Emperor—a resanctification of the place in the interest of that religion. There is a Hindoo temple, too, with subterranean ramifications stocked with shrines and idols; and now the Fort belongs to the English, it contains a Christian Church. Insured in all the companies.

From the lofty ramparts one has a fine view of the sacred rivers. They join at that point—the pale blue Jumna, apparently clean and clear, and the muddy Ganges, dull yellow and not clean. On a long curved spit between the rivers, towns of tents were visible, with a multitude of fluttering pennons, and a mighty swarm of pilgrims. It was a troublesome place to get down to, and not a quiet place when you arrived; but it was interesting. There was a world of activity and turmoil and noise, partly religious, partly commercial; for the Mohammedans were there to curse and sell, and the Hindoos to buy and pray. It is a fair as well as a religious festival. Crowds were bathing, praying, and drinking the purifying waters, and many sick pilgrims had come long journeys in palanquins to be healed of their maladies by a bath; or if that might not be, then to die on the blessed banks and so make sure of heaven. There were fakeers in plenty, with their bodies dusted over with ashes and their long hair caked together with cow-dung; for the cow is holy and so is the rest of it; so holy that the good Hindoo peasant frescoes the walls of his hut with this refuse, and also constructs ornamental figures out of it for the gracing of his dirt floor. There were seated families, fearfully and wonderfully painted, who by attitude and grouping represented the families of certain great gods. There was a holy man who sat naked by the day and by the week on a cluster of iron spikes, and did not seem to mind it; and another holy man, who stood all day holding his withered arms motionless aloft, and was said to have been doing it for years. All of these performers have a cloth on the ground beside them for the reception of contributions, and even the poorest of the people give a trifle and hope that the sacrifice will be blessed to him. At last came a procession of naked holy people marching by and chanting, and I wrenched myself away.

Chapter L

The man who is ostentatious of his modesty is twin to the statue that wears a fig-leaf.

—Pudd'nhead Wilson's New Calendar.

The journey to Benares was all in daylight, and occupied but a few hours. It was admirably dusty. The dust settled upon you in a thick ashy layer and turned you into a fakeer, with nothing lacking to the role but the cow manure and the sense of holiness. There was a change of cars about mid-afternoon at Moghul-serai—if that was the name—and a wait of two hours there for the Benares train. We could have found a carriage and driven to the sacred city, but we should have lost the wait. In other countries a long wait at a station is a dull thing and tedious, but one has no right to have that feeling in India. You have the monster crowd of bejeweled natives, the stir, the bustle, the confusion, the shifting splendors of the costumes—dear me, the delight of it, the charm of it are beyond speech. The two-hour wait was over too soon. Among other satisfying things to look at was a minor native prince from the backwoods somewhere, with his guard of honor, a ragged but wonderfully gaudy gang of fifty dark barbarians armed with rusty flint-lock muskets. The general show came so near to exhausting variety that one would have said that no addition to it could be conspicuous, but when this Falstaff and his motleys marched through it one saw that that seeming impossibility had happened.

We got away by and by, and soon reached the outer edge of Benares; then there was another wait; but, as usual, with something to look at. This was a cluster of little canvas-boxes—palanquins. A canvas-box is not much of a sight—when empty; but when there is a lady in it, it is an object of interest. These boxes were grouped apart, in the full blaze of the terrible sun during the three-quarters of an hour that we tarried there. They contained zenana ladies. They had to sit up; there was not room enough to stretch out. They probably did not mind it. They are used to the close captivity of their dwellings all their lives; when they go a journey they are carried to the train in these boxes; in the train they have to be secluded from inspection. Many people pity them, and I always did it myself and never charged anything; but it is doubtful if this compassion is valued. While we were in India some good-hearted Europeans in one of the cities proposed to restrict a large park to the use of zenana ladies, so that they could go there and in assured privacy go about unveiled and enjoy the sunshine and air as they had never enjoyed them before. The good intentions back of the proposition were recognized, and sincere thanks returned for it, but the proposition itself met with a prompt declination at the hands of those who were authorized to speak for the zenana ladies. Apparently, the idea was shocking to the ladies—indeed, it was quite manifestly shocking. Was that proposition the equivalent of inviting European ladies to assemble scantily and scandalously clothed in the seclusion of a private park? It seemed to be about that.

Without doubt modesty is nothing less than a holy feeling; and without doubt the person whose rule of modesty has been transgressed feels the same sort of wound that he would feel if something made holy to him by his religion had suffered a desecration. I say 'rule of modesty' because there are about a million rules in the world, and this makes a million standards to be looked out for. Major Sleeman mentions the case of some high-caste veiled ladies who were profoundly scandalized when some English young ladies passed by with faces bare to the world; so scandalized that they spoke out with strong indignation and wondered that people could be so shameless as to expose their persons like that. And yet 'the legs of the objectors were naked to mid-thigh.' Both parties were clean-minded and irreproachably modest, while abiding by their separate rules, but they couldn't have traded rules for a change without suffering considerable discomfort. All human rules are more or less idiotic, I suppose. It is best so, no doubt. The way it is now, the asylums can hold the sane people, but if we tried to shut up the insane we should run out of building materials.

You have a long drive through the outskirts of Benares before you get to the hotel. And all the aspects are melancholy. It is a vision of dusty sterility, decaying temples, crumbling tombs, broken mud walls, shabby huts. The whole region seems to ache with age and penury. It must take ten thousand years of want to produce such an aspect. We were still outside of the great native city when we reached the hotel. It was a quiet and homelike house, inviting, and manifestly comfortable. But we liked its annex better, and went thither. It was a mile away, perhaps, and stood in the midst of a large compound, and was built bungalow fashion, everything on the ground floor, and a veranda all around. They have doors in India, but I don't know why. They don't fasten, and they stand open, as a rule, with a curtain hanging in the doorspace to keep out the glare of the sun. Still, there is plenty of privacy, for no white person will come in without notice, of course. The native men servants will, but they don't seem to count. They glide in, barefoot and noiseless, and are in the midst before one knows it. At first this is a shock, and sometimes it is an embarrassment; but one has to get used to it, and does.

There was one tree in the compound, and a monkey lived in it. At first I was strongly interested in the tree, for I was told that it was the renowned peepul—the tree in whose shadow you cannot tell a lie. This one failed to stand the test, and I went away from it disappointed. There was a softly creaking well close by, and a couple of oxen drew water from it by the hour, superintended by two natives dressed in the usual 'turban and pocket-handkerchief.' The tree and the well were the only scenery, and so the compound was a soothing and lonesome and satisfying place; and very restful after so many activities. There was nobody in our bungalow but ourselves; the other guests were in the next one, where the table d'hote was furnished. A body could not be more pleasantly situated. Each room had the customary bath attached—a room ten or twelve feet square, with a roomy stone-paved pit in it and abundance of water. One could not easily improve upon this arrangement, except by furnishing it with cold water and excluding the hot, in deference to the fervency of the climate; but that is forbidden. It would damage the bather's health. The stranger is warned against taking cold baths in India, but even the most intelligent strangers are fools, and they do not obey, and so they presently get laid up. I was the most intelligent fool that passed through, that year. But I am still more intelligent now. Now that it is too late.

I wonder if the 'dorian', if that is the name of it, is another superstition, like the peepul tree. There was a great abundance and variety of tropical fruits, but the dorian was never in evidence. It was never the season for the dorian. It was always going to arrive from Burma sometime or other, but it never did. By all accounts it was a most strange fruit, and incomparably delicious to the taste, but not to the smell. Its rind was said to exude a stench of so atrocious a nature that when a dorian was in the room even the presence of a polecat was a refreshment. We found many who had eaten the dorian, and they all spoke of it with a sort of rapture. They said that if you could hold your nose until the fruit was in your mouth a sacred joy would suffuse you from head to foot that would make you oblivious to the smell of the rind, but that if your grip slipped and you caught the smell of the rind before the fruit was in your mouth, you would faint. There is a fortune in that rind. Some day somebody will import it into Europe and sell it for cheese.

Benares was not a disappointment. It justified its reputation as a curiosity. It is on high ground, and overhangs a grand curve of the Ganges. It is a vast mass of building, compactly crusting a hill, and is cloven in all directions by an intricate confusion of cracks which stand for streets. Tall, slim minarets and beflagged temple-spires rise out of it and give it picturesqueness, viewed from the river. The city is as busy as an ant-hill, and the hurly-burly of human life swarming along the web of narrow streets reminds one of the ants. The sacred cow swarms along, too, and goes whither she pleases, and takes toll of the grain-shops, and is very much in the way, and is a good deal of a nuisance, since she must not be molested.

Benares is older than history, older than tradition, older even than legend, and looks twice as old as all of them put together. From a Hindoo statement quoted in Rev. Mr. Parker's compact and lucid *Guide to Benares*, I find that the site of the town was the beginning-place of the Creation. It was merely an upright 'lingam,' at first, no larger than a stove-pipe, and stood in the midst of a shoreless ocean. This was the work of the God Vishnu. Later he spread the lingam out till its surface was ten miles across. Still it was not large enough for the business; therefore he presently built the globe around it. Benares is thus the center of the earth. This is considered an advantage.

It has had a tumultuous history, both materially and spiritually. It started Brahminically, many ages ago; then by and by Buddha came in recent times 2,500 years ago, and after that it was Buddhist during many centuries—twelve, perhaps—but the Brahmins got the upper hand again, then, and have held it ever since. It is unspeakably sacred in Hindoo eyes, and is as unsanitary as it is sacred, and smells like the rind of the dorian. It is the headquarters of the Brahmin faith, and one-eighth of the population are priests of that church. But it is not an overstock, for they have all India as a prey. All India flocks thither on pilgrimage, and pours its savings into the pockets of the priests in a generous stream, which never fails. A priest with a good stand on the shore of the Ganges is much better off than the sweeper of the best crossing in London. A good stand is worth a world of money. The holy proprietor of it sits under his grand spectacular umbrella and blesses people all his life, and collects his commission, and grows fat and rich; and the stand passes from father to son, down and down and down through the ages, and remains a permanent and lucrative estate in the family. As Mr. Parker suggests, it can become a subject of dispute, at one time or another, and then the matter will be settled, not by prayer and fasting and consultations with Vishnu, but by the intervention of a much more puissant power—an English court. In Bombay I was told by an American missionary that in India there are 640 Protestant missionaries at work. At first it seemed an immense force, but of course that was a thoughtless idea. One missionary to 500,000 natives—no, that is not a force; it is the reverse of it; 640 marching against an intrenched camp of 300,000,000—the odds are too great. A force of 640 in Benares alone would have its hands over-full with 8,000 Brahmin priests for adversary. Missionaries need to be well equipped with hope and confidence, and this equipment they seem to have always had in all parts of the world. Mr. Parker has it. It enables him to get a favorable outlook out of statistics which might add up differently with other mathematicians. For instance:

'During the past few years competent observers declare that the number of pilgrims to Benares has increased.'

And then he adds up this fact and gets this conclusion:

'But the revival, if so it may be called, has in it the marks of death. It is a spasmodic struggle before dissolution.'

In this world we have seen the Roman Catholic power dying, upon these same terms, for many centuries. Many a time we have gotten all ready for the funeral and found it postponed again, on account of the weather or something. Taught by experience, we ought not to put on our things for this Brahminical one till we see the procession move. Apparently one of the most uncertain things in the world is the funeral of a religion. . . .

In Benares there are many Mohammedan mosques. There are Hindoo temples without number—these quaintly shaped and elaborately sculptured little stone jugs crowd all the lanes. The Ganges itself and every individual drop of water in it are temples. Religion, then, is the business of Benares, just as gold-production is the business of Johannesburg. Other industries count for nothing as compared with the vast and all-absorbing rush and drive and boom of the town's specialty. Benares is the sacredest of sacred cities. The moment you step across the sharply-defined line which separates it from the rest of the globe, you stand upon ineffably and unspeakably holy ground. Mr. Parker says: 'It is impossible to convey any adequate idea of the intense feelings of veneration and affection with which the pious Hindoo regards "Holy Kashi" (Benares).' And then he gives you this vivid and moving picture:

'Let a Hindoo regiment be marched through the district, and as soon as they cross the line and enter the limits of the holy place they rend the air with cries of 'Kashi ji ki jai—jai! (Holy Kashi! Hail to thee! Hail! Hail! Hail)'. The weary pilgrim scarcely able to stand, with age and weakness, blinded by the dust and heat, and almost dead with fatigue, crawls out of the oven-like railway carriage and as soon as his feet touch the ground he lifts up his withered hands and utters the same pious exclamation. Let a European in some distant city in casual talk in the bazar mention the fact that he has lived at Benares, and at once voices will be raised to call down blessings on his head, for a dweller in Benares is of all men most blessed.'

It makes our own religious enthusiasm seem pale and cold. Inasmuch as the life of religion is in the heart, not the head, Mr. Parker's touching picture seems to promise a sort of indefinite postponement of that funeral.

Chapter LI

Let me make the superstitions of a nation and I care not who makes its laws or its songs either.

—Pudd'nhead Wilson's New Calendar.

Yes, the city of Benares is in effect just a big church, a religious hive, whose every cell is a temple, a shrine or a mosque, and whose every conceivable earthly and heavenly good is procurable under one roof, so to speak— a sort of Army and Navy Stores, theologically stocked.

I will make out a little itinerary for the pilgrim; then you will see how handy the system is, how convenient, how comprehensive. If you go to Benares with a serious desire to spiritually benefit yourself, you will find it valuable. I got some of the facts from conversations with the Rev. Mr. Parker and the others from his Guide to Benares; they are therefore trustworthy.

1. Purification. At sunrise you must go down to the Ganges and bathe, pray, and drink some of the water. This is for your general purification.
2. Protection against Hunger. Next, you must fortify yourself against the sorrowful earthly ill just named. This you will do by worshiping for a moment in the Cow Temple. By the door of it you will find an image of Ganesh, son of Shiva; it has the head of an elephant on a human body; its face and hands are of silver. You will worship it a little, and pass on, into a covered veranda, where you will find devotees reciting from the sacred books, with the help of instructors. In this place are groups of rude and dismal idols. You may contribute something for their support; then pass into the temple, a grim and stenchy place, for it is populous with sacred cows and with beggars. You will give something to the beggars, and 'reverently kiss the tails' of such cows as pass along,

for these cows are peculiarly holy, and this act of worship will secure you from hunger for the day.

3. 'The Poor Man's Friend.' You will next worship this god. He is at the bottom of a stone cistern in the temple of Dalbhyeswar, under the shade of a noble peepul tree on the bluff overlooking the Ganges, so you must go back to the river. The Poor Man's Friend is the god of material prosperity in general, and the god of the rain in particular. You will secure material prosperity, or both, by worshiping him. He is Shiva, under a new alias, and he abides in the bottom of that cistern, in the form of a stone lingam. You pour Ganges water over him, and in return for this homage you get the promised benefits. If there is any delay about the rain, you must pour water in until the cistern is full; the rain will then be sure to come.

4. Fever. At the Kedar Ghat you will find a long flight of stone steps leading down to the river. Half way down is a tank filled with sewage. Drink as much of it as you want. It is for fever.

5. Smallpox. Go straight from there to the central Ghat. At its upstream end you will find a small whitewashed building, which is a temple sacred to Sitala, goddess of smallpox. Her under-study is there—a rude human figure behind a brass screen. You will worship this for reasons to be furnished presently.

6. The Well of Fate. For certain reasons you will next go and do homage at this well. You will find it in the Dandpan Temple, in the city. The sunlight falls into it from a square hole in the masonry above. You will approach it with awe, for your life is now at stake. You will bend over and look. If the fates are propitious, you will see your face pictured in the water far down in the well. If matters have been otherwise ordered, a sudden cloud will mask the sun and you will see nothing. This means that you have not six months to live. If you are already at the point of death, your circumstances are now serious. There is no time to lose. Let this world go, arrange for the next one. Handily situated, at your very elbow, is opportunity for this. You turn and worship the image of Maha Kal, the Great Fate, and happiness in the life to come is secured. If there is breath in your body yet, you should now make an effort to get a further lease of the present life. You have a chance. There is a chance for everything in this admirably stocked and wonderfully systemized Spiritual and Temporal Army and Navy Store. You must get yourself carried to the

7. Well of Long Life. This is within the precincts of the mouldering and venerable Briddhkal Temple, which is one of the oldest in Benares. You pass in by a stone image of the monkey god, Hanuman, and there, among the ruined courtyards, you will find a shallow pool of stagnant

sewage. It smells like the best limburger cheese, and is filthy with the washings of rotting lepers, but that is nothing, bathe in it; bathe in it gratefully and worshipfully, for this is the Fountain of Youth; these are the Waters of Long Life. Your gray hairs will disappear, and with them your wrinkles and your rheumatism, the burdens of care and the weariness of age, and you will come out young, fresh, elastic, and full of eagerness for the new race of life. Now will come flooding upon you the manifold desires that haunt the dear dreams of the morning of life. You will go whither you will find

8. Fulfillment of Desire. To wit, to the Kameshwar Temple, sacred to Shiva as the Lord of Desires. Arrange for yours there. And if you like to look at idols among the pack and jam of temples, there you will find enough to stock a museum. You will begin to commit sins now with a fresh, new vivacity; therefore, it will be well to go frequently to a place where you can get

9. Temporary Cleansing from Sin. To wit, to the Well of the Earring. You must approach this with the profoundest reverence, for it is unutterably sacred. It is, indeed, the most sacred place in Benares, the very Holy of Holies, in the estimation of the people. It is a railed tank, with stone stairways leading down to the water. The water is not clean. Of course it could not be, for people are always bathing in it. As long as you choose to stand and look, you will see the files of sinners descending and ascending—descending soiled with sin, ascending purged from it. 'The liar, the thief, the murderer, and the adulterer may here wash and be clean,' says the Rev. Mr. Parker, in his book. Very well. I know Mr. Parker, and I believe it; but if anybody else had said it, I should consider him a person who had better go down in the tank and take another wash. The god Vishnu dug this tank. He had nothing to dig with but his 'discus.' I do not know what a discus is, but I know it is a poor thing to dig tanks with, because, by the time this one was finished, it was full of sweat—Vishnu's sweat. He constructed the site that Benares stands on, and afterward built the globe around it, and thought nothing of it, yet sweated like that over a little thing like this tank. One of these statements is doubtful. I do not know which one it is, but I think it difficult not to believe that a god who could build a world around Benares would not be intelligent enough to build it around the tank too, and not have to dig it. Youth, long life, temporary purification from sin, salvation through propitiation of the Great Fate—these are all good. But you must do something more. You must

10. Make Salvation Sure. There are several ways. To get drowned in the Ganges is one, but that is not pleasant. To die within the limits of

Benares is another; but that is a risky one, because you might be out of town when your time came. The best one of all is the Pilgrimage Around the City. You must walk; also, you must go barefoot. The tramp is forty-four miles, for the road winds out into the country a piece, and you will be marching five or six days. But you will have plenty of company. You will move with throngs and hosts of happy pilgrims whose radiant costumes will make the spectacle beautiful and whose glad songs and holy pans of triumph will banish your fatigues and cheer your spirit; and at intervals there will be temples where you may sleep and be refreshed with food. The pilgrimage completed, you have purchased salvation, and paid for it. But you may not get it unless you

11. Get Your Redemption Recorded. You can get this done at the Sakhi Binayak Temple, and it is best to do it, for otherwise you might not be able to prove that you had made the pilgrimage in case the matter should some day come to be disputed. That temple is in a lane back of the Cow Temple. Over the door is a red image of Ganesh of the elephant head, son and heir of Shiva, and Prince of Wales to the Theological Monarchy, so to speak. Within is a god whose office it is to record your pilgrimage and be responsible for you. You will not see him, but you will see a Brahmin who will attend to the matter and take the money. If he should forget to collect the money, you can remind him. HE knows that your salvation is now secure, but of course you would like to know it yourself. You have nothing to do but go and pray, and pay at the

12. Well of the Knowledge of Salvation. It is close to the Golden Temple. There you will see, sculptured out of a single piece of black marble, a bull which is much larger than any living bull you have ever seen, and yet is not a good likeness after all. And there also you will see a very uncommon thing—an image of Shiva. You have seen his lingam fifty thousand times already, but this is Shiva himself, and said to be a good likeness. It has three eyes. He is the only god in the firm that has three. 'The well is covered by a fine canopy of stone supported by forty pillars,' and around it you will find what you have already seen at almost every shrine you have visited in Benares, a mob of devout and eager pilgrims. The sacred water is being ladled out to them; with it comes to them the knowledge, clear, thrilling, absolute, that they are saved; and you can see by their faces that there is one happiness in this world which is supreme, and to which no other joy is comparable. You receive your water, you make your deposit, and now what more would you have? Gold, diamonds, power, fame? All in a single moment these things have withered to dirt, dust, ashes. The world has nothing to give you now. For you it is bankrupt. . . .

Benares is a religious Vesuvius. In its bowels the theological forces have been heaving and tossing, rumbling, thundering and quaking, boiling, and weltering and flaming and smoking for ages. But a little group of missionaries have taken post at its base, and they have hopes. There are the Baptist Missionary Society, the Church Missionary Society, the London Missionary Society, the Wesleyan Missionary Society, and the Zenana Bible and Medical Mission. They have schools, and the principal work seems to be among the children. And no doubt that part of the work prospers best, for grown people everywhere are always likely to cling to the religion they were brought up in.

Chapter LII

Wrinkles should merely indicate where smiles have been.
—Pudd'nhead Wilson's New Calendar.

In one of those Benares temples we saw a devotee working for salvation in a curious way. He had a huge wad of clay beside him and was making it up into little wee gods no bigger than carpet tacks. He stuck a grain of rice into each—to represent the lingam, I think. He turned them out nimbly, for he had had long practice and had acquired great facility. Every day he made 2,000 gods, then threw them into the holy Ganges. This act of homage brought him the profound homage of the pious—also their coppers. He had a sure living here, and was earning a high place in the hereafter.

The Ganges front is the supreme show-place of Benares. Its tall bluffs are solidly caked from water to summit, along a stretch of three miles, with a splendid jumble of massive and picturesque masonry, a bewildering and beautiful confusion of stone platforms, temples, stair-flights, rich and stately palaces—nowhere a break, nowhere a glimpse of the bluff itself; all the long face of it is compactly walled from sight by this crammed perspective of platforms, soaring stairways, sculptured temples, majestic palaces, softening away into the distances; and there is movement, motion, human life everywhere, and brilliantly costumed—streaming in rainbows up and down the lofty stairways, and massed in metaphorical flower-gardens on the miles of great platforms at the river's edge.

All this masonry, all this architecture represents piety. The palaces were built by native princes whose homes, as a rule, are far from Benares, but who go there from time to time to refresh their souls with the sight and touch of the Ganges, the river of their idolatry. The stairways are records of acts of piety; the crowd of costly little temples are tokens of money spent by rich men for present credit and hope of future reward. Apparently, the rich Christian who spends large sums upon his religion is conspicuous with us, by his rarity, but the rich Hindoo who doesn't spend large sums upon his religion is seemingly non-existent. With us the poor spend money on their religion, but they keep back some to live on. Apparently, in India, the poor bankrupt themselves daily for their religion. The rich Hindoo can afford his pious outlays; he gets much glory for his spendings, yet keeps back a sufficiency of his income for temporal purposes; but the poor Hindoo is entitled to compassion, for his spendings keep him poor, yet get him no glory.

We made the usual trip up and down the river, seated in chairs under an awning on the deck of the usual commodious hand-propelled ark; made it two or three times, and could have made it with increasing interest and enjoyment many times more; for, of course, the palaces and temples would grow more and more beautiful every time one saw them, for that happens with all such things; also, I think one would not get tired of the bathers, nor their costumes, nor of their ingenuities in getting out of them and into them again without exposing too much bronze, nor of their devotional gesticulations and absorbed bead-tellings.

But I should get tired of seeing them wash their mouths with that dreadful water and drink it. In fact, I did get tired of it, and very early, too. At one place where we halted for a while, the foul gush from a sewer was making the water turbid and murky all around, and there was a random corpse slopping around in it that had floated down from up country. Ten steps below that place stood a crowd of men, women, and comely young maidens waist deep in the water- and they were scooping it up in their hands and drinking it. Faith can certainly do wonders, and this is an instance of it. Those people were not drinking that fearful stuff to assuage thirst, but in order to purify their souls and the interior of their bodies. According to their creed, the Ganges water makes everything pure that it touches—instantly and utterly pure. The sewer water was not an offence to them, the corpse did not revolt them; the sacred water had touched both, and both were now snow-pure, and could defile no one. The memory of that sight will always stay by me; but not by request.

A word further concerning the nasty but all-purifying Ganges water. When we went to Agra, by and by, we happened there just in time to be in at the birth of a marvel—a memorable scientific discovery—the discovery that in certain ways the foul and derided Ganges water is the most puissant purifier in the world! This curious fact, as I have said, had just been added to the treasury of modern science. It had

long been noted as a strange thing that while Benares is often afflicted
with the cholera she does not spread it beyond her borders. This could
not be accounted for. Mr. Henkin, the scientist in the employ of the
government of Agra, concluded to examine the water. He went to
Benares and made his tests. He got water at the mouths of the sewers
where they empty into the river at the bathing ghats; a cubic centimetre
of it contained millions of germs; at the end of six hours they were
all dead. He caught a floating corpse, towed it to the shore, and from
beside it he dipped up water that was swarming with cholera germs; at
the end of six hours they were all dead. He added swarm after swarm
of cholera germs to this water; within the six hours they always died, to
the last sample. Repeatedly, he took pure well water which was barren
of animal life, and put into it a few cholera germs; they always began
to propagate at once, and always within six hours they swarmed—and
were numberable by millions upon millions.

For ages and ages the Hindoos have had absolute faith that the water
of the Ganges was absolutely pure, could not be defiled by any contact
whatsoever, and infallibly made pure and clean whatsoever thing touched
it. They still believe it, and that is why they bathe in it and drink it, caring
nothing for its seeming filthiness and the floating corpses. The Hindoos
have been laughed at, these many generations, but the laughter will need
to modify itself a little from now on. How did they find out the water's
secret in those ancient ages? Had they germ-scientists then? We do not
know. We only know that they had a civilization long before we emerged
from savagery. But to return to where I was before; I was about to speak
of the burning-ghat.

They do not burn fakeers—those revered mendicants. They are so
holy that they can get to their place without that sacrament, provided
they be consigned to the consecrating river. We saw one carried to mid-
stream and thrown overboard. He was sandwiched between two great
slabs of stone.

We lay off the cremation-ghat half an hour and saw nine corpses
burned. I should not wish to see any more of it, unless I might select the
parties. The mourners follow the bier through the town and down to the
ghat; then the bier-bearers deliver the body to some low-caste natives—
Doms—and the mourners turn about and go back home. I heard no
crying and saw no tears, there was no ceremony of parting. Apparently,
these expressions of grief and affection are reserved for the privacy of the
home. The dead women came draped in red, the men in white. They are
laid in the water at the river's edge while the pyre is being prepared.

The first subject was a man. When the Doms unswathed him to wash him, he proved to be a sturdily built, well-nourished and handsome old gentleman, with not a sign about him to suggest that he had ever been ill. Dry wood was brought and built up into a loose pile; the corpse was laid upon it and covered over with fuel. Then a naked holy man who was sitting on high ground a little distance away began to talk and shout with great energy, and he kept up this noise right along. It may have been the funeral sermon, and probably was. I forgot to say that one of the mourners remained behind when the others went away. This was the dead man's son, a boy of ten or twelve, brown and handsome, grave and self-possessed, and clothed in flowing white. He was there to burn his father. He was given a torch, and while he slowly walked seven times around the pyre the naked black man on the high ground poured out his sermon more clamorously than ever. The seventh circuit completed, the boy applied the torch at his father's head, then at his feet; the flames sprang briskly up with a sharp crackling noise, and the lad went away. Hindoos do not want daughters, because their weddings make such a ruinous expense; but they want sons, so that at death they may have honorable exit from the world; and there is no honor equal to the honor of having one's pyre lighted by one's son. The father who dies sonless is in a grievous situation indeed, and is pitied. Life being uncertain, the Hindoo marries while he is still a boy, in the hope that he will have a son ready when the day of his need shall come. But if he have no son, he will adopt one. This answers every purpose.

Meantime the corpse is burning, also several others. It is a dismal business. The stokers did not sit down in idleness, but moved briskly about, punching up the fires with long poles, and now and then adding fuel. Sometimes they hoisted the half of a skeleton into the air, then slammed it down and beat it with the pole, breaking it up so that it would burn better. They hoisted skulls up in the same way and banged and battered them. The sight was hard to bear; it would have been harder if the mourners had stayed to witness it. I had but a moderate desire to see a cremation, so it was soon satisfied. For sanitary reasons it would be well if cremation were universal; but this form is revolting, and not to be recommended.

The fire used is sacred, of course—for there is money in it. Ordinary fire is forbidden; there is no money in it. I was told that this sacred fire is all furnished by one person, and that he has a monopoly of it and charges a good price for it. Sometimes a rich mourner pays a thousand rupees for it. To get to paradise from India is an expensive thing. Every detail connected with the matter costs something, and helps to fatten a priest.

Sir Edwin Arnold

A Handsome City Seated
on Two Bays

The transformation effected in this great and populous capital of Western India during the past twenty years does not very plainly manifest itself until the traveller has landed. From the new lighthouse at Colaba Point, Bombay looks what it always was, a handsome city seated on two bays, of which one is richly diversified by islands, rising, green and picturesque, from the quiet water, and the other has for its background the crescent of the Esplanade and the bungalow-dotted heights of Malabar Hill. He who has been long absent from India and returns here to visit her, sees strange and beautiful buildings towering above the well-remembered yellow and white houses, but misses the old line of ramparts, and the wide expanse of the Maidan behind Back Bay which we used to call 'Aceldama, the place to bury strangers in.' And the first drive which he takes from the Apollo Bunder—now styled the Wellington Pier—reveals a series of really splendid edifices, which have completely altered the previous aspect of Bombay.

Close to the landing-place the pretty facade of the Yacht Club—one of the latest additions to the city—is the first to attract attention, designed in a pleasing mixture of Swiss, and Hindu styles. In the cool corridors and chambers of that waterside resort we found a kindly welcome to the Indian shores, and afterwards, on our way to a temporary home, passed, with admiring eyes, the Secretariat, the University, the Courts of Justice, the magnificent new Railway station, the Town Hall, and the General Post Office, all very remarkable structures, conceived for the most part with a happy inspiration, which blends the Gothic and the Indian schools of architecture. It is impossible here to describe the features of these very splendid edifices in detail, or the extraordinary changes which have rendered the Bombay of to-day hardly recognisable to one who knew the place in the time of the Mutiny and in those years which followed it. Augustus said of Rome, 'I found it mud; I leave it marble,' and the visitor to India who traverses the Fort and the Esplanade-road after so long an absence as mine might justly exclaim, 'I left Bombay a town of warehouses and offices; I find her a city of parks and palaces.'

Even the main native streets of business and traffic are considerably developed and improved, with almost more colour and animation than of old. A tide of seething Asiatic humanity ebbs and flows up and down the Bhendi bazaar, and through the chief mercantile thoroughfares. Nowhere could be seen a play of livelier hues, a busier and brighter city life! Besides the endless crowds of Hindu, Gujarati, and Mahratta people coming and going—some in gay dresses, but most with next to none at all—between the rows of grotesquely painted houses and temples, there are to be studied here· specimens of every race and nation of the East. Arabs from Muscat, Persians from the Gulf, Afghans from the Northern frontier, black shaggy Baluchis, negroes of Zanzibar, islanders from the Maldives and Laccadives, Malagashes, Malays, and Chinese throng and jostle with Parsees in their sloping hats, with Jews, Lascars, fishermen, Rajpoots, Fakirs, Europeans, Sepoys, and Sahibs. Innumerable carts, drawn by patient, sleepy-eyed oxen, thread their creaking way amid tram-cars, buggies, victorias, palanquins, and handsome English carriages. Familiar to me, but absolutely bewildering to my two companions, under the fierce, scorching, blinding sunlight of midday, is this play of keen colours, and this tide of ceaseless clamorous existence.

But the background of Hindu fashions and manners remains unchanged and unchangeable. Still, as ever, the motley population lives its accustomed life in the public gaze, doing a thousand things in the roadway, in the gutter, or in the little open shop, which the European performs inside his closed abode. The unclad merchant posts up his account of piece and annas with a reed upon long rolls of paper under the eyes of all the world. The barber shaves his customer, and sets right his ears, nostrils, and fingers, on the side-walk. The shampooer cracks the joints and grinds the muscles of his clients wherever they happen to meet together. The Guru drones out his Sanskrit shlokes to the little class of brown-eyed Brahman boys; the bansula-player pipes; the sitar-singer twangs his wires; worshippers stand with clasped palms before the images of Rama and Parvati, or deck the Lingam with votive flowers; the beggars squat in the sun, rocking themselves to and fro to the monotonous cry of 'Dhurrum;' the bheesties go about with water-skins sprinkling the dust; the bangy-coolies trot with balanced bamboos; the slim, bare-limbed Indian girls glide along with baskets full of chupatties or 'bratties' of cow-dung on their heads, and with small naked babies astride upon their hips.

Everywhere, behind and amid the vast commercial bustle of modern Bombay, abides ancient, placid, conservative India, with her immutable customs and deeply-rooted popular habits derived unbroken from immemorial days. And overhead, in every open space, or vista of quaint roof-tops, and avenues of red, blue, or saffron-hued houses, the feathered crowns of the date trees wave, the sacred fig swings its aerial roots and shelters the squirrel and the parrot, while the air is peopled with hordes of ubiquitous, clamorous grey-necked crows, and full of the 'Kites of Govinda,' wheeling and screaming under a cloudless canopy of sunlight. The abundance of animal life even in the suburbs of this great capital appears once more wonderful, albeit so well known and remembered of old. You cannot drop a morsel of bread or fruit but forty keen-beaked, sleek, desperately audacious crows crowd to snatch at the spoil; and in the tamarind tree which overhangs our verandah may at this moment be counted more than a hundred red-throated parrokeets, chattering and darting, like live fruit, among the dark-green branches. India does not change!

—originally published in Edwin Arnold, *India Revisited* (1886), pp. 54–8, and reprinted from R.P. Karkaria, ed., *The Charm of Bombay: An Anthology of Writings in Praise of the First City in India* (Bombay: D.B. Taraporevala, 1915), pp. 75–9

Nissim Ezekiel

Irani Restaurant Instructions

Please
Do not spit
Do not sit more
Pay promptly, time is valuable
Do not write letter
without order refreshment
Do not comb,
hair is spoiling floor
Do not make mischiefs in cabin
our waiter is reporting
Come again
All are welcome whatever cast
If not satisfied tell us

otherwise tell others
GOD IS GREAT

—from *Collected Poems 1952–88* (Delhi: Oxford University Press, 1989),
p. 240.

Nissim Ezekiel

A Morning Walk

Driven from his bed by troubled sleep
In which he dreamt of being lost
Upon a hill too high for him
(A modest hill whose sides grew steep),
He stood where several highways crossed
And saw the city, cold and dim,
Where only human hands sell cheap.

It was an old, recurring dream,
That made him pause upon a height.
Alone, he waited for the sun,
And felt his blood a sluggish stream.
Why had it given him no light,
His native place he could not shun,
The marsh where things are what they seem?

Barbaric city sick with slums,
Deprived of seasons, blessed with rains,
Its hawkers, beggars, iron-lunged,
Processions led by frantic drums,
A million purgatorial lanes,
And child-like masses, many-tongued,
Whose wages are in words and crumbs.

He turned away. The morning breeze
Released no secrets to his ears.

The more he stared the less he saw
Among the individual trees.
The middle of his journey nears.
Is he among the men of straw
Who think they go which way they please?

Returning to his dream, he knew
That everything would be the same
Constricting as his formal dress,
The pain of his fragmented view.
Too late and small his insights came,
And now his memories oppress,
His will is like the morning dew.

The garden on the hill is cool,
Its hedges cut to look like birds
Or mythic beasts are still asleep.
His past is like a muddy pool
From which he cannot hope for words.
The city wakes, where fame is cheap,
And he belongs, an active fool.

—from *Collected Poems 1952–1988* (Delhi: Oxford University Press,
1989), pp. 119–20.

Gieve Patel

City Landscape

Day after day the sea enchained
Behind granite buildings,
And workers' shanty towns roll
Like shed leaves at their feet.
I pick my way
Step by ginger step between

Off-Lamington Road, 1983–86, oil on canvas, approx. 9 feet x 4.5 feet, collection of Mick Yates; Painting credit and courtesy: Gieve Patel

Pokharan; Painting credit and courtesy: Sudhir Patwardhan

Muck, rags, dogs,
Women bathing squealing
Children in sewer water,
Unexpected chickens,
And miles of dusty yellow
Gravel straight
From the centre of some planet
Sucked dry by the sun,
And as radio-active as you wish,
Emitting haloes of wavering mirage
Air. The sea daily changes
From blue to green, to gray,
And breezes vaguely
Pull at the season. The sea holds
Netfuls of possibility,
Silver fish shining
Under a thin skin of water. My sight,
Like an angler's rod,
Springs across dust and buildings
To claim a few fish.
They tickle the inside of my chest
As I carry them across the city
Dancing on a scooter.

—from Gieve Patel, *How Do You Withstand, Body*
(Bombay: Clearing House, 1976).

Dilip Chitre

My Father Travels

My father travels on the late evening train
Standing among silent commuters in the yellow light.
Suburbs slide past his unseeing eyes.
His shirt and pants are soggy, and his black raincoat

Is stained with mud, his bag stuffed with books
Is falling apart. His eyes dimmed by age
Fade homeward through the humid monsoon night.
Now I can see him getting off the train
Like a word dropped from a long sentence
He hurries across the length of the grey platform,
Crosses the railway line and enters the lane
His chappals are sticky with mud, but he hurries on.
Home again, I see him drinking weak tea,
Eating a stale chapatti, reading a book.
He goes into the toilet to contemplate
Man's estrangement from a man-made world.
Coming out, he trembles at the sink,
The cold water running over his brown hands.
A few droplets cling to the graying hair on his wrists.
His sullen children have often refused to share
Jokes and secrets with him. He will now go to sleep
Listening to the static on the radio, dreaming
Of his ancestors and grandchildren, thinking
Of nomads entering a subcontinent through a narrow pass.

—from *The Oxford Anthology of Modern Indian Poetry*,
eds, Vinay Dharwadker and A.K. Ramanujan
(Delhi: Oxford University Press, 1994), p. 60.

Gieve Patel

From Bombay Central

The Saurastra Express waits to start
Chained patiently to the platform,
Good pet, while I clamber in
To take my reserved window seat
And settle into the half-empty compartment's
Cool; the odour of human manure

Vague and sharp drifts in
From adjoining platforms.
The station's population of porters,
Stall-keepers, toughs and vagabonds relieve themselves
Ticketless, into the bowels of these waiting pets:
Gujarat Mail, Delhi Janata, Bulsar Express,
Quiet linear beasts,
Offering unguarded toilets to a wave
Of non-passengers, Bombay Central's
In-residence population.

That odour does not offend.
The station's high and cool vault
Sucks it up and sprays down instead,
Interspersed with miraculous, heraldic
Shafts of sunlight, an eternal
Station odour, amalgam
Of diesel oil, hot steel, cool rails,
Light and shadow, human sweat,
Metallic distillations, dung, urine,
Newspaper ink, Parle's Gluco Biscuits,
And sharp noisy sprays of water from taps
With worn-out bushes, all
Hitting the nostril as one singular
Invariable atmospheric thing,
Seeping into your clothing
The way cigarette smoke and air-conditioning
Seep into you at cinema halls.
I sink back into my hard wooden
Third-class seat, buffered by
This odour, as by a divine cushion.
And do not suspect that this ride
Will be for me the beginning of a meditation
On the nature of truth and beauty.

—from Gieve Patel, *Mirrored, Mirroring* (Madras:
Oxford University Press, 1991), pp. 3–4.

Vertigo

Tuesday evening, he almost has a fight getting off the train at lower Parel. He hopped on to a Virar fast at Churchgate, and now the entrance is crammed with long-haul blue-collar types. They stolidly refuse to let him out. A penalty for riding this local: If he wanted to go a short distance, he should have caught any of the other locals, why did he make the mistake of boarding this one, they say. He has heard about this fierce possessiveness the distant suburbanites have about their trains; but this is the first time he is facing the brunt of their unwritten law. He pleads, then argues all the way from Bombay Central to Lower Parel. The irony is that he has been standing just six feet from the entrance, suspended on one toe, a dozen limbs digging into parts of his anatomy. But the sheer determination—and impenetrably thick crowd in the bogie—make it impossible for him to force his way through those six feet of human flesh and bone. Therefore the argument. Jay appeals to a well-dressed spectacled man standing next to him: 'But I have to get down at Lower Parel.'

The man smiles apologetically, shakes his head.

Jay tries again, desperate. 'Please, can't you understand my situation? Is this a crime or something?'

The man turns his face away and begins rattling off something in Marathi to another man. Jay watches them laughing, looking at him; the others in the compartment, three to a square foot, sweating, playing cards standing up, glance at him with amusement, cracking jokes in Marathi and Gujarati at his expense. Jay remembers a line somebody told him awhile back: 'India's the only country where the poor oppress the poor.' He realizes, as the train slows down at Lower Parel, that these guys really don't give a damn if he's forced to ride all the way to Andheri. As it is, he's lucky this is a mill-worker special; it stops at Lower Parel. Most Virar fast trains jump from Bombay Central to Bandra to Andheri. Some consolation. A grimy-necked clerk with a Hindi semi-pornographic paperback novel clutched in one hand, the other straining to cling on to a rail, mutters something to Jay in Gujarati.

'Huh?'

'You want to get down, no? Lower Parel? Get down this side, baba. Why you wasting time?'

Jay claws his way around the two or three men who stand between him and the nearest door, the one that isn't on the platform side. The train pulls up at the station. Someone's briefcase slams his groin, he ignores the pain in his testicles and sticks his head out of the door. Looks left and right. No approaching trains. The train lurches; Jay hesitates. Someone laughs, curses; someone kicks him in the back of the leg. His knee buckles. He falls, gasping, almost dropping his briefcase. Free fall, a moment of panic, visions of himself lying on the tracks, hip broken, blood trickling from the mouth, fast train approaching, people laughing on the platform.

(Should have caught that Andheri slow, should have should have. . .)

He lands with one foot on a rail, the other between the rails. Something splatters on the ground beside him, a rat scurries into the dark; he realizes it's tobacco juice—one of his excellent co-travellers has spat him a farewell.

******

The streets are still bursting with hordes of people hurrying home. An Irani restaurant has a blackboard placed outside the entrance; a crowd has gathered around it. Taller than most of the throng, Jay raises himself on his toes and can see part of the sign. It is in Hindi. It announces that Smt. Indira Gandhi was shot this morning by unknown assailants. Jay pushes past the crowd and goes into the restaurant. It is decorated in the typical style of Irani restaurants: back carved chairs, wooden tables with glass-tops, mirrors on the walls, rows of shelves displaying canned foods, toothpastes, toiletries, a heavy florid-faced old Iranian Indian at a counter with a glass-top under which cigarettes and chocolates are arrayed, non-uniformed waiters standing around casually, a hairy-armed cook in a dirty banian leaning at the kitchen serving counter, waiting for orders. Jay sits down and looks at the menus placed under the glass-top of the wooden table; there are four menus, each arranged to face one of the four seats; long lists of egg dishes, chicken dishes, mutton dishes, 'snacks' and 'bovarages'. He orders a double omelette with bun maska. The waiter calls out the egg order to the bored cook who grunts and sets about the job slowly but efficiently. The waiter goes over to a glass sideboard inside which dozens of buns, burn paos, sliced bread are kept, along with a dish of butter. He takes out a sweet bun, slices it in half horizontally, applies two precise licks of butter to each half, sticks both halves back together, then cuts the bun into strips. He sweeps the buttered sliced bun off the marble-top on to a stainless steel plate and brings it over to Jay's table. From his pocket he extracts a knife and a teaspoon, wipes them with the cloth hanging over his arm, and sets them down on the table. The sizzling of oil from the kitchen ceases and the burly cook reappears with a steel plate which he sets on the counter. The waiter brings the omelette over to Jay. It's large, greasy, a strange yellow-brown which Jay has only seen in Irani restaurants, and crisped around the edges which is how he likes it. With the maska pao—this crumbles in his hand and melts in his mouth with a unique salty sweetness—it makes a delicious meal. He goes through two more bun maskas to finish the egg using the strips of soft crumbly bread to scoop up pieces of the omelette. Then he orders a pani kum chai and another bun maska. He sweeps the buttered sweet bun in the concentrated tea, absorbing the entire cupful in this way by the time the bread is over. Only then does he feel the lightness in his head reduced, his bilious stomach settling.

The crowd outside the restaurant has increased. People are standing outside and staring at the blackboard for much longer than it takes to read the brief message. Jay realizes with a little shock that most of them probably can't even read and are simply staring at the meaningless chalked squiggles. At the counter, the florid old Iranian Indian talks in loud voice to a younger Iranian who must be his son. The son is fiddling with a cricket ball, rubbing it with his fingers, holding it to his ears. As a crackling static-distorted voice emerges from it, Jay realizes the 'ball' is a transistor-radio. The son is trying to find the news. 'Hah', he says in triumph as a droning Hindi monotone comes on: Vividh Bharti. The four waiters sidle over slowly to the counter, hands leaning on the backs of empty chairs, listening casually. Jay and two men drinking tea at another table are the only customers in the place. The two men stop talking and listen to the broadcast. Jay tries hard to follow it but the tiny speaker of the little radio and the 'shudh' Hindi of the newsreader makes it all but unintelligible to him.

He asks the waiter for the bill and pays it, feeling good about the one hundred and forty thousand sitting in his bank account. He likes having all that money and coming into a little café like this and paying a bill of Rs 17.75. He leaves the change from the twenty as a tip and....

—from Ashok Banker, *Vertigo* (New Delhi: Penguin, 2005 [1993]), pp. 78–9, 336–7.

A Voyeur is Born

Before my feet acquired sight, I had travelling eyes. Since home life—having the walls and roof attached to your skin—was a shell you couldn't cast off, windows served as a lookout. There were twelve of them starting from floor level and reaching seven feet up, plus the slats in the toilet and ventilators in the bathroom, providing extraordinary views of neighbourhood life. The verandas running all along the back and the front of the house were like gallery seats respectively to a backyard drama and a constantly unfurling spectacle on the front stage of the street. It was easy becoming a voyeur.

I spent hours hanging over the balcony railing—when I was old enough to rest my chin and elbows on the top—observing the street's activities. Early morning, it was the scratching of the municipal brooms, the rattling of the milk crates in the school next door which doubled as a milk distribution centre twice a day, the newspaper boys on foot or bicycles lugging bundles of newsprint, women hefting water out of the well across the street, the tailor shop, the barber and other provision stores opening for business with flocks of school kids stopping to replenish their supplies.

Next came the garbage truck, stopping in front of the house to clear the dump located right outside, which offered a variety of stinks from run-over animals to rotting watermelons, mango skins and much worse. Cows hung around the container, which invariably spilled over on all sides, and vied with urchins for whatever could be salvaged as food. The rag boys and girls who collected bottles, tins, cardboard, paper and pieces of cloth visited regularly, sorting out the stuff neatly in piles and leaving with bulging gunny bags. They supplied to local recyclers.

From my 180 degree panoramic view of the street, two disembodied images in black and white rose to the surface: smoking ice and boiling tar. At the end of the western arm of the street was an ice factory. Trucks and carts transported huge bricks of ice to restaurants all across the suburbs. Our street was serviced by a bullock cart—a sleep-walking, flat-backed open cart with three or four blocks of ice clothed in sawdust and blanketed in gunny bags. The man, the animal and the two-wheeled cart seemed to be part of a well-rehearsed pantomime. Unless the man had a back door delivery or wanted to chat a while, the cart never actually stopped moving. Sliding off his perch, 10 yards before his port of call, the man would swiftly carve off a slab of ice, deliver it to the customer at the door and amble back to his cart which was steadily making its way forward along the pavement. The bullock *and* the man could have been blindfolded and the operation would have run as smoothly.

What I watched out for was a misstep, a flaw in the timing. Counting, keeping score, matching time with appearance in the street, I gave the iceman a lead part in my dreamy-alert state on the balcony. But I kept score on everything—the colours and makes of cars, the licence plates, and route numbers on the red-and-cream BEST buses and the frequency with which they plied the street, familiar faces floating past the proscenium all added up in my day-long mental arithmetic.

We usually bought ice from the restaurant, but if we needed more than the normal supply for a big party, I got to buy it off the cart. A demonstration in the art of detaching a 6 × 6 × 6 inch cube of ice came with it. Using a pencil point icepick, the man would etch neat lines, and with just a couple of ice pick jabs, separate a clean-cut cake of ice from the parent block.

Sneaking into the factory to watch the smoking slabs of ice come off the assembly line was like going backstage. Using giant scissor-tongs, workers slid the slabs along the floor and hauled them into the delivery trucks. The trucks raced all over town with its frozen cargo—ammunition against the steamy vapours of an overheated city.

For us kids, it was the ice-ball doused in sweet sherbets that was mouth-cooling and deliciously stinging. This temptation came on a four-wheeled hand cart gaily decorated with bottles of coloured liquid along the cart's perimeter. A simple wooden contraption with a blade served to shave the ice into a packed snowball.

An advanced version of this device was a machine on which a chunk of ice was clamped, and a rotating handle turned the ice on the blade. Both were manually worked; the sound of the grazing ice, the flakes collecting in the palm held underneath, the ball fitted like a bulb around a stick, the sprinkled juices all came via the eyes drippingly into my mouth. Some of these carts did the rounds of the neighbourhood, summoning up business with a ringing bell; others were stationed invitingly on street corners. Buying the gola was not an everyday indulgence. So, most of the time I just watched, swallowing my saliva—a trainee in the art of self-restraint.

Street repair work went on almost continuously all over the city: dug up streets slowed down traffic, blew dust into houses, messed up walking spaces and generally elicited curses all round. After the heavy monsoons had torn up the roads, trucks and buses continued the battering: potholed streets and bumpy, lurching rides were a way of life eliciting more curses. With ineptitude, inefficiency and shortages becoming the norm, cursing and berating figured a great deal in normal Indian speech.

From my perch on 134 Versova Road, the gumbooted road worker walking in the black shimmer of tar mending potholes was more than a figure out of a recurring dream. He was very much a fixture. His tools of trade—a wagon, drums of tar, brooms, pickaxes, water cans and the steamroller—were permanently parked outside the yard.

—from Saleem Peeradina, *The Ocean in My Yard*
(Delhi: Penguin, 2005), pp. 28–31.

Saleem Peeradina

Death of a Well

The most magical spot in the garden for me lay in the northwestern corner. The well was forty feet deep, fed by a natural clear-water spring, though the water level would be brimming after the rains. I spent hours gazing at the reflection of trees, looking for some mystery at the centre of this calm surface. My most meditative poems have to do with water, trees and landscapes—and I can do no better at this point than to quote the third section of 'Still Life', which recreates my experience of the well:

Reciprocal

Along the semi-circular rim we ran
to where
The well was cut eye-high.
The reflection the dark stone wall
threw
Into the clear water and which the water held
By keeping still made the water
look
Dark-coloured.

So a stone became the mode of up-setting
Wall's repose to set the water free to see
hurriedly
Our lit faces.

In times of water shortage—a chronic problem that became a permanent feature in a city whose every resource was being worn thin—the well water proved a handy substitute. As the suburban population grew, water cuts became institutionalized. The hours allotted to each zone were bizarre—sometimes in the dead of night. I remember my parents taking turns, waking up at 2 or 3 a.m. to fill the water drum and an assorted collection of pots, rows of buckets, even cooking utensils. Sometimes, before going to bed they would leave the taps on with a pipe attached to the drum, and set the alarm for an approximate hour, resulting in overflows that flooded the room, involving brooming and mopping up—a backbreaking task at that ungodly hour. The luxury of running water and liberal showers was over: we had to measure out every mugfull.

The well, like everything else, was subject to changing municipal codes. Someone once threw seeds which germinated, spreading a thin layer of green slime on the water. Fearing contamination, the municipality ordered the well to be closed. The walls were levelled, the trucks brought in silt and stones to dump into the well, and the job was done efficiently, mechanically without much ceremony or tears. Except for my mother, who railed bitterly against civic shortsightedness when running water became a thing of the past. In the 1980s, in a water-starved metropolis of ten million, water contractors selling water all over the city became big business. The buried wells, their moisture blotted up, languish underground.

—from Saleem Peeradina, *The Ocean in My Yard*
(Delhi: Penguin, 2005), pp. 51–2.

Song of the City (Nagar-sangit)

Where has it gone, that noble calmness,
Fresh and pure and graceful greenness,
Edged with a hem of shining blueness,
    Beautiful, kindly world?
Sky's delight by light excited,
Secretive gardens, coolly shaded,
Where have the buzzing bees retreated—
    What brings us to this pass?
O city, city, jungle of people,
Road after road, buildings innumerable,
Everything buyable, everything saleable,
    Uproar, hubbub, noise.
Enormous profits, thumping crashes,
Sky-polluting foul dust-flurries,
Whipped by the sun into swirling eddies,
    Soiling heaven and earth.
Everything fitful, broken, fleeting,
No lasting sign behind remaining,
A quick combining, fast dividing
    Dash to the sea of death.
Pathetic weeping, raucous revelry,
Tyrannous arrogance, abject slavery,
Futile striving, malicious raillery,
    Hurtling forward *en masse.*
Nothing fixed for a single moment,
No desire for anything permanent,
Constant activity, ceaseless movement
    By day and by dark of night.
Each in pursuit of a gleaming fantasy,
Desperate to hunt and catch an illusory
Golden deer that dances endlessly—
    Old and young rush on.
It's like a ritual bonfire leaping,
Snouts and trunks of fire flailing,

Scrabbling and scratching the sky with raging
  Hunger for more and more.
Crowds of men and women around it,
Hurry to heap and stoke and worship it,
Break and smash their lives to nourish it,
  Offer their souls as fuel.
Fanatics serve it with butchered bodies,
Feed it with bones and gushing arteries,
Feeling in all their rites and ecstasies
  Death's golden allure.
Flames rise high with roaring menace,
Sky is clouded with smoke from the furnace,
Sun and moon disappear in a thunderous
  Universal blaze.
Winds whipped up by heat to a frenzy
Circle the dazzling fire in a fury,
Dismally roam and howl frustratedly,
  Whoosh and hiss and sigh—
Flutter and flap with the helpless terror
Thousands of mother-birds showed at that horror:
Holocaust when the forest of Khandava
  Fell to Agni's greed.[1]
Brahmins, Kshatriyas, Vaisyas, Sudras,
Age and status no longer matters,
All converge as the burning gathers,
  Hurl their lives right in.
Seeing this massive fiery spectacle,
Heart, like a fly, is drawn to the dazzle,
Longs to add to the wild hubble-bubble
  Blood of self-slashed veins.
City, O city, rushing and pouring
Constantly forth like foaming and bubbling
Wine—let me lose myself by drinking
  Deep of your essence today.
Stony nurse of human endeavour,
I shall become your fellow-traveller,

---

[1] In the *Mahabharata*, Agni (god of fire) exhausted his strength by consuming too many offerings. In order to revive himself, he devoured the Khandava forest— aided by Krishna.

Stay awake with crowds that stagger
   Through drunken, sleepless nights:
Whirling along with the communal frenzy,
Joining the great unfettered orgy,
Sinking my inmost dreams recklessly,
   Let me be part of you.
Peace and calm I'll treat as nothing,
Plunging down to the depths and soaring
Up on a comet's tail and stretching
   My arms towards the sun.
Whatever the games that fate has planned for me,
Some of them right and some of them wrong for me,
Some of them sweet and some bitter agony—
   I'll take them as they come.
Round on the wheel of joy and misery,
Riding high on poetry's fantasy,
Swooping down with prose's gravity,
   Swung by the merry-go-round.
Seizing the city's trumpet of conquest,
Grabbing all that is hardest and furthest,
I the unstoppably wildest and strongest
   Will take what I want by force.
Joining the ranks of the bullies and predators,
Will and desire foisted on others,
Snatching food from my fellow-creatures,
   I'll tighten my violent grip.
The world in my mind will now be merely
A place for me to stamp on freely:
Kingly rule and daylight robbery
   Seen as different no more.
Wealth and assets I'll raid and shatter,
Reap my harvest by looting the farmer,
Unleash the king's great horse to wander
   Brazenly over the world.[2]
Newly thirsty and newly eager,
Hungry for new kinds of work and power,

---

[2] An allusion to the ancient Indian *asvamedha* or horse sacrifice. The sacrificial horse was set free to wander at will. The king and his army followed the horse, and claimed as the king's own any territory that it crossed unchallenged.

Page after page swiftly turned over
    In life's unfolding book.
Crooked and tortuous paths ahead of me,
Start unknown and end not clear to me,
Forward I'll rush and cross unstoppably
    Rivers, mountains and seas.
Looking ahead and never behind me,
A nestless, restless bird-of-the-night I'll be,
You, fickle Fortune, laughing, will race me,
    Bewildering will-o'-the-wisp—
I shan't bow down or beg before you,
I shan't sit back and passively wait for you,
Let us fight—you'll see who'll master you,
    I'll bring you back in chains.
Human life is not for ever,
Fame and wealth and status and power
Are not the slaves of any owner—
    The river of time takes all.
So for a few days, a few nights only,
Let the clashing and crowded city
Fill the glass of my life completely
    With churning, heady wine.

—translated by William Radice, and first published in *Tagore: Verse and Versatility*, eds, Udayan Bhattacharya and Pathikrit Bandopadhyay (Mumbai: Shahana, 2001)

Buddhadev Bose

Calcutta

At one time, Calcutta to me was unique, marvelously beautiful
Like the birth of a dream, a flower sprung
On the stalk of imagination;
Its dust, its breeze, its warm metallic breath

Shouted my desires.
The evening lights in Chowringhee, the afternoon fragrance
Of the asphalt,
The huge swirling currents of strange crowds
On the footpaths,
And the descent of blue clouds on thousands
Of white rooftops
Made me mad with delight.
None can claim you: 'You are mine alone',
You are illusive, daughter of commerce
Parcelled out to the world—
But I gained my freedom when I was able
To whisper into the ears of your air:
'I'm yours.'
Freedom!—I sought that—and gained it from you,
The impulse to live, the freedom to be revealed;—
The freedom that the river gains by reaching the banks,
The poet by acquiring the tune,
The insect by its fleeting life
On a happy day in spring.
That was long ago.
Years were shed like the yellow leaves,
Stormy eras swept away pages from history.
You dressed up yourself in new robes—
Revealing a part of yourself which till then had
Remained outside our acquaintanceship.
Famine swooped down upon us,
Sparks of destruction came flying.
Your nerves became strained,
The streams of your blood broke into a flood;
The last breath of my youth drifted away with
Fears, restlessness, outbursts of enthusiasm
And the tears of skeletons.
The mangled flesh of human beings
Were swept away by your rains.
The feeble whimperings of the hungry
Were drowned by the sounds of your traffic.
The grass that gathered during the black-outs
Were wiped out by the wandering footsteps of the refugees.
The struggles during the famine,

The death of the heart,
The darkness of anarchy,
The partition and the partings,
The arguments gritty like stone chips,
Theories honed by grinding of teeth—
It was on this lacerated soul of Bengal
That the 'gulmohar' of my last summer blossomed—
And drooped.
Whatever we loved—
The fragrance of the learned aristocracy,
Friendship, love, grace,
The developed personality—
One by one all collapsed,
Rolled down upon the stones of your pavements.
The trees died. There were no birds left.
How many holocausts do you need
For your rebirth?
How many more deaths will you invite?
Yet, dreams are immortal.
I can never think of a civilization disappearing;
Go, my wishes are shouting.
I don't have any power, but my wishes have.
I'm dropping the seeds of my wishes
On the soil of your future.
Are you planning to collect their harvest
In some distant future—
Won't you let me know even this?

—excerpted, and translated, from a longer poem by Sumanta Banerjee;
translation first published in the *India International Centre Quarterly*, 17,
nos 3–4 (Winter 1990–1), pp. 10–11. The translator added this
note: 'Buddhadev Bose (1908–1974) was one of the pioneers of the
modernist movement in Bengali poetry which began in the 1920s. This
tribute to Calcutta spans an important era in the city's life with which
Buddhadev grew up and which ended with the 1947 partition of the
subcontinent and its aftermath. The references are to the 1943 Bengal
"famine", the impact of the "sparks" of the 2nd World War, the
"black-outs", the 1946 communal riots, the arrival of the
refugees from the then East Bengal, following partition.'

calcutta
if you must exile me

calcutta if you must exile me wound my lips before I go

only words remain and the gentle touch of your finger on my lips calcutta
burn my eyes before I go into the night

the headless corpse in a dhakuria bylane the battered youth his brains
blown out and the silent vigil that takes you to pataldanga lane where
they will gun you down without vengeance or hate

calcutta if you must exile me burn my eyes before I go

they will pull you down from the ochterlony monument and torture each
broken rib beneath your upthrust breasts they will tear the anguish from
your sullen eyes and thrust the bayonet between your thighs

calcutta they will tear you apart jarasandha-like

they will tie your hands on either side and hang you from a wordless
cross and when your silence protests they will execute all the words that
you met and synchronised calcutta they will burn you at the stake

calcutta flex the vengeance in your thighs and burn silently in the despair
of flesh

if you feel like suicide take a rickshaw to sonagachhi and share the sullen
pride in the eyes of women who have wilfully died

wait for me outside the ujjala theatre and I will bring you the blood of
that armless leper who went mad before hunger and death met in his
wounds

I will show you the fatigue of that woman who died near chitpur out of
sheer boredom and the cages of burrabazar where passion hides in the

wrinkles of virgins who have aged waiting for a sexless war that never
came

only obscene lust remains in their eyes after time has wintered their
exacting thighs

and I will show you the hawker who died with calcutta in his eyes

calcutta if you must exile me destroy my sanity before I go

—first published in Pritish Nandy, *Masks to be Interpreted in Terms of
Messages* (Calcutta: Dialogue Publications, 1971).

Nirendranath Chakravarty

Calcutta's Jesus

There was no red stop light.
Yet Calcutta, usually driven
by flurries of tempestuous activities,
suddenly came to a stop.
All taxis, private cars, double-deckers
with Tempo advertisements or Tigers
for symbols,
somehow, precariously
halted.
Stop! Do Something! They had screamed,
rushing from both sides of the street—
the coolie, the pedlar, shopkeepers and their
customers.
And even now, they are held in the stasis
of an easel, watching a naked toddler
toddle across the street.
A while ago, it had rained
at Chowringhee. And now, the sunlight,

like a long spear, reaches
through the cloud's lungs.
Calcutta is floating in a magic light.
I turn away from the sky,
press my face against the window
and watch you, beggar woman's child,
Calcutta's Jesus.
Your subtle enchantment
has brought all traffic to a halt.
You are indifferent to all;
the crowd's cry, the impatient drivers
gnashing their teeth,
death impending
on both sides.
You stumble your way between. As if at the moment
of incarnation,
in sheer pleasure of learning
how to walk, gripping
whole worlds in your fists,
you move with hesitant steps
from earth's one end
to the other.

—translated from the Bengali by D.K. Banerjee; taken from *Signatures:*
One Hundred Indian Poets, ed., K. Satchidanandan
(New Delhi: National Book Trust, 2004), pp. 122–3.

Sunil Gangopadhyay

City of Memories

Neera's Illness

When Neera is ill, all Calcutta mourns.
After the sun is quenched, before neons blink on,

They ask, 'Is Neera well today?'
The ancient cathedral clock, the ruddy grace of shops—
They know Neera is well!
In offices, parks, that news goes
The round of a million tongues:
The news of Neera.
The keenscented *bokul* garland brings
The news that Neera is glad today
Suddenly melancholy winds rise helter-skelter
And ring in sport
The alarums of the sky.
All Calcutta smiles softly
Knowing Neera has gone for a walk today.

Under an overcast sky, when the city chokes in misery
When the taxi collides with the belly of a tram,
Joyless jams choke intersections,
In restaurants and all the roads
People roam with darkened faces behind vexed masks,
All Calcutta is awash in anger,
Strikes and hell will break loose,
When setting fire to telephones and post offices
Each one will declare a strike
Against his own heartbeat
I start in fear, I know, I go in a trice,
I go and say,
'Neera, are you sad?
Sweet girl, look at me, as in a mirror
Show me the blossom of that face
In that voice full of laughter as the newborn waters
Answer a riddle!'
Just then barriers vanish, rains descend,
People leave for movies or games with comforted faces.
The snarled traffic unravels, the cycles, three-wheelers,
Cars, rickshaws go their ways in harmony.
Cigarette between their lips, some folks exclaim,
'It isn't bad to be alive!'

At me tugs night's sleepless river,
At me pulls the secret dark
Breaks my sleep and opens wide
The locked doors of midnight.
Torn clouds scatter in the wind.
Time's blue crystals circle the moon
Outdoors I see a deserted earth
All the roadways filled with sky.

The first call came in primal boyhood
On a maddening day of aches
Bugles of war rang through my flesh,
Then my dreams were first unchained.

I sought no one, yet suffered parting
The loss of a love I had never known
Then I remember the beckoning night,
Desire haunts the riverbends.

All rules, all duties fade
Familiar roads turn labyrinths
My beguiled eyes touch horizons:
To barriers false I take my axe.

Through whores' neighbourhood and crashing glasses
I walk beyond to the river's edge
A new odour pervades the city
To west and east, the world lies open.

Now awakens the worm and flowers
Darkness drinks the warmth of day
In the dust lie diamondshards:
Sin and Virtue now depart.

Shacks in lanes trip my heels—
These fragile households—whose are these?

In a profound comedy of Death and Birth
Lies the essence of mirth and tears.

The nighthag's call, a ghostly beckoning
These are the seeds of sorcery—
Such enchantment that all seems nothing,
Conjured gold dug from the heart.

Yet I must leave, I must go far
A ghostly vigil waits for me
Where yearning rocks to rhythm of waves,
Sounds gather to devour Memory.

A naked Shiva rules the roads
In baritone sings a glorious song,
Holding aloft his magical palmwand
He seems to smell the fragrant sea.

I show him deference with a bow
But on my way I cross the road
The pariah dogs in soundless stare
Watch him who stands tall as a tree.

Temples face temples, great locks on gates.
On Kali's stone breast a swirl of ants.
Earthen lamps dim, the stairs echo
A leperwoman's harsh cough.

Leaves of *sal* fly stained with food,
With sacred marigolds roll in dust.
A sleepy boy pisses on a wall
The outline of a woman's form.

Now festive burning ground I see,
Hibiscus flames and murmuring crowds,
Shadows' tumult, shadows' uproar
A frantic bodiless multitude.

Here's no night, nor is there day
The magnet's kiss arrests life's clock

The dead laugh carefree and the living
Indifferent flings Charon's coins.

Ganja seeds crack in lighted chillums
Shiva's followers sit in a circle, still
Twin tridents glow red in the flame
Fireflies sparkle upon the river.

More than my eyes, I have seen:
A change of scene, the wind has turned
Smoke from pyres chokes breath, burns eyes
All around lamentations rise

To the bank I go: no one is here.
The river's body lies supine.
I was called here by a dream
Dark as hair, deep mountainshade.

Shadows awaken from the river's body.
Forgotten, the city fades into sky.
I give, I take, and life goes on
But that city I never forget.

City of Memories 4

Like a horde of vandals, rain assaults
Helter-skelter upon Chhatubabu's market
On this festival of Shiva. In the carnival
One acrobat hangs, suspended in space—
In the heartrending thunder no one notices
If he plummeted or soared.
Suddenly the electric brilliance of the evening
Sweeps all other scenes from sight
Runaway folks with pigeons take flight.
Each loses the way, calls out,
Seeks another. Hordes of women dash
Towards Rambagan, the neighbourhood of whores:
But that is a road to exile!
Trucks and pushcarts choke traffic.
In the pandemonium of the carnival ground

Rises the shrill of a young girl,
Pierces the torrent and the dark:
'Papa, O Papa! Papa!'
No one answers.
Now the acrobat who swung high on the bamboo pole
Has catapulted into another century!

City of Memories 10

In Chinatown our friend was Sheikh Suleiman
　　His wife's name was Wah-ling
A red magic lantern hung above their home.
They were people of the night,
Had little to do with the sun.
They had never heard of Jean-Paul Sartre
But in their very lives had easily kept
　　His philosophy alive.
Suleiman had no childhood, has no tomorrow,
Wah-ling keeps a tight circle:
　　Suleiman, a goat, and a monkey.
They see rain and the dark
Exactly as rain and darkness.
On either side of them
The river and the open drain flow past alike:
Manusamhita, the *Hadith*, and Marx's message
　　Creep around under their makeshift cots.
Spry as a cane stands Suleiman
There's no telling his age.
I have never seen such a lean waist
　　On another man
He could easily be a god of ancient Greece
As indeed he might have been.
Lately he has been busy turning the Calcutta dust
　　Into gunpowder.
Beardless, hair thinning on his head,
He has the gleaming eyes of a true killer.
Barechested, he ties and reties his *lungi*
At the waist, an old habit
His sibilant spit darts out
　　Against all systems.

We sit face to face on two rickety cots.
Into our glasses he pours moonshine.
On the tinroof like a circus aerialist
    Chatters Wah-ling's monkey.
He leaps up the lamppost, and slithers down to show
His sly face, straightens up between us,
    And puts out his hand.
He too is given a glass.
If Wah-ling's goat begins its urgent bleat
It is given a tin bowl, not a glass.
Wah-ling moves, now in light
    Now in shade,
Bringing us shrimp dumplings, fried fresh.
We drink that harsh liquor.
The evening of our intense intimacy
    Hurtles toward midnight.
A few words from Suleiman have made it clear
That he has been baptized by many kinds of fire.
He has had blood on his hands
    His body not unfamiliar to sharp steel
And he knows
The thing called hunger is unclean
And there is no substitute for love,
And Death is his distant cousin
Who lives in an alien land,
And life is the savour of friend lentil
With cold steeped rice.
He has heard of no religion.
He is a stranger to silk,
Sometimes on a moment's whim, Wah-ling
Stands entranced, a hand on his shoulder:
A family portrait, as if
The Bourne & Shepherd Studio camera is ready.
In a show of envy
The monkey nudges her loins
They exchange amorous words in a private tongue
While Suleiman launches on his tales of the police.
In their contexts appear
The whore, the tout,
    Illicit brewers, lunatics incognito.

As each bottle is drained
Wah-ling takes our money,
Leaves us her free and spectacular smile,
And dangling our legs from the cots
The three of us grow warm.
With the slightest booze the monkey begins to sob.
The goat sings.
As the night deepens, Wah-ling's laughter
    Seems to speak.
Her breasts, fuller than other Chinese women's,
    Sway in rhythm with her laughter.
Sitting in the heart of Calcutta
We are transported
To the Saonthal province, where the heart
Soars skyward like the young *sal* tree,
Where joy is a gust amid the *polash* branches.
Amidst all this, suddenly, before this room
    A Black Maria halts.
From it dismounts
Some character from Suleiman's own story.
He keeps his eyes much more carefully on us
Than on Suleiman and Wah-ling
And we three comrades are so used to arrests
That we are unmoved even by a police sub-inspector.
Towards him we proffer a glass
Or a five rupee note
But some days obstinately
    He drags us to the police station.
The next evening Suleiman asks,
'You forgot your matches,
Did you manage to get a light?'
Within half-a-mile there are
The sharemarket and the secretariat,
Open to all comers,
Where the pandemonium
Of well-groomed slavetraders rises all day—
Life insurance and provident funds
Volley of bullets and accidents—
The jokes and laughter of the wilfully blind
The dialogue in signals between parasites and touts,

The rise and fall of the unreal.
Each one tries to make his bread in another's pan
Yet each day, newspapers with frowning foreheads
    Are delivered at dawn,
The airplanes fly on,
Even the child in the mother's womb
    Hears its roar.
Millions of monsoon insects
Flit towards the moon,
The river's profound sigh touches the grieving fishermen
The world moves on in its own way.
Indeed, of Suleiman's three selves
Only one survives
Having murdered the other two.
Of Wah-ling's three selves, only one.
    Has found her reliable man.
Goats and monkeys have no such problem.
They are not bothered by who survives, who falls.
Uncovering his naked thigh, Suleiman whets his knife.
A red lantern glow licks Wah-ling's breasts.
Between them they present a powerful advertisement
    For survival.
Three callow youths from respectable homes watch them.
Then they interchange their names,
The night nurses their bewildered heads,
Their roar of laughter mingles with their weeping.
Suleiman scales the world's highest peak
    And flies his colours;
Wah-ling, a second earthmother, begins her dance
As if there is no more time
And they are about to vanish from sight,
Their magic prsence sways on an aerie column.
We spring up, facing three directions.
From our lips flash the arsenal of alphabet,
At the infinite expanse of the sky
We fling
Our chestrending unspoken song.

—translated from the Bengali by Kalyan Ray and Bonnie MacDougall;
extracted from Sunil Gangopadhyay, *City of Memories*
(Calcutta: Indiana, 2006), pp. 7–8, 12–20.

Lina Fruzzetti
In conversation with MJ Akbar, Satindranath Chakrabarty, and Sunil Ganguly

Calcutta Conversations

LINA: How do you deal with society's values, tradition, problems in the city?

MJ Akbar: Problems in the city are the most obvious area for a newspaper. I think we've done more to protect the city's environment than anyone else. In the last two months we have had major victories through our campaigns. One is the Rawdom Square Project, which has been stalled. A park in the heart of the city which the government had handed over to the Birlas to set up another theater complex. Destroying every bit of green in the city. The government became very hostile to us. Mr. Basu [the Chief Minister of West Bengal] abused me personally and the paper—because there was inevitably corruption there. Corruption I didn't care about, but how can you destroy what little greenery there is in the city? There's no excuse any more. It's the last city which can afford this—it's been much raped. And the second one was the cemetery which the church was handling. Both these projects have been stalled.

LINA: That's one way that you deal with problems.

MJA: That's a real way. Identify problems and solutions. You're right about the feeling that Calcuttans seem to have given up.

LINA: It's like they're waiting for someone else to come and do something.

MJA: I think the newspaper has a very real role to play in the atmosphere of apathy. We have to take the lead even if the people aren't taking the lead. I used to get phone calls from readers. We were going through a bad phase with the government harassing us, so I told them, 'Why don't you get into the streets and protest?' People weren't willing to do that. They want the projects to stop but they're not willing to do anything about it. But I think they're grateful.

LINA: But the sense of values is not something that the paper picks up on.

MJA: Values have to be common to every newspaper. You have to have a certain commitment to your readers. I don't think *The Telegraph* is any better or worse. I think we put extra effort into investigative

Handa story. Other papers have refused to touch this story because a
particular financier has bought all the manuscripts. He's even sat in this
chair trying to do the same to me.

LINA: What about an article on high-rise buildings? My concern is
about the two-storey house which was replaced by a 12 floor building
without provision for parking, water, garbage collection.

MJA: I'd like to leave you with one thought. An interesting thought
that comes from living in the city. In the 60's the concept of living in
Calcutta was living in a nice one-storied house. In the 80's that has become
a multi-storied house. The unique conversion of this city to apartment
living is fascinating. These tall apartment buildings have become, in fact,
vertical *paras or mohallas.* This is not true of Bombay for example, where
neighbors don't really know each other. The building in which we're
staying, I would not want to leave it. Although the company is ready to
give me a house with a garden, I won't leave it because my children were
born there and I have a lot of friends. Just like in the traditional *mohalla*
where I was born and grew up, when we could walk into anybody's house
and come out of anybody's house; the only boundary line was that of the
mohalla, if the child went outside that, people would worry. Otherwise,
people assumed that you were around. At dinner time; you'd check at
whose house the child was. The 50 families who share this building have
religious differences, regional differences, but there is interaction.

✳✳✳✳

LINA: What do you think is the problem with Calcutta? Is it too political?

Satindranath Chakrabarty: To my mind—when I was young, Calcutta
was a decent city despite the fact that it was a colonial creation of the
British. We carry forward the legacy of Partition. That is the most
important historical factor. Because of the Partition of India and West
Bengal, so many refugees came over since 1947. Then there was the Great
Calcutta Killing and riots, the famine. So the social fabric was really
destroyed by (1) the partition, (2) the influx of refugees, (3)…

LINA: Migrant laborers…

SC: Laborers were there—but the partitioned state had to
accommodate millions of refugees. And they are truly the alienated. They
could not be rehabilitated in a proper manner. That constituted a great
strain on the economy of West Bengal. And the politics of West Bengal
revolved around that problem. The refugees grabbed land and in a way

developed the suburbs of Calcutta. At the same time there was a large concentration of people. Colonies developed in a haphazard manner. No minimum amenities.

LINA: I heard they improved *bustees*, and the water and sanitation problems?

SC: Peripheral. Instead of ordinary toilets, we have scientific toilets. But then slum life hasn't been remodeled. In any slum you'll find people bundled together—husband, wife and children. No separate bathroom. Their lives are absolutely different—even from that of the lower middle class. Amenities have been provided to some extent but they do not constitute any fundamental improvement so, to my mind, the post-war Calcutta changed fundamentally because of the refugee influx. It constituted a great strain on the economics, politics, culture and morality of entire Bengal. Added to that, after Independence, was the planned "development" of this country. One peculiar phenomenon of West Bengal was that, during the British days, West Bengal didn't develop an entrepreneurial class because of the land tenure system of the Permanent Settlement. The landed interest in rural areas received a fixed quota of rent, the land was tilled by peasants who had to pay *khajna* [revenue on land] to the landlords.

LINA: Why didn't they have a sense of investment?

SC: Because it was a life of ease. Money flowed in—they started schools. Excavated ponds. Built temples. But this class of *zamindars* did nothing to radically reform the land, augment production, introduce new technology. They amassed wealth, purchased houses in Calcutta and stayed here. We are all middle-class people and if you trace the history—we are all children of the Permanent Settlement system. My grandfather's father held some land and lived on it. Then because of certain factors, his son went off for English education and then his son joined a profession. So, many professional people like doctors, lawyers and clerks, etc., are coming out of that Permanent Settlement system. But they all cast aside the land. And what professions were they in? Either doctors, or lawyers, or clerks, or serving in British courts. You won't find a Bengali industrialist. You won't find a Bengali who had a lot of land and contemplated using tractors. No enhancement of production. That line, Bengalis were never accustomed to.

LINA: It's as if they despise it.

SC: Then again, for *bhadralok* and ordinary people—the term is there—*babu* class. This didn't happen in other parts of India— Punjab, Bombay, the Parsi community, etc. So there is this difference between the Bengali set up and that in other states: (1) the refugee influx; (2) the paucity of land; (3) the paucity of industries—Bengalis have no industries. At this time something happened—namely, the development of the Indian economy. Planning was introduced not only on the basis of private enterprise but also in the public sector. In basic fundamental industries, the state must interfere. The state pumped a lot of money into the economy. Doing that opened up opportunities for contracts.

LINA: Bengalis took up contract working for Marwaris?

SC: Also independent small contractors. Avenues opened up for different kinds of middlemen. If a factory purchases different things, I appoint you and then you appoint others to get them. *Dalal* or middlemen. This way new openings became available, which were mostly unproductive. Salesmen, middlemen, *dalals*, black marketers; paucity of goods but flow of money. Productively, the Bengali economy didn't develop but there were unproductive expansions: (1) refugees; (2) Bengalis having no other skill, owning no industries. Bengalis acting only as clerks, lawyers, and doctors—mostly unproductive—you can say, tertiary sector jobs. Not primary or secondary.

LINA: They don't have the entrepreneur spirit but one thing did develop in Bengal—the arts, literature.

SC: The Bengali middle class, children of the Permanent Settlement, imbibing British ideas (Calcutta was a city where English education started very early). The Bengali middle class took to English education whereas the Muslims did not accept it. Because of cross-fertilization we have a tradition of our own. Bengali is a rich language. We have our own folk songs, folk music, and dance tradition. Because of cross-fertilization—new ideas from the West and our own indigenous ideas came together. The nineteenth century was a century of genius so far as West Bengal was concerned. All sorts of ideas—social reform movements, religious movements, debates—if there was any golden age in recent times, it was the nineteenth century. On the plane of ideas, the Communists did not give any new ideas.

LINA: So how are they maintaining this city?

SC: What happened is that Calcutta is suffering from 'giganticism.' It's too big. It can't accommodate its sewer system built for a population of 10 lakhs[1]. Now with the outlying areas occupied by refugees and all that we have a population of 100 lakhs or 10 million.

---

[1] 1 lakh—one hundred thousand.

So, per square mile it has the highest density of population (in the world). The sewer system is at least 70 years old. But you can't shape it, because of the influx. This is the mischief this Communist government has done—and where my criticism lies. So it developed in an unplanned, haphazard manner. So many people came here and were allowed to occupy land forcibly and this has been legalized now. Refugees have been settled. But then, no planning took place. And because of the accretion of wealth in so many hands, you can just pay the Corporation and construct houses illegally. Bengali political parties did not emphasize planned development at all. The Congress was there when there was an imaginative chief minister, Dr. B.C. Roy. He couldn't think of such huge numbers of people in Calcutta and started satellite towns. He started Kalyani (a satellite town in Nadia district). And because of his initiative we have Durgapur, Digha. The positive things, he did. During the Congress regime, he was the topmost in this respect. There is such a large population but the electricity production has not kept pace with the growing numbers. For the last ten years there have been tremendous power cuts, load-shedding for 12–13 hours, shortage of water supply, sanitation problems.

What we Indians lack, despite the political movements, what we lack is collective action and discipline.

LINA: Is it because of the breakdown of the family? Loss of values?

SC: I feel there is less of values because of disruption in the social system. Village life was disrupted. Millions uprooted from the soil. Living the life of animals in refugee colonies for many years. No organic tie between man and woman. Victims of exploiters/money lenders. So many factors. The social fabric was destroyed and values distorted. The emergence of black markets and parasites started. The growing *bustees* or 'slumization' of Calcutta. Rash Behari Avenue was one of the finest roads thirty years ago—now it has become a slum.

Calcutta could be saved if we had a master plan. But there is no such plan. And, because of our false sense of democracy. If you've read Gunnar Myrdal's *Asian Drama*, he emphasises the situation aptly—he says that the Indian state is a false state. On paper it arrives at many decisions but cannot implement a single one because of franchise.

LINA: On the issue of lack of discipline. In Hinduism, discipline was always embedded in the family.

SC: But we had a national movement stretched over a 100 years.

LINA: But you had leadership and that national movement was a temporary one.

SC: The communist movement is 60 years old in India—in West Bengal, and Communists are known for their organization and party discipline. It's a monolithic party. But in society they can't take any decision. Why? The chance of adult franchise and the existence of plurality of parties and social forces create a situation where you can't take a quick decision. There are too many bidders. Congress says they'll do this much and if you want to bid you'll have to say you'll go further. When the streets were occupied Congress supported it, when the Communists are in power—Congress opposed it. Eviction of hawkers and all that. Why didn't they (the Communists) remove the hawkers from the start? Humanitarian considerations were there but the material considerations were stronger. The election agents work as party cadres! Because of this anarchic situation and lack of discipline Calcutta is in a bad way.

LINA: So what's going to happen? Are people moving out of the city?

SC: But West Bengal is so small…

LINA: The people who are most affected are the middle classes. The lower classes are here for temporary jobs. They don't have homes, schools and children to worry about.

SC: Also they (the unorganized sections of the people) have no awareness at all. They are the majority. They feel this is their destiny and they can eke out an existence.

LINA: The middle class will lose out. There will be 3–4 percent upper classes and the middle classes will move out to the districts and satellite towns.

SC: There is racketeering in land sale.

LINA: Everyone is selling their homes!

SC: They can't maintain it. Near the railway station, you have three famous men, three brothers, and after their demise their children left, rented the houses. Now, if you have to whitewash the house it will cost you 5000 rupees. You'll have to procure masons and all. But the son lives in Bombay. He is not interested. So the rooms were partitioned. Now you have shops there. Every bit of space has been utilized and in 15 years it will pass out of their hands. If you want to purchase a flat in Calcutta now, because of the racket—for 1000 sq. feet you'll have to pay 5.5 lakhs. Middle-class people have no chance of purchasing! For example, when my son was here—this is my house (my father's house since 1937). On the first floor is my doctor brother and my mother. I have three rooms on the ground floor. A drawing room (baithak-khana), etc. When my son joined Jadavpur—there was a problem of accommodation. So we gave him this room. My wife had one and I had one. Very difficult. I told him if he stayed he should rent a flat. He appointed *dalals*. You can't find a house on your own. In Regent Estate—not a very good locality—he found a two-room apartment house. They charge 2000 per month and 12 months' advance! When enquiry was made about purchase of an 800 sq. feet flat—very small rooms, one verandah, toilet, kitchen—would cost 3.5 lakhs!

LINA: These are problems that happen in all major cities. The way they happen in Calcutta is interesting.

SC: My point is—who are now owning flats? Non-Bengalis. Bengalis purchase, but the next generation can't maintain. Maybe the top level of 4 percent and those below the poverty line—these will be in the city. The middle class will be driven outside the city into the suburbs.

LINA: A circle around the city. What about the sense of culture? Do you think what they call Bengali culture today, corresponds to your sense of culture? Of course, when we talk about Bengali culture we are talking about middle-class culture. The culture formed here.

SC: There has been a plethora of cultural organizations—so many drama groups, cultural experiments, films, there is a quantitative increase. But qualitatively, no.

LINA: What about revolutionary theater?

SC: All superficial, catering to the taste of the middle class again who idolize revolution. They can't make revolution—mimic revolution.

LINA: What remains in Calcutta that is positive today?

SC: Positive is the fact that urban anonymity is not too advanced. There are still *addas* and chats at the local teashops. Religious congregations, meetings. Parties where you have heart to heart talks. In Delhi you won't find it. It's more drab in that sense.

LINA: Do you have a group that you have *adda* with daily, here.

SC: Occasionally. We are organizing a meeting for someone who was a victim of the Communists. Four years he spent fighting the politicization of Calcutta University and then retired. But we are giving him an ovation. He was the Vice Chancellor [the effective presiding officer]. We'll meet tomorrow and arrangements for transport will have to be made. We meet occasionally and discuss things. If you have a party (political) you have to do these things. If you have religious feelings you can go to Ramakrishna Mission. There are talks daily on various subjects, biology, the *Gita*, Ramakrishna.

LINA: Do you go?

SC: I don't. Occasionally, for a talk that I have to give! Recently I haven't on account of my eyes.

SC: I am very pessimistic because with hope you can't deal with politics.

LINA: I don't think the CPI (M) can do anything.

SC: The CPI (M) is a replica of the Congress. It has no life force, no ideal, no idea for leadership.

LINA: How about a new party?

SC: No sign yet.

LINA: There was the *Amra Bangali* but people didn't respond to it.

SC: *Amra Bangali* will cut no ice because it has no economic or social program. Bengalis (it must be said to their credit) are less chauvinistic because of our nineteenth century tradition.

LINA: But for how long. What about all this sale of houses, etc.? Will that create/continue with existing chauvinism?

SC: There is chauvinism but not really of the aggressive type—the vulgar type. You talk to a Bengali. They have anti-Marwari feeling. Very strong. They hate Marwaris. You talk to a Bengali—he will exaggerate his importance by recalling the past. Glorious culture. That sort of tendency.

LINA: But they don't use it to fight.

SC: Even here, the communal feeling—relatively speaking, is not so high. That is because of our liberal culture promoted by nineteenth century stalwarts. Not a 'Renaissance' of the European variety but still a great one. So, in a desultory way I have answered you.

*****

SUNIL GANGULY: I am basically a writer—I write poetry and fiction. I also work for a newspaper—*Ananda Bazar Patrika*—a Bengali language paper. The house which publishes it has other newspapers and journals, like *The Telegraph, Sunday* in English and Hindi papers like *Ravivar*. I work with the literary weekly *Desh*. I grew up in this city though I was born in a village in what is now Bangladesh. We immigrated during the time of the partition.

LINA: Do you consider yourself a Calcuttan?

SG: Now I can claim myself a Calcuttan, but most pure Calcuttans do not consider me a Calcuttan. They still treat me as a refugee.

LINA: How many generations before one can become a Calcuttan?

SG: At least three.

LINA: What are some of the issues you find most interesting? Do you deal with social problems of Bengalis?

SG: Of course. I write about the modern period, the situation around me, the people I meet every day. Social problems crop up all the time. I have seen very poor people, lower middle class, and middle class. I think I've just moved a way up into the middle class but I was born in a poor family. I know how the lower middle class lives.

LINA: How do you bring this concern into your writing?

SG: In literature it's not a case where I write to make people socially aware. Essentially you write about life as it is—the problems of life. When people read a novel or a poem, they enjoy the music of the language. But underneath every story or poem there must be a social reality. This is also felt by the readers.

LINA: How do people respond?

SG: Here people are very conscious. For instance, if I attack any social taboo or religious practice in one of my writings then immediately a lot of letters come to me and are published in journals. Some people support me, some don't agree with me. There are always people who are against any criticism of religion. Here we have many problems, but to me the most urgent one is the problem of religion, the tension of communalism, also among Hindus there is still casteism.

LINA: Do you think that caste is still an important issue in Calcutta?

SG: Not in the city. But if you go out into the villages, yes. In Calcutta also, all you have to do is scratch someone and you'll find he's 'Brahman' or something.

LINA: So caste has not really been replaced by class.

SG: No. In arranged marriages, they still consider caste. You can see the 'matrimonial' ads in the newspapers.

LINA: Do you do contemporary writing?

SG: Yes, I mostly write autobiographical work, my experiences. I have written historical novels also, but mostly I write about contemporary times. Two of my novels have been filmed by Satyajit Ray, *Days and Nights in the Forest* [Aranyer Din Ratri] and *Pratidwandi* or *The Adversary*. In both I have described the lives and problems of young people.

LINA: In looking at Calcutta in the nineteenth century, *bhadra* society, the culture which emerged then incorporated the best of British and Indian society, discarding some of the more strict traditions reflected in Bengali society. Later, in the 1920's and 30's, things changed. Some of the changes had to do not just with economics but with people developing values slightly contradictory to their culture.

SG: Yes.

professionalism brought change?

SG: Calcutta was one of the first places where English education came into India, so people around this new city started to get ideas from the West. Also, in the very beginning, people got so westernized that they forgot about their heritage. Later there was a realization that it was good to get the best of both worlds. That's how the culture developed here. About our literature: it is very fortunate that at the very beginning the standard was very high. Bankim Chandra Chattopadhyay, our first novelist, a great novelist, set standards which people subsequently sought to follow. Now with the media explosion, there is 'trash' in magazines, potboilers—still literature has a good standard not only by Indian but by world standards.

LINA: You don't think that people are moving away from Bengali as medium of communication?

SG: There is a section of our people who want to hold on to English education only. But that is a minor section, the upper classes. Not the middle class, about three to four percent not more.

LINA: How much power does this three to four percent have on determining policy?

SG: At least about two percent migrate to other countries. Until now this has been the trend.

LINA: I talked to some people from the 3 to 4 percent group and one thing that struck me was that while I reacted strongly to what was happening in Bengal and to Calcutta, they say that it is good to have universal Indian identity. Identification with Bengal and Bengali doesn't really matter. Then there is the middle class complaining about how fast things are moving. People talk about a 'Calcutta culture' which I never heard of before.

SG: Calcutta culture was labeled the 'babu' culture of the *nouveau riche* in the nineteenth century. The new generation of rich people acquired some western knowledge and ideas and also had a fancy for wine and womanizing. Now you cannot label anything as 'Calcutta' culture. It should be Bengali culture. In Bengal, the *nouveau riche* are aloof from the mainstream. They don't contribute at all. Their eyes are always on the West and they try to send their children to the West.

LINA: Bengalis move out of Calcutta: I understand that 46 percent of Calcuttans are Bengali and the rest are non-Bengali.

SG: No, it's good that Calcutta is metropolitan and the population is mixed: I appreciate it that there is no 'sons of the soil' attitude. There has never been a language law in the city. In Orissa and Bihar there have been incidents but not in Calcutta. Never a language riot though there have been communal riots.

LINA: Are these people who share language and culture?

SG: Well, most of the Muslims lived in separate parts of the town. Even in modern buildings like this one you will rarely find a mixed population of Hindus and Muslims. A Muslim friend of mine tried to buy a flat in this apartment block and was denied, but the committee would take a Marwari.

LINA: I'm surprised they allow a Marwari.

SG: They would allow a Marwari grudgingly—but they'd allow a Marwari. Maybe there are some residents of the building who work in a Marwari firm. But religious bias is so strong. This grew after partition, because the refugees here (I am a refugee) are still very anti-Muslim. A section of the refugees mixed with the Muslims, mind you but I find that many pure Calcuttans, 3 to 4 generation Calcuttans, have never had Muslim friends. Interaction between Hindus and Muslims is very little.

LINA: In the last fifteen years there haven't been many riots.

SG: 1964 was the last big one. But there is tension all the time.

LINA: Now there is tension among all the ethnic minorities.

SG: For instance, if there is a football match between Mohammedan Sporting and Mohan Bagan or East Bengal [popular Calcutta sporting clubs]. Afterwards there's bound to be a clash and it may take a more serious turn.

LINA: Are you concerned about the out-migration of the middle classes into satellite towns? The sale of old houses and the building of high-rise apartments?

SG: I am personally very concerned about this. All these beautiful mansions sold and demolished with match-box houses coming up. Anyone concerned for the city should be sorry about that. For a long time the corporation or the municipality was suspended and there was a minister of the government who looked after municipal affairs. So they didn't bother. Most of these buildings were demolished and sold to non-Bengalis. Declining old Bengali families are forced to move out of the city. A sad state of affairs.

LINA: Is there a law to stop the tearing down of buildings? I feel that some of the problems of multistoried buildings are not addressed by the government.

SG: There is no proper planning. These high-rise buildings grew up haphazardly and now the city fathers are thinking about restricting high-

called 'the city of palaces,' but no longer. Many Bengali families have become poor and are unable to maintain their ancestral homes and are forced to sell. I know a family on Lansdowne Road—now Sarat Bose Road—who owned a beautiful house, the Bhowal Sanyasi family home. In East Bengal there was a small *zamindari* called Bhowal, the site of a famous case about 40 years ago, 'the Bhowal Sanyasi case.' Many books have been written about it. The Bhowal Sanyasi was a prince or landowner (jamidar) and was supposed to have been killed by his wife and his wife's brother. He was cremated. After twelve years he returned as a *sanyasi* and claimed that he had escaped, become a *sadhu* [mendicant, holyman] and come back. People thought he was an impostor but he seemed well rehearsed—even knew of certain marks on his wife's body. The case went up to the Privy Council in England. The *sanyasi* won the case. Anyway, that house was very beautiful, and now it's been demolished.

LINA: It's not just demolishing a mansion but a whole way of life, and a class. The concept of *para* is destroyed by high-rise buildings.

SG: In north Calcutta there was a building which was so big and sprawling that they needed a small train to travel from one part of the building to the other, now it's no longer there.

LINA: Do Bengalis feel affected by this?

SG: You see, Bengalis write letters to the newspapers but do nothing about it. Is it in their power to stop it? A particular person or group can't resist but the government should take action to protect some historical buildings. But they were careless and busy with infighting.

LINA: What if you had a political party that addresses issues like a return to an awareness of who you are, a pride in the language, and policies which protect Bengali rights. Is that possible?

SG: There is a trend among Bengalis: the educated Bengali will not utter that 'I am a Bengali'—by nature they are universal types, they think about the whole world. I have a theory that the whole world won't care about Calcutta but Calcutta is caring about the burdens of the whole world. Talk to an ordinary Calcutta man. He'll discuss Vietnam, South Africa, Ethiopian famine but not the condition of Calcutta.

LINA: I used to think it's because of apathy or an expectation that something better will happen soon. It's like they're waiting for leadership. And I don't see another renaissance in the near future.

SG: No, I don't foresee one either.

LINA: At the same time there is a liveliness. You are writing, there are theater groups, painters.

SG: Culture sometimes thrives in poverty. Because the upper class, the rich, don't care about culture. It's mostly the middle class.

LINA: The repository of 'Bengaliness' remains with the middle classes and yet they are not in a position of power.

SG: But politically, especially after the coming of the Marxist government, the middle class has something to say.

LINA: What can they say that will change the situation?

SG: If you go to the villages, I think lots of work has been done by the political parties. Now almost every village has a political consciousness. They know what is their right. In other parts of India they do not have this consciousness.

LINA: I find it interesting that many people say that Calcutta would not exist unless it's run by a Marxist government, yet I don't think the Left government has addressed some problems but the Congress (I) would not do that either.

SG: Actually there is no hope for the Congress here, now. There was so much infighting and bad elements in the party that people have got disgusted. And unfortunately, there is no alternative. The Left is strong and they have shown for the last ten years that they can govern and hold on.

LINA: Are you working on a novel about Calcutta at present?

SG: I am working on a big novel now—it has a simple name—'The East and the West,' *Purba Paschim*. It has three levels of *purba/paschim*. In the first part there is the division of Bengal into East and West. I have described the conditions, the migration of Hindus and also of Muslims. In the second part is an eastern hemisphere and western hemisphere division. In the 1960's, many of our bright boys and girls migrated to the West leaving their parents here. Believing like Rimbaud, that they would come back with gold and make their parents happy, but many never returned. There is a third kind of east and west. I think in every individual's mind, there is an east and west, philosophically speaking. The center is Calcutta, but the novel goes to Dhaka, England and America.

LINA: In looking at two or three generations you are bound to be looking at changes in the city as well. Will you include the breaking down of houses? I feel that when you break a building you lose a sense of community, *para*, you move from a horizontal *para* with events, *pujas* and communication to a vertical one.

SG: You are very right. I feel I have lost contact with the people in the streets. I don't hear the sounds of people talking, the peddlers—once I come up to my floor I am unaware of what goes on outside.

LINA: If residential planning were different would there be less antisocial elements?

SG: You can think of these houses as villages.

LINA: Yes, I have never associated Calcutta with fear, though I am a woman and an outsider. In Delhi, after six pm, I would not walk outside. I used to take music lessons in Kalighat and return home by tram at eleven at night and never feared anything. I had a sense of security and it had to do with Bengali attitudes towards women. But now I am not so sure.

SG: It's not so bad yet. There are some notorious localities but otherwise it's not bad.

—from *Calcutta Conversations*, eds, Lina Fruzzetti and Ákos Östör, with notes by Tarun Mitra (New Delhi: Chronicle Books/ DC Publishers, 2003), pp. 36–7, 40–8, 86–93.

Kedarnath Singh

Banaras

Spring enters this city
without warning.
But before it comes
from Lahartara or Maduwadeeh
a squall rises to leave dust
on the tongue of this
city more ancient than any.

Everything that is
is more restless than
everything that is not tries to be.
On visiting Dashashwamedh
even the stone-steps of the ghat seem soft,
and the eyes of the monkeys
water strangely.

The emptiness in the beggars' bowls
begins to brighten.

Have you ever witnessed
the filling of empty bowls by the spring?
This city unfolds thus,
thus it fills and then it empties out.
Day after day
the endless chain
of bodies carried on shoulders
to the shining Ganga
from night's dark streets.
Dust in this city rises slowly,
slowly people walk,
slowly the gongs peal,
slowly it is evening.

This slowness,
this collective rhythm
of everything happening slowly
tightens up the whole city.
So that nothing ever falls,
nothing is shaky.

Everything keeps
its accustomed place Ganga
The anchored boat
and the wooden shoes
Tulsidas walked in
are all in their timely place.
If you ever happen
to be in Banaras unexpectedly
some evening
and see it in the glow
of lamps, lighted:
you shall see a Magic City,
partly in water, partly in mantras
partly in conches, partly in flower
partly in corpses, partly in sleep.

If you see carefully
partly it is and partly it is not.
what there is
stands without support,
What is not
is held up
by tall
pillars of ash and light, pillars of fire,
pillars of water, pillars of smoke
and fragrance,
pillars of human hands upifted.

Offering water to an unseen sun
for centuries
the city stands on one leg in water,
without knowing
where its other leg is.

—translated from the Hindi by Sunita Jain; taken from *Signatures: One Hundred Indian Poets*, ed., K. Satchidanandan (New Delhi: National Book Trust, 2004), pp. 236–8.

Ravi Dayal

A Kayastha's View

Seminar's letter seeking contributions to this issue on Delhi refers to 'Your city—where it is at, how it has changed and grown, and whether it has changed its identity.' Many solemn books on Delhi have been published over the years to confirm in stodgy detail what amateur eyewitnesses have long taken to be self-evident—that Delhi has, of course, changed enormously since the inauguration of New Delhi in 1931 and, more so, since 1947.

In 2001 the extravaganza of *The Millennium Book on New Delhi*, edited by B.P. Singh and Pavan K. Varma, OUP, was published. It deals with many of the issues now sought to be raised by *Seminar* and the bibliography of even that unscholarly volume lists some 80 titles. People have not only written on the monuments and history of medieval Delhi, but a great deal on the 20th century city, including its obsession with politics, and the fact that jackals could be heard on the outskirts of Barakhamba Road in the 1950s and nilgai roamed until later in the scrub now occupied by Pragati Maidan.

Many other details could be filled in to show how Delhi has changed: the expansion of the population from less than a million in 1946 to more than 12 million by 2000; the fact that you didn't need to boil or filter drinking water until the 1970s; could eat kakri and chaat from pavement vendors without falling terminally ill; could walk on grassy sidewalks in leather-soled shoes without damaging your heels and shins, as you would now on concrete pavements; could enjoy a boat ride on the Jumna rather than be driven to attempting to do so in a fragment of the stinking moat below the Purana Qila, and so on.

Delhi is vast, and it is said to be a microcosm of India; it is inhabited liberally by people from all parts of the country and shared by all. *Seminar*'s letter refers to 'Your city'—but apart possibly from the politicians who infest the city and have appropriated the prettiest real estate in it for themselves, do people still think of themselves as Dilliwallahs, as the Mathur Kayasthas of Delhi once did?

Born of Mathur parents, and having had an association with Delhi for as long as I can remember (i.e. from *circa* 1940), I have periodically thought of myself as an authentic Dilliwallah. Although much of my childhood was spent outside Delhi, we were annual winter migrants to the city over sixteen years when I joined Delhi University and stayed for the next five (1954–9). Thereafter, I was based outside Delhi for the next eleven years as a student and then a publisher, and have been a publisher here since 1971. My genes, college days and profession have conspired to tie me to the city and coloured my view of it, so in this brief piece I will restrict myself to what flows from these three elements.

One of the traditional conceits of the Mathurs of Delhi is that they consider themselves the highest form of a high species perhaps less flamboyant than the Mathurs once based in Lahore, but infinitely more refined as speakers of a tongue untainted by Punjabi; a cut above those in Rajasthan, who servilely served provincial rulers and said *hukum*; somewhat similar to members of the community in Agra and Lucknow, but free of the small-town smugness of urban U.P. The Mathurs of

Delhi also considered themselves Dilliwallahs *par excellence*, forgetting that the city is now barely aware of them.

My father's family was originally from Peepalmandi in Agra, but with innumerable relations in Delhi; my mother's family was once based in Chelpuri and Chiraykhana in the Old City—always referred to as *shahar* by insiders, and never as Shahjahanabad. Early in the 20th century some Mathurs from these *mohallas* colonized spacious houses with large gardens in the Civil Lines area, mostly a swathe of land with her orchards enclosed by Commissioner's Lane and Usmanpur (now Jumna) Road. Many of them were lawyers, some became civil servants, others taught Urdu and Persian in colleges, and some concentrated on enjoying good food and music. Qudsia Bagh and the Jumna across Bela (now Ring) Road were abiding factors in their lives—the river kept the area fragrant and comparatively cool, its sandy banks yielding walks and melons.

Some Mathur families were persuaded by the early developers of New Delhi to move to the new city. They clustered around Connaught Place, on Barakhamba and Curzon (now Kasturba Gandhi) Roads, and areas like Babur Road and Hanuman Road. All retained strong connections with their kin in 'Shahar' and the Civil Lines, and all the major shopping—whether for clothes, jewellery, spices, paan, tin boxes, books and stationery—was still done in the Old City.

You couldn't bypass Shahar. The entry into Delhi was always by train, at the Old Delhi railway station (the New Delhi station was largely ceremonial until the 1950s). There were usually prolonged unscheduled halts of the train at the Ghaziabad and Shahdara railway stations and, invariably, on the old iron bridge spanning the Jumna, from where passengers had the classical view of the *dhobis* of Delhi washing and drying clothes on the river bank. The last phase of the journey was exhilarating as the train chugged through the Salimgarh fort and skirted the walls of the Lal Qila: the sense of entering a great and historic city was palpable.

The journey to a home in very central New Delhi was done in a *tonga* or two, with tin trunks and holdalls and baskets piled high. The route was well-trodden, the streets the *tonga* clattered through celebrated: it went past the Public (now Har Dayal) Library, down Nai Sarak, then Chawri Bazar, past Qazi Hauz and on to Ajmeri Gate (through which the tonga went, the horse's hooves echoing), past Delhi (now Zakir Husain) College and eventually down and up the Minto Bridge slope (where the tonga moved at the pace of a pedestrian and a gleaming Connaught Place came into view). Old Delhi was not only an essential and hallowed part of the route, but also the place where people indulged in sharp practices (with elegance), sharp talk and, generally, were city-slickers in a city they ardently believed to be the acme of creation.

As late as the 1950s the most trusted doctors in Delhi were located in Chandni Chowk or Daryaganj, and the great tailor was Mohammad Umar, who functioned in a lane not far from Atma Ram's, the best bookshop in Delhi, and in the Kashmiri Gate area. You didn't know good cuisine unless you had eaten in Shahar, and of the four stylish hotels in Delhi, only the Imperial was in New Delhi: the rest—the Cecil, the Swiss and Maidens were in the Civil Lines area. When a West Indies cricket team first toured India, it was housed at Maidens, which rocked with calypso rhythms for the likes of Wallcot, Weekes, Gomez and George Headley.

And yes, people went to Shahar to see and ride in trams, perhaps the ricketiest, slowest and oldest trams in the world, but the only ones in north India. Not even Lahore could boast of trams. Shahar remained the heart and soul of Delhi throughout my days in Delhi University. Our movements circumscribed by poor public transport (perhaps the only element of continuity in Delhi), the lack of personal scooters, motorcycles and cars, an outing from the campus usually led to Kashmiri Gate or the Jama Masjid area: we often walked there, and the route to Chandni Chowk meant using the high pedestrian bridge across the railway track near Kash Gate and often emerging from that exercise covered with soot from the puffing steam engines below as they pulled wagons to or from the Old Delhi station.

Until the late 1950s even those living outside the city walls knew Shahar reasonably well. New and Old Delhi together still formed a comparatively compact unit, with New Delhiwallahs making regular forays into Shahar and the Civil Lines areas: Moti Mahal was a premier attraction, and the bar and nightclub at Maidens' the fanciest in town. The Ring Road hadn't yet come into being, so people couldn't ignore the Old City.

The journey to the university meant rides through Daryaganj and past Lal Qila, frequently involving prolonged halts in these areas as buses were changed. During these halts one got to know the *dhabas* and stalls near the bus stands, and, if a suitable bus failed to turn up, the journey was often continued on foot or temporarily abandoned in the *galis* of the Old City. Commuters thus got to know the book-shops in Daryaganj and Nai Sarak, and the *kabariwallas* near the Jama Masjid. These meanderings also prevented some of us from forgetting the Urdu script entirely, for the hoardings and signboards in the Old City were still mostly in Urdu and it was reassuring to be able to decipher them.

The cohesive, urbane combine of New and Old Delhi no longer exists and while Delhi has grown into a vast city over the last few decades, its different parts don't seem to make up a whole. The area covered by it appears to have reverted to what it was before Shahar came into being—a collection of disconnected villages, each with its own ways and mannerisms, and altogether more provincial than the stylish, integrated city of not so long ago.

The village I inhabit, roughly extending from the Lodi Gardens to the Purana Qila, with Khan Market, several schools and Sujan Singh Park as its focal points, and the IIC, IHC, Humayun's Tomb, the Oberoi Hotel and Taj Mansingh at its periphery, is agreeable enough, but it's not a distinctive civilization, as Delhi once was. It is, nevertheless, a central area in a city that has expanded thirty kilometres afield in all the cardinal directions, and is visited by and known to people living in the outbanks. But most of the outbanks are less fortunate and remain strangers to each other.

There is, thus, no such thing as a Dilliwallah any more, and this absence seems to be part of the present, amorphous identity of the city. There are Londoners and New Yorkers, Parisians and Mumbaikars, Mysoreans and Hyderabadis, but the inhabitants of Delhi are now anonymous. Even the Mathurs have stopped calling themselves Dilliwallahs. How can it be otherwise if you live in GK II, your spouse perhaps a Sikh, your son an investment banker in New York, your daughter-in-law an Italian and your grandson unable to digest a decent, spiced kabab made of goat meat?

While the Dilliwallah may have gone into oblivion, the other Kayastha conceit—of being traditionally literate and literary and, generally, good pen-pushers—has prospered in the changed environment. The Mathurs were quick to take to the new educational system introduced by the British and soon entered professions that needed the skills so acquired. Pedigree Mathur that I am, I became part of a comparatively new form of pen pushing in 1961—publishing, and from my publishing peep-hole have not only witnessed and participated in the flowering of publishing in Delhi over the last few decades, but also been struck by the spectacular growth in Delhi's educational system and intellectual infrastructure which catalyzed publishing.

India's educational system is much derided, no doubt with good reason, but the good should not be interred with the bones: one of the good things is that in the hurly-burly of the last five decades, as Delhi shed its old scales and didn't quite refashion itself as a cohesive whole, it also became India's premier educational centre and a magnet for the country in this area. If Delhi has more automobiles than Mumbai, Kolkata and Chennai put together, it also probably has more authors than in these cities put together, and produces books in a similarly excessive proportion.

This wasn't always so. Until the mid-1960s Bombay was the major publishing centre in the country, with Calcutta and Madras not far behind. The best book printers and binders were in these cities, and even in 1971, when the OUP opened its office on Ansari Road, its bigger books were usually typeset there or in Pondicherry. With every major publishing house shifting base to Delhi around then or soon after, the skills needed to make a decent book rapidly developed in the region, and Delhi now leads the field both in printing and publishing.

Initially it was Ansari Road in Daryaganj that hosted the publishing renaissance, and manuscripts from Delhi University that nourished it, but matching the expansion of the city further south and the growth of author-yielding institutions in other parts of the city, publishing too is no longer concentrated along the rim of the Old City. Penguin are now in Panchsheel, OUP on Jaisingh Road, IndiaInk in New Rajendra Nagar, Permanent Black in Patparganj and Ravi Dayal in a back-room facing a garden and a pomegranate tree in Sujan Singh Park.

While the Delhi I knew and sometimes felt I belonged to has been obliterated, its new and, in many ways, much nastier incarnation has nevertheless nourished me enormously with the ideas its contemporary scholars, thinkers and writers have generated. A live but violent and corrupt Delhi is not a pleasurable creature to endure, but for a publisher in India, 'If on earth there is a place of bliss/It is this, it is this, it is this' crazy city.

—*Seminar*, no. 515 (July 2002), pp. 21–3.

Ghulam M. Sheikh

Delhi

Over the fort like a broken loaf
sunshine sharp like radishes.
Grass and stones nestling in the ruins
of Tughlaqabad.

Shadows within arches: arches shadowed: Khirki Masjid.

Steps in rows fleeting through the eyes like a needle
at Jama Masjid.
The Qutb erect, stretching from root to throat.
Smells all around,
of food, flesh, blood, prisons and palaces,
yesterdays', centuries'.
Breath caught and fixed to this moment,
the eye alive wheeling through the past
enters the cracks in Ghalib's tomb.
seeking Khankhanan's fossilised bones,
wanders from tomb to tomb
with the restless fate of Jahanara.
Still, dust and mist
still, nothing separates flesh and stone.
A sunbeam
slipping through the vagina of a dove
asleep upon the western arches of the Red Fort
pierces my eye.
Still, dawn.
Dreams mate with reality
What will be the face of morning?

—translated from the Gujarati by the poet and Mala Marwah; taken
from *Signatures: One Hundred Indian Poets*, ed., K. Satchidanandan
(New Delhi: National Book Trust, 2004), p. 278.

Sarnath Banerjee

Corridor: A Graphic Novel

Early October

Still an hour or so of peace and quiet before the mad rush of office-goers floods the streets of old Delhi

Nearby, at Turkman Gate, a retired Tongawala
eats breakfast with his horse

The elaborate breakfast ritual of old Delhi is about to begin

The first prayers of the day will soon come alive on the loud speakers

As of now, the Jama Masjid sits quietly at the edge of Meena Bazaar

North of Daryaganj is altogether a different planet

Here the immeasurably old rub shoulders with the very new

Last year around this time Shintu got married

He was happy, maybe a little apprehensive

Till then his knowledge of sex and stuff came from reading Cosmopolitan

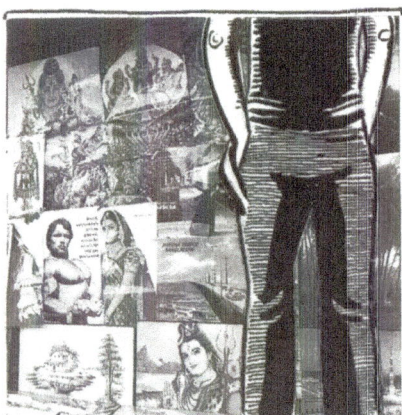

Therefore, it wasn't a surprise ...

... That on their wedding night, Shintu and Dolly played Scrabble

Which, according to Shintu's mum is a good sign

What's the hurry

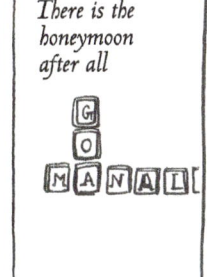

There is the honeymoon after all

And Shintu is a good boy isn't he?

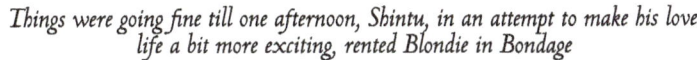

Things were going fine till one afternoon, Shintu, in an attempt to make his love life a bit more exciting, rented Blondie in Bondage

Not that anything was wrong

KUKREJA VIDEO PALACE

DVD 12/-

NEW RELEASE

TAAL

Heh, Heh, Shintubabu, I've changed the cover

Mary poppin's

Daily Hurts

A routine affair

Malti was already running late by the time she left the house that morning. The autorickshaw driver delayed her further. For some reason, she had been unable to sleep well last night. She was tired of her mother's daily abuses. She walked along the road thinking death relieves many. That's how it seems from newspapers at least. Alas, I'm not fated even for that!

What turn will life take now?

Maitri Devi of South Delhi's Durga Vihar was busy preparing for her daughter Vineeta's wedding. The wedding party was grand. A few days later, the truth of the marriage emerged. Vineeta's husband is mad. Or, we could say, he is a little weak in the head. Now we wait to see what turn Vineeta's life will take.

Ill omen of the garland

Ruheena of A Block, Milan Vihar, was getting married. Her house filled with guests on her wedding day. When garlands were being exchanged by the bride and the groom, a garland broke. An ill-omen, people declared.

Hotch-potch

The house was ready for the girl's wedding; the groom's procession was being awaited. Then a brand new manoeuvre from the groom's side: A demand of one lakh rupees. The bride batted well: She called up the police. Everyone is now behind bars. It was the guests who won in this duel! They ate heartily and slept contentedly.

Peepul Chowk

Sitting in an autorickshaw, one boy is saying to the other, 'His days are numbered.' Of course, the eavesdropper wants to know who is being talked about. The one being referred to here is about twenty-four years old. It is now known that he drank up his innards with alcohol.

The abundance of water

It has been heard that on the hillock near the jungle, fountains of water have appeared. But in every neighbourhood, people sit clenching their parched throats. Investigations have revealed that the water-pipe line had burst.

Household tale

Divorce papers were filed on the morning of the day the husband was to receive his monthly salary. Reason: Why did the wife demand that the pay be handed to her, even though the husband's mother lives with them? Result: The girl is now at her home and the boy at his.

Mobile love

In a small area in New Delhi, Rahul and Sunita struggled to give their relationship a name. As time passed, they became so close that they started to make social appearances together. They ended up being made to marry each other at least four times as a result.

The effect of films

In this fast changing world, the love people have for film songs remains unchanged. Year 2008, Wednesday, 9.45 a.m. Seeing a young woman pass from in front of an autorickshaw stand, a young man broke into song to express the feelings she had stirred in his heart, 'Your height is just-a-super, and on top of that you're such a looker.' The girl was no less than Malika Sherawat. She turned and walked back to where the boy was standing, and asked him, 'Are you speaking the truth?'

I love you very much, my dear

Love is getting a bad name these days. Everyone seems to have turned into a lover. In Tigri, Nilu has put his mother to a deep, dreamless sleep for the sake of his girlfriend. Fear has sealed his father's lips.

The fire of revenge

It has been seen that the moment someone buys a refrigerator, a long queue of people requesting a drink of cold water forms outside his door.

If the owner of the new refrigerator makes the mistake of saying he has no cold water to serve, his neighbours begin scheming to avenge this refusal. Today, one neighbourhood has seen a man take his revenge two years after the seeds were planted: The first thing Ramesh has done after buying a refrigerator of his own is to cut his neighbour Manoj's electricity cable. Now only his fridge will work, while Manoj will be left pining for cold water.

Burtar Singh held at gun point

Burtar Singh lives in an informal settlement. On Sunday he was at home with his entire family. Suddenly he heard a loud voice call out to him, 'Kakke...' As soon as his son stepped out to see who it was, he was grabbed by a group of boys. When Burtar Singh learnt of this, he rushed out to help him. One among the group held a gun to Burtar Singh's head. A crowd of people gathered to watch, but no one stepped forward to intervene.

The bus journey

A young woman sat by a window seat in a bus, immersed in her own thoughts. Some boys got into the bus and started to tease her. All the other passengers kept watching, as if this were a show. Is a film hero about to appear to save her?

Near Lal Building School, Ambedkar Nagar

Tuesday, 11.00 a.m. Satish's motorcycle was hit by another motorcycle. Not a big injury, only his leg got fractured. Sadly, his marriage was due to happen in two days.

School shoes

Tension mounted in the household over a minor matter. The son demanded a new pair of shoes for school. His mother's response: 'Next month.' On hearing this, the boy left home, vowing never to return. Will he leave school as well? What will happen next? We do not know.

In the fear of a bad name

Uday set out in the streets of the city to look for his wife. A month later, he was spotted again, doing the rounds of the same lanes. People advised him to seek help from the police. He replied his name would be disgraced if he does that.

Surprise in the feast

Anita's wedding was held in M Block in Ambedkar Nagar on the fourth of December. The group that had been helping Anita dress got delayed in reaching the tent to partake of the feast. By then there was no food left! Some 'exchanges' had transpired with the outside from the back of the tent.

Power failure

Khan bhai's life was made hell by his neighbours who kept gathering in his house after every power cut in the locality. Khan bhai grew so frustrated that he ended up breaking his own inverter.

The arrival of the sister-in-law

Four years have passed, but Sonia is still waiting to hear her in-laws' decision. Four years ago she was living happily with her husband. Everything changed after her husband's sister came to live with them. It has been very difficult to ascertain who is to be blamed.

In a hurry to create

In the middle of the game they were playing in the lane, these young boys between four and six years of age became inextricably caught up in trying to sort out what belongs to them and what to others. Now they spend all their time preparing to set up a gang.

In lane number four

Drops of rain fell from the sky. It brought everyone respite from the heat. People who live in lane number four of Dakshinpuri sent for mud to tackle the sludge caused by the rain. But they refused to contribute money to pay for it. By the end of 2006, mud has become a major issue.

The neighbours' medicine

Her neighbours created a furore because her husband came home drunk every night. She thought, 'Let me end this daily tension once and for all.' She hung herself.

In the heat of the summer

In this severe summer season, water is terribly scarce. The empathetic have set out earthen pots to provide cool drinking water to the passer-by; but they contain no water! Heat continues to tease the thirsty city traveller.

Love over the telephone

A boy fell in love with a girl. The girl is unaware of this. What is this mystery? The girl clarifies, 'How can someone who has never seen me be in love with me?' The boy can't bear the girl's refusal. He jumps into the river and ends his life.

Trust

Nutan has complete faith in her landlord, which is why she is not anxious that her daughter return from his house, where she has now been for three days.

Reason: Too many children. The daughter has gone elsewhere to find love.

Tuition centre

With Independence Day round the corner, students got together and decided to celebrate. They all went up to the roof of the tuition centre to fly kites. By the time the teacher arrived, two of the students lost in flying kites got stuck to the electricity cable.

Teasing at the temple

The priest snatched away Mira's purse when she went to the temple to pray. He accused her of having come to the temple with the intention to steal. Will Mira find justice in God's courtroom?

A Friend comes clear

Anil and Manoj set out together from Anil's home, but it was only Anil who came back. When Manoj didn't reach home, Anil was asked about it. He maintained silence, which only landed him behind bars. Anil has now revealed that to clear his path to Manoj's girlfriend, he has cleared Manoj off.

Reform

Sahil was alone at home. His neighbour accused him of stealing and beat him up. When his mother came back home and saw Sahil's condition, she too beat him up. What will Sahil do now? Mend his ways or lose his path?

When it rained bread

An uproar was reported at Sangam Vihar at 10.30 at night: A husband beat up his wife mercilessly. When people inquired, they were informed that she had made four extra rotis. Making sense of the turmoils in society is becoming extremely difficult. It is impossible to predict what might happen next.

Unyielding brother

A boy sent a proposal to this household, asking for the daughter's hand in marriage. The girl made one mistake after seeing the photograph of the boy. She said she liked him. This infuriated her brother. He put her to sleep forever.

When the belt speaks

The husband would get drunk and fight with the wife every night. The wife threw him onto the floor and whipped him with a belt.

An impossible account

Children in the lane have fought among themselves.

Reason: An argument that no one has heard, and about which none of the children seem to be able to give an account.

Injured in the drain

An accident has occurred in a drain pipe in Dakshinpuri's J Block. A two-year-old-girl was found inside it. According to information gathered, she was playing outside her house. On not finding anyone about her, she started crying and went towards the drain and, unseen by anyone, fell into it. She has been taken to the nearest hospital, where doctors have declared that her condition is critical. Is the municipal corporation now sparing a thought for this drain?

A bird in hand

It was Tuesday. When the mother noticed that the bottle of jam was broken, she called out to her son. Her son didn't respond. Time ticked on. When, after searching for him for long, she could not find him, she informed the police. Everyone who knew her also set out looking for the child. The mother, her tears flowing uncontrollably, lay down on the floor. That is when she saw her son was asleep under the bed.

The future of the eggs

There was a power cut. The egg-seller made the most of the darkness: He teased a girl who happened to be passing by. It was only later that he found out that she was Bhim wrestler's sister. Will the egg-seller be spared by the wrestler? He waits to find out.

Mouth shut

In Madangir, a woman chose a man as her brother. Her husband found this brother's visits to his home unpalatable. He slit his wife's throat and finished her off.

The family's deception

Under pressure from her family, a girl threw her newborn child into a drain. Her family told her that her being unmarried was the reason for her child's death. Why had her family deceived her for nine months?

Peeping out from a window

His lips curled as if ready to blow a whistle, this man must be about fifty years old. Such mischief fills those eyes! What is the secret? It's now been told there is a girls' school right in front of his house.

Eyewitness account

Two passengers travelling by autorickshaw grew tired of the length of the journey and decided to make the most of their time by silently making out. Suddenly the driver spoke up, 'I hope you don't mind that I have fixed in my auto one small CCTV camera recently.'

The conclusion of an argument

Two women were overheard chatting at a crossroad in their locality. One said these are days for lazing around. The other disagreed. Their argument became so heated that their husbands came out of their houses and slapped them. We now understand it is futile to argue.

—from *Trickster City: Writings from the Belly of the Metropolis*, translated from Hindi by Shveta Sarda (New Delhi: Penguin/Viking, 2010), pp. 88, 90, 92, 94, 96, 98, 100, 102, 104.

Ranjit Lal

Wild City: Nature Wonders Next Door

City Simians

They're easily Delhi's most notorious denizens: the huge population of rhesus macaques that thrive on the patronage of the capital's denizens and play havoc everywhere—from the corridors of power to hospital wards and school classrooms. Up close and personal, they'll behead your carefully nurtured chrysanthemums and check out your fridge and dare you enter your own front door.

It was a mistake never to be repeated. I left the balcony door of my bedroom slightly ajar one morning and went out of the house. When I returned, my room looked as if the CBI had been visiting, and with very specific search orders. Every single wildlife magazine I possessed—as well as a music book—had been shredded and was scattered all over the place. No other magazine or book had been touched. And even my dog apparently had had no idea when the raid had taken place. And there, on the boundary wall outside, a monkey sat holding a page of guitar chords to its face, before ripping it up. These are the city simians, the rhesus macaques—those tough, hairy, red-bottomed monkeys—who have made Delhi, and almost every major city in the country, their home. (In the southern states, the smaller, more delicate-looking bonnet macaques predominate.) They've always made me wonder whether we have evolved from them, or they from us. They sport a comic starburst hairstyle complete with a neat centre parting. Some monkey experts tell us that there are probably more of them living in cities than there are in the jungles. Well, obviously. No smart twenty-first century *bandar* would want to live in the jungle, for heaven's sake! There are wild beasts there. Besides, one of the indicators of a developed society is that most of its population lives in cities.

We must catch them, the experts say—entire families, of course, so that there is no trauma of breakup—and transport them back into the salubrious lap of nature; from where they promptly make a beeline back to the cities. And why wouldn't they?

In the wild, you have to find your own food—fruits, berries, seeds and whatever else. Right, it may be organic, but there are also leopards in the wild, for whom monkeys for breakfast is a nice way to start the day. In the city, pious city folk who revere the monkey-god Hanuman come searching for them, crying, 'Aao, aao, aao!' They are laden down with boondi ladoos, paranthas, bananas, litchies, watermelons, mangoes, oranges and left overs from last night's dinner. It is no wonder, then, that hungry urchins hang around the main feeding spots like the Ridge, grab a banana and flee; often being chased by the monkeys. The pious souls, would, of course, be horrified if they knew that little boys were stealing from the monkeys.

Naturally, in such an environment, where meals are served regularly and the parks are shady and cool and there are no nasty leopards about, city simians thrive. There are well over 5,000 of them in Delhi living in parks, gardens, marketplaces and housing colonies. And the pressures of big-city life tell on them too. While the number of monkey-bite cases probably doesn't come anywhere near the number of cases of people killed or injured by vehicles, we are naturally more outraged by the former. So we get after them with sticks and stones, which, coming after a breakfast of aaloo paranthas and boondi ladoos and pious incantations turn them completely schizophrenic in their relations with us. For some reason, the rhesus in Delhi—and perhaps other towns too—think of langurs as their bogeymen, so langurs and their handlers, kalandars, have to be hired to scare the rhesus away from some prestigious localities like the North and South blocks, as well as residential colonies. In the wild the rhesus and langur species cohabit quite companionably.

Just like humans, some city simians can't take the pressure of urban living. One venerable old gent took to spending his time under our van and would grab at a leg every time someone passed by. The monkeys of Mathura have a liking for spectacles and will snatch yours off before you can blink. In fact, the simian inhabitants of places like Haridwar and Rishikesh, and probably every other temple town, have become dangerously brazen and fundamentalist in their behaviour. Others, like the perverts of our own society, pick soft targets on quiet afternoons—women and children—to hound and terrorize. And like us, might appears to be right.

In rhesus society, however, a male with an ambition to become the don of his group needs more than just brute strength to achieve his aim. The real power lies with the ladies of the troupe, viragos every one of them. If he can win them over by charm, flattery, charisma and courage, he'll succeed. But if he puts them off, he can be Tarzan's uncle and they still they won't accept him.

Like those of us afflicted with instant attacks of road rage, monkeys too appear to have dangerously inflammable tempers, albeit for different reasons. Quiet, blissful Sunday afternoons are suddenly shattered by enraged grunts, ear-splitting screams, pounding feet, as tempers ignite and haunches and faces are bitten—very badly on occasion—over such trivials as 'you intruded into my private space without permission', or 'you made eyes at my baby'. The females are equally vicious fighters.

The old and sick, alas, are not respected and keep away from family groups—a trend that we're slowly beginning to follow too. And, of course, infants and juveniles throw the most incredible tantrums when they don't get their way. Human parents of spoilt brats can take some consolation.

But even in the cities there are happy times. Huge families will bask together in the winter sun, grooming each other with great care and concern. Infants gambol fearlessly over great, beer-bellied dons, who wear ludicrously benign expressions on their faces. The infants, of course, can provide more entertainment than forty-five television channels. Like us, they have their crazy moments. I once watched, with amazement, as a youngster went swimming in a pond on the Ridge on a crisp, cold winter morning. He would jump into the water from an overhanging branch, surface sputtering and covered with duckweed, paddle to the shore, climb up to an exposed perch and sit there shivering and teeth chattering. After a few moments, there'd be another sploosh and he'd be back in the water again.

The Ridge

Delhi's beautiful, notorious Ridge forest is no gift of god, but the work of man. Planted by the British, the Ridge is the largest and most effective air-conditioning plant in Delhi. And ten minutes from Connaught Place, you can quite literally be lost in the jungle.

I am constantly taken aback by the number of born-and-bred, dyed-in-the-wool Delhites I meet who are completely blank about Delhi's most prominent, valuable and beautiful physical feature and capital asset: the Ridge.

The Ridge forms the tail end of the Mewat branch of the ancient and rugged Aravalli mountains and enters Delhi from Gurgaon in the south, in the form of a plateau some six kilometres across. One branch turns back on itself while the other bisects the city in a northeasterly direction tapering off on the west bank of the Jamuna near Wazirabad. It has been divided into four zones: the vast southern Ridge (6200 ha) lies outside the city limits; the south-central Ridge (626 ha), much ravaged by quarrying and construction, lies in the Mehrauli area; the central or New Delhi Ridge (864 ha) lies between Sardar Patel Road and colonies like New Rajinder Nagar; and the northern Ridge which (87 ha) lies like an emerald flinthead between Delhi University and Civil Lines. It is the latter two that are the invaluable 'green lungs' of the city. Look out from the terraces of any of the big hotels on Sardar Patel Road and you will be amazed at the extent of the woolly green pelt of forest stretching before you. And this, smack in the middle of the city.

Even more amazing is that this forest is not a gift of god but mostly the work of man! Way back before the rebellion of 1857, the Ridge comprised of hard, rocky country that supported little more than thorny scrub foliage. Then, in the torrid summer and monsoon of 1857, the British encamped in the inhospitable gullies of the northern Ridge while attempting to retake the city and more soldiers succumbed to heatstroke and disease than to enemy fire. Afterwards, they swore to afforest this barren, heartless wilderness and change its face forever. Afforestation would also protect the new residential colony of Civil Lines from being blasted by the heat reflected off the hot rocks of the Ridge. Actually, they were not quite the first to do so. Some six hundred years ago, the emperor Feroze Shah Tughlaq afforested a section of the northern Ridge, turning it into a hunting park.

The big drive to afforest the Ridge began in 1912 when Lutyens arrived to design the new capital. It was a tough task as the elements were hostile and the soil was poor, but eventually, with much tree planting and zealous protection, the great forest did come up. The trees that grew here had to be tough and several species of acacia—most prominently, the well-armed babul (*Acacia nilotica*)—fitted the bill best. Others, like neem, flame of the forest, gulmohar, laburnum, desi papri and peepal did well too, and today, driving along the Ridge road beside Buddha Jayanti Park is a pleasure at any time of the year, with some tree species or the other in brilliant flower.

This wonderful city forest is naturally a haven for animals and birds. Sadly, most of the large animals like the leopard, wild boar, wolf, blackbuck and most of the nilgai that were reported from the Ridge in the 1920s and 1930s are not around. Today, you will be lucky to see a jackal scamper off or a black-naped hare lollop across a path. The most common mammals on the ridge are, of course, the roving bands of rhesus macaques, though even these seem to prefer built-up, inhabited areas to the wild hinterland, so completely dependent they are on human handouts. Happily, bird life still remains remarkably rich. About 200 species have been counted on the Ridge, including breeding residents, winter migrants and those that drop by on their way to other destinations. Here, you can catch a glimpse of the glamorous paradise flycatcher and the little known blue-capped rock thrush, as well as most of Delhi's common resident birds—its woodpeckers, barbets, hornbills, owls, parakeets, babblers, bulbuls, and prinias, et al. Not much is known about the wealth of 'lesser' life—reptiles, amphibians and insects—that the Ridge supports. There certainly are lizards and snakes though they tend to keep a low profile. In the monsoons, great orchestras of raincoat-yellow bullfrogs will serenade you from impromptu ponds and pools, then vanish without a trace. A study in the 1960s indicated at least seventy species of butterflies on the Ridge.

Modern Delhites have not treated the Ridge very kindly. Some estimate that up to 40 per cent of the Ridge has already been destroyed. People, both in and out of the government, have used the Ridge like it was their private property, encroaching and building on it in the most malignant manner possible. Everything, from schools, temples and farmhouses to satellite-tracking stations and open-air auditoria have come up on what was meant to be left to nature. But happily, the Ridge has its protectors too. Back in the 1970s, a group of students squatted in front of government bulldozers to prevent them from illegally destroying what they were meant to be protecting. A few years ago, the Supreme Court ordered that all encroachments on the Ridge be removed, a very welcome move. Till 1998, some 60 per cent had been.

For the capital's citizens, the Ridge is invaluable. It works like a gigantic central air-conditioning and air-purifying plant bringing down temperatures and removing noxious gases from the air. Drive along the Ridge in peak summer and you can feel the perceptible drop in temperature. It is a place you can go to walk, meditate, jog and exercise, nature ramble and bird watch, hold hands or just stand and stare. A ten-minute drive from Connaught Place can see you surrounded by greenery, listening to a classical flute concert by a magpie robin. In front of you on the path, a covey of sprightly grey partridge look back and trundle on, quite obviously giving you the come hither. What choice do you have?

—from *Wild City: Nature Wonders Next Door* (Delhi: Penguin Books, 2008), pp. 123–8, 224–9.

Kunwar Narain

Lucknow

Lucknow: a half-dead, debilitated fogey
Half-lying,
Coughing on a broken armchair;
Dead Set against the devil-may-care
Insouciance of its young busters.

Lucknow: chewing up its slices
Of four mores
Sweeping from the Coffee House
And Hazratganj
To Ameenabad and the Chowk.

Lucknow: checking out its forked youth
Who had thumped their jowls
Over lambasts and lairs,
Bumping along to take a bum-rap here
And a bush-wah there;
Burning up time, battling their gums

Going the full yard to go snooks
On gloom, grief and grouch.

Lucknow: in whose markets
Indispensables are dispensed with;
In whose streets
Multitudes pushover centuries;
On whose roads
No one fits into place
In the pell-mell of crushing bustles
Through the traffic circles of
Their hustlers and of haberdashers.

Lucknow; a morgue of perished glory
A penance of a widow,
Holding the canopy of dismal evenings
Over its decrepit cupolas.

Lucknow: an invitation of a hooker
With every tomorrow bearing
The fragments of its yesterday;
Crabbing and courting,
Bending its brows like a bowed baron.

Lucknow: a dazzle of a femme fatale
Sobbing in a mass of ruins,
With a fragility of a delicately flowered
Embroidery on a frail voile.

Lucknow: a *quawaali* celebrating
The raptures of its bygone deluges.

Lucknow: an ode acclaiming
The habitat of Sarshar and Majaaz

Lucknow: an animus, agog with
Scouted faithlessness.
Lucknow: a divination, aglow with
Prescient phosphorescence.

That, folks,
Is Lucknow: yours and mine!

—translated from Hindi by Deepak Sharma, originally published in
The Little Magazine (July–August 2000), p. 69.

K.S. Narasimha Swamy

From House to House

At the end of every year
Movement from one outhouse to another,
This means
Once again
Packing up of bags and gunny bags
The fatigue
Once again, the procession
Of lanterns without screws, baskets without bottoms,
The sieve, the cradle and the pestle

How heavy, these things! Can't we throw them out?
'Throwing out is no solution. Get new ones first'
Not enough place in the truck. 'Carry them, then.'
I must carry them? That is done after darkness.
'Yes, let's wait for the night!'
(The mother of ten children, the friendly one, laughed)
Hate is less killing than laughter. Get up,
Let us first go to the new house. After evening,
Let me transport them.
The red-tailed fish stirred
The dark pond. The woman had won.
We too can laugh at times in life

2
A new excuse every time for leaving the house

The reason this time: the owner was nice;
His wife and daughter?-could also be nice
Never did they say: 'Quit the house'
They did something entirely different!
They arranged music lessons for their daughter
Who could never be good at studies
So that at least her voice could improve
And take her close to marriage
During those eight months full of rains and frogs
She went on learning just one line:
'Carrying water from tank to tank'
This is what we all do

At dawn, in the afternoon and evening
We carried water from tank to tank
Till there was no place in the house
Any more for water
When we came out on streets
Roared the landlord
'You poured out water,'
And forced on us the entire water-tax
The water meter had spoken the truth
The door of another house opened for us

3

The owners of a house have just one house
But those without have a hundred
I cannot guess how many children
The previous occupants had
They have dug up the floor
Broken the taps
Put out bulbs
Scattered away the flower pots
Inscribed zero on every door
Tomorrow, these boys will be the same
Where is the novelty here? To the house someone else lived in
We have come. Are we strangers? We are not
The charcoal curtain on the brown wall carries
The name of the next play: 'Novelty'
We moved in just today

We are not in a hurry
To repair glasses of photo frames
Polishing of vessels
Can wait for another week

The new doormat to rub the feet—
Can't we get it tomorrow?
'What shall we do now?' Why ask again?
Whichever house we move into we will call it new
With new buntings on the old door
Like school children learning new things
We will spend another year

4

Just one year for each house
Nothing is new about tomorrow's news
Memory's silver thread is unwinding its skein

The back is bent carrying worthless things
The eyes have turned blank
Carrying water from tank to tank
The zero boys wrote; the landlords' words;
Laughers and tears—
Not just one or two, but many our blessings
For which we need the dark
Let's wait for the night

5

From house to house
From outhouse to outhouse......
From the first house
To another without love, door or name
We are moving with everything, old and new
No-one will stop us
No-one will call us in
There is not even a house
Or even a shadow of an outhouse
Those who reach there cannot come back
For there are no roads
That will be the last house!

Beneath the sideways glance of stars on the horizon
Often blows
The breeze of void

> —published as 'Maneyinda Manege', from the book *Malligeya Maale: Collected Poems of K.S. Narasimha Swamy* (Bangalore: Lipi Prakashana, 1986), translated from the Kannada by H.S. Shivaprakash.

Dhoomil

The City, Evening, and an Old Man: Me

I've taken the last drag
and stubbed out my cigarette in the ashtray,
and now I'm a respectable man
with all the trappings of civility.

When I'm on vacation
I don't hate anyone.
I don't have any protest march to join.
I've drunk all the liquor
In the bottle marked
FOR DEFENCE SERVICES ONLY
and thrown it away in the bathroom.
That's the sum total of my life.
(Like every good citizen
I draw the curtains across my windows
the moment I hear the air-raid siren.
These days it isn't the light outside
But the light inside that's dangerous.)

I haven't done a thing to deserve
a statue whose unveiling

Would make the wise men of this city
waste a whole busy day.
I've been sitting in a corner of my dinner plate
and leading a very ordinary life.
What I inherited were citizenship
in the neighbourhood of a jail
and gentlemanliness
in front of a slaughter-house.
I've tied them both to my own convenience
and taken them two steps forward.
The municipal government has taught me
to stay on the left side of the road.
(To succeed in life you don't need
to read Dale Carnegie's book
but to understand traffic signs.)

Other than petty lies
I don't know the weight of a gun.
On the face of the traffic policeman
doing his drill in the square
I've always seen the map of democracy.

And now I don't have a single worry,
I don't have to do a thing.
I've reached the stage in life
when files begin to close.
I'm sitting in my own chair on the verandah
without any qualms.
The sun's setting on the toe of my shoe.
A bugle's blowing in the distance.
This is the time when the soldiers come back,
and the possessed city
is now slowly turning its madness
into windowpanes and lights.

—translated from Hindi by Vinay Dharwadker; from *The Oxford
Anthology of Modern Indian Poetry*, eds, Vinay Dharwadker and
A.K. Ramanujan (Delhi: Oxford University Press, 1994), pp. 139–40.

Nirupama Dutt

Cityscape

Leave this city if you must
but you will not
be able to leave yourself
For a while you will live
the anonymous life
of an alien city
Then you will seek
someone to walk with you
on the unknown city roads
You will weave webs
of relationships to
adorn the walls of
your rented room
We know you well
You won't be able to resist it
You will fall in love yet again
just to make sure you are there
Perhaps they were right
It is difficult to live
in a city where the
breeze has no caress
where the night has
no secret to hide
Difficult like hell
to live in a city
that has no tale to tell

—translated from the Punjabi by the poet, and first published
in *The Little Magazine* (May–June 2001), p. 91.

Imagination of the City,
the City of Imagination

Folktale from West Bengal

Oh! Calcutta

Once there lived a rich man in Calcutta. Because he was rich, he naturally indulged in all sorts of dirty games: he used to drink a lot, gamble a lot, and do a lot of womanizing. Besides, he thrived on corruption, bribery, and dishonesty. In short, the man was rich but also sinful and dirty.

Now you know, rich people don't die young. So this man also enjoyed life till the end. He died at the ripe age of eighty. And as I said, the man was loaded with sin. Therefore, soon after his death, he was transferred to *Yamaloka*, the realm of the dead. There he could be seen in the long queue of dead people waiting for their turn to have an audience with Yamaraja, the god of death. All were waiting to find out their fate after death. Those who spent virtuous lives on earth would be sent to *Swarga* (paradise) and those who spent sinful lives would be sent to *Naraka* (hell).

Soon this sinful man had his turn. Yamaraja had his deeds on the earth assessed, and then declared, 'your place is in hell.' This verdict did not disturb the man at all. He kept on smiling. Yamaraja was surprised. 'I never saw anyone smile when being sent to hell!' said Yamaraja. 'Sir, I have lived my whole life in Calcutta. Hell cannot be worse than that,' replied the sinful, dirty man.

—from *Folktales of India*, eds, Brenda E.F. Beck, Peter J. Claus, Praphulladatta Goswami, and Jawaharlal Handoo, with foreword by A.K. Ramanujan (Chicago: The University of Chicago Press, 1987), pp. 207–8. The editors noted: 'This example of urban folklore must have its counterparts in nearly every industrial nation. While it is doubtful that India can claim originality for the story, Calcutta can possibly make the best claim to being a place worse than hell!'

Rabindranath Tagore

City and Village

When the bee first made its hive, its main object was food. But when bees banded together to gather honey from many flowers and stored them up against inclement seasons, they also found in the hive their community. This had not merely the mathematical feature of numbers but also the moral aspect of mutual service.

That which begins thus in the enjoyment of the many, ends in the renunciation of the many. Work for all takes the place of work for self; the individual life finds wider scope in the life of the community. So does one transcend the actual and realize the yet-to-be. Even the effort that fails to be fruitful in one's lifetime is not lost. The community becomes a common ground where relations are extended from the self to others, from the present to the future. And food, becoming abundant, transcends its materiality and expresses a spiritual value, revealing the infinitude of *Anna Brahma*.

In the primitive age men wandered alone, each in pursuit of his precarious livelihood. Their temper was fierce, their habits predatory, their behaviour unsocial. As, on river banks, food became plentiful, communities took form and civilizations were born.

Tilling the alluvial soil, men grew rich crops, year after year. They began to see that individuals could gain much more by mutual aid than by trying to deprive one another. With the food problem solved, the social instinct inherent in the nature of man was stimulated. When, at the invitation of the Earth-Mother, men sat down to feast together, their isolated lives found a basis of brotherhood through their common food.

The realization came that in union there was not advantage alone but also satisfaction. For its sake the individual would accept suffering and even death. The Earth gives us food in such a way that it gladdens our eye and enraptures our mind. The golden sunlight, flung from sky to sky, finds a response in the golden harvest from horizon to horizon. This splendour makes man think not only of his meals, but of festive rejoicing.

In the storehouse of the Earth there is, above the provision for our hunger, the nectar of joy. Lakshmi, the Goddess of Plenty, is beautiful as well as benign. The fruit tempts us not merely with its nutriment, but with its form, sweetness and fragrance. As the fruits of the Earth are beautiful, so also is the fellowship of man. The food we eat in solitude may have nourishment, but the food that we eat in fellowship has, in addition, loving-kindness. In such a feast of hearts the utensils become elegant, the serving decorous, the viands refined.

Dearth cramps the hospitality of man, on which society is founded. That is why villages had to grow on the threshold of the Earth's store of food. It was through his re-unions that the immortal in man has expressed itself: his morality, his literature, his music, his art, the variety of his ceremonials. It was through these that he began to be conscious of his own depths, and the ideal of his own perfection became manifest to him.

With the growth of the villages evolved the town. There became focused the forces of government—forts for soldiers, emporiums for merchants, colleges for teachers and students in their pursuit of knowledge, centres of commerce and communion with the outside world. There the soul is encased in hard stone, living is arduous, force contends with force. There the individual seeks to grow at the expense of others. So long as it is not carried to extremes, all this has value. If individuality be suppressed overmuch, man cannot attain fullness of stature. The young forest tree gets stunted if it is smothered under a profusion of undergrowth. On the other hand, the volcanic fire of individual ambition forces up the level of the masses. The standard of achievement is heightened. Competition enhances the output of energy. There is ever-fresh creativity in the fields of knowledge and work, and the sphere of wisdom is enlarged by the influx of the cultures of diverse peoples and countries. And so in the town, where the pressure of the community is relaxed, the individual mind gets a chance to rise superior to the low uniformity of the mass mind—'rustic' is everywhere a synonym for the mind's narrowness.

In their natural state—that is, when the community does not incline too much to one side—the village and the town have harmonious interactions. From the one flow food and health and fellow-feeling. From the other return gifts of wealth, knowledge and energy. A civilization which comprises mainly village life cannot advance very far. There the individual is unimportant, the community predominant. There we have, not the divine warrior, Kartikeya, on his winged steed, but King Demos—pot-bellied, elephant-headed Ganesha. On the other hand, where the town pre-dominates, the individual is all-powerful, the community negligible. There civilization burns itself in its own fires; the more brilliant its flame, the blacker its fuel, until at last it is reduced to ashes. Many civilizations have thus been destroyed by preying on themselves. It is yet too early to say that the civilization of modern Europe is not of this self-exhausting type.

The town is a point where activities are concentrated. The vital forces of our body are gathered at various centres. In the lower types of life these centres are not organized; with evolution, the brain, the lungs, the heart and the stomach gain in their functions. These may be compared with towns.

Towns are organized centres for serving the special needs of the body politic. Of old, machines played a minor role in fulfilling those needs. The joy of creation was the chief motive for manufacture, not the hunger for results.

In the modern age the machine has not only multiplied working capacity but also the hunger for gain and the scale of profit. That is why there is disharmony between the interest of the individual and the community, leading ultimately to conflict. Greed severs the relations between town and village. The town has become a drain on the village because it has ceased to make its contribution to the village. The artificial lights of the town are ablaze—lights that have no connection with sun, moon or star—but the humble lamps of the village are dead. The siren of the factory lures men away from the peaceful refuge of their community. And man is fast reverting to his primeval forest instincts. The individualism of those days has come back to life, but with a new, gigantic stature.

In the beginning, men had grouped themselves in villages to gather and store for mutual benefit. Now they have crowded together in much larger numbers, but each one is the centre of his own accumulation and enjoyment. So, in place of social regulation has come a more rigorous police rule. The solidarity of fellow-feeling has been replaced by the more stringent pressure of a complex system of laws. Where self-gratification is thus exclusive, we are either our own slaves, or slaves of others—in either case slaves. The work that has no room for voluntary renunciation is but a bondage. As an ever increasing number of people get tied together by necessity, with no internal bond of relationship, rivalry and malice rear their heads higher and higher.

The task before us today is to make whole the broken-up communal life, to harmonize the divergence between village and town, between the classes and the masses, between the pride of power and the spirit of comradeship. Those who rely on revolution to achieve this end seek to curtail truth in order to make it easy. When they are after enjoyment, they shun renunciation; when they incline to renunciation, they would banish enjoyment from the land and subdue man's mind by cramping it. What we, of Visva-Bharati, say, is that the nature of man is denied if truth is not offered to him in its wholeness. From this deprivation comes his despair and his ailments.

The factory may be an instrument of much wrongdoing, but it is not a thing that we can reject. The machine is also an organ of our vital force. If our hands have committed robbery, the remedy does not lie in cutting them off: they must be purged of their sin. To try to improve ourselves by crippling ourselves is a counsel of cowardice. All the powers of man seek development and expansion. From the earliest times man has sought to make tools. No sooner had he discovered a new secret of Nature than he tried to capture it with the help of some machine and make it his own. It is in this way that his civilization has advanced.

The day man first drew out the fertility of the soil by making the plough, a hurdle was removed from the path of his progress. This not only revealed the source of his food, but also illumined an obscure chamber of his mind. When he first devised the spinning wheel and the loom, they not only enabled him to cover his nakedness, but also roused the sense of beauty which was to possess so much of his life. If, today, man's body is clothed, so is his mind. The Kingdom of Man depends on this dual clothing.

If any *sanyasin* would plead that this extended commerce with the outside world should be restricted, then he must begin by an indictment of man's pair of hands. And the extreme sanyasin does go to that length. He allows his arms to wither by his ascetic practice of keeping them perpetually uplifted, in a gesture of denial of the world, asserting that he has attained freedom. To restrain man's hands with the command, *Thus far you shall go and no further*, is equivalent to this cult of uplifted arms. Who has the right to lay down such an injunction, to cripple man's God-given powers by saying that he shall not advance as far as the World-worker calls upon to do? We can regulate the exercise of power to ensure our welfare, but we must not bar the way to its expansion.

In the old days man applied his plough and loom, his bow and arrow, his wheeled vehicles, to the purpose of life's progress. So today should modern machines be made to serve the needs of humanity. It is true that because of the machine one rich man is served by thousands; but this only proves that one man can acquire the strength of thousands with the help of the machine. The power thus attained should not be monopolized by the few; it should be used for the benefit of the many. Let not power be concentrated to keep men apart. Let it never be irresponsible.

Civilization has grown by the conjunction of man's intellect with the gifts of Nature. These two must always work in partnership. Whenever the acquisitions of the intellect are hoarded in some strong-room, the store goes on dwindling. We cannot live long on the accumulations of a bygone age.

This new power of man must be brought into the heart of our villages. It is because we have omitted to do so that whichever way we turn there is the picture of penury and defeat. Everywhere our countrymen are crying, 'We have failed.' From our dried-up hollows, our fruitless fields, our never-ceasing funeral pyres rises the wail, 'We have failed.' If we can possess the science that gives power to this age, we may yet win, we may yet live.

The ups and downs produced by the inequality of wealth are healthy only within a limited range. No great civilization is possible in a country divided by the constant interruption of steep mountains, as they retard the natural flow of communication. Large fortunes and luxurious living, like the mountains, form high walls of segregation. They produce worse divisions in society than physical barriers.

Some people believe that the solution is to be found in the abolition of the idea of property. But we have to remember that the urges which have created private property are rooted in human nature. If you have the power, you may abolish private property, but you cannot change human nature.

Property is a medium for the expression of our personality. If we look upon the negative aspect of personality, we see in it the limits which separate one person from another. And when, in some men, this sense of separate-ness takes on an intense emphasis, we call them selfish. But in its positive aspect, it is the only medium through which men can communicate with one another. If we seek to kill our individuality because it is apt to be selfish, human communion itself will lose its meaning. If, however, we allow it to develop, then being creative by nature it will fashion its own world. Most often and for most men, property is the only framework for the creation of a personal world. It is not just money or furniture. It represents not merely acquisitiveness, but also our taste, our imagination, our faculties, and our desire for self-sacrifice.

Through this symbol of our personality we receive, we give, we express. Our highest social training is to make our property the richest expression of the best in us, of our individuality whose greatest illumination is love. As individuals are the units that build the community, so property, when it is alive to its functions, is the unit of wealth that makes for communal prosperity. Wisdom lies not in destroying separateness of units, but in maintaining the spirit of unity in full strength.

When life is simple, wealth does not become too exclusive. Individual property then readily admits its duties to the people. But with the rise in living standards property changes its aspect. It shuts the gates of hospitality, which is the best means of social intercommunication. It displays itself in extravagance. It begets rigid class divisions. In short, it becomes anti-social. With material progress, property has become intensely individualistic: the method of gaining it has become a matter of science and not of social ethics. It breaks social bonds; it drains away the sap of the community. Its unscrupulousness plays havoc.

The forest-fire feeds upon the living wood from which it springs, till it is completely exhausted along with the fuel. When a passion, like greed, breaks loose from the barrier of social control, it acts in the same way and feeds upon the life of society; and the result is annihilation. It has ever been the object of the spiritual training of man to fight those passions that are anti-social and keep them chained.

There are insects in our fields which, in spite of their depredations, leave a surplus for the tillers of the soil, and it does not pay to try to exterminate them. But when some pest that has an enormous power of self-multiplication attacks our crop, it has to be dealt with as a calamity. In human society, in normal circumstances, there are a number of causes that make for wastage, yet we can afford to ignore them. However, the blight that has fallen today on our social life and its resources is disastrous, because it is not restricted to limited regions. It is an epidemic of voracity that has infected the total area of civilization.

We all claim the right to be extravagant in our enjoyment to the extent that we can afford it. We feel ashamed if we are not able to spend as much on individual gratification as our rich neighbour. The tyranny of respectability leads us to ruin.

There is a continual stress on the idea of convenience and comfort. The actual results fall short of the energy spent because of the wastage involved. The shrieking advertisements, which constantly accompany the increase in production, mean an enormous waste of material and life force.

Civilization has turned into a vast catering establishment. It maintains constant feasts for a whole population of gluttons. The intemperance which could have been tolerated in a few has spread to the multitude. The resulting universal greed is the cause of the meanness, cruelty and lies in politics and commerce that vitiate the whole human atmosphere. A civilization with an unnatural appetite must feed on numberless victims, and these are being sought in the parts of the world where human flesh is cheap. The happiness of entire peoples in Asia and Africa is being sacrificed to provide fastidious fashion with an endless train of respectable rubbish.

What in the West is called democracy can never be true in a society where greed grows uncontrolled and is encouraged, even admired, by the people. In such an atmosphere a constant struggle goes on among individuals to capture public organizations for their personal ends. Democracy is then like an elephant whose one purpose in life is to give joyrides to the clever and the rich.

Under such conditions the organs through which public opinion is formed together with the machinery of administration are all openly or secretly manipulated by the prosperous few. They have been compared of old to the camel, which can never pass through a needle's eye—the gate that leads to the kingdom of ideals. Such a society is callous and cruel to those who preach their faith in spiritual freedom. In such a society people are intoxicated by the constant stimulation of what they call progress, a progress which they are willing to buy at the cost of civilization itself, like the man for whom wine is more attractive than food.

Villages are like women. In their keeping is the cradle of the race. They are nearer to nature than towns, and in closer touch with the fountain of life. They possess a natural power of healing. It is the function of the village, like that of women, to provide people with their elemental needs, with food and joy, with the simple poetry of life and with those ceremonies of beauty which the village spontaneously produces and in which she finds delight. But when constant strain is put upon her, when her resources are excessively exploited, she becomes dull and uncreative. From her time-honoured position of the wedded wife, she descends to that of a maid-servant. The city, in its intense egotism and pride, remains unconscious of the hurt it inflicts on the very source of its life, health and joy.

In the Sanskrit poem, *Meghaduta*, we follow the path of the cloud messenger and in imagination pass over the old-world towns with their beautiful names. We feel that these towns expressed more than anything else the love and hope of man. They treasured some of the splendour of his soul in their houses and temples with the auspicious decoration daily executed by the women, and even in the picturesque bartering that went on in their market-places.

We can imagine what Delhi and Agra must have been in the time to which they belonged. They manifested the creative and human aspect of a great empire. Even in their decay these cities retain the glory of man. But modern cities merely offer opportunities, not ideals.

Cities there must be in man's civilization, just as in higher organisms there must be organized centres of life, such as the brain, heart, or stomach. These never overwhelm the living wholeness of the body; on the contrary, by a perfect federation of their functions, they maintain its richness. But a tumour in which the blood is congested is the enemy of the whole body upon which it feeds as it swells. Our modern cities, in the same way, feed upon the social organism that runs through the villages. They appropriate the life stuff of the community and slough off a huge amount of dead matter, while making a lurid counterfeit of prosperity.

Thus, unlike a living heart, these cities imprison and kill the blood and create poison centres. When men come together only for some material purpose, they form an aggregation but not a congregation, so that there is moral decay. This is the result of true civilization being substituted by what the West calls Progress. I am not against progress but if, for its sake, civilization is ready to sell its soul, I would rather remain in a primitive state.

In India we had for ages our family system. Large and complex, each family was a miniature society in itself. I do not wish to discuss the question of its desirability. But its rapid decay in the present age points to the nature and process of the principle of destruction which is at work. When life was simple and its needs normal, when selfish passions were under control, such a system was quite natural and happy. The family resources were sufficient for all, and no individual member made an inordinate claim. But such a group cannot survive when the personal ambition of one member begins to clamour for more than he needs, when the desire for exclusive advantages runs contrary to the common good. Brothers must then separate and even become enemies.

Goethe's Germany was considered poor by Bismarck's Germany. The standard of civilization, illumined by the mind of Plato, or by the life of Asoka, is perhaps scorned by the proud children of modern times. But are those who lived then to be pitied by the adolescents of the modern age, who have more of the printing press, but less of the mind?

I often like to imagine that the moon, being smaller in size than the earth, produced life on her soil earlier than the earth. Once, the moon too had her festivals of colour, music, movement; her storehouse was perpetually filled with food. Then, on the moon, a race was born that began greedily to devour its surroundings. It produced beings who had an excess of animal spirit coupled with intellect but lacked the imagination to realize that the mere process of addition does not create fulfilment; that acquisition because of its largeness does not produce happiness; that movement does not constitute progress merely because of its speed; that progress can have meaning only in relation to some ideal of perfection. Their plunder soon outstripped nature's power of recuperation. Their profit-makers created wants that were unnatural. They dug deep into the stored capital of nature and ruthlessly exploited her resources. When they had exhausted the limited supply, they fought among themselves for the lion's share. In their scramble they laughed at moral codes and took it to be a sign of racial superiority to be ruthless in the satisfaction of their desires. They exhausted the water supply, cut down the trees, reduced the surface of the planet into a desert riddled with pits. They made its interior a rifled pocket, emptied of its valuables. Like a fruit whose pulp has been completely eaten by insects which it sheltered, the moon at last became a lifeless shell, a universal grave for the voracious creatures who had consumed the world in which they had been born.

My imaginary selenites behave exactly in the way that human beings are today behaving on this earth. Mother Earth has enough for the healthy appetites of her children and something extra for rare cases of abnormality. But she has not nearly enough for the sudden growth of a whole world of spoilt and pampered children.

Man has been digging holes into the very foundations, not only of his livelihood, but also of his life; he is feeding upon his own body. The reckless wastage is best seen in the villages, where the light of life is being dimmed, the joy of existence dulled, the threads of social communion snapped. It should be our mission to restore the circulation of life's blood into these maltreated limbs of society; to bring to the villages health and knowledge; wealth of space in which to live; wealth of time in which to work, rest and enjoy; respect which will give them dignity; sympathy which will make them realize their kinship with the world of men, and not merely their subservient position.

Streams, lakes and oceans exist not for the hoarding of water exclusively in their own areas. They send up the vapour which forms into clouds, so that there is a wider distribution of water. Cities have their function of maintaining wealth and knowledge in concentrated form. They should do so not for their own sake alone; they should be centres of irrigation; they should gather in order to distribute; they should not magnify themselves, but should enrich the entire commonwealth. They should be like lampposts, and the light they shed must transcend their own limits.

Such a relationship of mutual benefit between the city and the village can function only so long as the spirit of co-operation and self-sacrifice is a living ideal in society. When some temptation defeats this ideal, when selfish passion gains ascendency, a gulf is formed and goes on widening. City and village then stand as exploiter and victim.

We have started in India, in connection with our Visva-Bharati, the work of village reconstruction. Its mission is to retard the process of racial suicide. If I try to give you the details of our work, they will look small. But we are not afraid of this appearance of smallness, for we have confidence in life. We know that if it represents the germinal truth that is in us, it will overcome opposition and conquer space and time. We believe that the problem of unhappiness, rather than of poverty, is the greatest problem. Wealth is a synonym for the production and collection of things and men can use it ruthlessly. They can crush life out of the earth and flourish. But happiness, though it may not compete with wealth in its list of materials, is ultimate; it is creative; it has its source of riches within itself.

Our object is to try to flood the silted bed of village life with the stream of happiness. For this scholars, poets, musicians and artists have to collaborate and offer their contributions. Otherwise, they too must live as parasites, sucking life from the people and giving nothing in return.

Most of us who try to deal with the problem of poverty think only of a more intensive effort of production. We forget that it brings about a greater exhaustion of materials as well as of humanity. It gives to the few excessive opportunities for profit at the cost of the many. It is food which nourishes, not money; it is fullness of life which makes one happy, not fullness of purse. Multiplying material wealth alone intensifies the inequality between those who have and those who have not, and it inflicts so deep a wound on the social system that the whole body eventually bleeds to death.

II

What I had to say I have said many times before, and left nothing out. I had strength then, and the current of my thoughts was unimpeded. Age and ill health have now impaired my strength and you should not expect very much from me any more.

It is after a long time I am here. Some of you I do see from time to time—and all I can give you now is my presence and company. When first I bought this house I had no special plans. This much I had thought: Santiniketan was far from crowded life, and while it helped its students also to pass examinations, it gave them something more than the ration stipulated by the Education Department.

But another current flowed in my mind. Living in the villages of Shelaidah and Patisar I had made my first direct contact with rural life. Zamindari was then my calling. The tenants came to me with their joy and sorrow, complaints and requests, through which the village discovered itself to me. On the one hand was the external scene of rivers, meadows, rice-fields, and mud huts sheltering under trees. On the other was the inner story of the people. I came to understand their troubles in the course of my duties,

I am an urban creature, cityborn. My forefathers were among the earliest inhabitants of Calcutta and my childhood years felt no touch of the village. When I started to look after our estates, I feared that my duties would be irksome. I was not used to such work—keeping accounts, collecting revenue, credit and debit—and my ignorance lay heavy on my mind. I could not imagine that, tied down to figures and accounts, I might yet remain human and natural.

As I entered into the work, it took hold of me. It is my nature that, whenever I undertake any responsibility I lose myself in it and try to do my utmost. When I once had to teach, I put my whole heart into it and it was a great pleasure. Setting myself to unravel the complexities of zamindari work, I earned a reputation for the new methods I evolved; as a matter of fact, neighbouring landlords began to send their men to me to learn my methods.

The old men on my staff grew alarmed. They used to maintain records in a way that I could never have grasped. Their idea was that I should understand nothing more than what they chose to explain. A change of method would create confusion, so they said. They pointed out that, when it came to litigation, the court would be doubtful about the new way the records were kept. I persisted, though, changing things from top to bottom, and the result proved to be satisfactory.

The tenants often came to see me—for them my door was always open, day and night. Sometimes I had to spend the whole day listening to their representations, and mealtimes would slip by. I did all this work with enthusiasm and joy. I had lived in seclusion since boyhood and here was my first experience of the village. I was satisfied and heartened and filled with the pleasure of blazing new trails.

I was anxious to see village life in the minutest detail. My duties took me to distant parts by river, canal and waterways, and here was a chance to see the changing panorama of life. The everyday tasks of village folk and the varied cycle of their work filled me with wonder. Bred in the city, I stepped right into the heart of rural charm and filled myself with it. Then, slowly, the poverty and misery of the people grew vivid before my eyes arid I began to wish that I could do something for them. I was struck with shame that I was a zamindar, impelled by the money motive, absorbed in revenue returns. Since that realization I awoke to the task of trying to stir the minds of the people, make them shoulder their own responsibilities.

To try to help villagers from the outside could do no good. How to kindle a spark of life in them—that was my problem. It was so difficult to help them because they did not have much respect for themselves. 'We are curs,' they would say; 'only the whip can keep us straight.'

One day a fire broke out in a village nearby. The people were so utterly dazed that they could do nothing. Then the men from a neighbouring Muslim village came rushing and fought the fire. There was no water and thatched roofs had to be pulled down to stifle the flames. The stricken ones had to be beaten up before they would let this be done. You have to use force in order to do good! And then they came to me saying, 'What luck that our roofs were dismantled—that is how we have been saved.' They were happy that the beating benefited them; but I was filled with shame at their submissiveness.

I planned to put up a small building for them at the centre of the village, where at the day's end they could get together, read newspapers, listen to the Ramayana and Mahabharata—it would be a sort of club. For, I had been unhappy, thinking of their cheerless evenings; it was as if the same tedious line of a verse was being endlessly sung. In course of time the building was erected. But, then, it was never used. I engaged a teacher, but the pupils kept away with all kinds of excuses.

In contrast, the Muslims from the other village came to me and said, 'Will you give us a teacher? We are ready to bear the expense.' I agreed and a school was set up in the village and probably it is still there. In my village, nothing could be done, its inhabitants had lost all faith in themselves.

The habit of dependence has come down to us from time immemorial. In the olden days one rich man used to be the mainstay of the village and its guide. Health, education and all else were his responsibility. I have praised that system, but it is also true that because of it the common man's capacity for self-reliance was enfeebled.

In my estate the river was far away and lack of water was a serious problem. I said to my tenants, 'If you dig a well, I shall get it cemented.' They replied, 'You want to fry fish in the oil of the fish itself! If we dig the well you will go to heaven through the accumulated virtue of having provided water for the thirsty, while we shall have done the work.' The idea, obviously, was that an account of all such deeds was kept in heaven and while I, having earned great merit, could go to the seventh heaven, the village people would simply get some water. I had to withdraw my proposal.

Let me give another example. I had built a road from our estate office up to Kushtia. I told the villagers who lived close to the road, 'The upkeep of this road is your responsibility. You can easily get together and repair the ruts.' It was, in fact, their ox-cart wheels that damaged the road and put it out of use, during the rains. They replied, 'Must we look after the road so that gentlefolk from Kushtia can come and go with ease?' They could not bear the thought that others should also enjoy the fruits of their labour. Rather than let that happen, they would put up with inconveniences.

The poor in our villages have borne many insults, the powerful have done many wrongs. On the other hand, the powerful have had to do all the welfare work. Caught between tyranny and charity, the village people have been emptied of self-respect. They ascribe their miseries to sins committed in previous births, and believe that, to have a better life, they must be reborn with a greater fund of merit. The conviction that there is no escape from sufferings makes them helpless.

Once upon a time the rich regarded it as an act of merit to provide water and education. Through their goodwill the villages were well off. But when they started to move away to towns, the water-supply ceased, malaria and cholera struck hard, and the springs of happiness dried up in village after village. It is hard to imagine a life as cheerless as in our rural areas.

I could see no way out. It is far from easy to do something for people who have cultivated weakness for centuries and do not know what self-help means. Still I had to make a start. In those days my only helper was Kalimohan. Fever used to grip him morning and evening. With my medicine box I treated him myself, and never thought that I could get him to survive.

The shastras say: *Shraddyaya deyam*—if you give, then give with respect. That is how I set to work. From my office building I had often watched the farmers going afield with bullock and plough. Their land was in small strips and each man tilled his own holding. That, I knew, was a great waste of energy. So I sent for the men and said, 'Plough all your land jointly. Pool the strength and resources of all. Then you can even use tractors. If you all work together, small differences in personal holdings will not matter. Whatever the profit, you will share it equitably. Store all the produce of the village at one place and you will get a fair price from the middleman.' They listened and said, 'The idea is good, but how to work it out?' If I had the knowledge and the training, I would have said, 'I will take the responsibility.' They all knew me. But one cannot do good simply by wanting to; there is nothing so dangerous as ignorant help. Young men from town once went to a village to help the people. But the people cried jeering, 'Look, there come the quarter-rupee gentlefolk!'

No wonder—these young men knew neither the language of the villagers, nor the workings of their mind.

Something had to be done. I sent my son and Santosh abroad to learn agriculture and dairy farming. And in several other ways I started to work and to think.

It was about this time that I bought this house. I thought I would continue here the work I had begun at Shelaidah. The tumble-down house was supposed to be haunted! I had to spend a lot of money on its repair. Then, for a while, I sat still. Andrews said, 'Sell off the house.' But I thought to myself, 'Since I have acquired it, maybe there is some significance. Maybe one of my two objects in life will be fulfilled here.' How and when? I had no idea. When seed is strewn in an auspicious moment even on barren land, it suddenly sprouts. At that time there was no such sign. Everything was scarce. However, slowly the seed started to put forth shoots.

My friend Elmhirst helped me a great deal. It was he who turned this place into an independent field of work where progress was steady. It would not have been right to lump it with Santiniketan.

I have one more word for you. We must see that a force from within the people starts functioning. When I was writing *Swadeshi Samaj* the same idea had struck me. What I wanted to say then was that we did not have to think of the whole country; we could make a start with one or two villages. If we could free even one village from the shackles of helplessness and ignorance, an ideal for the whole of India would be established. That is what occurred to me then and that is what I still think. Let a few villages be rebuilt in this way, and I shall say they are my India. That is the way to discover the true India.

—from Rabindranath Tagore, *Towards Universal Man* (London: Asia Publishing House, 1961 [1928]), pp. 302–22.

Majrooh Sultanpuri

This is Bombay, My Love!

(Male Voice):
Oh my heart, how difficult it is to live here
Be vigilant, be streetwise, this is Bombay my love...
Ha ha ha, ho ho ho, hi haa ha haa
Hm hm hm hm, hm hm hm, hm hm hm hm hm
Oh my heart...

Behold the buildings, and the trams
Behold the motor cars, and the mills
Everthing can be found here—except the heart is amiss
Not a trace anywhere of humanity
Be watchful, be streetwise, this is Bombay my love
Oh my heart...

Behold the power, the gaming, the betting, and deceipt
Behold the theft, the hunger, the betrayal and treachery
For the loafers and idlers, there is much work indeed
Be watchful, be street smart, this is Bombay my love
Oh my heart...

Amidst laughter and mirth, they describe the homeless as tramps
While they slit others' throats, calling it business
The game is the same, just known by many a name
Be watchful, be streetwise, this is Bombay my love
Oh my heart...

(Female Voice):
You say the world is so wily, don't feign innocence
One reaps what one sows, is how the world makes sense
Your plotting and scheming will not prevail
This is Bombay, this is Bombay, this is Bombay my love

Oh, my heart, how difficult it is to live here
Be watchful, be streetwise, this is Bombay my love
Oh my heart, such is it to live here

Listen mister, listen friends,
This is Bombay, my love

(Male Voice):
Oh, heart, how uphill a task is life here
Be vigilant, be street smart, this is Bombay my darling

> —from the film *C.I.D.* (1956), director Raj Khosla; sung by
> Mohammad Rafi and Geeta Dutt; translated from the
> Hindi by Vinay Lal

Salman Rushdie

Bombay was Central

Bombay was central, had been so from the moment of its creation: the bastard child of a Portuguese-English wedding, and yet the most Indian of Indian cities. In Bombay all Indias met and merged. In Bombay, too, all-India met what-was-not-India, what came across the black water to flow into our veins. Everything north of Bombay was North India, everything south of it was the South. To the east lay India's East and to the west, the world's West. Bombay was central; all rivers flowed into its human sea. It was an ocean of stories; we were all its narrators, and everybody talked at once.

What magic was stirred into that insaan-soup, what harmony emerged from that cacophony! In Punjab, Assam, Kashmir, Meerut—in Delhi, in Calcutta—from time to time they slit their neighbours' throats and took warm showers, or red bubble-baths, in all that spuming blood. They killed you for being circumcised and they killed you because your foreskins had been left on. Long hair got you murdered and haircuts too; light skin flayed dark skin and if you spoke the wrong language you could lose your twisted tongue. In Bombay, such things never happened. —Never, you say?—OK: never is too absolute a word. Bombay was not inoculated against the rest of the country, and what happened elsewhere, the language business for example, also spread into its streets. But on the way to Bombay the rivers of blood were usually diluted, other rivers poured into them, so that by the time they reached the city's streets the disfigurations were relatively slight. —Am I sentimentalising? Now that I have left it all behind, have I, among my many losses, also lost clear sight? —It may be said I have; but still I stand by my words. O Beautifiers of the City, did you not see that what was beautiful in Bombay was that it belonged to nobody, and to all? Did you not see the everyday live-and-let-live miracles thronging its overcrowded streets?

Bombay was central. In Bombay, as the old, founding myth of the nation faded, the new god-and-mammon India was being born. The wealth of the country flowed through its exchanges, its ports. Those who hated India, those who sought to ruin it, would need to ruin Bombay: that was one explanation for what happened. Well, well, that may have been so. And it may have been that what was unleashed in the north (in, to name it, because I must name it, Ayodhya)—that corrosive acid of the spirit, that adversarial intensity which poured into the nation's bloodstream when the Babri Masjid fell and plans for a mighty Ram temple on the god's alleged birthplace were, as they used to say in the Bombay cinema-houses, *filling up fast*—was on this occasion too concentrated, and even the great city's powers of dilution could not weaken it enough. So, so; those who argue thus have a point, too, it cannot be denied. At the Zogoiby Bequest, Zeenat Vakil offered me her usual sardonic take on the troubles. 'I blame fiction,' she said. 'The followers of one fiction knock down another popular piece of make-believe, and bingo! It's war. Next they will find Vyasa's cradle under Iqbal's house, and Valmiki's baby-rattle under Mirza Ghalib's hang-out. So, OK. I'd rather die fighting over great poets than over gods.'

I had been dreaming about Uma—O disloyal subconscious!—Uma sculpting her early work, the large Nandi bull. Like the bull, I thought when I awoke, and like blue Krishna of flute-and-milkmaid fame, Lord Ram was an avatar of Vishnu; Vishnu, most metamorphic of the gods. The true 'rule of Ram' should therefore, surely, be premised on the mutating, inconstant, shape-shifting realities of human nature—and not only human nature, but divine as well. This thing being advocated in the great god's name flew in the face of his essence as well as ours.—But when the boulder of history begins to roll, nobody is interested in discussing such fragile points. The *juggernaut* is loose.

. . . And if Bombay was central, it may have been that what transpired was rooted in Bombay quarrels. Mogambo versus Mainduck: the long-awaited duel, the heavyweight unification bout to establish, once and for all, which gang (criminal-entrepreneurial or political-criminal) would run the town. I saw something like this happen, and can only set down what I saw. Hidden factors? The meddling of secret/foreign hands? These I leave for wiser analysts to reveal.

—excerpted from Salman Rushdie, *The Moor's Last Sigh* (New York: Vintage Books, 1997), pp. 350–2.

Amitabha Bhattacharya

Satyajit Ray's Calcutta: Friend or Adversary?

It is a pity that the myths created by the dazzling international success of *Pather Panchali* (1955) have often blinded even the perceptive from appreciating Ray's ouevre in its totality. Stereotypes like poverty, death and rural Bengal came to be associated with his films, though only a handful of them really deal with such themes. And except perhaps in three feature films, Calcutta appears directly or makes its presence felt, in virtually all other Ray films. Films like *Parash Pathar, Apur Sansar,* (partly) *Mahanagar, Charulata, Mahapurush, Pratidwandi, Seemabaddha* and *Jana Aranya* and *Pikoo* have the city as the canvas. In some others, like *Kanchenjungha* or *Aranyer Din Ratri* or *Nayak,* or *Sonar Kella,* for example, the main characters are from this metropolis, and in works like *Aparajito* and even in *Devi* and *Teen Kanya* the poignancy of Calcutta is evident.

In Ray's films, Calcutta appears often as a frame of reference, sometimes as an adversary, often in the background and sometimes as dominant. Individual beings live and survive, sometimes innocently, sometimes acquiescing, not infrequently with a sense of guilt and a troubled conscience, in a society which is fast changing.

Yet, the primacy of the individual, caught in the vortex of events overtaking him, has been the central focus of Ray's cinema. In an interview with *The Cineaste,* he made his attitude clear:

> You can see my attitude in The Adversary (*Pratidwandi*), where you have two brothers. The younger brother is a Naxalite. There is no doubt that the

elder brother admires the younger brother for his bravery and convictions. The film is not ambiguous about that. As a film-maker, however, I was more interested in the elder brother because he is the vacillating character. As a psychological entity, as a human being with doubts, he is a more interesting character to me. The younger brother has already identified himself with a cause. That makes him a part of the total attitude and makes him unimportant. The Naxalite movement takes over. He as a person becomes insignificant.... . If you took the controlling characters (of the movement), *that* would be interesting.

Illuminating the human soul has been the raison d'etre of Ray, while exploring the psychology of individuals affected by change that has been caused elsewhere. The causative factors—of zamindari and its decline, of rural people's migration to urban areas either by choice or compulsion, of man-made famine, the partition of Bengal (1905) and India, the annexation of Oudh, the Naxalite movement and such major events—are all palpable. But to Ray, the artist, what is more fascinating is to understand the man reacting, or failing to react to such signals.

The city assumes such importance, for much of the change in the late nineteenth and this century has been fostered and witnessed by the city, best epitomised by Calcutta. And to Satyajit Ray, Calcutta is much more than a living presence. It is in his blood-stream. A third generation Calcuttan, Satyajit grew in the city passing through its most profound transition. In his younger years, he came in direct contact with the great minds of India's modernisation like Rabindranath Tagore and later, personally experienced the trauma that metamorphosed the city and its psyche. He allowed himself to be exposed to all the influences that the city brought to bear on him, for he likes big cities 'to engulf and bewilder' him. He took the adversity in his stride and, therefore, could see both faces of the city—the humanising and the dehumanising. Ray's films, attempting to capture this flux, would quite naturally be informed by a vision that is essentially urban.

Ray's love for the much-maligned city is too well known to be repeated. He told Ved Mehta a quarter of a century ago:

> I love Calcutta, I have lived here all my life. The best of whatever is being done in the arts in India is being done here. There is great intellectual vitality . . . Only film-making has not attracted many intellectuals, yet from a film-maker's point of view no city could be better, ...

The assault that present-day Calcutta makes, especially in terms of civic and municipal inadequacies, has not deterred him. In 1966 he wrote:

The studios in Calcutta show their hallowed past in every crevice on the wall, in every tatter of the canvas that covers the ceiling ... The floor is pitted, the camera groans as it turns, the voltage begins to drop ... The general air of shabbiness is unnerving ... And yet I do not mind these at all. I don't think of these as hindrances ... It is the bareness of means that forces us to be economical and inventive and prevents us from turning craftsmanship into an end in itself. And there is something about creating beauty in the circumstances of shoddiness and privation that is truly exciting.

Calcutta is manifested as the seat of British power in films like *Shatranj, Charulata, Devi, Ghare Baire* and *Jalasaghar*. Calcutta of the twenties, by which time much of its colonial glory has faded with India's capital having been shifted away to Delhi, has been captured in the *Apu Trilogy* and partly in *Teen Kanya*. The early forties, when the famine ravages Bengal against the backdrop of World War II, is experienced in *Ashani Sanket;* and the mid-fifties, with the wounds of partition bringing in its wake such multitudes of rootless people still afresh, in *Mahanagar. Kanchenjungha, Kapurush* and *Nayak*, through their characterisations, evoke the spirit of Calcutta of the sixties, before the revolutionary fervour gripped the city. The late sixties and early seventies find their expression directly in *Pratidwandi* and *Jana Aranya* and, somewhat differently, in *Seemabaddha* and *Aranyer Din Ratri*. The mid-seventies and eighties politically meant a great deal to the rest of India, but Calcutta was relatively calm.

Traditionally, Ray scholars have been grouping *Pratidwandi, Seemabaddha* and *Jana Aranya* to form the Calcutta trilogy. Some other critics, notably Chidananda Dasgupta, classify Ray's films into two distinct categories, one covering the films upto *Charulata* and the other covering his later films. Arguments have been advanced how *Charulata* marks an important watershed in Ray's creative evolution. However, it is not difficult to find major flaws in such arguments. After all, the attitude of Ray is not markedly different in *Ghare Baire* (1984) than in *Charulata* (1964). The difference, if any, flows from the requirements of the players who are placed in different space-time contexts. In this article, an attempt will be made to underscore the great artistic and historical consistency in his films that chronicle the city's development in the last hundred years. As such, historical time has been followed in this discussion.

Calcutta of the mid-nineteenth century is glimpsed in *Devi,* symbolising the newly awakened spirit through Umaprasad fighting his goddess-addict superstitious father whose irrational belief leads to the human tragedy. It was Calcutta as the seat of learning, the city of social reforms and of the spirit of 'Young Bengal'. In both *Devi* and *Charulata,* the Calcutta of the last century has been framed, viewed from the angle of the landed aristrocracy, with superb grace and finesse, more through suggestions and images and sounds which have heightened the human drama instead of overshadowing it.

Urbanity, as is understood today, gets manifest in *Charulata* and *Ghare Baire*, set in late nineteenth and the first decade of the twentieth century, respectively. There is a great deal common between Amal and Nikhilesh as also between Charu and Bimala. The western liberal influences are visible. Both the husbands are English-educated zamindars, benevolent and broad-minded, rational and questioning, secular in outlook, and exhibit a cautious awareness of women's progress. But to Charu, the city reveals itself mainly through images and sounds, through books and journals since she is confined to her mansion. Though the film is set in Calcutta, its impact on Charu is marginal, more by way of providing fun and excitement as the bored wife watches the vignettes of life outside through the window-shutters. Using a lorgnette, she observes the monkeyman, the palanquin bearers pass by....

Two decades later, when Curzon would divide Bengal and the Swadeshi movement spread, the zamindar's wife cannot remain unaffected—even in rural areas. The privileged position of zamindars came under strain and, therefore, remaining indifferent to such a challenge would become increasingly difficult. The zamindar of *Ghare Baire* had to react differently to the emerging challenge. Compared to Charu's, Bimala's predicament was far more complex, the pulls and temptations of the outside world becoming irresistible. Calcutta is never explicit in *Ghare Baire*, but its presence felt, as a city of prosperity and the centre of colonial power "malignant and vigorous", pursuing the divide-and-rule policy.

The decadence of feudalism against the rise of a new capitalist class forms the canvas of *Jalsaghar*. Both the sophisticated zamindar and the boorish businessman are exploiters and beneficiaries of the colonial rule. Yet the latter attempts to emulate the behaviour of what he considers the "group superior". The zamindar is a tragic character because he refuses to see change, let alone accept it. No wonder he refuses even to go to Calcutta to protect his property-interest. His Calcutta is not the same as the Calcutta of Bhupati and Umaprasad. To the proud and ostrich-like Bishwambhar Roy, Calcutta hardly exists. It is natural, therefore, that the city would not be shown in the film. Nevertheless, the educated spectator is aware that Calcutta was witnessing the rise of a nouveau riche class of traders, businessmen and contractors, and

prosperity.

Looking from the angle of the poor, *Pather Panchali* acknowledges
Calcutta, somewhat indirectly. Somewhere away from the village, the
train whizzes past, telegraph poles inspire awe, letters are delivered
in the village. Impoverished bandsmen in shabby British uniforms
play English tunes. 'Look ... Calcutta's Kalighat ...' urges the village
showman inviting children to his peepshow. Through [an] improved
communication network, Calcutta is touching the fringe of the poor's
consciousness.

Aparajito starts with the family's entry to Banares. It stands somewhat
in between a village and Calcutta, measured by the degree of urbanisation.
Apu's bewilderment when confronted with Calcutta has been filmed by
Ray with a degree of sensitivity unsurpassed in the history of cinema.
Calcutta was a crucial factor in Apu's development, from a priestly
brahmin boy to a secular, sensitive and progressive human being. He
was transcending a painful adolescence as also experiencing the pulls of
contrary forces— between mother-home-root on the one hand and the
calls of a liberating outside world on the other. Calcutta saves Apu.

Apur Sansar opens with Calcutta. Apu is unemployed and life is far
from comfortable. But these things are not allowed to suppress his love
for the city. The freedom struggle that was sweeping the city is not
visualised, since that hardly affects Apu. His basic reverence for life that
Calcutta celebrates with such abandon, makes Apu retain his dignity. He
draws his sustenance from the city—the spirit of one reinforcing the
other. Only his wife's death makes the city unbearable to him—that too
for a while.

After the twenties, the most significant event of Bengal is the famine
of 1943 in which millions of people perished, without much protest.
That was a man-made scarcity while the second world war was being
fought. Satyajit's *Ashani Sanket* depicts how the impending calamity is
going to affect a Bengal village, especially a Brahmin family. In the
film's analysis of human relationships under stress and its perceptive
study of the caste-structure (compare the behaviour of the Brahmin
priest in *Ashani Sanket* with that in *Sadgati*), where does Calcutta fit in?
Much of the problems were caused there and strangely, people from
the countryside would start flocking to the city just to die in hordes.
The film ends before, just when the ominous clouds of doom surface.
Ray, therefore, uses animated Calcutta-shots of people dying on streets
to enhance the dramatic appeal of the film as also perhaps to instill

a feeling of guilt. What were the Calcuttans, with all their sense of rationality and justice, doing in the face of such a catastrophe? Four years later, a greater tragedy would befall the city.

The migration of people from rural to urban areas has been focussed in Ray films time and again. Calcutta became the home for people coming from all parts of Bengal and other parts of India—for different reasons. Apu moved to Calcutta. So did people driven by scarcity when the city started sucking up more and more of the rural produce. But nothing would equal the magnitude of partition in 1947, when most of the brunt of mankind's greatest migration had to be borne by Calcutta. Already ravaged by famine and a stagnant economy, and communal riots, the influx of millions of refugee families from East Pakistan would see Calcutta gasping for life.

Mahanagar is to deal with one such family. This film has been hailed as one of Ray's major works. Even thematically, the film traverses a path hitherto uncharted—a traditional housewife going out to take up a job to support her family, propelled by acute economic compulsion. But while working, she tastes the freedom which the city and the job provide her. The city also gives her the strength and courage to resign it on a moral ground. The dingy living condition of a lower-middle class family, lack of privacy, the next-door radio blaring day and night, and the bell in a nearby temple tolling in the evening—against this ambience a family of three generations fight for their existence.

If the big city has a benefic influence on the two lead characters, it has wrought havoc on the idealist school teacher who has now been reduced to a pathetic figure, going to the houses of his ex-students to beg favour. He cannot reconcile himself to his daughter-in-law taking up a job, musing 'even she has changed' and lamenting 'something has gone wrong in God's ruling—somewhere some injustice has taken place'. Calcutta of all hues comes alive in the film—Calcutta of the lower-middle class, of private banks, of the affluent upper class where Arati goes selling knitting machines, the Calcutta of the Anglo-Indian community and the posh office-locality.

All these images coalesce and create a city, where at least the young can live with hope, where morality has not become irrelevant.

What happened to the upper-class Calcuttans, pampered by the British, proud of their affluent heritage? For this, Ray takes us to Darjeeling where an oldish man goes with his family on a holiday. In terms of structure and its deep study of relationship between a group of men and women, all of whom are from the city, *Kanchenjungha* is one of cinema's masterpieces. Calcutta is never shown but all the characters of the film bring with them their slices of the city, the city of the high-brow Presidency College as also of the low-brow Bangabasi. Unlike *Charulata*, *Jalsaghar* or *Devi*, in *Kanchenjungha* the authority of powerful Indranath Chaudhury, recipient of a British title and Chairman of five companies in Calcutta, is challenged by a young, ordinary Calcuttan.

The angry young Calcuttan occupy the central stage in *Pratidwandi*. Calcutta becomes the adversary to Siddhartha, the protagonist. Calcutta is no mere backdrop; it interplays with the characters. As a force, it challenges, often threatens to overshadow the people. This is the city of the violent days, of radical politics. The naxalite movement which, according to many scholars, is the most important political movement of the country after "Quit India", torments Calcutta's soul. As if this were not enough, hordes of refugees arrive from East Pakistan while the liberation war is waging there. The nightmare city of 1970-71 towards which Siddhartha, an educated unemployed from an East Bengal family, develops a love-hate kind of ambivalence, is portrayed magnificently in this film.

Trams were burning, policemen were being murdered, statues of renaissance figures defaced, the Government was taking every measure to combat the situation—but to Satyajit Ray more important things were happening inside the frustrated younger generation. A high point of the film is where Siddhartha is interviewed for a job. As Andrew Robinson puts it:

> When Siddhartha without rhetoric replies to the interviewers that in his opinion the most significant world event of the last ten years is the 'plain human courage' shown by the Vietnamese people, rather than the moon landing (as they suggest), Ray is speaking through him about his own values ... 'You see, no one knew they had it in them' Siddhartha tells the stolid bureaucrats who then pointedly enquire, 'Are you a communist?'

Siddhartha is not selected, and learns the lesson that moral victory does not pay. Yet Siddhartha does not yield to just what pays. The value-frame that Siddhartha articulates is shared by many Calcuttans, young and old. There lies the moral triumph of the film.

The city has been handled by Ray with extraordinary care. Again the lower-middle-class household, the upper-class locality where Siddhartha's sister's boss lives, its prostitute-den, cinema hall where a bomb is exploded, its college life and coffee houses, the restaurant by the side of the Ganges, its hippies, its massive public rally seen from the top of a skyscraper, its radical politics and wall posters and graffiti—all these make the city pulsate with enormity and contradictions. The city overpowers Siddhartha who reconciles himself to a job outside the city. Ray's Siddhartha is Calcutta's Hamlet. From so many angles, no other film has illuminated Calcutta with such empathy. Relatively, the Calcutta of *Jana Aranya*, has lesser dimensions. Of that, later.

If *Pratidwandi's* Calcutta is the romantic young man's vision of the city, *Seemabaddha* forays into the Calcutta of the corporate management class. The city, as seen through the eyes of the successful business executive and his ambitious wife. They take to Calcutta as the proverbial duck to water. Calcutta of the clubs, race-course, new-market and luxurious multi-storied apartments, of corporate business houses, of retired civilians and company directors, of beauty parlours and restaurants, of parties and cabarets. Here also, Calcutta is observed from a high-rise building, but unlike in *Pratidwandi*, one does not see multitudes of people in the Maidan; there is instead the sprawling metropolis with concrete structures. The sounds of bombs (or of gun shots, as the sensuous wife wonders) are fading. But *Seemabaddha*, while showing the immorality of this class beneath its veneer, also shows the industrial units, where the workers toil and are manipulated, the strikes and lock-outs.

In *Seemabaddha*, the hero is not much troubled. He is a boxwallah in the making. He has learnt the rules of the game well. And this is what perhaps pains Ray, as is expressed by the protagonist's sister-in-law from Patna. In her eyes, the brother-in-law has changed which accounts for his material success. But at what cost?

The naxalite movement over, Calcutta is calm, yet to apprehend fully what really went wrong. But life's struggle continues. *Jana Aranya's* city is not the one of corporate houses or banks or factories, but the city of degrading poverty and squalor, of slum-like refugee colonies and lower-middle-class households, of traders and middlemen and burrabazar, of power cuts and petty politicians, of call girls, pimps and prostitutes, and a city where even some housewives have taken to part-time whoring. The film studies the murky side of Calcutta with such authenticity that one feels Ray has allowed his film to touch raw life itself. This is the Calcutta of Somnath, the vacillating lead character of the film.

Here is an interesting piece of conversation with Mitter, the P.R.O. who would introduce Somnath to that layer of Calcutta:

Mitter. Are you prepared to die for a cause? Somnath: I doubt it.

Mitter. Could you work as a labourer? You would earn a lot more than you do now. Somnath: I know.

Mitter: But you can't. Have you the guts to be a factory worker?
Somnath takes off his glass and rubs his eyes.
Mitter: You admit you are a weakling in mind and body.

Which Somnath is. And for the youngman who is a "weakling in mind and body", Calcutta is no easy place. Its soul has hardened.

Even in *Apur Sansar,* Apu is rejected for a primary school teacher's job, plainly because he is over qualified. But in *Jana Aranya,* Somnath, having answered a barrage of questions, is confronted with the ultimate, "What is the weight of the moon?" Calcutta was difficult even in Apu's days, but not absurdly ruthless.

Within a hundred years, *Charulata's* Calcutta has metamorphosed into *Jana Aranya's.* The days of innocence and anglo-saxon morality are over. A new set of values are emerging. Urbanity as a way of life is demanding new kinds of adjustment. The rise of the middle class as a major political force has changed the complexion of Calcutta life. Nuclear family, alienation, the gap in communication between man and woman as also between generations, dominance of the city over the people's lives, the lack of old-world social grace and of leisurely life are all factors becoming acutely felt in the city films. For self-introspection, the city characters, as in *Aranyer Din Ratri* or *Shakha Prashakha,* have to go out, to have a close look at themselves.

While exploring the human psyche against the changing Calcutta, can there be a fixed value-frame? All Ray's films raise this question. He understands the process of history too well. At the same time, he has an abiding faith in man. His artistic conscience is hurt when he sees the inanimate suppressing the human spirit. He feels for troubled young men and women, successful or frustrated, responding and adjusting, often against their wish, to the process of change.

To say Ray has not understood these characters, or he has lost faith in them, as some critics allege, is more than unfair. Gunter Grass once told me "In India, old people are young, the young are old". Does Ray seem to share such a perception? He is not angry with the younger generation or with the city. He is sad and perhaps anguished at the city increasingly assuming a domineering role over individual human lives. Nevertheless, his films keep fanning the embers beneath the ashes, for he has not lost faith in mankind. The glorious documentary on *Rabindranath Tagore,* in which Calcutta's live footage has been used with such brilliance, echoes this optimism.

His practical approach to life notwithstanding, he is the lone philosopher-moralist of cinema. He does not see man and the city from a distance, as some critics argue. Ray's holistic view stems from his ability to see them with piercing eyes, very closely but from every conceivable angle—which accounts for the enormous richness of his characters and for the city to acquire such fullness. Its comic aspect, as in *Parash Pathar*, its tragic form and various other nuances of temper are faithfully sketched.

Tagore dominated the Calcutta of the first four decades of this century, and Satyajit Ray the last four. The reason is not difficult to fathom. David Shipman once summarised Ray aptly, "... But Ray's greatness as a film-maker goes beyond his influence. The moral complexities of his character and the notion of 'right living' may be found in the great writers of the world, from Jane Austen to Tchekhov; but in very few film-makers." Right living, even in the context of Calcutta.

List of films discussed with their years of release

1. *Pather Panchali* (Song of the Little Road), 1955.
2. *Aparajito* (The Unvanquished), 1956.
3. *Parash Pather* (The Philosopher's Stone), 1958.
4. *Jalsaghar* (The Music Room), 1958.
5. *Apur Sansar* (The World of Apu), 1959.
6. *Devi* (The Goddess), 1960.
7. *Teen Kanya* (Three Daughters), 1961.
8. *Rabindranath Tagore*, 1961.
9. *Kanchenjungha*, 1962.
10. *Mahanagar* (The Big City), 1963.
11. *Charulata* (The Lonely Wife), 1964.
12. *Kapurush-O-Mahapurush* (The Coward and the Holy Man), 1965.
13. *Nayak* (The Hero), 1966.
14. *Aranyer Din Ratri* (Days and Nights in the Forest), 1969.
15. *Pratidvandi* (The Adversary), 1970.
16. *Seemabaddha* (Company Limited), 1971.
17. *Ashani Sanket* (Distant Thunder), 1973.
18. *Sonar Kella* (The Golden Fortress), 1974.
19. *Jana Aranya* (The Middle Man), 1975.
20. *Sadgati* (Deliverance), 1981.
21. *Ghare Baire* (The Home and the World), 1984.

—first published in *India International Centre Quarterly*, 17, nos 3–4 (Winter 1990–1), pp. 301–13.

Banaras: City of Death

No other city on earth is as famous for death as is Banaras. More than for her temples and magnificent *ghats*, more than for her silks and brocades, Banaras, the Great Cremation Ground, is known for death. At the center of the city along the riverfront is Manikarnika, the sanctuary of death, with its ceaselessly smoking cremation pyres. The burning *ghat* extends its influence and the sense of its presence throughout the city. Entering Banaras from the villages to the south, one sees, leaning against the walls of the shops on Lanka Street, stacks of bamboo litters for carrying the dead. Along the main roads of the suburbs or in the dense lanes of the city one suddenly hears the familiar chant of a funeral procession on its way to Manikarnika: '*Rama nama satya hai! Rama nama satya hai!*' 'God's name is Truth! God's name is Truth!'

In Kashi, life is lived in the perpetual presence of death. One of the most popular couplets of the poet Kabir, painted upon the walls of buildings throughout the city, reminds the passerby of death's inevitability:

Seeing the grinding stone turning, turning,
Kabir began to weep.
Between the two stones, not a single grain is saved!

The verse is often accompanied by a vivid folk art depiction of a woman turning the simple domestic grinding stone, throwing not grains but people into the mill, where they are sure to be crushed between the two stones. Death is as common, as certain, as the grinding of wheat once it is thrown into the mill. Rounding the corner of a narrow lane, or glancing up from a streetside market, one will see this famous couplet, next to the advertisements for the newest movie, or the slogans of the latest political campaign. The rickshaw-pullers and vegetable vendors know it by heart. Kashi is comfortable with the fact of death.

For death in Kashi is death transformed. As the saying goes, 'Death in Kashi is Liberation'—*Kashyam maranam muktih*. It is dying that unleashes the greatest holy power of Kashi, the power of bestowing liberation, *moksha* or *mukti*. Death, which elsewhere is feared, here is welcomed as a long-expected guest. Death, which elsewhere is under the terrifying jurisdiction of Yama, is free from that terror here, for Yama is not allowed within the city limits of Kashi. Death, which elsewhere is polluting, is here holy and auspicious. Death, the most natural, unavoidable, and certain of human realities, is here the sure gate to *moksha*, the rarest, most precious, most difficult to achieve of spiritual goals.

'Bound for Moksha'

Kashi's greatest gift is the bestowing of *moksha*—the final fording of the river of *samsara* to the far shore, beyond birth and death. Here, as the Puranas put it, 'the ferryboat is set for the crossing.' But the fare cannot be purchased with any of the other *purusharthas*. No amount of wealth, no accumulation *of punya*, no perfection of *dharma* can qualify one for *moksha*. Only that wisdom that completely floods one's consciousness with light will enable one to make that final crossing.

Moksha is the fourth of the *purusharthas*, but as an aim of life it constitutes a qualitative break from the others. *Kama, artha,* and *dharma* are pursued by those who still consider this world to be their home—students, householders, even retired people. But *moksha* and the wisdom by which it is gained are pursued only by those who have 'left behind' (*sannyasa*) their worldly home. These renouncers may be seen in the streets of Banaras, dressed in faded orange garments, carrying only a wooden staff and a coconut husk water vessel. Although they may belong to an order of *sannyasins* and live in a *matha*, they are, strictly speaking, homeless in this world. They are called *mumukshus*, those 'bound for *moksha*.'

Since the era of the Upanishadic sages and the Buddha, Banaras has been a gathering place for those who have renounced the world. They have come to the groves of the Forest of Bliss to practice asceticism, to pursue disciplines of yoga, and to strive toward wisdom. For them, Banaras is famous as the 'Bestower of *Siddhi*'—the spiritual attainments, the perfections, which are the goals of those who devote themselves totally to spiritual disciplines. It is called the 'Birthplace of *Siddhi*.'

Jaigishavya is one of the ancient legendary yogis in the Hindu tradition, and it is well known in the Puranas that his yogic practice was brought to fulfillment in Kashi, by the grace of Lord Shiva. His story is taken as a paradigm for the fulfillment of spiritual goals in Kashi. It is said that when Shiva left Kashi to dwell on Mt. Mandara, during the reign of Divodasa, Jaigishavya established a *linga* and vowed that he would neither eat nor drink until Shiva returned. Jaigishavya sat in meditation until his limbs withered. When Shiva returned, entering the city from the north,

upon this yogi a much-deserved boon:

'I give you the wisdom called *Yogashastra*,' said Shiva, 'which is the means to *nirvana*. May you be the teacher of yoga to all yogis. O sage, rich in ascetic practice, you will know the whole secret of yogic knowledge, by my grace, and by that knowledge, you will reach *nirvana*.'

Shiva pledged to dwell in the *linga* which Jaigishavya established in order to bestow *siddhi*, 'fulfillment,' upon all who practice yoga.

The *linga* of Jaigishavya may still be seen today. Its temple is in a small, peaceful monastic compound in the northeastern sector of the city. Here the ancient traditions of the yogi Jaigishavya continue. The *linga* in the temple is striking: an enormous, rounded stone some five feet tall.

There are many renouncers who have emulated Jaigishavya's severe ascetic practice, the most radical being those called the Aghoris, who not only renounce the world for a life of asceticism, but turn the values of the world upside down and fasten upon the reverse side, so to speak. Their name is euphemistic, meaning 'Not Terrible,' but in truth they are the most terrible of all from a worldly point of view. They haunt the cremation grounds and sleep upon graves. They drink wine, sever and cure a human skull to use for collecting food, and cook their food on the embers of cremation pyres. Like Shiva, who is also known by the name Aghora, they seem deliberately to adopt the things the world scorns, following a path of spiritual tempering that ensures their liberation from the values of *dharma*. If all, indeed, is Brahman, then one must not spurn any aspect of life or death. It is no coincidence that a modern Aghori, Baba Bhagavan Ram, has established the most active center for the treatment of lepers in Banaras.

The goal of the renouncer, whether the ordinary yogi or the radical Aghori, is to become 'liberated-in-life,' a *jivan mukta*. Such a person has transcended the tensions, the dualities, the anxieties of life and of death, even while living on 'this shore.' When he dies, he will make that final crossing, never to return.

Renouncers, of course, are not the only ones bound for *moksha* in Kashi. In a sense, this city, while it is famous for its ascetics, yogis, and renouncers, constitutes a challenge to their labors, for everyone here is bound for *moksha*. We have already heard that sleep is yoga in Kashi, and it is said that what is discovered by studying the Vedanta and all the Upanishads may be learned playfully in Kashi, with no effort at all. The Puranic *mahatmyas* are filled with the radical juxtaposition of the hard path of the ascetics and the easy path of those who do nothing more than meet their death here in Kashi.

Here why should a man dwell in a solitary place?
And what is the use of turning from the pleasures of sense?
And what is the use of practicing yoga or sacrificing to the gods?
For without these one gets mukti *easily in Kashi.*

Not only is living in Kashi as good as the ardent seeking of the professional *mumukshus*, but it is a more certain path. The yogi may not reach his desired goal in this lifetime, perhaps not in many lifetimes. But the rickshaw-puller, haggling over the price of a ride, peddling through the streets all day, waiting for a few late customers at night, is following a spiritual path that leads directly to *moksha*.

People come from all over India to live in Kashi until they die. They come for *Kashivasa*—'living in Kashi.' Having come to Avimukta, they never leave. For them, this is the final stop on a pilgrimage that has lasted for many lives, through birth and death and birth again. Dying in Kashi, they make the final crossing which ends the pilgrimage of this life, and of all lives.

Through the ages, Banaras has been colonized in its various sectors by these Kashivasis. The Madrasis have settled at Hanuman Ghat, the Bengalis in Bengali Tola, the Maharashtrians near Rama Ghat and Panchaganga Ghat. Some have come here to retire. Some are widows, who are left without recourse in their old age. They have been the pillars of their family religious life for decades. They have gone barefoot on more pilgrimages, observed more fasts, sung more devotional hymns than either their husbands or their sons. And now, thin and almost invisible in their plain white *saris*, they are among the most pious of the Kashivasis.

In addition to the Kashivasis, there are others who have come to Kashi at the eleventh hour. They come for what is colloquially called Kashi Labh—'The Benefit of Kashi.' They make it just in time. They are brought to hospices such as Kashi Labh Mukti Bhavan, near Godaulia crossing. Here they may die in peace, for dying a good death is as important as living a good life.

Entering the Kashi Labh Mukti Bhavan from the street, one passes into a garden compound where the two-story hospice building is located. There are sacred *tulsi* bushes on either side of the path, with little signs set amidst the plants saying 'Ram, Ram—Remember the name of Ram.' Entering the hospice, there is a *puja* room, with an altar and many deities. There are attendants and employees of the hospice who take turns chanting 'Hare Krishna! Hare Rama!' throughout the day and night. And if the attendants are all busy at other duties, there is a record player which carries the sound of sacred *mantras* softly through the quiet building. Around the center courtyard are the small, bare rooms where the dying may be cared for by their families. There is no conventional medicine here, however, for the patients have come, not to recover, but to die in an atmosphere in which their final thoughts may be directed toward God. Every few hours they are given some *tulsi* leaves and Ganges water, the finest medicine there is for the dying. On the wall of the hospice, as one enters, the rules of the house are painted. Here are the first few: (1) Only those sick people who are dying and who believe in liberation in Kashi and have come especially for 'The Benefit of Kashi' may stay here. The ill who wish to get well by taking medicines should stay elsewhere in a hospital. (2) Those good people who are followers of the Hindu *varnashrama dharma* may stay in this place. (3) One may stay here for fifteen days. After that, one may stay, if there is special necessity, by the permission of the director.

The praises of dying in Kashi are well known to those who have come here to die. There are thousands of verses, any two or three of which they may know by heart:

Where else does a creature obtain liberation as he does here, simply by giving up the body, with very little effort at all!

Not by austerities, not by donations, not by lavish sacrifices can liberation be obtained elsewhere as it can be obtained in Kashi simply by giving up the body!

Even the yogis practicing yoga with minds controlled are not liberated in one lifetime, but they are liberated in Kashi simply by dying!

—excerpted from *Banaras: City of Light* by Diana L. Eck,
copyright © 1982 by Diana L. Eck.

Amitava Kumar

In the Light of Small Towns

In a few minutes, the dog had retrieved Laloo's slipper. The master said, 'Shake hand *karo*,' and the dog, saliva dripping from its jaws, raised its paw. Johnny had recently won an award in a dog show. The show had been held in a park in front of my parents' home in Patna. My nephews told me that Johnny, a black labrador, had won the award also because there were no other dogs in his category. I asked them if the other competitors had withdrawn voluntarily, but my nephews felt that it might have been more because there are no other labradors in Patna. Both possibilities are equally plausible—and this too reveals a great deal about my hometown.

During my visit, Laloo was now out of jail, although there was talk of his return to custody. I was visiting him in the official residence of the chief minister of Bihar. There were policemen—and one policewoman—scattered around us. Away in the distance, to my right, stood a Black Cat Commando silhouetted against the yellow walls of the bungalow. The house is only a few minutes' drive from Patna's nondescript airport, and every few minutes a small-engine plane flew over us. Laloo, wearing a shabby white cotton undershirt, would look up momentarily and then cover his ears. A silver amulet hung from thick red strings around his neck.

As long as I was there, Laloo's wife, Rabri Devi, the chief minister of Bihar, sat a few feet away on a plastic chair. One of Laloo's lieutenants, Shyam Rajak, bearded and in a black *kurta*, or shirt, sat in another plastic chair at a respectable distance. I looked at Rabri now and then while Laloo talked to me. Rabri seemed fairer in person than in her photographs. Her neck bulged above the line of her blouse, as if she had swallowed a small bird. She was wearing a pale blue sari. I began to wonder whether it was the smell of Rabri's shampoo that was carried over to me when the breeze stirred.

The smell had a faint sweetness to it that I found agreeable. It returned me to my childhood, and to the memories of my aunts in Bihar's small towns and villages. They were simple women, only mildly literate, and they stuck to the routines of housework and worship. None of them would have dreamed of becoming the chief minister of Bihar. I am sure Rabri hadn't either. As she sat there, behind her husband, smiling occasionally and saying nothing, Rabri was only a middle-aged housewife who had just finished taking a bath to get rid of the heat.

Laloo spoke to me in Hindi. Much of our conversation was about our hometown. Laloo spoke briefly about his arrival in Patna from his village, Phulwaria. He said his village 'was in a remote area.' He had taken the ferry across the Ganges. In Patna, he said, 'everything looked new and mysterious.' Then, he added, 'When I came here I got an opportunity to learn about the wider world.' That remark gave me pause. The town that I had sought to escape in order to get a sense of the world outside was the one that had been for Laloo the introduction to the world outside the village. I remembered the story I had heard my father tell us about his coming to Patna from the ancestral village to the north. Like Laloo, my father had taken the ferry. He had slept on the banks of the Ganges after spreading a towel on the sand. I thought also about my mother, taking a train from Ara to come to Patna for her college. It was in Patna that one was afforded a chance to meet writers, artists, and musicians. During Dussehra festival each year, there would be all-night performances by the best Indian artistes. A cousin remembered one year having had the privilege of listening to the legendary Ustad Bismillah Khan playing the *shehnai*. The next day, the cousin was taking a train out of Patna, and he saw the Ustad strolling on the station platform and then squatting on the concrete edge to piss on the tracks.

At some point, Laloo decided to deliver a brief lecture to me on history. He recited the ancient name for our town, Pataliputra, and then mentioned the Chinese traveler, Hieun Tsang. He looked at me and said, 'Itihaas padhne ki zaroorat hai' (It is necessary to read history). Then, Laloo mentioned other names, Ashok, Chanakya, Guru Gobind Singh. Rather pointedly, he said, 'It was here that we had Chandragupta II. His reign is called the Golden Period in Indian history. Chandragupta II was a shudra. Ask the historians.' Actually, the ruler that Laloo had in mind was not Chandragupta II—a ruler in the fourth century A.D., in what is described in school textbooks as India's Golden Age—but Chandragupta Maurya, a ruler in the third century B.C., who, it is speculated, was the illegitimate son of a ruler and a palace maid. Clearly, what was more significant in Laloo's mind, and what he wanted to convey to me in passing, was that Bihar had been ruled by a person who had been born low.

The recognition of this plain but radical truth imparts a moral legitimacy to Laloo's immense, albeit waning, popularity in Bihar. Laloo understands the appeal of this idea. Born in a rural, milkman's family, he has made his own rise to the top the powerful narrative for others to identify with. But it is only through an ideological sleight of hand that the difference between him and today's Bihari poor can be erased: Laloo is only in a very narrow sense like those who vote for him. He is powerful and rich. Further, his irresponsible and corrupt rule takes him away from any comparison that could possibly be made with any of the Chandraguptas in Indian history. For Laloo to invoke that comparison, in however veiled a manner, is the more egregious misreading of history.

When the history lesson was over, it was time for me to leave. I finished the lemon tea that had been delivered in a tiny cup. The conversation had begun to peter out. Suddenly, Laloo shouted that he wanted water. A servant in a dirty white uniform, with a faded gold comb in his turban, came bearing a plastic tub. It was brimming with water.

The tub was placed in front of Laloo, and he proceeded to put his feet in the water. Another servant rushed forward with a bar of Lifebuoy and a brush. The servant sat on his haunches and started soaping Laloo's feet. But the servant's motions weren't vigorous enough. Laloo spurred him on. He said, 'Khakhoro! Khakhoro! Aur nahin ho to chhuri se khakhoro!' (Scrape. Scrape. And if it doesn't work, scrape it with a knife).

I wanted to take a photograph but thought it would be impolite to ask. When I got up to leave, I asked Laloo what was wrong with the soles of his feet. He explained the matter to me patiently. Each morning he rubbed oil on his feet. But when he walked out to a place under the tree to pray and perform *puja*, pebbles got stuck to his soles. He preferred walking barefoot when he offered his prayers. This explanation was given to me so directly that it appeared that I could, indeed, have gone ahead and taken the photograph. It probably would not have struck Laloo that in trying to take a picture of the servant washing his feet, I would have been portraying him in an unfavorable light. For Laloo, nothing that he did was wrong. He was now a member of the elite in our town. He behaved in the way that he had always, from a distance, seen the elite behave.

*****

I disliked Patna when I lived there as a boy, but what I remember most clearly is how much I disliked myself. The loathing diminished when I grew up and found words and started to write. I began to see myself and the place Patna as two different, distinct entities. But I also learned how both of them had always been very close if not also the same.

I grew into puberty in Patna. Around the same time that adolescence began changing my voice and the way in which I looked at the world, a boy who was a year or two senior to me stunned me by making a sexual remark in the schoolyard about my elder sister. Rage caught me by the throat. Everyone thought my elder sister was very pretty. I adored her. But I stayed silent. I might have been afraid of the older boy, but I was also confused by the anger and desire I felt in myself. The greater part of this confusion was that it seemed to seep into me from my surroundings in Patna: what I despised in the boy who had offended me was not particular to him at all; I saw it as a standard Patna trait. Both the boy and I belonged to this place: how could we have behaved otherwise? To realize this truth was to feel very alone.

I was eleven when I entered a medicine shop on Station Road and asked for a packet of Carefree sanitary napkins for my mother. The man behind the counter said something to the other two men sitting on stools beside him. They laughed. What were they saying? I was upset at my mother for having sent me on this errand. I was learning as I grew into manhood in Patna that I must become distant from the women I had loved the most in my family.

In a sense, Patna forced this on me. My sisters would hire rickshaws to take them to their friends' houses or the cinema. I would be asked to get on my bicycle and accompany them. The men on the streets always made passes at them. In my mind, each street of Patna looked like a permanent leer. Once a young man, chewing *paan* outside a shop on the crowded Boring Canal Road, said 'Ehhh, ehhh, dekho, dekho, Red Roj.' A film called *Red Rose* had recently been released. Years later, I incorporated that remark in a routine I used to do on Bihari street talk for my friends in college in Delhi. I never mentioned my sisters. I found my trips on the bicycle humiliating. My sisters were much calmer, even indifferent about it. I refused to escort them anymore. But when I quarreled with them at home, I found that I would repeat things that I had heard strange men say about them on the streets. The experience gave me my first divided sense of home and outside.

In a year or two, I became an expert at making remarks about other boys' sisters myself. I remembered my boyhood hurt, so I made sure that the brothers of the girls I was insulting were never around to hear my words. But there were no other restraints. I poured everything I had learned in the classes in physics or geography or biology into my description of bodies and acts that I was, in reality, utterly ignorant about. From the febrile imagination of a characteristically repressed Indian school boy poured out a Sadean fantasy of pulleys and hydraulics, elevation and latitudes, skin and glands that sweated sexuality.

All of this did nothing to lessen the confusion or the anger. It was only a part of a process that took me away from home to a life in which I was more and more on the street. This meant that I did no reading or writing; I had nothing that could be called an interior life. My elder sister began to keep a diary. But there was nothing in my life that I felt I could record on a page.

There was a time in the years that immediately preceded my unruly adolescence when I had wanted to write and to draw. When we took the ferry up the Ganges to our ancestral village, I studiously observed the scenes I wanted to paint. I remember a stretch of sand and a small red flag on a bamboo pole. Some afternoons, I saw men on the riverbank pulling a boat upstream with the help of a rope. I wanted to paint the shape of tall egrets near the water. I wasn't very successful. After a painting competition one Saturday, my art teacher told me that he had tried hard to give me the third prize. With a resigned shake of the head he stopped in mid-sentence, and I remembered the slim trees and the mountain peaks I had painted for him on far too many occasions. Seen from the window of my classroom—the school was built close to the water—the Ganges did not appear beautiful to me. Crows rode on the carcasses that floated on the water, pecking. I also wanted to write for the school magazine. At a relative's house, I read old copies of *Reader's Digest* and tried to write jokes like the ones I saw printed there. Those jokes had been sent in by ordinary readers. But nothing remotely funny seemed to be happening around me. I had tried to write a story, but I had to abandon that too. And then, within a year or two, none of this mattered anymore.

For, what seemed like the rest of Patna, we discovered girls. Neither I nor any of my friends knew a single girl, but in the abstract, girls dominated our lives. We rode our bicycles obsessively past the girls' school, but I could not bear to look at the red-skirted figures milling around. My sisters were among them and I kept hoping they would call out to me. We also began to haunt the 11:00 a.m. Sunday shows at Veena Cinema. We told our parents we were watching the old Hollywood films to improve our English. Very few in the audience understood or spoke the language. We were all there for the same thing: any hint of female flesh. Whenever there was any suggestion of sex on the screen, the theater resounded with loud whistling. The whistles would only grow louder a moment later because the censors' scissors would already have cut out the rest of the scene. Life seemed caught in an endless cycle that promised cheap excitement but inevitably led to frustration.

2

The older youth in Patna also lived through a cycle of frustration that had in it an element of sexual denial. But their experiences of frustration were also more complex because of their meager prospects in life. Colleges were often shut down. Unemployment was high and corruption was rampant. On the day after my eleventh birthday, this frustration found its release in a huge protest against the faltering government of the Congress chief minister Abdul Ghafoor.

The date was 18 March 1974. The students took out a procession in Patna and the police fired on them, killing several of the protesters. A curfew order was 'clamped' immediately. Some of my relatives—cousins and their spouses from a nearby town who had come for the party at our house the previous night—were unable to return to their homes.

The party got extended. We stood on the roof of the house and played *antakshri*. There was one young woman in the group, a distant relative, who was a wonderful singer. She was also beautiful with light eyes and hair that strayed from her forehead in the manner made popular by Bombay film actresses. While this woman sang songs from old Hindi films, in the distance we could see smoke rising from the buildings that had been set on fire.

The students' agitation that had begun that day would bring down the government in Bihar and face the brunt of Indira Gandhi's emergency rule the following year. The leaders who emerged during that movement, the old and ailing J.P. Narayan and a new student leader by the name of Laloo Prasad Yadav, were to change the political landscape of India in the years to come. In the large sprawling family on my mother's side, my male cousins had so far been inactive and unengaged in campus life. One of them, only a few months earlier, had consumed a pesticide and had laid down on a sack of potatoes prepared to die. That same cousin had now joined the fray as a follower of JP. Other cousins courted arrest.

There were huge gatherings in Patna's Gandhi Maidan. The students were on the rise in the rest of Bihar too. The movement was met with very little repression at first. Then, as a result of other disturbances, Indira Gandhi's rule at the center was suddenly threatened. She imposed the emergency rule; the fundamental rights were suspended; many of the leaders who had gained popularity were thrown in jail.

The superintendent of the Patna jail was my maternal uncle. His house, located right outside the jail's walls, faced the Sujata restaurant, which had been torched during the students' riots the previous year. When I went to eat at my uncle's house, I would hear of the arrests and my uncle would tell me about the leaders in jail. I would get chicken for dinner at my uncle's house. The Emergency didn't mean much to me. People spoke of trains running on time. The landscape in Patna showed a change. Suddenly, new billboards sprouted on the streets; they carried slogans that proclaimed our march toward a golden tomorrow. One of Indira Gandhi's slogans was borrowed for our new urinal in school. On the wall that we faced when we stood in a line to pee, someone had written in pencil: 'Aaapka bhavishya aapke haath mein hai' (You hold your future in your hand). This was the way in which politics entered our adolescent universe—as a private part of the human anatomy. This might have been because of our youth, but Patna made it very easy for this to be so.

The 1970s had come to town, for most of us in Patna, after half of that decade was over. The Emergency, as far as I can remember, didn't change our entry into the borrowed culture of the age. We wore bell-bottoms and grew our hair long. We tried to acquire other affects. There was a bookstore in Patna called Tricel—there were excellent bookstores for Hindi books near the Patna College, but only one as far as I could tell for books in English—which sold stickers suitable for the new Zeitgeist. I bought one that said 'Love' in funky, psychedelic colors. I did not buy any books.

As I look back on those years, I am struck by the absence from my life of all matters literary. I remember reading the report of the local, well-known Hindi writer Phanishwar Nath Renu raising his arm to protect JP from the stick-wielding policemen in Patna. Renu was imprisoned soon thereafter. I discovered Renu's fiction two decades later. Ten years would pass before I'd watch *Teesri Kasam*, starring Raj Kapoor and Waheeda Rehman, a film based on one of Renu's stories. By then, I had already left Patna. And Renu was dead. But back in the 1970s, when I first came across him in the news in Patna, I had not read any of Renu's writings. The report in a Hindi weekly about the writer's protest meant little to me. What stayed in my mind was only a small detail about how Renu's long, curly hair was dry and unkempt in prison. In his cell, the writer lacked hair oil.

The paltry evidence in my life of the aesthetic—if we can call it that—was only the annual elocution at school. At this event, during the final years of my school life, I must have heard Lord Tennyson's 'The Charge of the Light Brigade' recited more times than I had even read the poem on paper. For the Hindi version of the event, a popular choice was Ramdhari Singh Dinkar's jingoistic poem 'Samar Sesh Hai' (The War Is Not Over). I had declaimed it with appropriate passion myself and won a prize. The poem was actually a critique of Nehru's pacifism, but once again, I did not know any of this. The poet, who had died some years before I had read out his poem in our school auditorium, had also lived in the same city as I. Dinkar was one of the giants of post-independence Hindi writing. But this didn't mean much to me either. His home was

—from Amitava Kumar, *Bombay London New York* (New York: Routledge,
2002), pp. 78–89. 'In the Light of Small Towns' is the chapter from
which the first four pages are excerpted.

Aditya Nigam

Theatre of the Urban: The Strange Case of the Monkeyman

In April-May 2001, the eastern outskirts of Delhi were suddenly gripped
by a strange fear, occasioned by widespread reports of a creature said to
be stalking lower class neighbourhoods. Not many had actually seen the
creature—or at any rate, not seen it well enough to be able to describe
it, though quite a few claimed to have actually been injured in its attacks.
Consequently, it was described by different people in many different ways,
though generally *kaala bandar* or *bandar aadmi*—that is 'black monkey' or
the 'Monkeyman'—was how it came to be described in popular parlance.
    In about a month and a half of its existence the Monkeyman had
acquired the character of an urban legend, going through many mutations
through the various tellings of the stories of its exploits. The creature was
variously described as a 'half-monkey, half-man', 'a strange creature with
a machine-like body with glowing lights' and in some cases, a 'man with a
mask'. According to one news report, although the first complaints were
filed at the Vijaynagar Police Station in Ghaziabad, starting from April 5,
records do not show any mention of a 'man wearing a mask'. Except for
one, 'all the complaints ... are about nocturnal monkey attacks, mainly
on people sleeping in their terraces, a common practice in the summer'.[1]
The first complaint at the police station, that suggests anything out of

---

[1] Nistula Hebbar, 'Rumour evolution: It was a monkey till April 30, man after',
The Indian Express (Express Newsline), 17 May 2001, 3.

the ordinary appeared as late as April 30, when a local resident Anil, alias Kapil, claimed that he had been attacked by 'a dark shadow-like creature which seemed like a monkey', and which had hit him 'through his stomach'. The report adds, 'His wounds seemed to correspond with his version'.

The police however claimed that on investigation they found that Anil had made a false complaint 'to save himself from arrest as he had actually had a violent fight with his brother, and disturbed the peace'. In order to mislead the police, therefore, he had created the story of the Monkeyman.[2] According to the report, however, this angle was revealed much later, by which time the rumour of the Monkeyman had acquired a life of its own. 'After the story appeared in the press, people became desperate despite the fact that victims of attacks such as little Guddi's father in Ghaziabad, positively identified the attacker as a monkey, but with black hair', says the report.

As the stories began circulating, with new accretions at every step, the Monkeyman began taking shape in popular imagination. The Hindi daily *Amar Ujala*, reported that on May 2 residents congregated at an open field near Vijaynagar, after someone claimed having seen a 'monkey like shadowy figure'. Gradually, the terror of the creature also built up. So much so that on May 10, the district administration gave shoot-at-sight orders in order to control the situation.[3] From May 13 onwards, the Monkeyman carried on his activities in the capital, especially in the eastern outskirts bordering Ghaziabad. By this time, interestingly, the creature had mutated into a kind of cyborg—a kind of computerised/robotised figure with almost supernatural powers. It was claimed that it had green eyes, that it presumably had a springboard under its feet and a green belt with buttons for navigation.[4] Some other reports however, showed that at least some of these characteristics had already been acquired by the Monkeyman by the time it entered Delhi. The Superintendent of Police (City) of Ghaziabad, Mr. R.K. Chaturvedi, for instance told *The Hindu* reporter that while initially most reports came from Vijay Nagar, Raj Nagar and Sanjay Nagar—areas with 'a high simian population'—and people mostly 'reported attacks by a dark monkey with lips cut', descriptions soon changed to those of a 'masked figure'.[5] Very soon, according to Chaturvedi, people were speaking

though there were no first-hand accounts.[6]

Whatever the point at which the new features may have got added to the Monkeyman, there is little doubt that by the time the scare became rampant in Delhi, this mutant cyborg was 'in existence'. In my discussions with ordinary folk, a kind of deductive reasoning was offered for the claim that the creature had intricate electronically operated/computerised systems to keep it going. They claimed, for instance, that at one house where the Monkeyman attacked, a pitcher of water got spilt in the course of the attack and seeing the water 'he' took to 'his' heels. Water, they reasoned, would have destroyed his electronic system, which was why he ran away.[7] In one version, this was then extended into a different narrative that is already available these days for any such oddity, namely the narrative of the Pakistani enemy: it was claimed that the creature was a robot with remote control that had been sent in by Pakistan to create terror.[8] The episode thus became the occasion for the externalisation of a whole series of latent fears—often of a deeply pathological nature. Some of them may not even have been entirely innocent, as for example the one expressed in the Shiv Sena's bizarre claim that the Monkeyman was a handiwork of the Pakistan secret service, the ISI, which had sent '131 monkeys from across the border to create terror'.[9] So great was the scare that for some days people stopped sleeping on the terraces, night patrols of neighbourhood youth were formed to reinforce the patrolling by the police. *Havans* and *yagnas* (Hindu rituals) were performed in different parts of the city to exorcise the evil.

Undoubtedly, once the legend took on a life of its own, it seems that a whole series of otherwise unconnected, often innocuous incidents started getting inserted into the larger stories of the Monkeyman's exploits. Descriptions about its height varied, indicating that either people had not seen the creature or that they were generally mistaking different creatures for the elusive Monkeyman. One person in NOIDA claimed, for instance, that he had been attacked by it but when he turned to catch

---

[6] Ibid.

[7] Conversations with a *paan* shop owner in Rajpur Road.

[8] Narrated to me by a resident of Shastri Park area.

[9] 'Monkeyman gives power to the people: parties score points', *The Hindustan Times*, 17 May 2001, reported that the Shiv Sena's Delhi Unit claimed that 'The ISI is behind it; 131 monkeys have come across the border to spread terror'. I am grateful to Prakash Upadhyay for this reference.

it, it turned into a cat with glowing eyes. Some others claimed that it came on wings and disappeared into thin air when attacked.[10] One of the rare 'sightings' in a well off middle-class colony, for instance, occurred when a gentleman standing on his balcony at 5:30 in the morning, 'saw a speeding Maruti Zen which braked suddenly' and 'a man dressed as a black monkey reportedly stepped out of the car which then sped away'. Injuries that may have been caused by entirely unrelated incidents now came to be cast within the larger narratives about the Monkeyman.

While speaking to *The Hindu*, the SP of Ghaziabad, Chaturvedi also made some other perceptive observations. Some things, Chaturvedi claimed, remained unchanged through the changing narratives. For one thing, 'all cases were reported from lower-middle-class [and] jhuggi clusters with a very high population density'. And in all cases 'the attacks took place within about half an hour of a power breakdown after nightfall'. He further stated that, 'all cases were reported from residential areas and there was not a single incident in which a person travelling home alone on a road at night had been attacked'.[11] This last feature of the Monkeyman's exploits remained unchanged through all its excursions in Delhi too. Settlements of the poor, largely labouring populations, living through prolonged spells of power cuts and darkness, sweating it out on the terraces that join together with those of other houses, was the theatre of its activities.

There have been many occasions in the past too, when Delhi has witnessed the sudden eruption of rumours that have had large sections of the city on its feet, running around in panic and/or excitement. One of the most recent ones, of course, was the rumour of the Ganesha idols 'drinking milk', in 1995. That was, however, a rumour that had a much wider spread both within the city, enveloping within its ambit its more affluent sections too, and outside—reaching out to expatriate Hindus living abroad. The Monkeyman, on the other hand, confined its activities to the subaltern neighbourhoods of Delhi.

The Space of Subaltern Existence

One of the distinctive—and interesting—things about the recent episode of the Monkeyman is the spatial span of its activities. In a sense, the

---

[10] This last story was told to Sanal Edamaruku of the Rationalist Association, 'It is a mass delusion, say rationalists', *Express Newsline*, 17 May 2001, 3.
[11] Ibid.

very fact that the activities of this creature were limited to the lower and lower-middle-class neighbourhoods indicates its close link with a subaltern imagination and existence. What are the kinds of spaces invoked in the course of these descriptions? What do they tell us about life in subaltern Delhi? Let us look at the spatial descriptions more closely. These descriptions continuously refer to densely populated settlements of labouring populations, usually located on the peripheries of the city—in this case, the eastern outskirts. These constitute the theatre of the Monkeyman's activities. The Ghaziabad police chief in fact, reminds us that on no occasion was anybody attacked while returning home at night—that is to say on the main roads—open spaces—leading to the residential areas. The Monkeyman's appearances were in places where people sleep on terraces—and in lanes outside their houses—in the dark and hot summer nights, densely populated areas with winding lanes and bylanes, where the creature could easily disappear into thin air. We hear of small open fields in the vicinity, characteristic of suburban, relatively 'undeveloped' areas, where people collect to exchange notes after a series of attacks by the creature. We also hear of 'tall buildings' that the Monkeyman is able to jump off with ease—which probably mean, in this context, low-rise three or four storey buildings of Delhi's 'urban' villages, and 'unauthorised' and resettlement colonies. Stories of these sightings thus provide a glimpse of one kind of space of subaltern urban existence. We can also see that these areas are entirely segregated from the affluent colonies—most of which are located in New Delhi, especially its southern parts. Even when there are some relatively affluent areas nearby, they remain effectively cordoned off by huge iron gates and a certain social distance. The spatial re-ordering of the city that has taken place in the last two decades has now made this segregation almost complete. As a result, the only reported 'sighting' of the creature in a middle-class colony is when somebody 'sees' a 'man wearing a mask' from the balcony of his house, from a considerable, safe distance.

From my own observations of these neighbourhoods over the years, what I have found interesting about these spaces is that subaltern life here continues to reproduce the patterns of *qasba* of small-town life. The internal spatial layout of these areas gives a strange sense of distance from the speed and movement that characterise the life of the metropolis, embodying as it were, almost a different sense of time. Life inside these colonies and neighbourhoods provides a kind of refuge from the hectic pace of life that the mostly male workers—especially factory workers—experience from the moment they step out for work and within which they live till they return. The spatial organisation, as well as the specific histories of these neighbourhoods, also ensures a kind of life where a community existence is reproduced on a daily basis and one that stands in sharp contrast to the atomised existence of middle-class and affluent sections of the city. Networks of communication here, therefore, tend to be quite active and live, organised as they are around certain kinds of sociality centering mainly on tea shops and *paan* shops. The lanes and bylanes where people simply sit outside on cots and spend their free time provide another mode of exchange of information, gossip and rumours. Unlike the middle-class and affluent colonies, where contact with the locality is minimal and where the routine trips to the markets too are likely to be purely commercial transactions with minimal human interaction, in these subaltern spaces the rapidity with which information travels through informal channels can often be truly mind-boggling. Interesting however, are the ways in which, through repeated tellings and retellings of stories and news, different angles emerge, new accretions take place and occasionally, some things are also lost. If the representational mechanisms through which information gets broadcast in the mass media transform their object in some, often predictable, ways, the transformations here are likely to take very unexpected directions—as some of the descriptions above reveal. The easy insertion of the ISI/Pakistan angle into these transmissions also indicates the activity of certain right-wing political groups that exist there and make good use of such opportunities.[12]

It is really difficult to say, for instance, whether there was ever such a thing as the Monkeyman or whether it was somebody—or a group of people—playing mischief. In one early instance, as we saw, we did hear of a 'false complaint' being registered after a fight between two brothers. In a sense, the question as to its actual existence is not really as interesting as the glimpse that the episode might provide into the daily existence of subaltern Delhi. Take for instance the following reading of the episode. Extrapolating from the life of small towns, where joined and continuous terraces become, in the monotonous lives of people, a theatre for the playing out of sexual desire, noted Hindi intellectual Sudhish Pachauri, in fact, perceived a libidinal dimension in the matter. Pachauri alludes here to the *meaning* of the space that we can roughly translate as the roof

[12] Of course, these kinds of narratives draw on certain mindsets that are already in place and do not require organised political intervention. However, in this case, the fact that the Shiv Sena did take such a public position indicates that such might have been the case.

the site of the play of a generally unrequited desire. The *chhat* or *baam* (as Urdu poetry would have it) and in some cases the *chhaj-ja* (an extended 'balcony' or roof) becomes the place where initial furtive glances are exchanged, often developing into bolder exchanges leading up to written notes setting up [a] secret rendezvous. The continuity of the terrace provides the place where the rigidly guarded boundaries of sexuality and domesticity stand potentially threatened. It is not uncommon therefore, or so Pachauri suggests, for such transgressive acts to be played out in the darkness of the summer nights—nights of surreptitious wakefulness when someone 'accidentally' strays into somebody else's terrace.[13] The suggestion in Pachauri's reading is that there was, in all probability, one such angle in the initial incidents that led to the appearance of this mysterious creature who merely gently 'scratched' his victims—often women.

Whatever be the case, it seems unlikely that the Monkeyman's exploits can be separated from the specific spatial layout and structure of the lower-class neighbourhoods. The Monkeyman could not have animated the imagination of the middle and upper-class residents of the city of Delhi in the way the self-fulfilling story of the Ganesha idols drinking milk did. Ganesha was fixed to his place in the temple and you had to go out, to see him 'drink milk'. The location of the action was in the temples not in the isolated homes of the rich, where there is a singular absence of the networks that animate life in subaltern settlements. The networks of communication mobilised in the Ganesha episode characteristically, were long-distance telephones and the rudimentary electronic mail service that was available those days, not as with the Monkeyman, spatially internally situated networks within and between localities.

Another space

There is another kind of space that this episode draws our attention towards. We can begin to outline this space by looking at the reaction of rationalist public opinion to the episode. It was in some senses classic. The key spokesperson of the Indian Rationalist Association, Sanal Edamaruku dubbed the entire episode a 'mass delusion'. Similar opinions were expressed by many others too. *The Hindu*, for example, editorially commented on the entire episode, as did many other newspapers—apart from a flurry

[13] Sudhish Pachauri, 'Naye zamane ki vaanar leela', *Jansatta Ravivari*, 3 June 2001.

of articles that appeared subsequently. This editorial in a way sums up best what came to become the rationalist consensus on the issue. 'It is not for the first time in recent memory', it averred, 'that *civil society in Delhi has shown signs of cracking up*'. It recalled the Ganesha incident when, it lamented, 'even those from affluent sections' were seen moving about with glasses of milk, and marked these incidents out as occasions when 'rational behaviour took a beating'. It criticised the instruments of the state and the police in particular for adding to the crisis.

After trying to give a rational explanation of what might have happened, the editorial added that, 'The only way to put a stop to such things is to deal firmly with the rumour mongers'. However, it also underlined that this will not be sufficient. Therefore, it is important 'to *infuse the fundamentals of a scientific temper among the people*' so that they learn to react in a rational manner. It concluded by observing that '*this is where institutions of civil society ... will have a role to play* ... A vibrant civil society is the only way out of such situations'. An editorial in the *The Indian Express* too expressed concern at the 'galloping spread of unreason' which it saw as a global phenomenon.[14]

Civil society—or its conscience keepers—lashed out at the institutions of the state, particularly the police force, for falling prey to the same 'irrational forces' and forced it to intervene, in order to rein in 'the galloping spread of unreason'. And sure enough, the state fell in line—one of the very rare occasions when it showed inclination to do so. Within a month, the Delhi Police produced a 200-page report debunking the 'monkey business' as a myth.[15]

What, we might ask, has all this got to do with space? My argument here is that this comment is also about a different kind of space—what we might call a social or conceptual space.[16] There is a certain spatial imagination that becomes evident in our theorisations of the social when we start dealing with modernity and the urban transformations that it brings forth. These are abstract spaces but terrains nevertheless, on which we situate different layers of the social. There are three distinct social/conceptual terrains that the comments above, for instance, identify. At one level is

[14] *The Indian Express*, 19 May 2001. I am only referring here to some of the articles out of a much larger number which came out in those days. Also see, for instance, Ashok Vardhan Shetty, 'Imagination on the prowl', *The Hindu Magazine*, Sunday 10 June 2001.

[15] *The Hindustan Times*, 18 June 2001.

[16] See also Henri Lefebvre, *Production of Space* (Blackwell, 1990).

the terrain of *civil society*—the ground that is the bearer of rationality and scientific temper. Even though the editorial commentator is worried about its occasional 'cracking up', s/he sees it as the high ground of modernity on which alone can 'unreason' be reined in. This is also the ground, we can see, that is inhabited by the atomised, individuated, rights-bearing citizen. The other terrain in this narrative is the state and its instruments like the police, who seem too, to occasionally slip into roles not quite becoming of them. Even though the comment does not make it explicit, we could say that the occasional 'lapsing back' by the state into such behaviour has to do with the fact that it is not quite insulated from the third and most problematic terrain. This third terrain is relatively unnamed and unspecified. Its existence here is acknowledged merely as 'the problem': 'the people' who inhabit this ground, figure in this discourse as the objects of the pedagogical activity of the state and civil society—into whom 'scientific temper' is to be infused. The agency of its inhabitants goes unacknowledged for they have to be taught to 'respond to such situations in a rational manner'. Following from our discussion above, we could say that this terrain is also the domain of community existence. At any rate, it is the terrain where the imaginative power of smaller, face-to-face communities is still quite strong and is reproduced daily in the life conditions of these subaltern settlements. Because they are seen as the domain of the pre-modern and the irrational, their very existence constitutes an always-present threat to both civil society and the state's 'instruments'. This third terrain, if it cannot be eliminated, must at least be controlled and assimilated.

The terrains identified here function *as sites* of the theatre of the urban. The simple representations of the non-urban/rural spaces as in some sense continuous, linked to a kind of singular temporality and rhythm of agrarian life, give way here to a more complex, layered, segregated and somewhat enclosed spaces where the 'modern' and the 'non-modern', the 'enlightened' and the 'irrational' live.[17] The city represents what

[17] Premodern spaces too, undoubtedly have rigid hierarchies and many like those in and around temples or the residences of the upper caste and landed gentry are physically separated and inaccessible. Modern spaces of the city are not, in that sense, inaccessible. What is different however is that modern, urban societies, precisely because they are not in principle inaccessible to lower orders, need to be protected from them. They therefore call for a continuous activity on the part of 'civil society' and the state to discipline them. However, it seems to me that these premodern agrarian spaces, even when segregated, are marked by certain common rhythms and pace of life.

Foucault calls 'the epoch of simultaneity'. The urban, especially the post-colonial urban, brings together these different rhythms and times within the space of a single city, inaugurating a highly mobile and dynamic arena of contestation. To be sure, these conceptual representations are problematic insofar as the first domain, that of 'civil society', does not really correspond to the middle class and upper middle class living an atomised existence, in its entirety. For there too, in the post-colonial scenario, notions of community existence have a continuing power. The difference, however, is that here communication is mediated through technology—telephone, electronic mail, Internet—and ceases to be a locally grounded face-to-face community, as we saw in the case of the idols drinking milk. That kind of community, however, does not seem to present a 'problem' for the modern city. It is the existence of the subaltern, constructed through different imaginations of a spatially situated community life that presents a problem that the city and its citizens must deal with. If physical entry into the city cannot be prevented, there certainly are ways by which the enlightened citizenry insulates itself within this space and within the conceptual universe made possible by this experience of the city. In any case, there certainly are ways by which entry into the representational/conceptual domain of the 'civil' can be controlled. Civil society, as the domain of the rights-bearing individual citizen, marks itself out as the domain where entry is predicated upon a certain prior pedagogy: the rustic must first be 'civilised' before s/he can claim entry into its hallowed precincts. In a sense, this bifurcation of the abstract conceptual space of the city parallels efforts to cordon off and segregate its real-physical spaces.

—from *Sarai Reader*, no. 2: 'The Cities of Everyday Life'
(New Delhi, 2002), pp. 22–30.

Ooru and the World*

The Karnataka government officially changed the name of the city from Bangalore to Bengaluru on Rajyotsava Day, 1 November 2006.

Get famous, no matter through what route, goes a sarcasm-laced saying in Kannada. I had achieved that without building anything, destroying anything or even writing anything when the change of Bangalore's name to Bengaluru was in the news. Those were the days when BBC, the *New York Times*, *USA Today* and a host of Indian newspapers and television channels called me incessantly. My apologies, if that sounds a bit like boasting.

All my interviewers would start with the same question: 'So, was it you who proposed the idea of the change of Bangalore's name to Bengaluru?' I could often predict the next set of questions and answered without waiting to be even asked: 'Yes, of course, change of name alone will not ensure better infrastructure.' Or, 'You say Bangalore has a "brand value" today and it may lose out on all the economic gains that come with it by changing the "brand name". But kind sir, why don't we look at it in a slightly different way? Bangalore became a "brand" because of its great weather. But *because* it is a "brand", the weather went bad. Now we have so many people, so many cars, and so much dust and smoke that we can hardly breathe.'

A couple of Bangaloreans wrote letters to me in bad English, asking who on earth I was to suggest a change of name. Why should we learn Kannada, they asked; had I sought the permission for this name change business from 50 lakh people living in the city? My friends Ashish Nandi [Ashis Nandy] and H.Y. Sharada Prasad too are asking me questions, without getting so angry, though. 'Bangalore is not one city. It is both Bangalore and Bengaluru. Let them both be,' they say.

I feel inclined to accept their liberal line of argument. But I would still like to offer a counter-argument, though tinged with hesitation:

You see, most people of Bangalore are unaware of even the existence of Bengaluru. They come face to face with it when buses are burnt or stones come crashing at their expensive cars when Rajkumar gets

---

* The Kannada original of this piece was published in *Udayavani*, Bangalore, in November 2006.

kidnapped or dies. But that's a brief encounter. There was a time when people who didn't speak Kannada in their homes learnt the language. Someone like Masti Venkatesh Iyengar or Pu.Thi. Narasimhachar, who spoke Tamil in their homes, became great writers in Kannada. But these are times when you don't need Kannada to even buy brinjal in the market. There are food malls and food worlds where you can buy 'ladies' finger' and 'banana' without knowing they are called *bende kayi* and *bale hannu* in Kannada. Of course, there is no question of doing a bit of haggling with the seller there on the prices. Small retailers, with whom you could haggle, argue and exchange gossip, have shut shop. If they own the piece of land on which they have their shops, it is more lucrative for them to sell the plot and sit at home. Those who have rented establishments, of course, find themselves in a pathetic situation. The children of those who buy brinjals in food malls also grow up without a touch of the soil. The schools they go to and the school the Kannada children go to might well be on two different planets. By Kannada children, I mean here the children of poor people. The children of rich Kannada-speaking people also, of course, can get on in life without uttering a word of Kannada. They travel one and a half hours every day to go to schools that cost a lakh a year and remain untouched by Kannada children. No, no chance at all of lice from a poor child's head crossing over to a rich child's head!

It was just with the hope that these people would be compelled to learn at least a word of Kannada that I had proposed the name change to Dharam Singh, when he was the chief minister. That's all. No more than that.

Some people ask me if it's not hard for outsiders to get the 'la' sound in the word 'Bengaluru'. That reminds me of how I have spent the better part of my life trying to learn the distinction between the pronunciations of 'e' as in 'ye' sounds in English. Let those who speak English struggle a bit with the world Bengaluru, I would say. Then people warn me, 'Careful, if you start troubling business people like this, they will shut shop and go home. It's not a good idea to provoke the noble souls who have opened call centres here to improve our lot.' Then I extend my stupid argument without any sense of shame: *Tchu, tchu*, don't worry. Business people are a very wise lot. They will learn even Kannada if it will add to their profit. If the 5 million people (50 lakh, as we say in our language) here begin to read and write the language, they will not only have name boards in Kannada, but will also start using it in their transactions. They will speak Kannada like we speak English, I tell them. After all, it's not as if there is 'one' Kannada. Let's add to the already existing variety.

The British, who fancied they ruled an empire over which the sun never sets, did want everyone to speak their kind of English. But see how spectacularly they failed even in their own America, Australia and London! Think of why George Bernard Shaw wrote a play like *Pygmalion.*

I will tell you one of the many stories of my struggle with English. I went to England to study in the early part of the 1960s. When I went to the well-known historian K.M. Panikkar, who was then the vice-chancellor of Mysore University, to seek permission, he asked me what my area of research would be. Lawrence, I said. He asked me what new perspective I could offer on Lawrence without studying writers like Kalidasa, Bhasa, Bhavabhuti and so many more in my own language. There was a lot I could offer, I argued, with respect but not without the arrogance of modernity. He wished me well and granted me leave.

I left for Birmingham with my family. I got a pin-striped woollen suit, a prestige symbol in those days, stitched and worn with pride. But there I met Richard Hoggart, a brilliant scholar who came from a working-class background, wearing a cap typically worn by labourers. The much-respected man would be dressed in a faded coat and never wore a tie. He wore a black gown only when he taught. He would sit and chat with students in pubs. His book, *Uses of Literacy*, had won the praise of even someone like Raymond Williams.

Though I wanted to get close to this circle, they sent me to do English composition classes for six months. I put up with it, though I had already done my MA. After all, English is an alien language and there may be many more things to learn, I thought. I passed the exam. Then I had to discuss my area of research with my tutor. A great deal had already been written about Lawrence. I thought I should work on writers like Orwell, Auden and Isherwood, who wrote in the 1930s when almost all of Europe was in Hitler's clutches. I wanted to especially concentrate on a writer called Edward Upward, who had escaped the attention of critics. I had the support of Malcolm Bradbury of my own age, who was already famous as a novelist, critic and teacher. But the tutor had to agree to my proposal. He was a good man, but an old and old-fashioned man. He had just then returned from a tour of India. His advice to me was along these lines: 'Don't do literary research, do phonetics instead. If you learn the English phonetic system, you could even land a U.N. job. See how high Rajan, who studied in Cambridge, has risen. You know why? Because if you hear him speak in the dark, you would think you are talking to an Englishman. I met a big professor of English in India. I believe his name is Iyengar. But I could hardly make out what he was saying! Anyway, what do you want to do research on?'

I suppressed my embarrassment and said: Edward Upward. The tutor knitted his brows and asked again: Who? I cleared my throat and said in a clearer voice: Edward Upward. Running his fingers through his white goatee beard, my tutor told me in a voice dripping with pity: 'Do you know why I asked someone as intelligent as you to study phonetics instead of literature? Because you don't know the difference between "e" and "ye". Say "Edward", it's "ed" and not "yed".'

That was the limit. I blurted out: 'Sir, you don't know how to say "Iyengar", you say "Eyengar". Then why can't I say "Yedward"? If I speak as you do while teaching students in Mysore, they will call me an ape with silly English pretensions.'

I went straight to Richard Hoggart, after saying bye to him. He was a senior teacher there. I narrated what had happened and told him: 'I would rather surrender my Commonwealth scholarship and go back to Mysore than do phonetics.' Hoggart smiled and said:

'Your tutor is a good man, I will tell him. I will hold an MA exam for you at the end of the year. You take four papers of your favourite Shakespeare and pass the exams. Then you do research on whatever you want. The English I speak in my unselfconscious moments is the English spoken by the labour class. Your tutor could well have told me the same things!'

The same tutor was my examiner in MA. He liked my paper, and praised me to the point of making me feel embarrassed about what I had told him in those moments of anger. He approved my research proposal.

***

During My meeting with Dharam Singh I had proposed many things, besides the change of Bangalore's name: Karnataka should become a fully literate state; all children should get free and equal education in common schools; English should be taught to all in a way that makes it possible to use it the way we want to without illusions about its superiority; and an engineering and a medical college should be opened with Kannada as its medium of instruction.

Surprising how the high priests of globalization are threatened by the mere issue of a name change! Do our IT companies fear that the Sensex that fluctuates at everything from the tsunami to farmers' suicides, might be affected if Bangalore becomes Bengaluru?

I hope the name change is a symbolic step towards Kannadization. By Kannadization, I mean the ability to belong to the world at large even as one is rooted in one's Kannadaness. I hope it does not become a mere publicity gimmick that doesn't rise beyond symbolism.

I went to England to see daffodils celebrated by Wordsworth 'tossing their heads in sprightly dance'. And I have a dream. I dream of a time when people who visit Karnataka want to smell the fragrant Mysore jasmines, eat the bananas of Nanjangud and read the great *vachanas* of Basaveshwara and Allama Prabhu. I dream of a time when those who admire the wanderings of Joyce's hero Daedalus also open their eyes to the rich Dalit world that Kuvempu's character Nayigutti leads us into.

—translated from the Kannada by Bageshree S.; from *Multiple City: Writings on Bangalore*, ed. Aditi De (Delhi: Penguin Books, 2008), pp. 63–7.

Ashis Nandy

Time Travel to a Possible Self: Searching for the Alternative Cosmopolitanism of Cochin

For over a quarter of a century the Indic world confirmed what since my birth was only a blurred feeling: the self-identity of Man is transcultural, and thus cannot have any single point of reference ... Pluralism is not synonymous with tolerance of a variety of opinions. Pluralism amounts to the recognition of the unthinkable, the absurd, and up to a limit, intolerable ... Reality does not need to be in itself transparent, intelligible.

Raimundo Panikkar, 'Personal Statement'

Cochin (or Kochi) is one of the few cities in India where the precolonial traditions of cultural pluralism refuse to die. It is one of the largest natural harbours in India and has also become, during the last fifty years, a major centre of the Indian Navy. With the growing security consciousness in official India, it has recently become less accessible to non-Indians, particularly if they happen to be from one of the countries with which India's relationship is tense. Few mind that, for the city no longer means much to the outside world. For Indians, too, except probably for the more historically conscious Malayalis, Cochin is no longer the 'epitome of adventure' it was to Mohandas Karamchand Gandhi or a crucible of cultures, as it is to its former mayor, K.J. Sohan.[1] For most, it is now one of those regional cities not quite up to the standard of India's major metropolitan centres.

Yet, Cochin is for its residents, the ultimate symbol of cultural diversity and religious and ethnic tolerance or, to use the expression recommended by Madhu Prakash and Gustavo Esteva in place of secularism, hospitality.[2] The city still bears the imprint of its record, stretching across at least six centuries, as a place where China, Africa, Southeast Asia, West Asia, and Europe met. At least fourteen communities still live in the city—ranging from Jews and Eurasian Parangis to Tamilians and Saraswats. Some ethnic communities have blended with the locals and are no longer clearly identifiable, such as the Yemeni Arabs; some have moved away entirely, such as the Chinese; still others are about to, such as the Jews. Most of these communities are not even listed in the Indian census because they are identified with castes, and official India has given up caste enumeration after 1935, lest the data are misused politically.[3]

Cochin has seen adventurers, invaders, and pirates. It has seen people seeking refuge from oppression and discrimination in other parts of the world. It has also seen occasional communal skirmishes among different communities, but for centuries it has not seen any bloodbath, not even a proper riot. This does not mean that there is no hostility among communities. Nor does it mean that communities do not have their own distinctive written and unwritten memories of past injustices and violence against them. Syrian Christians remember the destruction of sacred books and documents by the Catholics, Jews the harassment of their forefathers by the Portuguese. The Chinese are said to have been driven away by the Arabs; Tipu Sultan, some believe, attacked the Jews at Cranganore; and Konkanis talk about how they fled to Cochin from the inquisition at Goa.

---

[1] 'Celebrating Diversity in Cochin', *Culture and Identity Newsletter*, October 1997, 1(3), p. 1.

[2] Madhu S. Prakash and Gustavo Esteva, *Grassroots Postmodernism: Remaking the Soil of Cultures* (London: Zed, 1998).

[3] That does not prevent political parties of all hues from maintaining their own secret data bases on castes for electoral purposes. However, these are not accessible to outsiders.

Virtually every community has its 'history' of struggle and believes it to be the best, if not in the world, certainly in Cochin. Every community also has its own hierarchy of communities, in which it places the others according to a remembered or mythic past. Each community sees some communities as good, others as bad. There are also, in many cases, apparently historicized memories of how other communities and one's own have fought in the past. Even these memories do not lead to impassioned hatred. The Jews and the Syrian Christians talk disdainfully about the Portuguese and their fanatic Catholicism, not about the Catholic communities that trace their origins to the Portuguese. The Konkanis talk of an attack on their temple by a king of Cochin, not of the hostility of any community. One comes to suspect that most memories of communal strife are props to a community's self-esteem and self-definition rather than stereotypes having murderous implications. Whether they can be used at some point to mobilize communities against each other remains an open question.[4]

There is little defensive search for purity in the communities of Cochin either. Probably because they have not sensed threats to their lifestyles and are culturally self-confident, they can borrow from each other with fewer inhibitions. Fort Cochin has mosques that are hundreds of years old and share the region's distinctive ancient style of Hindu temple architecture and sacred decorative designs; there are synagogues so unique that at least one has been dismantled and rebuilt by a Malabari Jewish community near Jerusalem: it has become a tourist attraction there.

During the last few centuries, Cochin seems to have thrived on the checks and counter-checks provided by its low-key communal loves and hates. Having stereotypes and disliking other communities, yet granting

---

[4] Perhaps this is not unique to Cochin; it has only been patterned and institutionalised in a somewhat unique fashion there. Compare, for instance the autobiographical account of the well-known New York designer, Anita Lobel, *No Pretty Pictures—A Child of War* (New York: Greenwillow, 1998). Lobel is a Polish Jew who, along with her brother, was protected during the war years by her Polish Christian nanny who, at the same time, was anti-Semitic. In the Sri Lankan context, Michael Roberts has argued against the 'simplistic argument' that a cosmopolitanism or cultural diversity cannot coexist within chauvinism and xenophobia. See Michael Roberts 'Prejudice and Hate in Pluralist Settings: The Kingdom of Kandy', paper presented at the Neelan Tiruchelvan Commemoration Programme, Colombo, 30 January–1 February, 2000. But it may be as simplistic to believe that cultural likes and dislikes and ethnocentrism automatically lead to xenophobic or rabid nationalist violence.

them a place in the sun and even the right to dislike and keep distance from one's own community, is obviously one of the building blocks of Cochin's version of cultural plurality. Hardboiled social scientists claim that three factors have contributed to Cochin's historic communal harmony. First, there has been trade, especially in spice, fishing, coir, and shipbuilding. Trade has made communities inter-dependent on each other; none can do without the others. Second, there has been a common language. Almost everyone speaks Malayalam in Cochin—from the European-looking white Jew to the language-conscious Tamilian. Even the smattering of white, former colonial bureaucrats or businesspersons who have stayed back in Cochin know the language. Third, Cochin is located in a part of India that is highly literate, urbanised and secular. Many like to see its communal peace as a triumph of modernity over an atavistic past.

While these factors might have played an important role in Cochin's civic culture, none seems an adequate interpretation. For economic interdependence means that each community has specialised in certain enterprises or professions. They are, therefore, badly represented in other kinds of jobs and professions. As we know from the experiences of other parts of India, this by contemporary standards is not 'real' equality. Ideally, in a modern fully individualised society, each community must be well represented in all sectors; or else dedicated ethnic chauvinists will exploit the under-representation of a community in some sectors of the economy. Similar situations have led to much bitterness and demands for affirmative action elsewhere. Likewise, instances of communal violence between two groups that speak the same language but are divided by caste or religion abound in India. India's worst communal riots took place at Punjab and Bengal, at the time of partition, between communities that were parts of the same culture and linguistic group. And education, industrialisation and urbanisation, combined with secularisation, have often stoked communal strife, instead of containing it. A huge majority of communal riots in India have taken place in large cities, despite three-fourths of Indians living in villages. The fear of losing one's faith can be a destructive force in a secularising world; it can hand over entire communities to venomous identity politics.

One will have to search elsewhere for the sources of Cochin's tradition of alternative cosmopolitanism and cultural pluralism. This paper represents such a search and should be read more as the diary of a personal, cultural-psychological journey rather than as professional ethnography.

The search is not grounded in history. It rejects history as a guide to the 169
'living past' of Cochin. The only kind of history considered relevant here
is the clinician's idea of case history, where the past is configured as an
immediate, felt reality—indeed as a part of the psychodynamics of health
and ill-health. In this instance I have focussed mainly on the perceived
sources of health in the remembered or fantasised past. There must be
other pasts of Cochin, but I leave it to others to excavate them. For me,
an exhaustive, fully objective pathological report usually comes in the
form of a post-mortem, not diagnosis or prognosis.

I

Cochin is one of three cities on the Malabar Coast—the other two
being Calicut and Mangalore—traditionally known as places where
West Asia, Europe, Africa, Southeast Asia and China meet. In the self-
definition of its citizens, Cochin's territoriality has two dimensions,
one land-based, the other determined by the traditional sea routes
converging at the city. As we were to find out, to many Cochinis, the
city is only apparently located in one corner of India, in the small state
of Kerala. To them it is at the centre of the Indian Ocean, presiding over
the memories of these sea routes, and of a once-flourishing, spice trade.
To these Cochinis, West Asia, parts of East Africa and Southeast Asia
often seem, defying their own nationalist sentiments, psychologically
closer than Delhi.[5]

Cochin is not a large city by Indian standards, though it is the largest
in Kerala. The population, according to the 1991 census, is a little over
1.14 million. *The District Gazetteer* says that nearly 95 per cent of the
residents are literate. Literacy is higher among women than among men.[6]
Cochin City is in the Ernakulum district, one of the smallest in India
(with a population of roughly 30 million). This leads to some confusion,
for Ernakulum city is now, for all practical purposes, a part of Cochin

---

[5] This is probably true not only of Cochin but of a number of cities of the
region. At this point, I shall also put on record my debt to Amitav Ghosh,
whose brilliant ethnographic novel, *In an Antique Land* (London: Granta Books,
1992), has been a source of my insights into the civic culture of the cities on the
Malabar Coast.
[6] S.C. Bhat (ed.), *The Encyclopaedia District Gazetteer of India: Southern Zone* (New
Delhi: Gyan Publishing House, 1997), vol. 2, pp. 727–41. Recent reports say
that the entire district is now 100 per cent literate.

[right margin, vertical text] Time Travel to a Possible Self

city, which itself was, until fifty years ago, part of a princely state, also called Cochin.[7]

Though the traditional spice trade survives, Cochin's economy now depends heavily on the coir industry and the shipyard. But, as will gradually become evident from this story, the spice trade—and the myths and fantasies surrounding it—define the city. Cochin without the spice trade is no Cochin. One of the characters in a Salman Rushdie novel, progeny of a family of spice traders, turns the link into a grander if comic vision:

> the pepper, if you please; for if it had not been for peppercorns, then what is ending now in East and West might never have begun ... we were 'not so much sub-continent as sub-condiment', as my distinguished mother had it. 'From the beginning, what the world wanted from bloody mother India was daylight-clear,' she'd say. 'They came for the hot stuff, just like any man calling on a tart.'[8]

Cochin lies in a particularly green part of India, though industries and urban growth have begun to take their toll. Despite its high population density, most visitors to the city are struck not so much by its civic structures and narrow, crowded streets as by the omnipresence of water and greenery. Quiet waterways and rich tropical lushness temper the sudden ferocity of heat and humidity that one faces when emerging from a plane. The small, humble airport, unable to cope with the new international stature given to it by the Malayali propensity to globetrot, complements that impression. It is built on the sparsely populated, thickly green Wellington Island, which the British artificially created during the high noon of the raj. The island strengthens the image of a large city that magically retains the touch of a tropical village.

There are various explanations of the name Cochin. Some say it is a derivative of 'Kochi', the name of a river nearby. Others claim Chinese settlers gave the city its name. There are other theories. It is possible that the name has meant different things at different points of time; it certainly means different things to different communities in the city. Even the geography of Cochin seems to change, depending on the person one is talking with. Some mean Cochin state when they talk of Cochin; others mean the present city, including Ernakulum; still others mean mainly Mattancherry or the area around Fort Cochin.

---

[7] Actually, each informant seems to have his or her own view of geographical Cochin, perhaps because the Cochin of imagination transcends cartography and official boundaries.

[8] Salman Rushdie, *The Moor's Last Sigh* (London: Jonathan Cape, 1995), pp. 4–5.

The official past of Cochin is well known and does not need 171 repetition. It is part of the history of the Malabar coast that, in the pre-colonial and early colonial period, Cochin played a central role in the world of the Indian ocean, with its crisscrossing sea routes connecting cultures, histories and geographies.[9] The erstwhile princely state of Cochin was a small state of about 1,400 square miles, with a population of around 25 million. Cochin's royal house, Perampadappu Swarupam, had its original capital at Vanneri. It moved to Mahodayapur in Cranganore in the late thirteenth century, after an attack by the Zamorin, the ruler of Calicut. Cochin became the capital of the Cochin State in 1405. Others say that Cochin became important only after the Portuguese came to India; the Portuguese saga in Cochin began when Vasco da Gama landed near Calicut in 1498. Cochin's kings were friendly towards the new immigrants, who gradually turned Cochin from a fishing town into an important commercial centre. The Portuguese were also enthusiastic builders. They built forts, churches and European style houses in the city. When the Dutch won control of Cochin from the Portuguese in 1663, they also turned out to be eager builders. Fort Cochin still has a large number of houses that are Dutch in style and distinguishable from other buildings. Despite the proliferation of standardized, tasteless structures, often built by newly rich Malayalis with a West Asian connection, these parts of Cochin still remain distinctive and identifiable. In 1795 the British wrested control of the city from the Dutch, but they did not interfere much with either the indigenous lifestyle or the Dutch political order.

Though historical Cochin is remembered mainly as a centre of the spice trade by many, it was also known for its shipbuilding facilities, which the Portuguese turned into an important trade. Some say that shipbuilding around Cochin began as early as the Sangham period, at Cranganore. The Dutch further developed these facilities. In independent India, too, Cochin continues to be a major shipyard: only, the Indian Navy now dominates the facilities. The Jews of Cochin played an important role in ship building during the Dutch period (1663–1795).

Official history, however, is not the last word in Cochin. There are shared memories, partly mythical, of Chinese fishermen and seafarers

---

[9] For a proper history of that part of the story, see Sanjay Subrahmanyam, *The Career and Legend of Vasco da Gama* (New Delhi: Cambridge University Press, 1997).

who inhabited Cochin till the fourteenth century. The Arabs reportedly defeated the Chinese and settled down in the city. These memories also claim that Cochin was cosmopolitan and international even before the Portuguese came. Many residents know that early European accounts talk of Cochin being a small fishing village next to the river Kochi (in Malayalam 'small place'), but many of them also know that the Sanskrit *Kerala Mahatmyam* already called it Balapuri, 'a small town'. While admitting that early travellers did not mention Cochin in their chronicles, some Cochinis point out that Ma-Huan, a Chinese Muslim was the first to mention the city in AD 1409. That was before Cochin became a 'proper' port. These memories are kept alive by popular 'histories' of Cochin, which sometimes confirm the memories, sometimes not, but always stoke a reactive return to unofficial memories.[10]

Particularly important in this context is Cochin's remembered historical geography, which includes elements crucial to its psychogeography. For instance, we are told that 'oceanic convulsions' in the fourteenth century turned Cochin into a safe natural harbour and threw up the Vypin Island. Previously, a small river near Cochin opened into the sea; the floods of AD 1341 created Cochin as we know it today. That creation shapes Cochin's self-definition even today.

People do not look at Cochin as an eternal city, in the way they look at Varanasi, Ujjain and Delhi. However, such memories do push the beginning of the history of Cochin as far back as possible, almost into a prehistoric mythic past. In that past a series of immigrant communities play an important part—as refugees fleeing from oppression, natural calamities and war. They brought to Cochin their distinctive skills in

[10] We met at the office of historian K.A. Kareem, the Secretary of the Kerala History Association, two local Christians, both highly educated professionals: Dr A. Noble, a retired government scientist, and Colonel K.I. Thomas, formerly of the Indian army. They were researching the historical roots of their family. They claimed that they had learnt from their elders that, when Tipu Sultan attacked the Jewish Kingdom at Cranganore and began a massacre, 10,000 Jews ran away and converted to Christianity. Our newly found acquaintances claimed they were the descendants of two such converted families. Kareem, a polite leftist, patiently explained to them that historical records showed that no such incident had taken place. The visitors did not look particularly happy but appeared convinced by these words of reason. Later, when we interviewed them at their homes, they were back to their original version of the story. One of them hinted that Kareem might have denied the story because he was a closet fundamentalist.

business, craft or art. These refugees—or *abhayarthis*, as the Konkani-
speaking Cochinis call them—have played an important role in Cochin's
well being and there are memories of local kings even quarrelling among
themselves for the privilege of having them as subjects. Perhaps these
memories give certain strength, resilience, and legitimacy to Cochin's
pre-modern culture, increasingly under threat from the quick urban
growth taking place in the city. Its residents like to see Cochin as a
place where the new has never defeated the old and is, in fact, parasitic
on the old.

The Two Wings of Mythic Cochin

However, sharable public memories are not the whole story. There
are also tacit memories, constituting an identifiable, communicable
'unconsciousness'.[11] It took me many months to find out that beneath the
social reality called Cochin there was also a mythic entity that went by
the same name. That other Cochin is not openly recognised in Cochin's
public life or its public self-reflection. Thanks to the long exposure to the
mechanical, state-centric, positivist cultures of Leninism and Nehruvian
socialism, to many sectors of Kerala's society, the mythic Cochin means
only a false, unreal Cochin—a collection of superstitions, stereotypes,
and surviving symbols of a lost 'golden' age. The mythic Cochin is the
opposite of the historical Cochin; it is what Cochin is not.

Only gradually does one realise that the mythic Cochin is at least as
important as the historic Cochin if one wants to grasp the city's culture
today. In many respects, the former is the heart of Cochin, for Cochin's
traditional cosmopolitanism lives to the extent that the mythic Cochin
lives. The city's political culture is organised around that city of the mind.
The day that phantom city dies, Cochin will die and become like any
other small South Asian city trying desperately to become a standard
metropolis.

[11] Elsewhere, I have called this a secret self, to distinguish it from the standard,
Freudian unconscious. The presumption is that the secrecy is imposed, in this
instance by categories associated with dominance, but is also partly internalised.
As a result, the socialised self learns to keep double ledgers, one for public or
official consumption, the other for private moments or for transmission as
unofficial memories or creation of contraband histories. This paper suggests
that not merely individuals but even communities sometimes have their secret
selves. See Ashis Nandy, *The Savage Freud and Other Essays on Possible and Retrievable
Selves* (New Delhi: Oxford University Press, 1995), pp. 53–80 and 81–144.

It is, however, not easy to identify the components of mythic Cochin. Many of them are probably inaccessible to outsiders, particularly if they do not speak any Malayalam. Not as it always possible to separate the private or tacit from the mythic or the unconscious. I have already mentioned how the co-ordinates of geographical Cochin are not merely land based but, perhaps in more important ways, also defined by the traditional sea routes to Cochin. One suspects that the latter is mainly tacit knowledge, part of the everyday wisdom within Cochinis, though never entirely acknowledged as such in school texts. But that does not make it a form of disowned aspect of the self. The first component of the disowned Cochin of the mind, though, is easy to identify. Cochin is a direct progeny and heir to the mythic epicentre of the Kerala society—Cranganore. Cranganore had to die—as a harbour, a habitat and the cultural capital of Kerala and Malabar—for Cochin to be created in 1341. People talk about the 'oceanic convulsions' that silted up and made Cranganore port unusable and created the Vypin Island and the natural harbour at Cochin as if the convulsions were the birth pangs of a unique city. The disaster that killed the former was the same one that created Cochin. The city not only has two histories, one realistic and the other fantastic, it also lives with two geographies; even physically, the city's past is part of a larger map of the mind.

Cranganore seems to have many names. It is also known as Kodungalloor. In earlier times it was also known as Muziris and in Tamil as Muchiri. It is not merely a sleepy city to the north of Cochin that once had a glorious past; Cranganore is the mythic capital of mythic Kerala and mythic Malabar. In the minds of many, it is still the first city of Kerala. The Malayali public consciousness and self-definition inextricably centre on that lost city. Unless you are talking to historians, everything began at Cranganore. Even the famous spice trade—mainly involving cardamom, cinnamon, ginger and the black gold, pepper—began at Cranganore. Some Cochinis make it a point to remember that, as early as in the first century, Pliny the Elder (AD 23–79) had grumbled about the drain on the wealth of the Roman empire due to heavy purchase of a 'useless' commodity, pepper, from Muziris. Others point out that in AD 403 Alaric the Goth lifted his siege of Rome reportedly in exchange for 3000 pounds of pepper-purchased from, where else, but Muziris.

Most communities link their remembered pasts to Cranganore. The Jews trace their origin to the city, so do some communities of Muslims, who talk of the city as one of the early bastions of Islam. Some of the most sacred texts of Tamilian Hinduism, especially Shaiva Siddhanta, are supposed to have been written at Cranganore. Christians, too, seem eager to point out that St Thomas landed at Cranganore in AD 52. No popular history is complete unless you have somehow related it to something that has happened some time in Cranganore. Though some members of Cochin's erstwhile royal family speak of the consolidation of the Cochin Kingdom as a slow and laborious process that lasted decades, in popular genealogy the dynasty emerged in a fully formed fashion at Mahodayapur at Cranganore.

So, we are told, did the city's religious and ethnic tolerance. Cranganore remains the ultimate symbol of Cochin's ecumenism. Balagopalakrishna Menon, a successful lawyer who has been close to the Cochin royalty for more than five decades, not only endorses the widely shared image of the mythic capital of Kerala and Malabar when he talks of the Cheraman Masjid at Cranganore. He claims that it is the world's only mosque that faces east because it was a temple that was allowed to be converted into a mosque by Cheraman Peruman, the legendary king of Kerala, a contemporary of Adi Shankara in the eighth century.

Why do all journeys begin from Cranganore? What is the magic of the city? One part of the answer is that Cranganore was a thriving port until 'natural calamities'—in some stories a flood, in others an earthquake—destroyed it. Others talk of 'the mysterious Malabar mud-banks' that moved inshore to clog the mouth of the river Periyar to end the long career of Muziris as a port that the Phoenicians, Egyptians, Persians, Chinese, Romans and Arabs frequented. In Cochini imagination, Cochin is the rebirth of that dead, ancient, cultural 'capital' of Kerala and, unless one knows about Cranganore, one cannot be expected to fathom its reincarnated version. Cranganore is the clue to Cochin's *karmic* past.

The Jewish synagogue at Fort Cochin, for instance, has a panel of paintings that depicts the Jewish journey through time at Cochin. This too begins at Cranganore. Only, for some unknown reason, the Jews call the city Shingly. It tells how the Jews not only saved themselves from a flood and an invasion, but also how its Jewish king escaped to safety in Cochin, according to one respondent by swimming with his Torah and the wife on his back and his people on his side. It is impossible to tell the Jewish story of Cochin without the Jewish construction of Cranganore and the small Jewish principality that once existed there.

The 'memories' of Cranganore are often bittersweet. Even among the Jews, the story of a unique Jewish kingdom is bordered by the myth of how Cranganore's first 800 Jewish settlers, under the leadership of a rather formidable widow called Kadambath-Achi, were doing well till the king's son fell in love with her daughter. As Ruby Daniel tells the story, the widow refused to marry her daughter to a gentile prince who, pining for the daughter, fell ill. The angry king ordered the Jews out of his kingdom and they ran away. The widow and her daughter stayed back to grind their jewellery and precious stones into powder, throw them into a pool, and commit suicide by swallowing diamonds. The pool is still called Jutha Kulam (Jewish pool) and the hill nearby Jutha Kunna (Jewish hill). 'People living there still say they sometimes find tiny pieces of gold in the sand of that pool. The memories of the Jews at Cranganore also survive in Malayali songs and stories. More 'realistic' are the stories about being expelled from Cranganore by the Portuguese and the Moors, which scattered the Jewish communities to places such as Mala, Chendamangalam, and Parur.

**

The story of the dead city of Cranganore, now surviving as an inconsequential district town with a magical past and serving as the underside of the story of the living city of Cochin, is incomplete without the story of the Cochin kings. The memories of its kings constitute the other pivot of mythic Cochin. After long lectures on feudalism, caste domination, and the oppressive ways of religious life, informants began to speak, diffidently and defensively, about the Cochin kings as the source of most things that are adorable in Cochin's culture. These kings helped communities to settle down in Cochin, ensured their security, and gave them a sense of participation in civic life. Though dynastic rule ended fifty years ago and royal privileges were abolished, the Maharajas of Cochin continue to preside over the minds of the Cochinis. This is a different kind of rule; most people do not even know the names of the members of the erstwhile royal family. But the family's contributions to the culture of the city remain alive in the minds of people, the same way they always come back to Cranganore.

Two caveats, at this point. First, the contradictions or inconsistencies in dates, figures and events in the following pages have been deliberately retained as parts of the narratives with which the people of Cochin live. Second, for the moment I have chosen the witnesses arbitrarily, only to flesh out the arguments already made and to hint at a few of the cultural-psychological principles of Cochin's ecumenism.

It is not easy to construct the story of Cochin by talking to its inhabitants; for, the past of Cochin has been aggressively historicized during the last fifty years. Like Gujarat and West Bengal, Kerala has undergone a middle-class revolution in recent years. Not only do cities now dominate the landscape of the state, differences between the village and the city are no longer sharp. Both have been heavily infiltrated by textbook-based, politically correct, stereotypes inspired by some rather crude, tropicalized versions of left-Hegelian European thought of the 1930s. It has become difficult to get private narratives reflecting much privacy or personal feelings.

At first, all witnesses seem brainwashed to believe in the right values and Cochin's cosmopolitanism seems to be a triumph of secularism, rationalism, high literacy, the rudiments of a welfare state, Indian nationalism, urbanity and egalitarianism. If one is to trust these witnesses, these values seem to have entered Cochini society in the early medieval period, if not earlier, uncannily before they were formally launched as parts of the Enlightenment project in South Asia, under the auspices of a series of colonial regimes. All Cochinis, in the beginning, seem to speak the same language, cite the same examples, and seem equally proud of Cochin's multiculturalism and 'perfect' communal harmony. As the ideological strands associated with [the] culture of the Indian state exercise lesser control over the life stories and memories of the interviewees, a slightly different set of categories take over. And one finds with some surprise that most Cochinis have a partly shared, quasi-private theory of what makes Cochin tick. Only gradually do they come out with personal experiences and family histories that are no ordinary histories but emotionally laden constructions of the city's past, transmitted over generations. They are first offered hesitantly, almost as skeletons in the family cupboard. Only after a while do some interviewees acknowledge them up as unofficial narratives, with which they 'partially agree'. In these narratives other communities, and, even parts of one's own community, emerge as scheming villains, conquerors, victims, traitors, friends, enemies and protectors. There are moving stories of how one's own community survived and grew through its ingenuity, courage, cunning, and sometimes with the help of other communities. Cutting across ideological lines, however, the city itself always emerges as the hero.

The First Family of Cochin

The concept of 'feudalism', when mechanically imported and indiscriminately applied to pre-colonial structures and experiences in

South Asia, often hides more than it reveals. In its decontextualized forms, it can even sometimes begin to underscore a self-serving, blinkered analyses of structures of authority that are unfamiliar and outside the range of one's own culture. Examined closely, these 'feudal' authorities often turn out to have enjoyed lesser privileges and standards of living than those enjoyed by their fire-eating critics adorning the academe, the press, and policy-making bodies, and passing casual summary judgements on entire ways of life and eras of history.

Thus, the Dutch Palace at Mattanchery in Cochin, the former residence of the Cochin kings and a favourite of tourists, looks more like an enormous, pretentious home of a village landlord. A successful businessperson in contemporary India will not want to be caught dead in it. It exudes considerably less opulence and comfort than even the homes of many who write fiery prose on the evils of feudalism. The royal temple adjacent to the palace, too, is a modest affair. Cochinis, however, are proud of both, for the Cochin kings are remembered with much reverence and fondness by their now-liberated subjects.[12]

The royal dynasty or Perumpadappu Swarupam is predictably Kshatriya. But they brought to their style of governance a touch of Brahminic austerity and self-denial. (As we shall see, some of their former subjects believe them to be Brahmins.) Indeed, almost all the members of the family I contacted referred to themselves as 'poor kings,' known for their piety and scholarship.

There are, it is said, 800 to 900 members of the royal family in Cochin itself; 716 members share the family estate. Though traditionally matrilineal, the family has acquired a touch of primogeniture in recent decades. Its religious identity, too, has

---

[12] Years ago, freedom fighter and alternative historian Dharampal told me of a letter from a viceroy he discovered in the India Office Library in London. In it, the viceroy complained that the Maharana of Udaipur, the doyen of Rajput principalities, did not know how to live in kingly dignity; nor did the British in India know how to treat their friends and allies. The viceroy grumbled that the Maharana received a monthly stipend of only Rs. 3000 from his own treasury. Of this, about half was spent on commensal lunches; every day hundreds of ordinary peasants came and ate with the Maharana. The viceroy recommended that the stipend be increased to Rs. 3000 per day. This was duly done. At first, nothing changed; only the number of peasants at lunch increased. However, in another generation and half, inter-dining had stopped and the dynasty had begun to show many of the 'classical' signs of feudal decadence including flamboyant, mindless consumption and wastage.

undergone subtle changes. Like most ruling Kshatriya families, it is technically Shaivaite; the family deity at Pazhayannur, Trichur, is an incarnation of the goddess Bhagawati. The temple, said to be an *Arjuna pratisthan* (that is, established by Arjuna, the hero of Mahabharata), is at some distance from Cochin. Previously, blood sacrifices used to be offered at the temple. Now, as a symbol of those days, cocks are flown from the temple. At some time, however, the Cochin kings have acquired the looks of a Vaishnava family. The deity in the family temple at Tripunithura, Sri Purnathrayeesa, is Vishnu.

Kerala Varma Thampuran, one of the four members of the family with whom we talked, is a cousin of the last king of Cochin, Pareekshit Varma.[13] The king was a scholar in Sanskrit and English; his cousin is an unassuming journalist and a former captain of the first batch of Cochin State Forces. Raised in the 1940s as the Nair Brigade, it was later integrated into the Indian army. The Brigade's name was changed in 1945 when the maharaja, Aikya Kerala Varma—so named because of his willingness to relinquish his throne to help the cause of India's unity or *aikya*—allowed other castes to join it. Kerala Varma has seen action in World War II. He also was on garrison duty at Mhow, Madhya Pradesh, where he looked after Italian prisoners of war. Afterwards, he managed for a while his brother-in-law's large rubber plantation. He could not manage it well, he admits, and it had to be sold.

Kerala Varma is now seventy-eight, but does not look it. He is slim, erect and projects self-assurance. With his white moustache, touch of army manners, his *vesti* and plastic sandals, he looks more like a retired petty army officer than an erstwhile prince. Actually, he identifies himself as a journalist. He is friendly and helpful and, after talking with me at some length, took me to meet some other members of his family nearby. He seems for some reason to be the obvious choice as a spokesperson for the family. A number of persons suggested that we meet him. . . .

Our interviewee's colourful past, though, belies his appearance. A leftist and a modernist, Kerala Varma has fought elections with the support of Communist party of India. He also was the architect of the late

[13] In the Cochin dynasty, the first three sons usually have the following names: Rama Varma, Kerala Varma, and Ravi Varma, though there are odd exceptions. The king who gave up his kingdom to join the Indian Union was named Aikya Kerala Varma because of his commitment to Indian unity; another king had come to be known posthumously as Madras Thampuran; he had died in Madras.

V.K. Krishna Menon's victory in an election to Parliament in the 1950s.

Menon, Jawaharlal Nehru's controversial friend and confidant, contested for Trivandrum; at the time, Menon presided over India's foreign office. 'I am a communist,' Kerala Varma blandly declares. He hastens to correct the 'general impression' that his entire family is communist. There are other shades of political opinion in the family; some are supporters of the Indian National Congress. Others supported the Gandhian freedom movement before Independence.

It soon becomes obvious that Kerala Varma tries hard to see the world through his ideology. The strain shows. Like some others in his family, he is obviously ambivalent towards his origins and one can detect a touch of defensiveness towards his family. To him, time is basically an evolutionary unfolding of hierarchical and more liberal social practices. He remembers his childhood mainly as days of unmitigated conservatism, when he and his brothers went to school on horseback, sit separately from other children, and were often surrounded by bodyguards. In sum, he almost grudges the fact that he was brought up as a prince. (In practice that means that, after the fourth grade, he was in a special school. That school was evidently special in more than one sense. It even had a Hebrew teacher though there were only three or four Jewish boys in the school.) The Cochin royalty, he also adds, was more conservative than the Travancore one. The family had at first opposed the entry of the lower castes into the palace temple. Only in 1950 did the Sri Purnathrayeesa temple allow the entry of low castes. This was despite the fact that, in the family, the males customarily married Shudras or low castes and the women Namboodiri Brahmins. (The family never marries within itself, because it traces its origins to two sisters.)

Gradually, as we continue talking, Kerala Varma becomes less self-aware and begins to talk more freely. He is unhappy that E.M.S. Namboodiripad, the communist politician and a former chief minister of Kerala, has called Aikya Kerala Varma a counterfeit coin and a hypocrite. He feels vindicated by the admiration that another communist chief minister, C. Achyuta Menon, had for the king. Kerala Varma now warms up to the subject and begins to talk about his family's ecumenism with a touch of pride. He points out that though people usually notice the synagogue close to the Dutch palace, there is also a mosque close by. He claims that ecumenism has coloured the personal lives of some of his ancestors and relatives. The first Hindu-Christian marriage in the family took place around 1990. One member of the family married a lowly Puleya at around the same time. He mentions the case of a relative,

Gopalika, who was trained as an Arabic teacher. When she, a Brahmin, was appointed in a Muslim school in Malapuram, there was strong opposition; she was made to resign. However, there was even greater opposition to that injustice and she was given her job back in 1987, during the Left Front rule. Islam comes back to the royal family in insidious ways. . . .

Venkitangu Jairaman supplies some of the missing notes to Kerala Varma's story. Jairaman is an art critic, writer and a journalist. He is fifty-four and has been writing in the *Indian Express* for years. Slim, bespectacled, with closely cropped greying hair, white shirt, a sandalwood mark on forehead and *vesti*, he look likes any other upper-caste Malayali. 'My father belonged to the royal family; I do not,' he said, probably hinting at the matrilinear traditions in his family. He has mostly been an independent writer, but has worked in a press for a while. He writes mainly on classical Carnatic music, theatre and paintings. He chose to meet me at a hotel, perhaps to spare me the problem of locating his house in the crowded city centre.

Like many others, Jairaman starts by saying that Cochin is a loveable city. It has retained a touch of its 'semi-urban', 'semi-pastoral' past and can be habit-forming; 'those who come to the city do not go back'. As a result, the older residents of Cochin are becoming a minority. Other cities are not like that, Jairaman insists. Trichur, another cultural centre of Kerala nearby, is meant for Trichuris; Cochin is for everyone. Jairaman traces this openness to Cochin's erstwhile monarchs. They were 'pious and Spartan'. They 'never amassed wealth' and were 'perfectly secular'. For these qualities, they were 'considered foolish by others'. Yet these qualities explain why they have survived the demise of the princely order. They can live within their means because their needs are few. Their emphasis on education has also helped. The entire family, including the women, are well educated. Today, all royal women are employed and almost all are college graduates. No royal family in India enjoys this advantage.

The family, because it was born from two sisters, was previously strictly exogamous. Now endogamy is not unknown to it. 'The texture of the family' has changed. There is much more intimacy within the family, Jairaman believes. In this respect, too, the family is different from the Travancore royalty. According to Jairaman, the looser family ties in the latter case are a legacy of Martanda Varma, the warrior-king of Travancore.

Jairaman moves on to an aspect of Cochin rarely talked about: its contribution to the arts, especially music. He points out that T.N. Krishnan, N. Rajan, L. Subrahmanyam are all from Cochin. The city has produced a large number of musicians and artists, less due to royal patronage than to royal openness to the new and the strange. Unlike other Indian princes, the Cochin kings never directly patronized music, nor did they produce anyone like Swathi Thirunnal, the king of Travancore who renounced everything to write devotional lyrics and compose music. But the Cochin kings had that crucial ecumenical attitude—'anything that came up, they allowed'. Cochin flourished culturally as a result. The family can even take credit for innovating the game of one-day cricket some fifty years before it was formally launched in world cricket.

Because the kings were liberal, Jairaman says, the people were also liberal. Cochin's 'soil has not been a fertile place for fundamentalism or communal riots'. This liberalism of the kings came from their piety. Foreigners were often 'at first taken aback by the simplicity and piety of the kings'. It is said that once, on the occasion of an eight-day ritual feast at the family temple, someone found out that systematic theft of foodstuff was taking place and complained to the maharaja. The maharaja took it calmly; he said that it was a good way for the consecrated food, *prasadam*, to reach a larger circle of people. Sadly, others interpreted such piety and tolerance as weakness. V.P. Menon swooned when the Cochin maharajah only asked for an almanac and a hand-fan in return for joining the Indian Union and giving up his royal privileges and rights.[14]

The same attitude of openness informed other areas of political action. When some members of the family turned anti-British in colonial days, no one interfered; it was seen as of their personal ethics. Once, during World War I, one king even had to abdicate because of his differences with the British: 'They were not supine or invertebrate, despite their piety,' Jairaman says. Probably this is his reaction to the feeling that exists even close to the family—that while the Zamorins courageously fought

---

[14] The belief is widespread that invaders often took advantage of the naive tolerance of the Cochin kings. According to Noble, the scientist researching the Jewish roots of his family, the Portuguese took full advantage of the religious tolerance of the ruling family to introduce religious chauvinism in Cochin. They destroyed the churches and sacred objects of Syrian Christians and harassed the Jews.

the Portuguese, the Dutch and the English, the Cochin's kings, like their counterparts in Travancore, 'adjusted' to changing realities.

The Jewish Diaspora

There are two main Jewish communities in Cochin: the white Jews and the Black or Malabari Jews. The latter are also known as Myuchasims. 'Black' and 'white' are terms the Cochinis and the communities themselves use; there is no defensiveness associated with them. In recent decades, however, subtle changes have crept into these self-definitions. As the Jews themselves have become a major symbol of Cochin's multiculturalism, the two main Jewish communities have simultaneously come closer and moved further away. Of the two communities, the black Jews claim to have a hoarier past, but the white Jews are the more conspicuous presence. That, too, is a source of a minor tension now; some black Jews feel that the white Jews are separating themselves from others; this they never did in the past.[15]

Even before the founding of a proper Jewish settlement and, later, a Jewish kingdom in Cranganore, Jewish oral traditions claim that Jews were in Malabar, in and around Cochin. Since the time of King Solomon, some of them say, they traded in gold, ivory, sandalwood, peacock feathers, and, of course, spices. This old connection is said to have encouraged the settlement of Jews after the destruction of the second temple and, in another wave, around 1000 AD. This was when full rights were given to them to settle in the area.

There might have been once a third community, the Meshuhrarim, literally 'freed slaves'. Much less is known about this, though a charming autobiography gives clues to their lifestyle.[16] We have not met anyone who admits being a Mushuhrarim; all of them might have by now migrated to Israel. In any case, it is a controversial category; some deny that such a community existed at all. We also heard of a few Baghdadi Jews who were at Cochin once, but they were individuals and families brought to the city mainly by work. Most of them migrated to Britain soon after independence. However, the most famous Baghdadi Jewish

---

[15] Some accounts suggest that the tension between the two Jewish communities was a gift of colonialism and the politics of colour. See, for example, Ruby Daniel and Barbara C. Johnson, *Ruby of Cochin: An Indian Jewish Woman Remembers* (Philadelphia and Jerusalem: The Jewish Publication Society), 1995.
[16] Ibid.

family in India, the Sassoons, established a more enduring connection with the city; one of the Sassoons married into Fort Cochin's most illustrious Jewish family, the Koders.

According to Samuel Halegua, the acknowledged leader of the community, at the moment there are about twenty families of white Jews left in Fort Cochin and thirty-four families of black Jews in Ernakulam. He says that in Cochin region, there are eight synagogues, two of them in Ernakulam. The Paradesi synagogue at Fort Cochin is the most famous of them. It is the oldest synagogue in the British Commonwealth.

We first met Samuel Halegua when he made a presentation at a meeting of community leaders at Cochin. He was introduced there as a leader of the city's Jewish community. He made an excellent and, in many ways, moving presentation on the history, experiences, and concerns of the Cochin Jews.

Later on, we met him, his wife Queenie, and a few others from his community, including Joseph Halegua, the sexton of the synagogue. Samuel Halegua is sixty-six but looks much younger. He is self-confident and articulate. Like some others in his community, he has the looks of a Southern European, but unlike some others cannot pass off as a North Indian. Though he does not say so, he began as mainly a leader of white Jews of Cochin who, according to some, came to India as late as in the thirteenth century. With the dwindling population of Jews, he has almost automatically become the main spokesperson of the city's Jews.[17] While talking to us, he shifts between the white Jews, all Cochin Jews (including the Malabari Jews) and Indian Jews; and the dates he mentions do not often sound right. However, as far as the Jewish history of India is concerned, he talks on behalf of all Jews and traces the origin of Judaism in India through its quasi-mythical history stretching two thousand years.

Samuel Halegua and Queenie stay in a large, modest but enchanting, two-storied house on the Jew Street, Fort Cochin. They are cousins and when they fell in love and married, their marriage was seen as a continuation of the long tradition of intermarriage between the Haleguas and the Koders, two of the most important families of Fort

[17] [Editor's Note: Samuel Hallegua passed away in 2009. For his obituary, see Vinay Lal, 'Cochin's Jews: History's Last Gasp—A Tribute to Samuel Hallegua (1930–2009)', *Journal of Indo-Judaic Studies*, no. 11 (2010), pp. 155–6.]

Cochin. The Halegua family has never had much to do with Cochin's famous spice trade; they have been mainly gentlemen-farmers. They still own some agricultural land, where they grow rice and coconuts. Some of his ancestors could be called merchant-princes. Samuel Halegua's grandfather brought electricity to Cochin and pioneered a highly profitable ferry service in the city. This gave employment to a number of Jews and the Jews usually travelled free on the ferries. The Cochin royalty valued the Haleguas; one in the family was given the title of Mudaliar (though the Levys produced the first Mudaliar among the Jews of Cochin). Evidently, the community did not put much emphasis on formal education the women in particular did not go in for higher education. Samuel's grandfather was the first to matriculate in the community, his aunt the first woman matriculate and graduate. Jewish society tends to be patriarchal, he adds almost apologetically.

Samuel and Queenie might have been brought up in an extended family-like environment, but now they have to live by themselves in a large house. Their children have migrated to Israel. But they continue to come back to Cochin every year, not merely to meet their parents but also to participate in various community festivals. The house the Haleguas live in is roughly 250 to 300 years old. It is on a narrow street, with a few well-stocked antique shops and a couple of small, attractive bookstores. The houses on the street are joined together by common walls. They all once belonged to Jews, but many have now been sold. Jew Street once had three synagogues, but only one, the Paradesi Synagogue, is still in use. It was constructed, Halegua tells us, in 1334.

Though well maintained, Halegua's home is not museumised. This is surprising, given his popularity among the scholars of Jewish history and anthropologists. There are a few artefacts that reflect the traditions of the house and the family, but they are not obtrusive. It looks very much the home of an easy, well-to-do, middle-class family in Kerala, with its usual touch of austerity and Edwardian charm. The language of Cochin Jews is Malayalam, and Halegua talks to his wife and the visitors who interrupt us in Malayalam. He calls it his mother tongue. It is a bit of a shock to some visitors to Cochin when they first hear two whites talking among themselves in Malayalam. However, Halegua speaks to us in fluent English. . . .

Halegua is proudly Jewish. Like many Cochin Jews, and unlike most Bene Israelis I have met, he carries a slight ambivalence towards Christianity.

Christ was born a Jew, and he lived and died a Jew, he says, but persecution and discrimination against Jews has been typical of Christian Europe. In Islamic countries they have been treated better. Though large parts of his family have settled in Israel, Halegua maintains a certain distance from present-day problems of the Israeli State. He is committed to Israel, but not blindly. He certainly does not sound like an Israeli nationalist. The distance may be due to the Israeli attitude towards the Arabs. He likes the Arabs because of their excellent past record of the treatment of Jews. This may also have something to do with Cochin's Arab connection.

Halegua is also a trifle distant from the conventional interpretations of the Holocaust. He has read much on the subject and, naturally, feels strongly about the genocide. But he has self-consciously tried not to be bitter. He finds it difficult to hate a 'whole nation' for the crimes of a regime and system. Apparently, in this respect, geographical distance and the Indian experiences have played a role. While the ideas of religious and ethnic hostility and violence have a place in his world, the industrialisation of homicide—the cattle trains and chimneys of the holocaust—remain alien to him. For that matter, he even found the 1984 riots against the Sikhs in Delhi 'unbelievable'.

Halegua is a proud Malabari and Indian too. 'I never wanted to live anywhere else,' he has more than once said. This is not merely nationalism; he is deeply attached to the Malabari, particularly Cochini Jewish traditions. His self-definition is that of a custodian of these traditions. They include everything from the distinctive liturgy and marriage rites of the region to the Jewish versions of pancake called pastelle, and hot chicken curry. They also seem to include his interest in cricket in football-crazy Kerala. He strongly disagrees with Hannah Arendt, whom he identifies as an 'American sociologist'. According to him, Arendt has argued that persecution and discrimination have ensured the survival of Jewish culture. 'Arendt is wrong', Halegua says. 'We have not been persecuted or discriminated against, yet we have retained our identity.'[18] He agrees with the news item published in a journal given to us by a resident of Cochin:

---

[18] He does not know that, living with the culture of Israeli politics, partly organized around competitive histories of discrimination, sections of the Cochin Jews in Israel seem to have developed a sense of loss for not having a 'proper' history of oppression. At least a few of them have invented a less peaceful history of the community at Cochin. Some expatriate Malabari Jews there spoke of harassment and discrimination against the Jews at Cochin. To the dismay of the

The only safe haven in the history of the Jewish Diaspora is disappearing ... India has been uniquely free from anti-Semitism ... According to oral history, Jews arrived in Shingly, Cochin, in the year of 72 (Common Era), shortly after the destruction of the Second Temple in Jerusalem. In the fourth century the Maharaja of Cochin granted them royal rights for 'as long as the world and the moon exist'.[19]

In 1492 the Jews were expelled from Spain, a few years after that from Portugal. But the Ottoman Empire welcomed them. The Halegua family came from Spain to Alleppo to India. It has always maintained close links with the Yemeni and Aden Jews. The Portuguese rule in Cochin, however, was a tough time for the Jews (AD 1505–1663). 'We have known religious intolerance only from the Portuguese,' Halegua says; the inquisition in India was crueller than that in Portugal. The Dutch rule between AD 1664–1773 was slightly better. The synagogue constructed in AD 1334 remains the centre of community life in Cochin. Halegua sometimes leads the prayers there. The Cochin kings used to visit the synagogues, often carrying gifts, another Jewish informant tells us; prayers were said for them there.

For Halegua the major problem of the Indian Jews is 'numbers'. Between 1950 and 1960 more than a thousand Jews left for Israel: that was the major exodus. Around 1700 and 1800 Jews were now left. Migrants return off and on to Cochin, mainly at festival times. All of them have 'strong attachments' to India, Halegua claims. There are between 4,000 to 5,000 Indian Jews in Israel. . . .

Malabari Jews, also known as the black Jews, are a shadowy presence for many scholars and historians who have studied the culture and history of Cochin's Jews. According to some accounts, fiercely disputed by others, Black Jews are freed slaves who were converted to Judaism and given a

---

anthropologist known for work on Indian Jews, who had taken me to meet the group, one of them talked with some relish about how St Thomas in the First century brought anti-Semitism to Kerala and precipitated a first-class conflict between the 'Jacobites' and the 'Catholics'.

[19] *Rotunda* 16 (1), December 1991. See also *Two Thousand Years of Freedom and Honor: The Cochin Jews of India*, Director: Johanna Spector (212), 666.9461. Halegua says that the Jews were given their rights in the Fourth century and the engraved copper plates, which formalised these rights, were given to them in the Fifth century. Others claim that the plates were actually given to the Cochin Jews in the Tenth century.

synagogue.[20] In the recent decades, White Jews have dominated the public imagination of the Cochin Jew. Self-confident and articulate, most White Jews also speak excellent English. Black Jews, on the other hand, give the impression of being ordinary, middle- and low-brow Cochinis. Yet, for that very reason, they have an especial place in the city's culture. White Jews are a part of Cochin's elite; the black Jews are the more accessible, everyday version. However, a slight resentment has grown among Black Jews towards White: not so much because of the latter's wealth, influence and social salience, but because of the feeling that, during the last fifty years or so, White Jews have tried to distinguish themselves from the Malabari Jews and have become more strictly endogamous. (This came out even in some of my conversations with the expatriate Malabari Jews near Jerusalem. They complained that only in recent times have White Jews claimed cultural distinctiveness and laid stress on their greater acquaintance with Jewish culture and rituals.) The complaint, however, has its other side. Samuel Halegua claims that White Jews tend to be endogamous not because of colour prejudice, but because they are protective about their liturgy. They find Yemeni Jews fully acceptable even though they are darker than Malabaris.

Eliavoo Abraham may not be old, but he looks elderly. Soft spoken, exceedingly polite (in the way people in Indian public life often are), he gives the impression of being nondescript not by default but by choice. His son, Sam, has an automobile garage in Ernakulam, which also sells luxury cars. It is located in Ernakulam's Jew Street. Like the other Jew Street in Fort Cochin, this one too is identified with a proud community that shows no sign of defensiveness. It is a community that has felt protected against most of the humiliating experiences of the Jewish Diaspora. We met Eliavoo and Sam Abraham at the garage for the first time. Hospitable and friendly, they invited us to their home for a chat.

During the first visit we found out that Eliavoo himself had moved to Kiriyathyovel, Israel, 25 years ago, in 1973. His other son lives there. Sam stays at Ernakulam and looks after the garage. Eliavoo now comes every year to Cochin to visit his family and is also active in community affairs in the city. The Abrahams are a reasonably well-to-do family that has had a long interest in Jewish culture. Eliavoo's uncle was a Hebrew teacher. His father, however, had less exalted interests; he supplied vegetables to the

---

[20] *The Cochin Synagogue: 400th Anniversary Souvenir* (Cochin, 1968).

Maharaja's palace for twenty-five years. In appreciation of his services, the
Maharaja gifted him a gold chain.

Eliavoo's grandfather died in 1940. He had been instrumental in laying the foundation stone of a grand synagogue the same year. Eliavoo was then very young. He does not remember his grandfather, but remembers the days when both synagogues of Black Jews were active. They are now closed. His grandfather used to tell him that the Abraham family had stayed in Cochin for 600 years, but Eliavoo himself had not taken much interest in the history of his family and never asked his grandfather about the history of the Cochin Jews. Eliavoo now seems to regret that lapse.

Eliavoo remembers his childhood with a touch of nostalgia. He studied in Maharaja's school, with the princes and princesses of Cochin, even though he himself came from a modest background. He married in 1950. Like him, his wife was also born on Jew Street. The 1980s were a bad decade for him. His father died in 1980, mother and wife in 1984. That past pulls him to Ernakulam's Jew Street every year and he has to repeatedly affirm that he was very happy in India. He had been a successful Class-I PWD contractor for seventten years—from 1954 to 1971. Though he claims that he is also happy in Israel, he seems to feel that his job in India gave him more prestige and dignity.

In Israel, he first worked in a post office. Now, he is an accountant in an ambulance service, a semi-governmental job. He had many difficulties there at the beginning, because he had to take care of everyone from his family who migrated to Israel. He also had to spend two years to learn Hebrew in a government language centre. His parents, sister and brother-in-law, who joined him in Israel, never learnt any Hebrew. Eliavoo also had to work as a watchman for a while. Now, he is better off, but there is something in his tone that suggests that, like many first-generation immigrants, he is ambivalent towards his adopted country.

That ambivalence has many sources, the most important of them being the youth culture of Israel. Like the sexton of Cochin's main synagogue, Eliavoo is uncomfortable with that culture, which he sees as amoral and decadent. He distinguishes himself sharply and sometimes aggressively from the many Israelis who come to India as tourists. He does not believe they are genuinely interested in India or Indian culture. They come to Goa mainly to smoke hashish, he claims. Of the 300 odd Cochini Jews who come to Cochin from Israel every year, he estimates that roughly 40 per cent are interested in Cochin's Jewish traditions; 60 per cent are not.

Yet, he is pretty certain that the remaining Jewish families in Cochin will also move to Israel. (According to him, there are about eleven Black

Jewish families left in greater Cochin.) This is because of the problem of marriage. In Cochin, there are just not enough marriageable boys and girls among Jews. Also, the heavy migration that took place earlier has taken its toll. Now they have to make an effort to assemble the quorum of ten for prayers. For his prayers, Eliavoo joins White Jews at the synagogue at Fort Cochin, where Samuel Halegua serves as the priest. The synagogues of the Malabari Jews remain closed.

As we talk and Eliavoo relaxes, his ambivalence towards Israel becomes clearer. He starts by saying that the Jews had some problems in India, such as those faced by schoolgoing children in the family. They could not observe many of the rites and rituals of Sabbath. They had to go school on Saturdays, and that was hard on the community.[21] Also, the better schools in greater Cochin were Christian missionary schools; the members of the community constantly feared that their children would be taught the principles of Christianity or inducted into the Christian worldview and would loose respect for their own faith. As with many others of his community, Eliavoo Abraham's image of the local Christians is split. He remembers the amicable relationship the Jewish communities had with the Christians, but he also remembers the Portuguese violence against the Jews as a defining moment in the life of the community.

Yet, now that he is in Israel, he says, he constantly remembers Cochin when in Israel, and Israel in Cochin.[22] As he says this, Eliavoo warms up to the subject, and is no longer that defensive or protective towards Israel. He says, 'we always tell our grandchildren that Cochin is the best place in the world, if you want to live peacefully'. Suddenly he blurts out 'I regret I went to Israel.' He adds that even people with money in India cannot go and buy a shop or a house in Israel. 'Israel is not an easy country.' But then, when they migrated, many Malabari Jews were poor; some 80 per cent of them,

---

[21] There is obviously a difference in the self-confidence of the Haleguas and the Abrahams. Samuel Halegua speaks of a cousin who joined the Indian Navy and was finding it difficult to go through the usual drill on Sabbath. When the cousin complained to Samuel's fa ther-in law, the latter directly wrote to the prime minister. The rules were quickly changed.

[22] Eliavoo is probably not an isolated case or individual whim. I remember Ichak Nehamia, a Malabari Jewish immigrant at Moshav Nevatim near Jerusalem, telling me on behalf of his community, 'We like to live as if we were in Kerala.' Indeed, Nehamia and his friends made a point to serve us typical Malayali food arid claim that the Malayali food the Cochin Jews prepared in Israel was better than that available in Cochin.

he estimates, 'lived below the poverty line'. That was why they emigrated.
Many of them are millionaires today. . . .

The Abrahams are finding out the hard way what Basil Elias, a Jewish urologist at the General Hospital, Ernaculum, articulates openly. Elias tells us that he is attracted to Cochin because it is a city of immigrants. 'Nobody here actually belongs to this place. It is built by immigrants.' Obviously, he looks at his community as one of those that have built Cochin over the centuries. Cochin belongs to the Jews as much as it belongs to the others. Elias' grandfather left for Israel in 1954 and he himself visited Israel in 1985. He now expects his children to go first to Israel and find out things for themselves. He himself is ambivalent towards the idea of immigration.

Other Cochinis see the future as less open. Many of those we met seem prepared for the loss of the city's Jewish community. But they are not reconciled to the idea. Some years ago in BBC's radio programme, 'The Last Jews of Cochin', the secretary of the city's spice traders' association compared the departure of the Jews with a daughter's marriage. One knows 'she may be doing well, but there is a sense of loss'.

Two 'Immigrants' Speak

Cochin introduces itself to you in unexpected ways. I remember the first afternoon of my first visit to the city for this study. We were having lunch at a seaside restaurant. Two persons, one with a vermilion mark on his forehead, came and sat at a nearby table. They immediately ordered rum and Coca-Cola. My associate, an anthropologist, guessed they were BJP functionaries and predicted that they would order beef preparations. They did. After lunch, we joined them uninvited at their table and had a chat. They were exceedingly friendly and told us that they were organising a BJP rally that evening. They were fortifying themselves for the job and were perfectly frank about what they were eating and drinking. They had to be strong, they claimed, as if mimicking BJP's critics who accuse the party of being pathologically masculinity-seeking.

Communalism has reached Cochin but failed to make any deep inroads into it. Hindu nationalist pamphlets in Malayalam, directed against the Christians and Muslims, are occasionally published from Cochin and distributed in some other cities of Kerala. But I am told that they are not easily available in Cochin itself. This has something to do with the warp and woof of Hindu-Muslim relations in the city, particularly their social perceptions of each other. Ostensibly, neither sees the other or itself as a monolithic community. Nor do the others see them as such. Despite the entry of modern categories and attempts to delegitimize older categories like caste, most Cochinis with whom we talked continue to see generic terms such as Hindus, Muslims, and Christians as representing confederations of living, identifiable communities. Many who claim to have risen above the traditional divisions of castes and sects slip into the use of these divisions when off-guard. As a result, there is no minority complex in the majority community, the sort that one finds in large parts of North India. The Hindus are a majority and the Muslims and Christians are minorities only theoretically. Two of those who told us the story of Cochin were Hasan Nasar and Muhammad Iqbal.

Hasan Nasar is a Malayali novelist in his late fifties. His grandfather migrated from Southern Yemen to Cochin. Their tribal surname was ba-Nasir. Nasar knows the names of seven generations of his ancestors. His grandfather made him learn the names. He, however, has not taught his own children any family genealogy: 'I want to mingle', he says. He adds that, over the generations, his family has lost some of its older characteristics. Previously, there was a surfeit of Arabic words in the Malayalam his family spoke. That is no longer the case. He does not say so directly, but his experience of working in Riyadh in Saudi Arabia has something to do with the erosion of interest in his Yemeni roots. He is still proud of his origins, but not of 'those people'—probably meaning the Arabs whom he came to meet at Riyadh. His discomfort with Riyadh has something to do with the lifestyle and consumption patterns in that city. Presumably, he did not like them. That sojourn has made him more proud of being a Cochini and strengthened his sense of belonging to the Cochini Muslim community.

Nasar proudly says, 'nowhere in the world will you find a community like this. Walk one kilometre and you will find more than one language and religion.' He quickly enters into a comparison between the cosmopolitan cultures of Dubai and Cochin. He does not like the former. 'Dubai has taken too much from the West; they spend their holidays in Europe.' On the other hand, Cochin has retained something of its self. It is still, Nasar feels, a city of communities and, despite many recent changes, the city itself also remains a community. There are not many instances of separate living or ghettos at Cochin; most of the localities are mixed. Yet the differences are not ironed out. 'If you go even ten kilometres away from Cochin, they speak perfect Malayalam, whereas there are so many dialects in the city. They add richness to its culture.'

In Cochin there is a custom, also found elsewhere in India, of people speaking one language at home, another at work, and still another for creative self-expression. Nasar proudly mentions Kunal Jussawala, a Gujarati journalist who has become a well-known writer in Malayalam.

Of course, there are intercommunal distances in the city. Nasar gives the example of Kutcchi Memons who do not allow the use of their cemetery to even other Muslims. But these distances are more than compensated for by Cochin's tradition of mutuality. Even in the fourteenth and fifteenth centuries, Nasar says, India was known for its tolerance; so was Cochin. Indeed, he claims that the Spanish and Portuguese Jews tempted Vasco da Gama with money and other incentives to find a sea route to India. For the Iberian Jews, da Gama's fateful trip to India in 1498 was a means of accessing Cochin's legendary ecumenism and generosity.

At this point Mohammed Iqbal, a journalist and a writer, intervenes. He is approximately sixty and is a Kutcchi Qazi, whose forefathers migrated from Kutch in north-west Gujarat. He speaks Kutcchi, too. From his tone it seems that he feels that Nasar has not been fair and assertive enough about the culture and the traditions of Cochin. (Iqbal, I suspect, thinks me to be a journalist, probably on a mission to dig out instances of Hindu-Muslim conflicts at the city. We are meeting soon after the Bharatiya Janata Party Government has come to power and the party's Hindu chauvinism is a much-debated subject in the newspapers. He seems to assume that I want to join the debate in my columns.)

Iqbal points out that not only in Cochin but in the whole of Kerala there has flourished a 'rich heritage of hospitality, since the time of King Solomon'. He has read somewhere that King Solomon's palace was adorned with teak wood and ivory. He is convinced that the wood and ivory came from Kerala. He claims that even a community of slaves from Mozambique played a role in the history of Cochin, not as slaves but, strangely enough, as a cultural symbol. The practice of *Kappirri Muthappan* (kafir grandfather) involved, what could be called, slave worship among low-caste Hindus, as a system symbolically analogous to that of *Yaksha* in Eastern India, for the protection of hidden wealth of a person or a family.

Apart from these transcontinental connections, the city itself, according to Iqbal, is a remarkable testimony to communal coexistence.

Apart from the communities usually mentioned, there are the Swetamber and Digamber Jains with their own functioning temples; Parsis, Sindhis, Dawoodi Vorahs, Maharashtrians, Konkanis (who have separate temples for Brahmins and Vaishyas, and even a special temple for Konkani goldsmiths); Bengalis, Kudumbis, Telugus, Tulus, two sects of Tamil Brahmins, of whom Palghat Iyers are particularly conspicuous. He proudly adds that Cochin is a mosaic of communities. I have heard Cochinis speak of their diversity on a number of occasions. All Indian metropolitan cities have hundreds of communities; in none of them have I found people as proudly speaking of their diversity and the 'different histories' of their people, as if diversity itself was a value, and by itself constituted the first marker of the uniqueness of a city.

Mattancherry, at one time, Iqbal says, was settled by a large number of Muslims. They are still there but, proportionately speaking, their numbers have dwindled. They also celebrate Deepawali like the Hindus. 'My father was a pious man. He used to take me for the Deepawali celebrations.' Every community has examples of how it went out of its way to acknowledge or interact with other communities. He gives example of the *Coonan Kurish* (Bent Cross) oath that the Christians took to defend the Cochin kingdom against European powers. There were nine synagogues at Cochin at one time. As opposed to this, 'see, what is happening in Northern India'. North India seems to haunt Iqbal. 'There is no threat to the culture of Cochin', he says confidently at one point and then quickly adds, 'but we are concerned when we see the national scene.'

Iqbal, too, believes that the Cochin maharajas had much to do with Cochin's ecumenism. They were, he seems to suggest, Brahmins, but not purists. Ten days before Onam they used to have a festival called Athachamayam. Technically, it was a Hindu festival and it involved a large procession. Invariably, the Naina Muslims were in the front row of the procession. Even low-caste Hindus, Iqbal adds, had a place in the procession.

The unique feature of the city, according to Iqbal, is that nobody has 'abandoned' his or her cultural background and yet everyone can appreciate other cultures. Even 'the advent of faiths like Christianity and Islam have been perfectly peaceful' in the city. The Arabs have maintained connections with Malabar since pre-Islamic days; one of the first groups to carry the message of Islam outside the Arabic tribes came to Cochin. It was led by Malik Ibu Deenar al Habeeb, a direct disciple of the prophet. The Arabs earlier lived in a settlement in Southern Cochin. The Chinese,

Sikh Riots Survivors, Kalyanpuri Sector 13, Delhi 1984; Photo credit and courtesy: Ram Rahman

Bhagirath Place, Delhi, 1993; Photo credit and courtesy: Ram Rahman

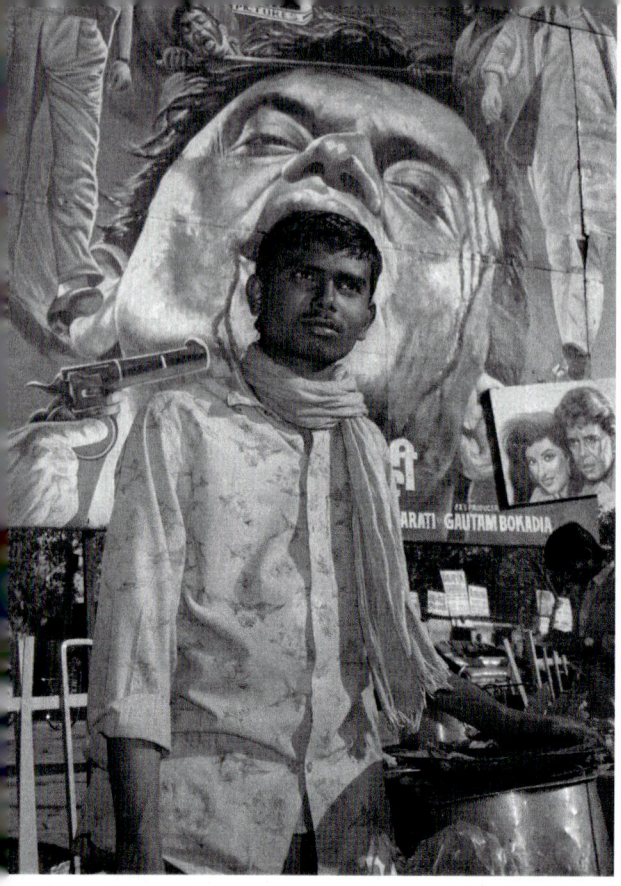

Peanut seller, Red Fort, Delhi, 1995; Photo credit and courtesy: Ram Rahman

Market in Old Delhi, around Id, 2007; Photo credit and courtesy: Ram Rahman

Playing with Pages; Photo credit: Vicky Roy;
courtesy: Vicky Roy and Ojas Art, New Delhi

Boys Dreaming; Photo credit: Vicky Roy; courtesy:
Vicky Roy and Ojas Art, New Delhi

Pappu and Nandu at Jorbagh, New Delhi; Photo credit: Vicky Roy; courtesy: Vicky Roy and Ojas Art, New Delhi

Untitled; Photo credit: Vicky Roy; courtesy: Vicky Roy and Ojas Art, New Delhi

too, lived in peace in a settlement at Fort Cochin and they built some pagodas there. Ma Huan was a Chinese Muslim. When a ship in 1963 hit the Malabar coast, some evidences of this settlement accidentally became available. ◄

Cochin's ecumenism, Iqbal claims, extends to humbler domains of life. Though they are exposed to Karnataki music, Cochinis can appreciate Ravi Shankar, Pankaj Mallik, and ghazals. He also talks of the 'Pottey Ramayana' of the Konkanis and the way it has influenced other communities. Indeed, Iqbal believes that Cochin's diversity has also allowed the influence and the customs of some communities to act as forms of cultural criticism of other communities. Thus, many of the 'regressive elements' in the culture of the Saraswats, such as the Devadasi system, have broken down under the influence of Christianity and the social status of the Saraswat women has improved.

III

This is not the full story of Cochin. It is an exploratory peep into its strange charms. The scraps of conversations I have strung together here are parts of a much larger narrative, and I have not told the story of the communities that may provide a glimpse of, what both communalised and secular India would call, Hindu Cochin. A few things, however, are relatively clear, even from this incomplete story.

Seemingly, Cochin does not offer any unique theory of communal amity or religious tolerance. It is multicultural not by design, but by being itself. As we have seen, the city does not ooze with brotherly love either: its easy communal amity includes communal distances and hostilities. But these distances and hostilities, because they operate within a widely shared psychological universe, have certain in-built checks against mass violence and nihilistic rage. Cochin, all said and done is a community where distances and hostilities, like closeness and friendship, have specific, culturally defined meanings. Like an annual Ramlila that cannot do without its demonic anti-hero, Ravana, in Cochin one has to relive one's self-definition as much through one's enemies as through one's friends. For within Cochin's psychological universe one needs one's enemies to define oneself and one is aware every moment that one is incomplete without them.[23] This need to have enemies (to spite

---

[23] Vamik D. Volkan, *The Need to have Enemies and Allies* (New York: Jason Aronson, 1988).

psychoanalyst Vamik Volkan) never acquires a passionate, homicidal edge (Volkan 1988). There is certain optimality about Cochin's loves and hates.

The beehive-like organisation of communities endorses this optimality. The communities in Cochin do not swim together in a steamy melting pot. Indeed, their lifestyles, while being intertwined, are also partly autonomous of each other. These sectors of autonomy, which can be called community affairs, subsume under them 'legitimate' differences in religion, caste, and sect. These differences in the city have not lost their meanings, value, and sense of continuity with the past, either in the communities or in their neighbours. As a result, after a point, despite ideological pretences, nobody seems particularly disrespectful towards or defensive about them. Communities can afford to take on the moderate hostilities of others because their self-esteem has not been badly damaged. Such hostilities do not constitute what psychoanalysts call a narcissistic wound.

'The future', Jim Hicks has recently reaffirmed while reviewing Bruno Latour and Ivan Illich, 'may ultimately be found in our premodern past.' Perhaps because in the high noon of modernity, that past, uncontaminated by modernity, allows a freer space for imagining a future less shackled by the present. Indeed, along with Mangalore and Calicut, Cochin is a window to a once-flourishing and now-forgotten alternative—probably threatened—culture of cosmopolitanism. That culture, I may have said at the beginning, refuses to die. However, I am more aware now that the refusal may end up guaranteeing an ugly, slow, painful death. In our times, the dice seems to be loaded against cultures dependent on the survival of communities and community ties. Cochin is constantly bombarded by ideologies that have little respect for the city's distinctive style of dialogue of cultures; it is subject to steam-rolling development and a style of random urbanisation that has become the hallmark of Asian and Latin American economic growth. The only saving grace may be that Cochin is still terribly habit-forming. It seems to socialise one very quickly to its algorithm of life, which is probably a way of subtly inducting one into the city's community-based normative frame. As sections of its Jewish population are finding out, just when you begin to feel you have washed Cochin out of your system, the city begins to haunt you likely a friendly, persistent ghost.

Is that too shifting and fragile a base on which to build upon? The question troubles one because, as we have frequently seen in this century, when proximity sours, it releases strange demons. The Hutus and the Tutsis, the Bosnian Muslims and the Serbs—and in South Asia itself, the Punjabi

Sikhs, Muslims and Hindus in the 1940s, and the Sinhalas and the Sri Lankan Tamils—they all are witnesses to the pathology of nearness rather than that of distance. Neighbourliness, Don Miller has recently reminded us, always carries a load of ambiguity; neighbours themselves are—or can turn into—strangers.[24] Some sections of Cochin anxiously wait to hear the verdict of contemporary India on its version of neighbourliness.

One final word on the nature of this enterprise. In contemporary critical theory, criticism has been mostly unidirectional. The idea of systematic, durable, cumulative social knowledge in such theory has come to mean knowledge that demystifies manifest social realities hiding less palatable truths (realpolitik, class relations or psychosexuality, for example). In the mainstream global culture of knowledge, it is seen as an act of intellectual courage to unmask the manifest, to unravel the hidden, the tacit, or the latent in their full ugliness—in turn seen as closer to truth for that very reason. During the last 100 years, new certitudes have been built on such demystification. From Nietzsche to Marx to Freud, it has been the same story.

For a long while, this model has served the social sciences well. It has deepened the awareness of economic and political power and psychological and cultural defences that have hidden subtler forms of violence and dominance, which previously seemed natural or legitimate. However, with the knowledge industry gradually domesticating critical theory into a new domain of expertise, the theory's one-way style of demystification has not merely become a new source of certitude, but also a new means of legitimizing the forced obsolescence for those marginalised by the world system. This study of Cochin once again suggests that the challenge is to redefine what Philip Rieff calls the analytic attitude, and to exercise a new scepticism in the case of the defeated cultures in the tropics. This scepticism may involve challenging a series of ideas—among them progress, rationality, development, and modern science—that at one time the victors of the world might have feared but have now come to adore. Critical theory will not be maimed if it borrows something from the idea of unending criticism or criticism of criticism implicit in Buddhist dialectics in general, and Nagarjuna in particular. In such criticism the unsightly that underlies the apparently trivial can also be further demystified to reveal a 'truth' that signposts alternative ways of organising a humane society.

[24] Don Miller, *Neighbours and Strangers* (Delhi: Rainbow, 1999).

The story of Cochin also suggests that multiculturalism need not be merely a political or social arrangement, nor even be a principle of citizenship that tolerates or celebrates disparate lifestyles. Multiculturalism may sometimes imply a culturally embedded identity in which the others are telescoped into the self as inalienable parts of the self. In that case, they survive not merely as fragments of a negative identity, but also as temptations, possibilities, and rejected selves. Such internalisation is not unknown to psychoanalytic psychology though there is in it, in this instance, a larger cultural dimension. The internalisation need not be of significant individualised others; it can be of culturally significant collective others.[25] This, in turn, means that the communities do not usually need any painful rite of exorcism, because the spirits that populate the inner world of the Cochinis are no strangers. They are more like friendly ghosts who occasionally become unfriendly enough to haunt one.

[25] This is a process vaguely parallel to the one Sudhir Kakar describes in folk therapeutic contexts in his *Shamans, Mystics and Doctors* (New Delhi: Oxford University Press, 1993).

Kaliprasanna Sinha

The Observant Owl: Hootum's Vignettes of Nineteenth-century Calcutta

[Calcutta's Charak Festival]
All of a sudden the morning guns fired! The crows cawed and got ready
to fly out of their nests. Shopkeepers opened the shutters of their shops,
sprinkled Ganga water all over the place, prayed to Gandheswari,[1] and got
down to dressing their hookahs. The horizon brightened by degrees. Fish
wholesalers began arriving in droves; fishwives ran after them shouting
and quarrelling! Barges loaded with potatoes from Baidyabati and brinjals
from Hasnan sailed in one by one. Native and English death-dealers set
out on home *visits* in coaches or palkis as their income and status dictated.
These blessed creatures don't smile till there's an outbreak of malaria or
a cholera epidemic somewhere! Even vets reportedly made a fast buck
when there was a malaria epidemic in the Ulo region! Some vets can
be seen *practising* even in Calcutta! Their medicines are wonderful. Some
treat their patients by boring holes into their nostrils as if they were bulls,
and some treat them by forcing plain water into their mouths! The city's
kavirajs are even deadlier: they use the same 'Killer Potion' to cure all
kinds of diseases! Many have taken to this profession after reading the
slokas of Chanakya and the story of Datakarna![2]
    Brahmin pundits walked by briskly for their baths with dhotis under
their arms. They were in a great hurry: they'd have to reach the homes of
their patrons early that day. Middle-aged rheumatics were creaking out

---

[1] A goddess worshipped by the gandhabaniks.
[2] The slokas of Chanakya and the story of Datakarna were popular reading
books for children.

of their houses for their *morning walks.* Oriya bearers brushed their teeth with twigs as they ran full tilt to have a bath. *The Englishman, The Bengal Hurkaru, The Phoenix* and *The Exchange Gazette* landed on the doorsteps of their subscribers. Bengali papers are like venison: subscribers don't get them till they've aged! This, however, doesn't apply to English papers; they're served hot with hot *breakfast!* By and by, the sun rose.

Like the change in shifts of *section writers*[3] in an office, the bullocks yoked to the oil-mills were changed. The first *instalment* of pagri-wearing men—the ship-sircars and *booking clerks*—made their appearance. A little later the barbers and darners showed up. *Government offices* were closed that day, so we couldn't catch a glimpse of the *clerks, bookkeepers* and *head writers.* Nowadays people go to *office* wearing all kinds of clothes, thanks to English education! Pagris have almost vanished; only a few old-fashioned clerks still wear them. They'll disappear forever once these clerks receive their *pension.* The only problem with a pagri is that one's *Albert fashion*[4] parting gets hidden under it when it's wound round the head! Even barbers and darners have given up wearing pagris.

Brokers have no holidays. They got out of their homes in the morning on an empty stomach as usual. Work or no work, they have to visit moneylenders and wealthy babus at least once every day. Gathering information—'Whose house is on sale?' 'Who wants to buy a garden-house?' 'Who wants to borrow money?' etc.—is their main job. Many moneylenders and rich babus engage brokers to hook prospective prey. Once they've found one, they suck him dry!

The brokers' job is splendid. Sweet is the money that's earned without toil! Many young men from respectable families have become brokers: they can be seen doing the rounds of the city, riding in their coaches. Cash-strapped commercial agents and four-times-insolvent babus have also taken up broking as a profession. Many have built big mansions out of their earnings. These fellows are veritable chameleons! It's very difficult to recognize their true colours; there's nothing in the world that they can't do. Professional moneylenders and wealthy babus spread their dragnets wide to catch a good haul. Brokers lie in wait to drag them in. If by chance there's a favourable tide, even small fish can't escape the net!

The church clock struck seven. The city grew intolerably noisy. The streets were crawling with people; drums boomed everywhere; fumes of

---

[3] A copying clerk in an office, native or European, was called 'writer'.
[4] A hairstyle after Albert, Prince Consort of Queen Victoria.

incense and the smell of liquor filled the air! The sanyasis were returning from Kalighat[5] cheerfully having pierced their sides and tongues with shafts, nails and iron rods. The verandas of brothels were swarming with fun-loving babus, amateur panchali singers, singers of *half*-akhdai troupes, and *members* of the garden-house fraternity. They'd been there since morning to watch the Charak festivities.

In the meantime, the sitting rooms of the wealthy babus began to warm up. Some, for the sake of *civilization, hate* Charak. Some, in spite of being Brahmos,[6] celebrate Charak because it's an old family custom. They detest the festival, but are quite helpless: their aunts and elder brothers are still alive; their grandmas are yet to peg out!

Many people love to watch hook-swinging and sanyasis torturing themselves during Charak. They set out with their little grandsons and daughters to watch the immersion of idols after the end of a puja. In spite of their age, many doddering old fools don't feel inhibited about going out on the streets wearing a diamond-studded topi, a kaba embroidered with gold thread, a pearl necklace, a diamond necklet, and rings on all the ten fingers, like small children! The man's son by his first wife may well be sixty years old, and his nephew's hair is perhaps grey!

Many rajas and zamindars from the suburbs visit Calcutta now and then to attend hearings of their cases in the Nizamat adalat,[7] or to file petitions. They take up lodgings at Bhowanipur during their stay in the city. Those who come to the city from the suburbs find Calcutta too hot. Earlier, they used to be plagued by loose motions on arriving in the city, but nowadays they're plagued by something more dreadful—wily brokers! These rogues keep them on tenterhooks all the time. They often 'fall' prey to the wiles of these scoundrels and lose everything. Some zamindars spend all twelve months of the year in Calcutta. With *crape* chadars wound round their heads and pearl necklaces round their necks, they wander about merrily in *phaetons* with their lackeys. They look like panchali singers, and their clothes are those of a courtesan's pimp! The minute you see them it's obvious that these creatures are from Bongaon! Their intellect is feebler than a mule's; in learning they surpass Saraswati![8] They're great enthusiasts of community pujas, immersion processions, khemta nautches and jhumurs! Sometimes they

---

[5] A centre of pilgrimage in Calcutta, famous for its temple of the goddess Kali.
[6] Followers of Brahmoism, a faith founded by Rammohan Roy.
[7] The court of criminal justice.
[8] The goddess of learning and the arts.

go to ground to evade arrest warrants in homicide cases and *decrees* for non-payment of debts to moneylenders! On high days and holidays they deck themselves out in their glad rags and roam gaily about in their coaches!

This doesn't mean that all zamindars from the suburbs are rascals. Some, in fact, earn great fame and respect during their stay in the city. In spite of taking up lodgings in Sonagaji,[9] they don't whoop it up in brothels! Many people from Calcutta are awestruck by their refined manners. Some, on the other hand, spend all twenty-four hours of the day in Sonagaji in spite of renting lodgings in places like Kashipur, Barisha, Bhowanipur and Kalighat! They storm into people's houses and act like louts. The next day they appear before the *police* with their paramours, clasping each other's hands like a married couple; senior male members of the family rush to the police station to bail them out! They buy elephants on credit, but brawls break out at the time of payment! When things get worse, they flee to their hometowns: it's a veritable paradise there!

Just as crooks besiege new *sailors*, the moment they alight from a ship, petty brokers trap rich men coming from the suburbs as soon as they set foot in the city. By the grace of the babu's attorney, petty brokers get the responsibility of renting lodgings for him, hiring coaches, arranging khemta nautches, and rendering sundry other services. They also act as *political agents.* The babus are given a tour of the important sites of the city: the Seven Tanks, the Asiatic Society Museum, the Bally Bridge, the lockgate in Baghbazar Canal, the swanky parlours of famous babus, and the brothels of eminent whores! If they can strike while the iron is hot, the brokers win a lot of favours from the babus! This fun and merrymaking lasts for some time. Finally, the babus go broke and flee to their homes. The brokers are then transformed into full-fledged *agents.*

There are two groups of anglicized babus in the city now. The members of one group are like cowdung-busts of well-bred sahibs, and the members of the other are crappy imitations of feringhees! The first group follows the English style in everything: having at-homes around tables and chairs, drinking tea from cups, smoking cigars, keeping water in *jugs*, serving *brandy* from *decanters*, covering glass tumblers with beautifully decorated lids, etc. They read *The Bengal Hurkaru*, *The Englishman* and *The Phoenix*, and talk about *politics* and the *best news of the day* all the time! They dine at tables, shit in *commodes*, and wipe their butts with paper!

---

[9] A famous red-light district in Calcutta.

However, they're quite amiable, compassionate, generous and gentle. Their only problem is that they're henpecked and plagued by illnesses all the time! Enthusiasm, fellow feeling and ambition have fled from their hearts. These fellows belong to the *old class*.

Members of the second group—Bagambar Mitra[10] and others—are more dangerous than snakes, and more ferocious than tigers! They're a distinct species of wild animal! Just as thieves smear their lips with alcohol and sneak into people's houses masquerading as drunks, these scoundrels masquerade as well-wishers of the country to further their own selfish interests. All their efforts are directed towards becoming rich, and getting the upper hand. Their *policy* is to make a cat's paw of another! They studiously keep away from charity: they never donate more than four annas!

There's a great buzz in the sitting rooms of the city's wealthy babus in the morning. Here the *head* clerk of a solicitor's firm can be seen sitting like a thirsty crow—three or four *equity* and *common law* cases are pending in the court! There creditors and moneylenders can be seen waiting with *bills* in their hands to receive their payment. They've probably visited the house several times in the last three months; each time the diwan invents some new excuse and sends them away. *Summons, warrants,* lawyer's notices and *subpoenas* have become the babus' ornaments. They don't care a fig for reproaches and insults: they dismiss them as senseless prattle, and wear rings on their fingers with the words 'This day shall pass' inscribed on them. But despite doing all this, peace eludes them.

Elsewhere a boy of a rich family can be seen spinning like a lopsided kite after coming into a fortune at an early age. He'd been playing horses and hide-and-seek just the other day; now he must watch out for irregularities in the diwan's account books. He has to keep a close watch on the family solicitor too, so that he doesn't checkmate him early in the game! Even crows snatch fruits from the hands of a child, let alone humans! The young babu's besieged by visitors all day. Someone walks in and introduces himself as 'a good friend of the late babu' and another as 'the son of the late babu's sister's uncle's niece's nephew!' The house is always filled with job seekers, fathers of unwed daughters (it may well be that the rascals, haven't married yet!), and other creatures like them.

[10] A veiled reference to Raja Digambar Mitra (1817–79). A student of Hindu College, Mitra began his life as a teacher. In 1864 he was appointed member of the Bengal Legislative Council. He became Sheriff of Calcutta in 1874. The title of Raja was conferred on him in 1877.

Their real motives lie buried deep within their hearts; they surface at the right moment!

The streets thronged with people. The shops were bristling with customers arrayed in all kinds of clothes. Some wore kameezes with *cuffs* and *collars*, and *shining leather* shoes with silver *buckles*; some wore *China coats* and shoes of *India rubber*, some wrapped themselves up in *crape* chadars; some had a *stick* in their hand and a *guard chain* around their neck and wore their hair in the *Albert fashion*. Calcutta is a veritable zoo, you'll find all kinds of creatures here! Fun-loving fellows parked themselves on either side of the road: the swarm mainly consisted of lawyers, *section writers*, spice-sellers, oilmen, blacksmiths and wretched brahmins. Some carried two daughters on their hips, some three sons!

A padre was distributing Bibles among the people. A *catechist* was standing close by, dressed like a *suburban* chowkidar: he was wearing a *pantaloon*, a short chapkan and a black top hat. He was speaking and gesticulating like a pleader and explaining the glory of the Christian faith to the crowd. At first glance one would mistake him for a puppeteer! A few porters, pedlars and schoolboys were listening to the *catechist* with rapt attention, but they couldn't make head or tail of what he said! Earlier, wayward boys used to quarrel with their parents and run away to the north of the country, or become Christians. But now, with the coming of the railways, running away from home has become a hazardous job! What's more, having seen the wretched condition of the converts, people are now terrified of becoming Christians!

The main road in Chitpur gets mucky the moment clouds appear in the sky! The place was already covered in filth, and to add to the horror, a Charak procession was passing along the road, accompanied by a horde of drummers. Two menials were carrying a big gong hung from a bamboo pole on their shoulders, and little boys were banging it merrily with mallets. Others went marching behind them with colourful banners in their hands. Some low-caste devotees were singing songs in praise of Shiva to the accompaniment of drums; they were followed by liveried darwans, hurcarras and sentries. Shongs dressed up as Shiva and Parvati[11] were walking in the middle; Shiva's body was smeared with ash and chalk dust, and his head was covered with a snake-like hood made of *tin*! A pack of sanyasis with bleeding bodies went dancing merrily after them, burning incense; they carried long canes topped with sola lobsters! The drummers were playing various beats on their drums. The babu's

---

[11] One of the many names of the goddess Durga, the consort of Shiva.

nephews, brothers and cousins rode coaches at the rear. They'd woken up at three in the morning that day; their eyes were bloodshot, and their heads were covered with the dust of Bhowanipur and Kalighat. Passers-by stood gawking at the pageant. The horses shied at the drumbeats. People ran pell-mell into the nearby shops in panic; some fell into the gutter! It was a blazing hot day, yet nobody wanted to leave.

Gradually, at the orders of the *police* all the Charak processions in the city broke up. The *superintendent* was out on the beat on his horse; he looked at his *pocket* watch and called time on the processions. *Martial law* was imposed; people were prohibited from playing drums. The constables smashed a few drums with their batons and the city grew quiet in an instant! People slid back to their homes furtively, with their drums on their shoulders. The spectators dispersed, cursing the *Queen's* regime!

The city suddenly grew quiet. The zealots pulled out the shafts and rods from their bodies and got into grog shops. The sanyasis were dog-tired; they got back to their homes and drank themselves unconscious on arrack. The Shiva temples in the Charak ground were closed for the year. The fun of boring bodies with shafts and rods also came to an end. The Sunday slipped away this way.

It was the last day of the year. Young men and women were sunk in sorrow; they'd lost one precious year of their youth! Jailbirds were in seventh heaven; they had one year less to serve! An old man passed away; a young lad shone in the prime of his youth! We consigned all our unpleasant memories of the old year to the bin of the past and looked with hope towards the future. The old year fled as if grimacing at us. The new year strode in gravely like a *schoolmaster*; we stood stock-still in awe and wonder. Indigo Cultivators are seized by fear when the old judge of their zilla's transferred! Students promoted to a new class have butterflies in their stomachs when they behold the face of their new teacher! A woman who's given birth to many stillborn babies in the past feels nervous when she gives birth to a son late in her life! People found themselves in a similar plight with the passing of the old year and the coming of the new!

Englishmen celebrate *New Year* with great fanfare. They drink themselves into a stupor and ring out the old year. Bengalis ring out the old year by chewing drumsticks and beating drums! Only babus who've dedicated their lives to the bottle, and shopkeepers who open new ledgers on the occasion, celebrate New Year's Day in a befitting manner!

******

Babu Padmalochan Dutta, Alias 'Chance Avatar'

Babu Padmalochan Dutta[12] was born in his maternal grandfather's house, the house of the famous Mitras, in Nauparamusuli in 1705. Nauparamusuli was a nice village. It was the home of many kayasthas and brahmins. Muzaffar Khan was the zamindar of the village. In spite of being a Muslim, Khan didn't indulge in such abominable acts as slaughtering cows! He showed equal respect to mullahs and brahmins, and was courteous towards everyone. He was fluent in Persian. He also knew Bengali and Urdu quite well. Though Muzaffar Khan was the zamindar of the village, the task of punishing people who broke social laws and communal customs was discharged by the Mitras. Earlier, the Mitras ruled the roost in the village. Deaths in the family and division of the property have robbed them of much of their former glory, but people of Nauparamusuli still regard them with great awe.

Padmalochan wasn't born on an ordinary day like other mortals. Thunder crashed in the sky and there was heavy rain throughout the day. A snake hissed before the labour room all night and the pet parrot of the house died in its cage suddenly! Pleased with these auspicious sighs, Padmalochan's grandma gave away one of her red-bordered saris to the midwife. Four-anna coins and coconut sweets were distributed among the invited drummers and musicians. Gifts were also distributed among the little boys of the village; they went home merrily with sweets, snacks and glittering one-paisa coins in their hands. After performing all the necessary pujas and rituals for a month mother and child were received into the house.

Gradually, Padmalochan began to grow like the waxing moon. He soon became a whizz at games like guli-danda, kabaddi, and cops-and-robbers. He was initiated into the world of learning at the age of five. He hid behind reedy edges of ponds, bushes and bamboo groves out of fear of the teacher, and was always plagued by mysterious ailments like stomach aches and nausea. And so the days flew by. One day, his father suddenly died. His mother immolated herself in his pyre. His grandfather, uncles and cousins also kicked the bucket one by one. The Mitra family became almost destitute of males. Some of the lands were grabbed by zamindars like Joykrishna[13] and some got auctioned off because of non-payment of taxes. Padmalochan was left with no choice but to rely on fate and his

---

[12] Padmalochan Dutta is probably a veiled reference to one Gorachand Dutta of Thuntuneah. He was a trader who dealt with Crooke and Gray Co. (Nag, *Satik Hutom Pyanchar Naksha*, p. 211)

[13] Joykrishna Mukherjee (1808–88) was the zamindar of Uttarpara.

own inner resources to earn a living. He went to Calcutta and worked as an errand-boy-cum-cook in a boarding house to earn a living, and honed his skills on other jobs during his spare time. The boarders promised to help him with his studies.

Padmalochan won the hearts of the boarders with his services. Gradually, he began to visit the houses of the well-known babus of the city, soliciting jobs. The sitting rooms of the babus of the city are always crawling with people. If you check, you'll find that the crowd mainly consists of debtors, moneylenders, shopkeepers, hoary bachelors and job seekers! Padmalochan was the latest addition to the list! After paying regular visits to the babus' houses for one year, he landed himself a few recommendation letters. Finally, a kind-hearted accountant gave him a good government job in the *House* that he worked in.

Padmalochan had to struggle very hard to earn his living. In spite of coming from a respectable family, he had to do all kinds of menial jobs—folding clothes, frying luchis, going to the grocer's, drawing water and so on. Gradually, he became so skilled in the art of frying luchis that even professional cooks couldn't beat him! Impressed by his skills, the boarders honoured him with the title '*Maker*'! He's been famous as *Maker* Padmalochan Dutta since then.

There's a saying that 'when luck smiles on a man, even sand turns into gold at the touch of his hand.' Gradually, the stars began to favour him. The accountant babu helped him to get the job of a ship-sircar. The sahibs were impressed by Dutta's intelligence and efficiency. Padmalochan did his best to please them with his services. Even a wild snake turns tame if served sincerely! There are also instances in the Puranas of men appeasing the ghostlike Hindu gods with austerities. Pleased with his work, the sahibs extended their full help and support to him. One day when the sudder-mate of the *House* resigned from his job, the sahibs asked the accountant to install Padmalochan in his post.

Padmalochan had continued to live in the boarding house even after becoming a ship-sircar. But having gained the post of a sudder-mate he felt it unbecoming of him to remain there. He rented a small piece of land and built a tiled hut of his own. But he didn't have to live in the hut for long. His fortune soon puffed up like a luchi, or, like a newly-wed bride! The accountant had differences with the sahibs and resigned. Padmalochan, the blue-eyed boy of the sahibs, became the accountant without having to deposit any security money.

Money can work wonders! Padmalochan began to feel the change in his life from the day he became an accountant. The next morning his tiled hut seemed to be pulling faces at the big mansions in the city! The house was filled with job seekers, brokers, darwans, shopkeepers and wholesalers. Some sat on their knees and spoke to him with folded hands and some began to puff him up like a roti. 'May you come to possess golden pens and inkpots!' 'May you become a millionaire!' 'May you have a son within a year!' 'This humble servant of yours has no one in this world except you', etc. Distress hid his face behind a cloth like daytime rakes! Dressed in vanity and egotism, Lady Luck held him in a warm embrace! The gossips spread the word across the city: 'Padmalochan is beyond our reach now!' Taking their cue from them, the do-nothing brahmins went about loudly proclaiming— 'Padmalochan is a big shot now!'

There are some good-for-nothing timeservers in the city. Whenever someone rises to a position of fame and power in society, they immediately ally themselves with him. He is declared the best specimen of his caste and worshipped as a god. Then if somebody else rises to a position higher than his, they quickly change sides and ally themselves with the new babu. We'd heard the story of the rope and the stick from our grandma in childhood; these good-for-nothings were like that rope and stick. In the story, the prince asks the rope and the stick: 'Who do you belong to?' The rope and the stick reply, 'No one. We belong to whoever uses us.' The timeservers would say the same thing about themselves—'We belong to whoever uses us.'

These wretched timeservers come from respectable families; many of them are educated too. The pack mainly consists of idolaters, kulin brahmins and kayasthas, idle *pensioners* and people who've gone *broke*. After a long time the city had witnessed a babu in the person of Padmalochan. Calcutta had produced no new babus in the last twenty years. The timeservers and toadies of the city had been moving around like floating crap all that time! The advent of Padmalochan provided them with a new shelter.

Gradually, the timeservers began to praise Padmalochan to the skies. Fortune continued to favour him as before. Padmalochan fell victim to *ambition*. By and by, he became extravagant and went underground like other bankrupt babus. Padmalochan made his appearance on the world stage wearing the mask of a true Hindu. He licked the holy feet of brahmins and took an active interest in factional intrigues and religious matters. As far as listening to devotional songs was concerned he was a veritable *blotting paper*! Padmalochan was a man of great power and influence. His sitting room was always teeming with brahmins and Sanskrit pundits.

Just as the *government* gathered *volunteers* indiscriminately during the Sepoy
Mutiny, Padmalochan began to gather brahmin pundits at random after
becoming a babu. Like the Asiatic Society Museum, his house was soon
filled with all kinds of weird creatures; most of them were live specimens!

Mischievous and crooked Bengalis can do no harm to the world if
their pockets are empty. But when money begins to rub shoulders with
mischief, enormous elephants too meet their doom! Even someone like
Sibkissen Banerjee succumbed to it![14] Padmalochan turned bitchy on
the advice of some rogues. He devoted all his energies to criticizing the
people around him, sneering at them and making caustic comments. His
faultfinding faculty slowly gathered such strength that he began to regard
himself as a saviour. His hangers-on praised him as an avatar; the rogues
honoured him with the tide 'Chance Avatar'! Seeing this, the good people
of the city began to *clap* their hands in wonder.

Padmalochan began to believe that he was no ordinary mortal. He was
either Hari,[15] a pir or the would-be *messiah* of the Jews! To prove this he
even tried his hand at confidence tricks.

Jesus Christ had fed one hundred people with a loaf of bread; he
could also cure the blind and lame with a touch of his hand. The Hindus'
Lord Krishna performed superhuman feats like killing Putana, slaying
Sakatasura[16] and things like that. To get himself accepted as an avatar,
Padmalochan claimed he'd once fed one hundred people with the food
of twelve people, that the blind and the crippled queued up at his door
to receive his blessings, and women flocked to his house with their
children to receive the touch of his blessed hand! On hearing all this, the
brahmin pundits jumped for joy like vultures during an epidemic! Money
inspires awe in the minds of people; such is its power! One gets to see
different kinds of insects in rich sweet shops: varied flies, reddish-yellow
wasps, humming bumblebees and so on, but one doesn't get to see this
wonderful variety in austere bookshops. They're filled with just lousy
white ants, filthy cockroaches and tiddly rats!

Nothing can cheer the spirits more than money, not even a puff of ganja!
One wasn't sure whether Padmalochan would give up his worldly pursuits
after becoming an avatar. Within a short time he became the most notable
Hindu in the city. His hangers-on got into a flap whenever he yawned or

[14] There is an account of Sibkissen Banerjee in the chapter, 'Gossip and
Rumours'.
[15] One of the many names of Lord Vishnu.
[16] A demon slain by Lord Krishna.

sneezed! Gradually, the news spread in the big factions of the city that Calcutta's *natural history* collection had increased by one more *number!*

Slowly, Padmalochan began to earn a lot of money by various means. In tune with his status, he bought a new house. His hangers-on began to fill the house with all the things that a man needs when he becomes rich. The babu (on his fiftieth birthday) also acquired a mistress of his choice.

Whoring is seen as a heroic job nowadays; the babus treat whores like everyday clothes. Many babus kicked the bucket long ago, but the houses they built for their mistresses still stand like *monuments* bearing their memory. Besides erecting a few two- and three-storeyed houses like these, the babus of the city have done nothing by which the common people may remember them. Many Hindu faction-leaders and Raja-titled dignitaries don't even see the faces of their wives at night; like other official work, the diwans and the clerks are charged with looking after them! Some lock their wives in the bedroom and spend the night in the sitting room with their mistresses. The babu sneaks into the bedroom after the mistress leaves the house at dawn in a coach or palki. Some young babus, out of fear of their parents, instruct their servants to sleep in the bedroom before slipping out of the house at night. The servants bolt the door from inside and sleep on the floor. The wife sleeps on the bed with a tulsi leaf beside her. The babu tiptoes into the house at midnight after having his fill of fun and knocks softly on the door. The servant opens the door and leaves. The babu quietly gets into bed. Nobody in the house ever comes to know that the babu stays away from home at night.

Readers, it's no surprise that those who've never heard the word 'dharma' in their life, those who can't discriminate between good and bad, and those who've been guided only by sycophants all their life, behave like beasts. Calcutta's become a city of whores, thanks to the lecherous babus! You won't find a single locality in Calcutta where there are less than ten whorehouses! The number of whores in the city multiplies every year. It's very risky to live near the house of a rich babu with a pretty wife or daughter; within ten days she'd elope with the babu and bring shame to the family. The babu would stand on the roof or in the veranda of his house for all the twenty-four hours of the day and keep smiling at her or waving notes at her till she relented. The hangers-on too can't rest in peace till they bring her to the babu: the babu's perhaps passed the sentence, 'Bury him alive with his family if he fails to bring her', like the nawabs of yesteryears. The woman or girl is raped and then driven away from the house. She's then left with no choice but to put herself on the market. This is not all. Some babus are so lecherous that even their wives and mistresses can't satisfy their lust; they rape their sisters and nieces! Many girls have committed suicide to save themselves from the lust of these lecherous babus. Like salt and cooking oil, herbs for abortion are regularly supplied to the babus' houses! Wherever there's an excessive show of prudishness, scandals like these are common.

> —from Kaliprasanna Sinha, *The Observant Owl* [*Hootum Pyanchar Naksha*]: *Hootum's Vignettes of Nineteenth-century Calcutta*, translated from the Bengali by Swarup Roy (Ranikhet and Delhi: Black Kite/ Permanent Black, 2008), pp. 11–19, 119–25.

G.H.

The Opening of the East Indian Railway

The 15th August 1854 is a date worth remembering, for it was the day on which the first passenger train steamed out of Howrah and the first section of the East Indian Railway was opened for public traffic; well may it have been called by the enthusiastic journalists of the times 'a red letter day in the ides of progress.'

It is not easy now to picture India without a railway of any kind, but we can imagine what an awakening the opening of the first section of the line must have been; what hopes were raised of future commercial enterprise; what anticipations were prompted as to its political and social effect on the people of the country. A leading Calcutta paper of the day wrote: 'The best which can be said of Bengal at this moment is bad. It is a wilderness, a great jungle.

'tis an unweeded garden
That grows to seed; things rank and
gross in nature
Possess it merely.

'Its resources are totally undeveloped, its natural products remain almost unknown,' and again: 'While Governors and Government and its Officials could only travel 16 or 20 miles a day, they lived, thought, wrote, acted, ruled at the rate of 20 miles a day. Now they will find where there is a railway we must all accept the high pressure principle. In twenty years hence the *dolce far niente* of Bengal will be slain.'

But let us endeavour to recall the scene at Howrah on this opening day. What is known to us as the 'old' Howrah Station had not yet been constructed; there was just a temporary shed five minutes' walk from the muddy bank of the river. It was one of the earliest grievances that there was no landing ghat on the Howrah side, and that more often than not there were no palanquins available to convey people from the foreshore to the trains. The town of Howrah as we know it now with its teeming population, its mills, factories and workshops, was then little more than a village. It is true that the site on which the new railway station now stands was a jumble of railway stores, and that the workshops of the locomotive department, where engines were put together and carriages constructed were already there, and also that there were a few small privately owned mills and workshops in the vicinity, but these were only the beginnings of Howrah as we now know the place. It was, at the time the Railway first opened, a sort of isolated suburb, completely separated from Calcutta by the river; for it was not till many years after that Sir Bradford Leslie's floating bridge connected the two places. In the meanwhile everybody who wanted to go by train had to cross the Hooghly by boat and we may imagine what a pilgrimage it was to get to or from the Railway station.

Having arrived at the temporary shed called the station, the intending passenger had to force his way through an excited and noisy crowd to the Booking Office, for there was only one small place at which tickets were issued to all classes of passengers and in this small place sat one or two Babus distracted by the requirements of the eager applicants, and unable to respond to the demands for tickets because they were new to their duties, untrained and unaccustomed to work at such high pressure.

As an instance of the difficulty of procuring a ticket one complainant wrote: 'To get a ticket is a work of time and most trying to the temper of the impatient traveller . . . . the whistle was screaming, but hardly louder than the Bengali writers who were vituperating each other instead of attending to our wants.' The complaint of another was to the effect that even if you secured a ticket you were by no means certain of a seat in the train, which by the way, was made up of the total coaching stock the line possessed: three first class, two second class, three trucks for third

class passengers and a brake van for the guard. All these vehicles had
been built in India without a model of any kind, under the supervision
of Mr. Hodgson, the first Locomotive Superintendent of the East Indian
Railway, the carriages sent out from England as models having been most
unfortunately lost a few weeks before in the shipwreck of the *Goodwin* at
the Sandheads.

There were no less than three thousand applications for tickets by
this first train and of course the great majority were disappointed as the
accommodation was barely sufficient for a tenth of that number. A public
holiday had been suggested, but this idea was not adopted as the Railway
was obviously not in a position to deal with an immense crowd; besides
this the official opening of the line was to take place later on, and as a
newspaper of the day remarked 'those who desire to treat themselves to
the novelty of the thing will have an opportunity of doing so every day in
the week except Sunday.'

Sunday was then a day of rest on the Railway; trains were not run, the
locomotives went to shed, the staff took a holiday; it was a printer's devil
who first proposed Sunday trains on the East Indian Railway. Three days
after the line had been opened to Hooghly an anonymous correspondent
who signed himself 'A Printer's Devil' wrote to the *Harkaru* paper in these
terms:—

'Attracted by the novelty of the Railway, thousands are daily
gathering to witness the running of trains and take trips to the places
on the line, but by the arrangements restricting the running to week
days, we who cannot be absent on one of these days are deprived of
obtaining a peep at the iron horse. May I therefore take upon myself to
suggest the propriety (impropriety rather) of running the locomotive
on Sundays also, to enable us *poor devils* to satisfy the curiosity which
now devours us.'

This suggestion was soon afterwards adopted, for on the 1st of
September, one of the earliest advertisements, signed from the first
Head-quarters of the East Indian Railway, 29, Theatre Road,[1] by
R. MacDonald Stephenson, Managing Director and Agent, a name
remembered by everyone as the Pioneer of Railway enterprise in India,
announced that two trains would start daily from Howrah for Pundooah,
to which station the line had by then been extended, one in the morning
and the other in the afternoon. The hours of arrival are not given, but the

[1] The Present Turf Club. The numbering of Theatre Road has since been
altered.—G.H.

The Opening of the East Indian Railway

same eight carriages ran up and down to form the service, and it may here be noted that trains ran in daylight only.

Of course there were many grumblers; the sheets of stagnant water, formed by the borrow pits along each side of the railway, were declared unwholesome, the presence of 'oily natives in a state akin to nudity in the first class carriages,' the overcrowding and so on were all themes for complaint. One writer to the public press gives his experiences in these words:—

'The up going passengers in the first class carriages on the day noted were for the most part exceedingly respectable, but all sorts of riff-raff of all colours were in the same carriages on the return trip. Some of the male gender were all the worse for their holiday making and two of them in the same compartment amused the other passengers with their amativeness. One very dark East Indian gentleman and his very dark lady stood up the greater part of the journey looking out of the window, the sterner sexed passenger winding his arm fondly round the neck of the passenger of the feminine gender. There was another billing and cooing couple of the Saxon breed and two who were almost vehemently affectionate—another gentleman treated his fellow passengers with a brief dance and various practical jokes, &c, &c.'

On the whole, however, early notices were complimentary. 'The speed at which travellers are conveyed,' writes one, 'leaves nothing to be desired. I travel up and down the line almost every day and I should declare the average rate to be about 45 miles an hour, although midway between the several stations, as high a rate as 60 miles an hour is attained. The motion of the carriages is extremely easy. The European officials are most attentive' and so on. The *Harkaru*, of the 23rd August 1854, has an amusing article on 'First impressions and first impulses of Railway travelling' full of poetical allusions—skipping the earlier part of this entertaining production, we quote the following as indicating the general views about the Railway at the time.

'Roopchand Ghose, a flourishing dealer in piece goods and perfumery, when set down at the end of the journey and told that he had arrived at Hooghly, felt strongly suspicious that he had been served out in the coin so often used in his own shop in the China Bazaar and that he had been fairly 'sold.' Arrived at Hooghly so soon—impossible! he thought—and when he saw the train was not going to move again immediately, he went about asking people what place it was, and if it was really Hooghly, and it took a long time before the conviction gained upon him that verily he *had* come to Hooghly.

'At five minutes past six o'clock on Wednesday evening, a native sircar was seen running incontinently from Armenian Ghat,[2] towards Chitpore Road. Those who saw him had their own charitable surmises, and the first chowkidar he came up to that happened to be awake stopped him, suspecting that he was running away under the cowardly impulse of a guilty conscience. This individual was no other than Kali Coomar Day, so well known to the Commanders of ships, and who having once 'realized' a full idea of Railway speed felt an irresistible impulse to accelerate his personal locomotion by running instead of walking.'

'One of the thrice born, Radhalunkur Banerjea, having made up his mind to make a trip on the Railway, duly consulted the stars with the help of the Almanac, and fixed upon Thursday for the journey as a "lucky" day. He fortified himself for the expedition by bathing three times in the river, and repeating the name of his tutelar god nine hundred and thirty-seven times. All the while he sat in the carriage he preserved the most serene and meditative silence as was very proper and becoming in so learned a person, though some took occasion irreverently to hint that the pundit was feeling *funky*. He went on as far as Hooghly but declined to undertake the return journey, because, said he, too much travelling on the car of fire is calculated to shorten life, for seeing that it annihilates time and space and curtails the length of every other journey, shall it not also shorten the journey of human life? Being asked by other pundits to furnish an exposition of the nature and properties of the Railway, our friend Banerjea gave utterance to a lot of Sanskrit maxims and verses, which very few could venture to pronounce and fewer pretended to understand. But his hearers were as perfectly satisfied with the explanation as if Watt himself had lectured to them on the Steam Engine. Indeed the learned Radhalunkur and his learned compeers feel a firm conviction that a mighty demon is kept imprisoned in the great green boiler of the Locomotive and made to work the machinery by the application of live coals to his tail, and that every time the stokers stir him up with their long hot pokers, he utters that dreadful diabolical shriek which the engineers facetiously call the 'whistle.'

'Many Europeans and East Indians have likewise performed their maiden journey on 'our own' Railway, and have also their 'first impressions,' which are doubtless as deserving of record as those of the individuals mentioned in the foregoing paragraphs,—but suffice it to

[2] For many years the East Indian Railway had a booking office at Armenian Ghat and passengers could take their tickets there before crossing the river.—G.H.

state one instance only. Mr. Jones 'regardless of expense,' made trips to Hooghly and back three successive days, and the consequence is that ever since his old horse has had to pay for it. Having acquired a notion of speed such as he never knew before, he can no longer reconcile himself to the jog trot of his buggy horse, and accordingly does nothing but whip the poor brute as soon as he gets behind him, in the vain hope of making him go at something like Railway speed.'

Comment is needless, although probably the article was merely intended for wit, it clearly indicates the feeling and style of talk at the time that Railway trains were first run in India.

We now pass to the official opening of the Railway. Saturday, the 3rd February 1855, was the day chosen and Burdwan was the scene of the festivities that followed, but unfortunately owing to severe indisposition, Lord Dalhousie, the Governor-General, could not do more than attend the ceremony at Howrah Station. Lord Dalhousie's absence was a great disappointment [as] he had taken the greatest interest in the Railway and had looked forward to being present, but it was out of the question and in a sympathetic letter to Mr. Stephenson he wrote:—

'I shall be present at Howrah but I am conscious that I am wholly unfit for the performance of the remainder of the task, which would involve a Railway journey of 150 miles, a midday banquet and the addressing of 400 people under a Bengal sun.'

The party invited to attend began to assemble at Howrah Station at 8 o'clock and by 9 a.m. about a thousand guests were ready to start for Burdwan. The Governor-General, with his staff, arrived shortly after 9.30 and the ceremony of the day was opened by the Lord Bishop of Calcutta, who, after reading several appropriate texts, offered up a prayer and gave the benediction.

Two trains had been provided for the occasion. Joshua Greenhow[3] was the driver of the first and Samuel Briggs was the driver of the second, and each train took 2 hours 50 minutes on the run.

On arriving at Burdwan Station 'the guests were conducted through an avenue strewn with leaves and overhung with arched bows and streamers to a pavilion decorated with corresponding taste, under which a sumptuous breakfast was laid out.'

In the absence of the Governor-General Mr. Stephenson took the chair. To his right was the Lord Bishop, to his left the Hon'ble Mr. Dorin and amongst the gentlemen at the same table were Sir J.W. Colville, Sir

---

[3] Both these drivers left the line in 1862.

Arthur Butler, the Hon'ble Mr. J.P. Grant, the Hon'ble Mr. Peacock, and many others whose names are still familiar in India.

After the banquet and the usual loyal toasts many speeches were made. Mr. MacDonald Stephenson proposed the health of the Governor-General and quoted largely from his despatch to the Court of Directors of the East India Company dated the 20th April 1853 which finally decided the fluctuating fate of the entire question of Indian Railways. Sir Arthur Butler proposed the Army, Brigadier Wakford replied—Captain Rogers proposed the Navy and Captain Crawford responded. The Hon'ble Mr. Dorin proposed the East Indian Railway Company. In the course of his speech he said that the Railway might justly be characterized as 'the greatest good that had been conferred on India by the application of European science. To the Government it would be of the highest value as a political engine; but its advantages in that point of view would sink into comparative insignificance when contrasted with the benefits which it would confer upon the country and people both physically and morally;' and again, 'the men of twenty years hence would indeed see and profit by the astounding works and results of which we had only been the Pioneers. But even we ourselves had seen great changes, and had found with astonishment the extraordinary demand which had already been created amongst a class of persons whom it had been thought it would be impossible to attract to that system of locomotion.' Many had been of opinion that natives would not use the Railway but from the day it opened this gloomy anticipation was dispelled. 'It must always be borne in mind,' said Mr. Dorin, 'that to the East Indian Railway Company we are indebted for the first great stride that had been made in Railway progress, that Company had already so far taken the lead amongst competitors that it appeared inevitable that they must maintain the position.' No truer words were spoken that day and the toast was drunk with loud and repeated cheers.

Mr. MacDonald Stephenson replied in a long and interesting speech, the key words of which may be said to have been 'modesty' and 'appreciation'—modesty in alluding to his own achievements, appreciation in referring to the good work of his staff. Space does not permit of our quoting from Mr. MacDonald Stephenson's speech on this auspicious day, nor is it easy to select any particular portion of it as being more interesting than other parts, but in the course of it he reminded those present that of the 20 previous years of his life devoted to the service and interests of India, the first six had been spent in contributing to secure steam navigation between Great Britain and India while the last fourteen had been 'steadily directed to those results, the first instalment of which we are this day assembled to commemorate.'

Many other speeches were made. The Hon'ble Mr. J.P. Grant, afterwards Sir John Peter Grant, Lieutenant-Governor of Bengal, Mr. Turnbull, the Company's first Chief Engineer, and Mr. Hodgson, their first Locomotive Superintendent, and several others spoke. Each one had something more or less interesting to say and as a matter of fact speeches were continued hour after hour until late in the afternoon when the party got into the return trains and were carried back to Howrah, the down run taking only 2 hours 40 minutes.

Hopes were high: '649 miles are under contract to be completed by the beginning of 1857,' said Mr. Stephenson in his speech at Burdwan. How little did those present realize what would happen in two short years time, but the history of the Railway during the Mutiny is another story!

—originally published in *Bengal: Past & Present*, vol. 2, part 1 (January–July 1908), pp. 55–61.

Amar Farooqui

Opium City: The Making of Early Victorian Bombay

Bombay and the Trade in Malwa Opium

Overwhelmed by nostalgia for the colonial era some popular works on Bombay revel in selective images of the city, choosing such landmarks and such moments in its history as might conjure pleasant memories for those who look back on the days of the British raj with longing. While there might not apparently be much harm in isolated nostalgic evocations, one has to guard against the distortions that could be, and often are, introduced by allowing a desire for some aesthetically more appealing experiences of that era to become desire for the days of the raj.

Further, one must be careful that the ugly is not easily ignored. As much
as one might like to suggest that learning to play cricket and thinking
'more or less in the European manner', gave indigenous groups the
wherewithal to participate in the economic development of Bombay and
that social intercourse with the British was responsible for the success
story of Bombay, the fact remains that the destiny of Bombay as a great
commercial and industrial centre was born of its becoming an accomplice
in the drugging of countless Chinese with opium, a venture in which
the Indian business class showed great zeal alongside the East India
Company. This is the sordid underside of Bombay's colonial past.

The story of the formation of the Indian capitalist class in Bombay
is a story both of collaboration and conflict. The feature of economic
activity in western and central India which illustrates, most vividly, the
vigour of Indian enterprise in the region during the early nineteenth
century is trade in opium. In the case of Bombay the significance of
trade in this commodity derives from the capacity of Indian merchants
to thwart attempts of the British Indian government to establish a
monopoly of the Bengal type over opium in western and central India.
They were encouraged in their truculence by the tacit or active support
of numerous other indigenous groups ranging from Indian rulers in the
region, with their curtailed authority, to armed bandits. The divergent
policies pursued with regard to the opium produce of the Ganga region
('Bengal' opium), on the one hand, and that of Malwa and Rajasthan
(Malwa opium), on the other, must be kept in view in the context of
far-reaching implications which a non-monopolistic policy, forced on
the British in western India, had on the development of Bombay.

Modern Bombay, in a sense, has its genesis in poppy fields of Bihar.
Large-scale exports of Indian opium to south-east Asia commenced in
the seventeenth century when the drug became one of the commodities
in the Dutch East India Company's intra-Asian trade. There were two
major opium producing areas in India: the Ganga region, where initially
Bihar was the main supplier, and Malwa. The Dutch procured most of
their opium from Bihar. By the mid-seventeenth century Bihar opium was
the principal commodity being carried by the Dutch company (VOC)
from Bengal to the Indonesian archipelago. According to Om Prakash
'the quantity exported had reached fairly important levels' towards
the end of the 1660s. Employees of the VOC also privately exported
substantial quantities of Bihar opium to ports such as Batavia, though
they were officially prohibited from trading on their own account. There
was almost an eight-fold increase in the profits earned by the VOC from

the sale of Bihar opium in Indonesian markets between the late 1670s and the 1740s. In 1745 the Dutch company set up the Opium Society so as to allow private traders to participate in the opium trade on a limited basis while ensuring overall control of the VOC. Private traders were already so numerous that the Opium Society was not entirely successful in regulating the commerce. In any case the VOC soon lost access to supplies of Bihar opium after the conquest of Bengal and Bihar by the English East India Company. They virtually withdrew from the trade during the latter half of the century.

From the early 1760s servants of the English East India Company in their private capacity, and eventually the Company itself, tried to corner the entire supply of Bihar opium. To start with, the head of the Company's factory in Patna attempted to personally monopolize the opium produce of the region for the purpose of export. Then in 1765 Company officials launched a joint venture to collectively trade in the drug. The size of profits from the trade was too large for it to be left in the hands of individuals, and 1773 Warren Hastings abolished free trade in it. Henceforth the Company had an exclusive right to all the opium produced in its territories in eastern India. When Banaras and the area around it were placed directly under the Company's administration in 1795 the opium monopoly was extended to Banaras-Ghazipur. This was another prime opium-producing tract. Opium from Banaras-Ghazipur and Bihar, officially referred to as 'Benaras opium' and 'Patna opium' respectively, were together marketed under the brand name 'Bengal opium'.

In 1797 the Company modified its earlier policy of purchasing opium through contractors and began procuring the entire produce directly. A comprehensive regulation of 1799 (Bengal Regulation VI) brought the cultivation of opium under the complete control of the Company. The cultivation of the poppy crop and extraction of raw opium from it was left to peasant producers. The peasants had to obtain a license from the Company that specified the actual area on which the crop was to be grown. The entire produce was supposed to be handed over to the Company's officials. Raw opium was processed and packed by the Company in its own establishments so that it was partly involved in production as well. All this opium was taken to Calcutta (some of the more inferior produce having been reserved for 'internal' consumption) where it was auctioned exclusively for export. The bulk of the opium purchased at Calcutta went to China. As Chinese imperial authorities had banned the import of the drug into the country, the Company found it more convenient to realize

profits through these auctions and then leave it to private traders to   221
fake the risk of carrying the contraband cargoes and smuggling them
into China.

The East India Company had barely settled down to enjoy the fruits of
its Bengal monopoly when disturbing reports began flowing in about the
export of opium from the west coast. One report suggested that perhaps
more than a thousand chests (a chest may be taken as containing 140
lbs of the drug) had been exported from Bombay alone between 1800
and 1803. Opium was also making its way to China from other ports
such as Goa and Surat. It was only then that the Company learnt for the
first time that opium produced in the Malwa region had the potential
of becoming a serious rival to Bengal opium in the China market. The
obvious response was a complete ban, in 1805, on the export of opium
through Bombay. Simultaneously the Indian states in Gujarat and some
other parts of western India were asked to restrict the production of
the drug in their respective territories and block its passage to the coast.
The company's objective at this stage was the 'ultimate annihilation' of
Malwa opium.

Malwa was well-known for its opium at least since the sixteenth
century. It would appear that the opium sold as 'Cambay opium' at
markets along the west coast in the sixteenth and seventeenth centuries
was in fact the produce of Malwa. The massive expansion of opium
exports from Bengal to China in the closing decades of the nineteenth
century drew Indo-Portuguese and Indian traders to this alternative
source of supply. The long association of Indo-Portuguese traders with
the sea-borne commerce of the west coast, combined with the links that
they had with the Portuguese at Macao who actively participated in the
smuggling of the drug into China, gave them a distinct advantage. It is no
coincidence that large exports of the drug from India's west coast were
more or less pioneered by Roger de Faria, an Indo-Portuguese trader
from Goa.

Roger (Rogério) de Faria was born in Goa in 1770. His father, João
de Faria, was connected with the China trade. João went to China for
a short while (in all likelihood to Macao) and on his return became a
partner in the firm Bruce, Faria and Co. at Calcutta. Roger de Faria too
was initially based in Calcutta. In his mid-twenties he was undertaking
regular voyages to Macao. We have a reference to a visit he made to
Macao in December 1798. Even before that, c. 1796, he had been granted
permission to trade at Macao, a privilege allowed at this time only to the
Portuguese. De Faria eventually settled down in Bombay sometime after

1800. He maintained close links with firms in Goa, especialy V. Nariana Camotim (Kamat).

De Faria was part of a group of Indo-Portuguese traders who procured Malwa opium from Bombay, Daman and Surat for onward shipment to Macao (though not necessarily as partners). These traders had set up their base at Bombay rather than at Goa since the capital of the Portuguese Estado da India was situated at too great a distance from the main Malwa supply networks. Bombay was their preferred port due to the facilities for export that were becoming available there. Further, just a stone's throw away from Bombay was the Portuguese enclave of Daman which was to play a crucial role in keeping the trade in Malwa opium alive following the restrictions that the East India Company imposed in 1805. Between 1805 and 1821 Daman was the main outlet for Malwa opium. However the big opium dealers conducted the trade from Bombay. In the long run most of the benefits accrued to Bombay rather than to Daman.

****

Urban Development in Early Victorian Bombay

The distinctiveness of the western Indian colonial situation had its impact on the urban development of Bombay as a capitalist port city. From an urban sociological perspective early Victorian Bombay was representative not so much of a colonial city with its colonial/indigenous spatial dualism, but was an easily recognizable capitalist city with class differentiation determining its spatial pattern.

In the early nineteenth century Bombay was fast acquiring an easily recognizable capitalist face. The city was well maintained in parts, it was squalid and congested in others. Population was expanding; there was growing functional specialization and division of labour; relations of the market were penetrating day to day life; and class differentiation was cruelly apparent. Urban development in nineteenth century Bombay has to be placed within the wider framework of the development of capitalism and the intervention of colonialism. It goes without saying that colonial rulers brought to urban development in India certain features which were inherited from the historical evolution of cities in the metropolis. At the same time it has to be borne in mind that such features were inescapable in so far as colonial rule drew various urban centres in India into a network of capitalist relations. Indian cities on which the British left their imprint became less or more capitalist cities depending upon the extent to which capitalism was able to develop/not develop in them or in the region/s in which they were located.

In Bombay, just as in Calcutta, Madras, Simla, Ootacamund or Pondicherry a pre-colonial city did not confine the colonial city. The, organization of space in colonial Bombay was therefore unencumbered by historical usage. In Delhi, Lucknow, Ahmadabad, Pune and other cities with a pre-colonial past the pattern of colonial urban development had to take into account space which had already been historically appropriated. It was often difficult to internally modify the usage of this space to suit colonial requirements: the colonial city had to be located externally. The example of Delhi is instructive. Here colonial rulers created two 'external' cities, at different points of time. One was in the middle of the nineteenth century, especially after 1857–58, when the area outside Kashmiri Gate was developed as an exclusively British 'civil lines'. Beyond the 'civil lines', troops were quartered near the Ridge. This was the time when a belligerent Delhi was being subdued after the 1857 Revolt. Before 1857 the British had shown a preference for the area lying north of Lal Qila. The residency, St. James' Church, Ludlow Castle and Metcalfe House were all located in this direction, close to the centre of the old city. As in the case of Hyderabad the location of the residency was intended to facilitate a live intercourse with the indigenous elite. There was a radical departure after 1857–58. Under the influence of military planners such as Robert Napier, who had 'cleaned up' Lucknow, the colonial civil and military establishment was now completely detached from the walled city. During the latter half of the nineteenth century urban Delhi conformed to the classical model of 'native city', cantonment and 'civil station' so characteristic of the colonial urban tradition in towns with a pre-colonial history. Then, after the decision to transfer the capital of British India from Calcutta to Delhi in 1911, a new external city was built, this time on a grand scale, on the southern outskirts of the old city. Raisina village was to house symbols of occidental despotism and ample space intervened between the new city and the old. The one did not easily impinge upon the other and the ivory tower feeling of the viceregal residence was complete.

In those cities which evolved largely as a result of British initiative, colonial urban development did not merely have to be the other of indigenous settlement. As there had been no initial appropriation of space in these cities, it was possible for the colonial rulers to take up the most favourable locations which then became the nucleus and raison d'etre of the city as a whole. Here too it would be inaccurate to talk of a uniform pattern. In the major colonial port cities—Calcutta, Madras and Bombay—where defence against external enemies had initially been an important consideration, a fortified European settlement became the starting point of development. The earliest model was provided by Portuguese factories with their defensive walls and looking out towards the sea. In these cities, however, a live economic and administrative contact with various indigenous groups was vital for the East India Company. Hence it was not feasible that the non-indigenous part of the city be isolated, permitting no interaction. Indigenous groups had to be allowed some access to a few prime locations either within or in the vicinity of the fortified settlement. In hill-stations where the British did not look forward to any intercourse with the 'natives', and which had been built at a time when British rule was relatively secure, far greater freedom in creating a non-indigenous environment was possible.

There is, therefore, no such thing as colonial urban development in the abstract. Various urban centres were products of specific historical conjunctures. The sanitaria apart, for strictly speaking their historical role was very limited, urban centres of colonial India reflected variations in the level of capitalist development in different parts of the country. Spatial organization therein was indicative of the relative strength or weakness of indigenous groups and their capacity to intervene in the control of urban space. The urban development of Bombay has to be seen in this context.

Here one might draw attention to the distorted nature of urban development which colonial rule set in motion. Urban centres developed or patronized by the metropolis in colonies often failed to generate economic activity concomitant with their expansion, since much of this expansion was often not the result of an organic growth but was related to specific colonial economic, military, administrative, strategic, and/or political considerations. The hegemony of the colonial power placed it in a position to intervene arbitrarily in according primacy to a particular urban centre in a given region so that frequently artificial, imposed and unintegrated urban development took place.

—from Amar Farooqui, *Opium City: The Making of Early Victorian Bombay* (Gurgaon: Three Essays Collective, 2006), pp. 17–22, 50–4.

A Parade of Diwans

Hyderabad had attracted people of all sorts right from the beginning. After 1763, when it became the capital city once again after a gap of seventy-six years, people from all parts of India started flocking here. Its name too had changed from Bhagnagar to Hyderabad. This name was now widely used, although old and poor people, especially amongst the Hindus, continued to call it by its original name of Bhagnagar. Not only Indians, but foreigners too came and settled down here. The French came in the wake of Bussy and Raymond in their brief period of power and glory. The English followed them for a prolonged stay. A colony of English people surrounded by the lesser mortals—Anglo-Indians and Eurasians—sprang up around the Residency in what came to be called the Chaderghat area. Missionaries did not lag behind. Church buildings arose in the vicinity. In the early nineteenth century Arabs in large numbers sought service here and they soon became strong and unruly enough to disturb the peace of the city. Adventurous Rohillas and Afghans from the northwest also gravitated to the Deccan during this period. Raja Chandulal, a Punjabi Khatri and the real power in the state for over thirty years, attracted a large number of Sikhs from the Punjab. With all these accretions, Hyderabad became a truly cosmopolitan city. Meadows Taylor described the city of the 1820s through the mouth of the Thug, Amir Ali, in his novel, *Confessions of a Thug:*

> We passed the village of Ulwal, its white pagoda peeping from among groves of tamarind and mango trees, and its large tank now glistening in the rays of the sun; and pursuing our way, we saw, on passing a ridge of rocks, the camp of the army at the far-famed Hussain Sagar, or, as it is more often called, Secunderabad. The tents of the English force glittered in the bright sun, and behind them lay a vast sheet of blue water.

We had heard much of this lake from many persons on our journey, and as we passed it a strong breeze had arisen, and the surface was curled into a thousand waves, whose white crests as they broke sparkled like diamonds, and threw their spray into our faces as they dashed against the stonework of the embankment. We stood a long time gazing upon the beautiful prospect, so new to us all, and wondering whether the sea, of which we had heard so much, could be anything like what was before us. I have since then, Sahib, twice seen the sea; I need not attempt to describe it, for you have sailed over it; but when I saw it [Hussain Sagar] first, methought I could have fallen down and worshipped it, it appeared so illimitable, its edge touching as it were the heavens, and spread out into an expanse which the utmost stretch of my imagination could not compass—a fit type, Hyderabad thought, of the God of all people, whom every one thinks on; while the hoarse roar of the waves as they rolled on, mountain after mountain, and broke in angry fury against, the shore, seemed to be a voice of Omnipotence which could not fail to awaken emotions of awe and dread in the most callous and unobservant!

... My horse slackened his pace when he reached the top, and allowing him to go on a few steps, Hyderabad opened my eyes, and glorious indeed was the prospect before me.

Beneath lay Hyderabad, the object of many a conjecture, of many an ardent desire to reach it—the first city of the Dukhun, justly celebrated throughout the countries I had passed. I had imagined it, like every other I had seen, to be in the midst of a plain, and that all that would be visible of it would be here and there a minaret rising out of large groves of trees: but Hyderabad presented a different aspect.

I stood on the crest of a gentle slope, which to my right hand was broken at some distance by rude, rocky hills, and to the left appeared gradually to descend into a plain, which stretched away almost uninterruptedly to the horizon. Before me, on the gentle rise of the valley, and beyond where Hyderabad supposed the river to be, lay the city, its white terraced houses gleaming brightly in the sunlight from amidst what seemed to me at the distance almost a forest of trees.

The Char Minar and Mecca Musjid rose proudly from the masses of buildings by which they were surrounded; and here and there a white dome, with its bright gift spire, marked the tomb of some favourite or holy saint, while smaller mosques, I might say in hundreds, were known by their slender white minarets.

Beyond the city rose another connected chain of rocky hills, which ran along until they met those on the right hand, and shut in the valley on that side. The city seemed to be of immense extent; but I thought from the number of trees that it was composed principally of gardens and inclosures, and was much surprised afterwards, when I entered it, to find its streets so filled with houses, and the whole so thickly peopled.

It was altogether a most lovely scene: the freshness of the morning, the pureness of the air, and the glittering effect of the city and its buildings caused an impression which can never be effaced from my memory. I have seen it since, and thought it is ever truly beautiful, it never struck me as it did that day.

... Crossing over an old but massive bridge, below which ran the river, now a shallow stream, we entered by the gate at the head of it, and inquiring our way went direct to the chowke, or market-place, where we trusted we should find goods exposed for sale similar to our own. The streets were narrow and dirty, and the interior of the city certainly did not answer the expectations we had formed from its outside and distant appearance; still there were evident tokens of its wealth in the numbers of elephants, on the backs of which, in canopied umbaras, sat noblemen or gentlemen, attended by their armed retainers.

... and here that noble building, the Char Minar, burst at once upon our view. 'How grand!' I exclaimed, stopping my horse and looking up to the huge minarets, which seemed to pierce the clouds; 'to see this alone is worth a journey from Delhi.'

The minarets formed the four corners of the building, and from them sprang immense arches which supported a roof, upon the top of which a small mosque was built. It did not look capable of supporting the immense weight of the whole, and yet it had stood for centuries, and the fabric was unimpaired.

... and passing by the Char Minar, we turned up a street to our right, and stopped our horses at the gate of the mosque.

A feeling of awe mingled with admiration came over me as we entered the courtyard and advanced along a raised causeway to the foot of a flight of steps which led up to the interior. On either side of us were the graves of princes and nobles, many of them of elegant forms and richly carved; but the building itself engrossed my entire admiration. Five lofty and wide arches opened to view the interior of the edifice, where an equal number appeared in depth; and where the arches met, the eye was perplexed by the innumerable points and ornaments, which, running into each other, completed a roof of exquisite design and workmanship. To add to its beauty, the whole was of stone, carefully smoothed; whereas the Char Minar and the other buildings I had as yet seen were, of stucco.

*****

Since the foundation of Hyderabad, the local chroniclers have recorded the occurrence of twelve major floods in the Musi.

The first great flood occurred in 1631. At that time the old bridge was overtopped and several populous quarters of the new city were swept away. This was regarded by the people of that time as the worst flood on record. Another flood occurred in 1831 and it was attended with considerable loss of life. The Chaderghat Bridge, which was then under construction, was seriously damaged by it. Again in 1903 there was a flood of moderate intensity in which over 1400 houses were destroyed. After that the government discouraged rebuilding of the destroyed houses and no permission was given for construction of new houses on the bank of the river.

The worst flood on record is the deluge of 1908. It occurred on Monday, the 28 September 1908, and was caused by a cyclonic storm in the Bay of Bengal. It had rained throughout Sunday. A cloudburst developed at midnight over an extensive area. Rain descended in sheets flooding small tanks and overburdening their weirs. As a result one tank after another gave way.

The flood rose about sixteen feet in less than three-and-a-half hours. All the four bridges were overtopped and their parapet walls were carried away. The approaches to the oldest bridge, the Purana Pul, were damaged but the bridge itself did not suffer any damage. The latest, the Afzal Jung Bridge or the Naya Pul, suffered the most.

The houses in Kalsovadi, along with the river, began to collapse on Sunday night and continued falling till ten the next morning. Yadgar Hussain Kunta, Shaheed Gunj, Char Mahal, Badri Alawa, and Anjee Bagh were the worst sufferers. Darul Shifa was also damaged extensively. Three thousand people were perched on the city wall near Petla Burj, which was washed away.

More than two-and-a-half kilometres of thickly populated area was devastated on the north bank and about half of that on the south bank. Nearly 19,000 houses collapsed and about 80,000 people, representing roughly one quarter of the entire population of the city, were left homeless. About 15,000 lives were lost and property worth Rs 30 million was destroyed.

Many eyewitness accounts have been written about the devastation caused by the Flood, mostly by those who suffered loss of property and some members of their family. One of them, Sayyad Ahmed Husain 'Amjad', the well-known poet, narrates the tragedy as it befell him:

> Since evening (on Sunday) the Musi was rising furiously. By 8 p.m. water was knee-deep in our house which was in Ghansi Mian Bazar. We urged our

mother that we should leave but she replied that if our end had arrived then it was better to die in our own house. By 10 p.m. water had surrounded us like a vengeful enemy. In panic we moved to a nearby house which was strong and which had survived a flood earlier. Many persons had already taken refuge there. We stayed in the sitting room. Soon the west wall collapsed and water started rushing in. We ran to the other side but there too water came gushing in from the courtyard. We put a wooden platform in the middle of the room and stood on top of it. Then we decided to move out of the room into the street. My mother, my wife, my little girl and I—all four—clung to each other. Water kept on rising even above the terrace. At 2 a.m., it touched our ankles, then came to our calves, then the knees, then our waist and finally, it reached our necks. We held each other tight so that if we got drowned, we would go down together. One step beyond—and plom—we fell into a ditch. At that time we lost hold of each other and got separated. My mother saw me swirl past her in a swift current. I shouted to her that she should catch hold of a branch of the tree overhead. She said, 'My son I can't. Your daughter is tied to my back and because of her weight I can't pull myself up.' Those were the last words I heard from her. My little daughter had become a millstone around my mother's waist. Both went down together. My wife was nowhere to be seen. I was swept towards the Maternity Hospital. Someone there pulled me up and saved me. Forlorn, naked and shivering, I was saved but there is no use of such escape. I could not even trace the dead bodies of the members of my family.

This was a story which applied to thousands of people. The Nizam, Mahboob Ali Pasha, came out on his elephant to survey the scene.

Some one suggested that the flood was caused by the fury of goddess Bhavani. He should placate her by doing an *aarti* for her. A silver plate with five earthen lamps and a sari were produced. He performed the *puja* in all solemnity. People believed that the water started receding because of that.

People wailed before him. 'We have lost our houses. We are ruined.' The ruler consoled them and told them: 'The house of your slave is there. It belongs to you.' People flocked to his palace, the Purani Haveli. The government set up refugee camps. Clothes were distributed to all. Five kitchens were opened for Muslims, five for Hindus, and one for the women who observed *purdah*. All government offices were closed for ten days. Employees were given one month's salary by way of advance.

This was the last great gesture of the ruler beloved of the people. It endeared him to them still more. That unprecedented tragedy reinforced the legend of the man.

The memory of this flood is so strong and so fresh that more than nearly a century after the event, people born long after the tragedy refer to it as *Parson ki Tughyani*—the Deluge of the Day-before Yesterday.

—excerpted from Narendra Luther, *Hyderabad: A Biography* (New Delhi: Oxford University Press, 2006), pp. 129–31, 176–8.

Sidney Low

Vision of India

You go outside into the white sunlight to find a cab. The Mussulman driver of the *tikka gharry* salaams to you with effusion as being a Sahib of inexperience, who will give a rupee where another would bestow eight annas. The short drive to the hotel takes you through what seems to be a fine modern town. You see handsome stone and brick buildings of great size, imposing frontages, clubs, hotels, public gardens, statues, fountains, well-stocked shop windows. But you have no eyes for such things. You are held and fascinated by the riot of colour and strange humanity with which you are assailed at once. Bombay is a generous and liberal hostess to the stranger within her gates. She feels the responsibility of showing him India, and she does not husband her treasures or reveal them grudgingly, but, on the contrary, throws them lavishly before him at the first onset. The great city is cosmopolitan and Pan-Asiatic. A fifth of the human race has its representatives within the island town where the white Power in the East found its first secure resting-place. Bombay is largely an epitome and abstract of the conglomerate of peoples and religions which we call by a single inadequate name.

The visitor will find out something of this later. But in the beginning he can only gaze in a sort of helpless amazement, stunned by the succession of living pictures which ring their chromatic chords upon his bewildered retina. His first impression is that he is taking part in a gigantic masquerade, with everybody in fancy dress of indiscriminate extravagance. Here are splendour, wealth, poverty, but, above all, colour and strangeness. All the hues of the rainbow, and many more, are displayed against a background

of white and brown, the white of cotton garments and the dusky tone
of bare legs and arms and bodies. The reflection you feebly make as you
survey the groups which move like ants over the broad roads is that in
Bombay any person may wear anything or nothing. He may go with a
wisp of rag round his loins. Here is a pudgy child, naked as nature made
him, save for two anklets of rough silver; here a Parsi lady in a robe of
sky-blue silk, and a filmy veil of muslin and silver tinsel drawn over her
black hair and round the pale oval of her dark face.

A porter strides along the tram-lines bearing a load of wood. His thin
legs, revealed in all their length, his bare arms and breast and shoulders,
gleam in the sun as if carved out of some smooth polished brown wood.
There is a shout of 'Ey-ah' behind him, and he jumps out of the way
to avoid being run over by the carriage in which his Highness the Raja
is seated with some of his suite. His Highness has come into Bombay,
where he is renting a bungalow for a fortnight on Malabar Hill for
20,000 rupees, in order that he may welcome the Prince of Wales on his
arrival, and he is in festal array. His coachman and his two grooms have
gold turbans and gold sashes, his landau is a noble vehicle, and it is drawn
by two high-stepping bays. He himself is attired in white silk trousers,
spangled with gold stars, a pink jacket, and a magnificent green and gold
turban with a high aigrette and brooch of diamonds.

The landau moves with stately slowness; its big horses are fat and out
of condition. It is easily passed, not only by the shabby gharry, in which
is seated an English lady in a white flannel dress with a huge sun helmet,
but also by the native bullock-cart, with its two little humped zebus
trotting smartly along. The cart is gaily painted, and a whole Hindu
family in striped cottons of various shades are stowed miscellaneously
inside.

Wherever the eye travels it catches some patch or point of colour;
and no combination seems to be excluded on the ground of extravagance
or excess. In most places, even in Cario, or Constantinople, or Tangier,
some notice would be directed to a stout man, with a sort of Roman
toga of vivid purple, drawn over a yellow under-garment, and crossed
by a sash or waistband of cerise, with a head-dress of red velvet and
silver braid, especially if the arrangement ended inadequately with tight
cotton drawers and canvas shoes in bad condition. In Bombay no one
is surprised at this decorative scheme; nor at others, such as that of
the man with bare feet, several inches of unsheltered skin above the
waist-line, and a turban of a pale lemon silk, of a quality and shade so
delicious that one would have liked to buy it on the spot.

There are Parsi gentlemen in grey bowlers provided with a particoloured roll instead of a rim, and Parsi clerks and shop assistants in black alpaca surtouts and high hats of shiny oilskin. A few Englishman are visible in sola topis and flannels, and there are Arabs, Armenians, veiled Mussulman ladies, ragged dervishes all hair and tatters, a watercarrier with his goat-skin bag across his back, and coolie women in bright-coloured *saris*. The novelty of the scene, and the flood of living light poured over everything, transfigure the commonest incidents to your enraptured senses. A Hindu with the caste mark on his forehead, under the white folds of his ample headdress, and two bullet-headed Goanese servants, are leaning from a low verandah to talk to a woman of the people on the pavement below. A crimson shawl drapes gracefully over her head and shoulders, leaving her shapely brown legs bare to the knee, and as she lifts an arm you see that it is clothed to the elbow in broad bands of silver. A carriage dashes through an open gateway, and two grooms leap down and run beside it, with long horse-tails fluttering from the staves they carry. In a hand-cart, heaped with garbage, a man is rooting and burrowing like a dog. All his raiment would not furnish the substance of a table-napkin; but gold loops depend from his ears, and a collar of dull blue stones is round his neck. As you drive in to the welcome coolness of the shaded hotel courtyard you feel that if your Vision of India were to be limited to a single morning spent in Bombay you would not have crossed the seas altogether in vain.

His first few days in the city, if the visitor has never set foot on the soil of India before, are likely to be a period of delighted amazement and most enjoyable confusion. He wanders about, drinking in the fullness of the new experience, perplexed and absorbed by all he sees, trying to wind his way through the jumble of novel human types and unfamiliar customs and costumes borne before him. Bombay is different from any other town outside India; the tourist will presently discover that India itself has nowhere anything quite like it. The Island city is unique—*a diluvies gentium*, a well into which the races of Asia have poured themselves, or, perhaps one should say, a reservoir out of which they pass as fast as they flow in. It is full of the wealth of the East and the wealth of the West, and of the poverty and vice of both. It has its palaces fit for a prince, and its human kennels unfit for a dog. The hand of Vishnu the Preserver, and Siva the Destroyer, are felt in their might daily. A splendid industrial and commercial activity makes Bombay rich and great, and a canker is working at its vitals. Every tenth person you meet is doomed to swift and painful death by a disease for which science has no remedy. It is the city of the Parsi millionaire. It is the city of the Plague.

When you have begun to disentangle your first impressions, you can appreciate the force of the contrasts which Bombay presents. The East and the West, the old and the New, are here in curious and piquant juxtaposition. A great deal of that part of Bombay which is called the Fort, and is the centre of the European business life, is very modern indeed. There are enormous ranges of huge public buildings, designed with a fine official disregard for all local associations, great blocks of flats, and flourishing shops, some of which might have been transported from Bond Street and others brought from the Edgware Road; and a life, essentially English and only touching the East at the fringes, is in being here. But a few hundred yards away are the bazaars and the native streets, and you are in the heart of Asia. This is true, more or less, of many Indian towns; but it is specially felt to be the case in Bombay, because there the Europeans are not shepherded apart in cantonments, or in any separate quarter of their own, but are physically, at least, in pretty close contact with the natives. The lines touch at many points, but they do not merge.

'Society' in Bombay, though the natives are knocking insistently at its portals, is still English in the English orthodox mode. It is more varied in its constituents, more permeated by the commercial element, and less dominated by the official factor, than in other Indian towns, except Calcutta. But its forms and customs are those to which we cling with fidelity wherever we settle. There are excellent clubs in Bombay, where the stranger, if properly accredited—much meaning in that 'if'—will be welcomed with a most agreeable hospitality; there is a relative abundance of ladies' society; tea parties, lawn-tennis parties, and dinner parties prevail; people dance, ride, play bridge, and go out with a good pack of hounds to hunt the jackal; they escape the heats of Bombay by ruralising in the hill stations of the Ghats, or they flit about the harbour in smart little yachts.

In the cool garden of the Yacht Club, from tea onward till dinner-time, the visitor may almost forget that he is in India. If it is on a Friday, the day when the P. and O. liner discharges its complement, the grounds will be thronged, especially during the weeks of the autumn rush eastward. Except for the dark faces and white cotton garb of the servants, there is little that is distinctively oriental, ladies are parading the green lawns, or taking tea and cooling drinks at small tables set out on the terrace which overlooks the shimmering waters of the roadstead. Immediately opposite lies the slate-grey guardship, and a wall-sided yellow-funnelled transport. The band of the Blankshire Regiment is playing a selection from the last new musical comedy. The fragrance of cigarette-smoke is wafted into the air; there is the tinkle of feminine laughter and the buzz of many voices; the women are in light European summer dresses; the straw hat has replaced the sun-helmet for the men; we might be on the Riviera, or at some fashionable country club in the United States, or perhaps even at Ranelagh or Hurlingham.

When you have stayed long enough and drunk your tea, and the sudden Eastern night has fallen in its pall of blackness, you will be asked to dine in some luxurious bungalow or well-appointed flat. Here, it is true, the flavour is slightly more Oriental. The punkahs will be flapping above your head; barefooted 'boys' will minister to you. But though there may be some unfamiliar dishes and a local fish, the viands presented will be in the main those of home. You will find a *menu* card, written in the usual culinary French; mutton cutlets and partridges and asparagus and ices and *olives farcies* will appear on the list; you will drink Mumm or Heidsieck, and talk to your neighbour about nothing in particular in a subdued undertone. It is a replica of those sparkling repasts with which we exhilarate ourselves during the London season. You will emerge into the starlight with the consciousness of an evening spent in a reputable and decorous dullness.

But get back into your gharry and tell the driver to take you by the Grant Road past the Munbadevi Tank, along Abdul Rahman Street, by the Bendi Bazaar, and about the native quarter generally. You will not lack entertainment: especially if you strike Bombay, as I did, on the eve of a Royal visit, and at the new moon of the month Kartik, which is the Hindu Feast of Lanterns. The entertainment begins even before you leave Malabar Hill, that most desirable residential region, where the luxurious bungalows have their place. Many of these have been rented for a fortnight by native chiefs and potentates, who have come into Bombay to pay their respects to the Shahzada. They are in a demonstrative mood; they attest their loyalty to the eye and ear. That is why 'the Queen Victoria Royal Band' has been brought up to the lawn of Bellaggio, and why its Eurasian artists are fiddling drumming and fifeing furiously among the flower-beds; that is why The Pines is a blaze of light, and why its compound is dotted all over with red green and white balls of tinsel stuck on little poles. If a man is a raja, and a ruling chief, and a K.C.I.E., entitled to be met at the railway-station by a Government House aide-de-camp, and to a salute of several guns, there is no reason in the world

perceptible fashion.

The night indeed, like Prospero's isle, is 'full of noises'; the Indian night always is, even in the quieter suburbs of the towns, for there are the noises of beast and bird, as well as the sounds made by human hands and throats. The field crickets and grasshoppers are chirping with a loud metallic clank; the grey-backed crows, which you have noticed all day feeding on dead rats and other carrion, retire to their nests with raucous cawings; weird squeals and chatterings are heard from a thicket, and you know—that is, you know when your driver tells you—that they are emitted by the monkeys who are swinging in the boughs.

When you reach the native bazaar, your coachman must drive at a foot's-pace, with many stoppages. The narrow twisting streets are swarming with people, spreading all over the roadway in close groups and solid columns. You will make better progress by leaving your carriage and walking; besides, this will give you an opportunity of observing the people in their various types and tribes. Your studies have not gone very far, but you make and attempt to classify and select. In India everybody bears the mark of his occupation, his religion, and his social status upon his person, so that his mere outward aspect should tell you who he is and what he does. It is as if you could wait for the nine-fifteen train at Ludgate Hill, and, as the crowd poured through the turnstiles, you could point a finger and say: 'Here is a Roman Catholic, here a member of the Church of England, here a Welsh Non-conformist; this man was born in Lancashire and is a member of the Stock Exchange; that other is very likely to be an auctioneer, though it is also possible that he does something on commission in coals and wine.'

There is ample opportunity for such exercises in the Bombay bazaar. Even a novice can distinguish between the Mussulman head-gear and that of the Hindu, between the sturdy, upstanding Sikh and the Mahratta, with his rat-like profile, little, restless eyes, and receding forehead; between the Brahman, with his oval face and pale yellowish skin, and the outcast, despised Mahar, a little blackened wisp of a man, stunted and ape-like. In honour of the Festival, many of the people have been to the priests and paid their fee to have their caste-marks repainted, so that their foreheads glisten with weird symbols, balls and lines and ovals, and smears of red and yellow.

The expert can tell you something about almost everybody you pass in the throng. Here is a baniya, or retail trader, with carpet slippers and a large gamp umbrella in his hand. The baniya is often fat; for, though he lives generally in the native quarter and in the native fashion, he may be quite rich, and wealth means to a Hindu more butter and ghee and rice and sweet meats and other viands that produce adipose tissue. Here is a man in white jacket and trousers of a somewhat European cut, carrying a child sitting astride his right hip, and followed by a woman in a purple *sari*, a square of cotton cloth, which serves for tunic and bodice and as much skirt as she needs. It is the prosperous upper servant of a well-to-do family, or perhaps the butler at a club, taking his youngest born and the more favoured of his two wives out to see the show. He shuffles along, in ungainly fashion, in his canvas shoes; his wife, in her graceful drapery, with silver earrings and anklets, is a more distinguished figure, and she walks like a princess, but she keeps respectfully a pace or two behind her lord, and does not speak to him except when he turns to address her over his shoulder. In Bombay and elsewhere in India the women of the lower classes have a dignity of carriage which is denied to their male owners. Some of them, of the coolie grade, are almost pygmies in stature, their features are blunt and shriveled, and they are black from exposure to the sun; but no wild doe on the mountain-side moves with more unfettered grace and freedom. The women walk better than the men, for they bear their burdens on their heads, while their partners and proprietors bend and slouch under the weight of heavy loads carried on the shoulders and back.

The bazaar is always crowded from early morning until late night; it is always full of people walking, sitting, lying on the ground, jostling against one another like ants. But perhaps the throng is a little more than normal on this Feast of Lamps, the *Diwali*, which is one of the great festivals of the Hindu year. The *Diwali* is held in honour of Lakhshmi, the Venus of the Indian Pantheon, the wife of Vishnu the Preserver. Lakhshmi, like her Hellenic antitype, arose out of the foam of the sea waves, and she is the Goddess of Beauty; but she is also the Goddess of Wealth and Prosperity, and is therefore held in special honour by shopkeepers and tradesmen.

On the Feast of Lamps the gains of the year are dedicated to the goddess, and every house is lighted for her. The larger Europeanised stores in the bazaar, the 'cheap jacks,' where they sell all sorts of things, from bicycles to safety-pins, the motor garage where the wealthy native buys his up-to-date car, are hung with tiers of electric lights and glow-lamps; but each little square booth has its own small illumination. All the shops are open, and the owners are seen sitting beside the implements and objects of their trade. The goldsmith has rows of candles to set off his golden bowls, his cups and chains and jewellery work; the *shroff*, the small moneylender or usurer, piles up his account-books in a heap, with a kerosene lamp on top. A white Hindu temple is all festooned with ropes and wreaths of flowers; a yellow Jain chapel sparkles with coloured lights, and looks rather like a Paris café, with its open rooms and balconies and lounging groups. Only the Mohammedan mosque stands grimly shut and dark and silent; for *Diwali* is a Hindu festival, and the children of the Faith have no parting it. There were times when the celebration was a fruitful source of faction-fighting and serious riot. But the vigilant Bombay constables, little sturdy men in blue, are scattered freely among the crowds, and in the very centre of the whole turmoil, where the chief Mohammedan street crosses the Hindu bazaar, there is a small square brick building, which is the police post. Here a couple of sepoys are talking to a khaki-clad sowar of the mounted force standing beside his horse, ready to ride to the barracks for assistance, if need be; and against the door-post leans a tall young Englishman, in white uniform and helmet, surveying the passing stream of humanity with good-humoured, but not inattentive, indifference—a symbol of that impartial tolerance, combined with the vigorous assertion of public authority in the maintenance of order, which is the attitude of the British *raj* towards the creeds and sects of India.

Some Rajput Capitals

The City of the Enchanted Lakes

The older un-Occidentalised Rajputana, which still clings to its feudalism and medievalism, finds its most favourable example in the State of Mewar; for the ruler of that territory, a dignified, upright, and conscientious prince, thoroughly loyal to the Empire, is, nevertheless, a steady champion of Hindu conservatism, who dislikes modern innovations, admits them grudgingly, and does his best to keep his country and his people to the older ways. The bluest blood of India runs in his veins: he can trace his lineage back authentically he goes further still, for he is the head of the Sesodia dynasty, the descendants of the Sun God, who have never sullied the purity of their race by giving a daughter in marriage to the Mohammedans. For this reason, his Highness the Maharana, Sir Fateh Singh Bahadur, G.C.S.I., is regarded with reverence all over the Hindu world; and partly on this account, and partly because he is an excellent man, who governs wisely and honestly according to his lights, we interfere with him as little as possible, and allow him to retain in being many vestiges of the past, which more progressive rajas have been induced to abandon. To the student of Eastern institutions, of sociology, of Asiatic history, and Indian politics, much fruitful material lies to hand in Mewar State. But that student must be 'more or less than man' if he can keep his mind on these matters during the first day of his sojourn in the distracting city of Udaipur. You cannot easily make statistical observations in Fairyland.

Conceive a rugged mountain country, of brown, bare, jagged peaks, and scarped, serrated hills; and in a broad valley or basin of this desolate land place a chain of still and silvery lakes, with palms and plantains, and blossoming wisteria, and cactus, and spiny jungle-grass, breaking the sandy hummocks in a belt of verdure at the edges of the pools. And plant, by the margin of the largest lake, and on the lowest ridges of the upland, a city of snowy palaces and gleaming towers and fretted minarets, and the great carved blunt pyramids of temples—a city which leans over the flood in long stretches of crenellated rampart and jutting bastion, or opens from it in arabesqued gateways, which reveal narrow streets, gay with many-hued life, and backed by a sheet of turquoise sky. It is a city of wharves and bridges, like Venice, and tiers of marble steps, leading down to the lapping water, and balconies, with delicate domes and threadlike mullions and shafts of embroidered ivory hung from high white walls. Stud the surface of the lake with islands, and make these visions of marble porticoes and cupolas and trellis-work and terraces, with the plumes of the palm and the broad green pennants of the plantain waving above them; and let castles and forts and shrines dot the mountain-sides, or rest like tiaras on the frowning headlands. Imagine all this, and you may get some faint idea of the earthly Paradise which the Children of the Sun created for themselves when the Moghuls sacked their ancient capital and drove them to find a home and resting-place behind the desert hills.

Udai Singh and his successors had a sense of the fitness of things. Perhaps they were not great designers; I do not know that there is a really fine piece of architecture in Udaipur, and whenever you pry into the details of the buildings you are met with something petty and insignificant, with silly pepper-pot turrets, domes with poor lines and bad curves and cemented verandahs that look mean at close quarters. Put all this confectionery under a dull sky and in a leaden northern atmosphere, and it might seem common and shabby. But in this fine air, picked out against the monotone of enameled blue, it is in its place. The old palace is an immense building, of high, blank, and nearly windowless, wall, which dominates the lake from its lofty terrace; but behind this massive screen one catches a glimpse of pinnacles and roofs in creamy marble, so graceful and so light that you almost think they must wave and quiver with the breeze.

The palace is a town of itself, so vast that the Maharana's stables, with all their horses and grooms, can be stowed away among the foundations of the great containing wall. The newer portion of the palace, built in the last century, with its courts and fountains and reception-rooms, occupies a mere corner of the huge fabric, a corner happily which does not too roughly depart from the style of the remainder. Seen from the lake, the palace is always the centre of the picture as it should be, standing, impassive and serene, with the clustering town at its knees, the green gardens at its feet, and the castellated brown heights, like kneeling elephants with their howdahs, shutting off the enchanted valley from the world beyond.

It would be hard to say at what hour of the twenty-four Udaipur is at its best. Is it when the touch of dawn turns the hills to gold and flushes the white walls and cold marbles with the rose of life? Or is it that magic moment just before sunset, when the heat-haze rises like thin smoke over the ridges, and when all the foreground, lake and town and islands, swims in a bath of thin and luminous azure? One has seen it at night, and on that special night when the Maharana clothed it in golden light in honour of his Royal guests. Illuminations are, as a rule, rather vulgar affairs; but I think all illuminations henceforth must seem cheap and tawdry to those who remember that November evening on the terraces at Udaipur. Here there were no electric arcs, with their cold and steel-like beam, no incandescent lamps, with hard unwinking stare, no coloured lanterns in garish green and red. Nothing was used but the common Eastern *butty*, the true 'Light of Asia,' a mere earthenware saucer, with a shred of cotton-wick and a tiny pool of oil. These humble nightlights were set by the thousand and the ten thousand, outlining every thing with a tender palpitating glow, as if streams and runlets of lambent flame were slowly trickling along every wall and pinnacle and projection, by the sides of buildings, and down the shafts of columns. The islands mirrored themselves in the lake in temples and palaces of softened fire; the forts flickered like giant fireflies on the distant hills. It was Fairyland—with the elfin lamps alight.

When you are recovered from your first ecstasy at the mere outward form and aspect of Udaipur, and you come to know it familiarly and to move about its streets and courts, you find it more delightful still. You are filled with a strange sense at once of novelty and reminiscence. You may go down to the lake-side, and there, on the broad steps of the palace itself, under the embossed and fretted arches of the gateway, you may see the women filling their water-pots at sunrise and evening: pots of gleaming brass and copper, that go dripping up the steps, or great red earthen *chatties*, balanced on dusky heads, under veils of purple or crimson, and held in place by a single curved brown arm. You can look over the low wall into the square arena of sand, with the circular stone pedestal in the middle, where the king has his wild-beasts fights on certain state occasions; or you may stroll down to the bottom end of the lake, and see the King's wild boars fed, and the King's tigers and black bears ramping at their bars. Walk down the narrow dusty street, through the *Hathi Pal*, the Gate of the Elephants, past the great Temple of Jaggernath, and by the Sarai, or caravanserai, where camels and bullocks and squealing stallions are tethered all over the open courtyard.

Peer into the rows of dim little booths as you pass. Here is the armourer at his work, and the goldsmith, and the man who puts spots and borders of silver tinsel on the cotton *saris*. The money-changer sits at his door with his scales and measures and his little heaps of coin; if you give him a quarter of a rupee, which is fourpence, he will fill both your hands with irregular square-shaped bits of copper, that represent the small currency of the Maharana's realm. A huge Brahminy bull wanders by, none making him afraid, for he can nose into what stalls and baskets he pleases, and is a licensed plunderer and drone. And here is the man whom the King delights to honour, resplendent in silk and cloth of gold, with his runners before him to clear the way; here a young cavalier, riding down the street with his falcon perched upon his gloved wrist; here a Rajput noble, in helmet and crest, with a hauberk of chain-mail descending over his shoulders, followed by his knot of armed retainers with long spears and rusty scimitars. In the cool of the evening you may see many people walking upon the flat roofs of the houses, even as King David walked when his eye lighted upon the wife of Uriah the Hittite; you may, perchance, come upon Jezebel, with her head tired, looking out from an upper window. After all, we are on familiar soil. We have come far from the world of the twentieth century. But we are close to countries which have been traveled ground to most of us at some period of our lives. We are in the land of the Bible and the land of the Romances.

—excerpted from Sidney Low, *A Vision of India* (2nd edn, London: Smith, Elder & Co., 1910), pp. 6–16, 95–100.

Man and Life in Calcutta

Calcutta grew enormously during the thirty-two years I lived in it, and became amorphous. Since 1942 it has received hundreds of thousands of additional immigrants and, according to old residents, is no longer recognizable as its familiar self. I have not seen Calcutta after this recent adulteration, but even in 1910 it was not one city. In certain of its quarters a man could easily fancy that he was in China. Other parts look like *mohallas* torn out of the cities of upper India, and, in fact, till recently Calcutta had the largest Hindi-speaking population of any city in India. Along the Chowringhee and south of Park Street the city had an appearance which probably was not materially different from that of the European adjuncts of Chinese, Malay, or Egyptian ports, but even here it did not exhale mere commerce, club life, sport, and turf. Those who were historically conscious could sense these parts of Calcutta to be very perceptibly breathing the spirit of the builders of the British Empire in India. The rest of the city was purely Bengali.

Between the European and the Bengali parts, however, there always was a Eurasian and Muhammadan belt, very characteristic in appearance and still more so in smell. One of the typical sights of these quarters were the butcher's shops with beef hanging from iron hooks in huge carcasses, very much bigger than the goat carcasses to whose size we the Bengali Hindus were more used. These wayside stalls were redolent of lard, and were frequented by pariah or mongrel dogs of far stronger build and fiercer looks than the dogs of the Hindu parts of the city. These animals always reminded me of the dogs in the butcher's shops of the *Arabian Nights*. All the components of Calcutta had personality and character, but the foreign elements seemed to be even more particularly assertive. In spite of the numerical preponderance of Bengalis the city was, and perhaps still is, an international concession, once flourishing but now moribund, on the mud-flats of deltaic Bengal.

Even when we first came to it Calcutta was vast. At the same time it was very close-knit and compact. It was not broken in relief like Rome with its Seven Hills, not scattered in space like Delhi with its seven historic sites. That did not mean, however, that from a height the city had a smooth appearance. Looked at from the top of the Ochterlony

Monument, or even from the roof of a high private house, the house-tops of Calcutta seemed in their crowded and untidy rows to bid the most solid and the ugliest imaginable defiance to the sky. They made a deep impression on me when I contemplated them with the newly acquired sense of being a citizen, immediately after our arrival in 1910. Our house, which was in the Bowbazar quarter, was a four-storied building, and as we went up to its roof an amazing confusion met our eyes. There was an immense expanse of house-tops fading away on all sides into the smoky horizon, but no two house-tops were alike in shape, height, colour or arrangement. If one had a parapet, another had a wooden or iron railing, and a third nothing. The levels were nowhere uniform, nor even rising or falling in any discernible pattern of tiers, banks, or terraces. Another extraordinary thing we noticed was that the roofs seemed to be the favourite dumping ground for lumber and waste of all kinds, from broken furniture to smashed earthenware and pieces of torn canvas or sack. The irregular upper surface of Calcutta was made more jagged still by the edges and points of this junk.

The only place where the skyline appeared to suggest architecture was the extreme west. There we could see in the one ample curve the tops of the well-known public buildings of the Esplanade and Dalhousie Square. The line began with the cupolas, small and big, of the new building of Whiteaways and ran through the tower of the High Court, the flat dome of the Government House, the square tower of the old Central Telegraph Office, the high dome of the General Post Office, the leads of Writers' Buildings and the statues on its cornices, to the steeple of the Church of St. Andrew. The scene gave the impression of an ugly sea of tossing brickwork contained along a clearly marked line by an architectural breakwater. If the view of Calcutta from above was ever softened it was only by its own appalling domestic smoke and the not very much more pleasant mist rising from the river to the west and the marshes to the east.

But three special features of the top face of Calcutta must also be mentioned, not only because they somewhat redeemed the squalid general effect, but also because they could not have been missed by anybody looking at Calcutta from an elevated point in the years following 1910. They were, first, chimneys and church spires. Two of each could be very prominently seen from the roof of our house. To the south-east rose the very tall chimney of the sewage pumping station at the Entally end of Dhurrumtollah Street, and the other was the ornamental chimney of the municipal waterworks on Wellington Square. Both the chimneys have now disappeared. The church spire nearest to us was that of the Roman

spire of the church on Wellesley Square almost equally distinctly. In
Calcutta of those days no temple or mosque rose into the air. If any
bells rang they were church bells. The people of Calcutta were so used
to church spires that they gave the distinctive name of Bald Church to a
steepleless church in our locality. In my time the church had disappeared,
but it had bequeathed its name to the quarter.

The second landmark in the Calcutta sky was the group of five
cranes on the site of the Victoria Memorial, then in the course of
construction. These impressive architectural ancillaries were not less
decorative and monumental than architecture itself, and for many years
these magnificently arranged objects, imprinted as they were on the
southern sky of Calcutta, created the illusion of a vast Brangwyn etching
overhanging the city or some colossal ghost ship working its derricks
in the upper air. When with the completion of the building the cranes
disappeared, with them also disappeared one of the most vivid and poetic
associations of my first years in Calcutta.

The third feature we noticed has also become rare, if it has not
disappeared altogether. Every thousand yards square or so of the top
face of Calcutta had a bamboo mast bearing on its head a bird-table,
consisting only of a trellised frame, for pigeons to sit on. At the foot of
the mast crouched a watchful man with an upturned face; he held a long
and thin stick in his hand and from time to time prodded the birds with
it. The birds at first tried to avoid the stick by changing places; then one
or two began unwillingly and lazily to ascend with laboriously flapping
wings; but as soon as three or four had gone up the whole flock rose
with a whirr and began to fly to and fro over an orbit of about a quarter
of a mile, keeping the trellis at the centre. They flew in one direction
to begin with, and then took a complete right-about turn towards the
other direction. At the turning points they wholly melted away in the
atmosphere, but as soon as they had taken their turn flashed back into
vision like silvery scales on the blue-grey sky. After about half-a-dozen
turns in this fashion they came back to their frame and began to drop
by twos and threes on it, and with a little jostling and elbowing-settled
down for the time being, to be prodded up again after a while by their
keeper. Eight, ten, or even a dozen flocks were seen flying at the same
time, and they gave a feathery and shot effect to the Calcutta sky. This
sky was never gorgeous, but it had at times a pearly tenderness, and to this
softness the flying birds added not only a suggestion of the pastel shades
of the pigeon's throat, but also a turtledove sensibility. The contrast of

such a sky with what lay spread out below was very marked. It seemed as if a crowd of misbehaved and naughty children were showing their tongues and behinds to a mother with the face of Michelangelo's Night.

Within a few days of my coming to Calcutta I learned with astonishment from my new school-fellows that the pigeons, and, even more so, their keepers were held in the worst possible disrepute by the human beings of the city. I casually mentioned to some of my school-fellows that I used to keep pigeons at Kishorganj. They looked with scandalized incredulity at me, because I had already given proof in the class that I was clever at books, and in my general behaviour, too, there was nothing to suggest a keeper of pigeons to these Calcutta boys: I showed no obvious signs of the moral degeneration which pigeons were supposed in Calcutta to bring on mankind. Fortunately, the boys took my former pigeon-keeping as the oddity of an East Bengal boy and did not report to the teachers. In the case of a Calcutta boy a cry would have arisen: 'Sir, this boy flies pigeons,' and at that cry the cane would have descended mercilessly on my back.

On the ground Calcutta presented a very impressive façade. But it was a façade which looked inwards, like the amphitheatre on the arena. The arena was formed by the famous Maidan or, as it is called in Bengali, the Field of the Fort, and the city stood in a rough arc round it like the inner face of the Coliseum. The parallel is not as correct for the two wings of the façade of Calcutta as it is for the eastern or Chowringhee section, for both the wings—the first from Hastings to St. Paul's Cathedral and the second from Esplanade corner to Outram Ghat—were leafy. To the north, the Government House was all but hidden by the trees which stood trunk to trunk along the low white balustrade which formed its outer boundary wall, and towards the river the long line of the beautiful *polyalthia longifolia* of the Eden Gardens hid the High Court and the Town Hall even more effectively. Only through the funnel-like opening of the road called Government Place West could a glimpse of the Treasury Buildings be caught. At this entrance a formidable group of statuary stood on guard. Queen Victoria, Lawrence, Hardinge, Canning in greenish bronze reminded everybody in 1910, even if the unobtrusive Government House modeled on Kedleston Hall did not, that he was very near the heart of the British Empire in India. To the south of the Maidan there was a similar line of trees along Lower Circular Road, and although there was not in that quarter the same reminder of British power in India as there was to the north, there was at least a reminder of British sickness, both civil and military. For one set of the buildings which could be seen through the trees constituted the British Military Hospital and the other the Presidency General Hospital. The first was reserved for British soldiers and the second for British civilians.

Although the wings of the façade of Calcutta were leafy, the brickwork on the eastern side was long, high, and solid enough to obliterate all sylvan atmosphere. This front would not have stood the scrutiny, building by building, of an architectural designer, but, seen from the distance and as a whole, it was not unimpressive. The skyline, though not absolutely uniform, was not unbalanced by any pronounced irregularity. I once saw the Chowringhee from the River Hooghly when going to the Botanical Gardens at Sibpur in one of the Port Commissioners' ferry service steamers, and the familiar line of buildings beginning with the Army and Navy Stores and ending in Whiteaways was estranged to my eyes by the beauty shed on it by the distance.

The central point in this façade of Calcutta was certainly the high pile of the Indian Museum, rather dull-looking from the outside but always enlivened by the thought of what it contained within. There was no place in Calcutta, unless it was the zoological gardens of Alipur, of which I was more fond. The huge galleries, each at least one hundred feet long, forty feet wide, and as many high, were always reeking of the sweating upcountry men who visited the museum as a matter of duty and trudged through the galleries as solemnly and steadily as my Kishorganj peasants marching to the field of Id prayers. They never stopped before anything unless they saw some visitor taking particular interest in one or other of exhibits or comparing something in a book with the objects. Then they crowded round that visitor and asphyxiated him with their body odour. It was, however, impossible to get angry with them. They were as natural and primitive as the exhibits, though not as monumental. In the entrance hall were the bull and lion capitals of the pillars of Ashoka, in the hall to the right were the highly ornamental red sandstone railings of the Bharhut Stupa, and in the hall to the left the Siwalik fossils together with the skeletons of the huge Hasti Ganesa or *Elephas Antiquus Namadicus Falc.* of the Nerbudda valley. It could be said that in these galleries of the Indian Museum were represented all the previous empires in India from that of the gigantic prehistoric elephants to that of Asoka the Buddhist and Samudragupta the Vishnuite.

Facing the Indian Museum across the Maidan stood Fort William equally silent from the outside but busy and humming like a beehive within with sun-helemeted British soldiers. It was impossible for any person endowed with the consciousness of history to overlook the correlation of the museum with the fort. It was as if those who were living for the time being in Fort William were saying to those who had been housed for all time in the Indian Museum—'Hail, dead emperors, emperors about to die salute ye!' In 1911, unknown to all of us, the shadow of death had already fallen. I still remember my father reading with his friends the news of the transfer of the capital to Delhi. *The Statesmen* of Calcutta was furious, but was thinking more of the past than of the future and was not inspired to prophecies like Cassandra. We were flippant. One of my father's friends dryly said, 'They are going to Delhi, the graveyard of empires, to be buried there.' Everybody present laughed, but none of us on that day imagined that although the burial was the object of our most fervent hopes it was only thirty-six years away.

Only one section of the façade of Calcutta had depth, and that was the section between Park Street and Lower Circular Road. The interior here was like the front, only quieter and more spacious. To walk down Middleton Street, Harrington Street, and Theatre Road was to walk into an area of large, still houses standing in their own grounds planted with *lagerstroemia indica*, canna, and ixora, and of wide silent streets shaded by *gul mohurs*, and cassias, and an occasional *lagerstroemia flos-reginae*. All these flowering trees and shrubs blossomed from April to September, making a gorgeous blaze of colours—scarlet, vermilion, pink, purple, lilac, blue, white, and golden yellow—in the midst of which the houses looked dull and ordinary. They did not, however, jar with any obtrusive ugliness. The majority were impressive by reason of their size and solidity, although not by their architecture. But a few had style. They were old buildings in the modified Georgian manner of the East India Company. Here too, as in the façade, it was the effect as a whole and not the details which constituted the attraction. And in this attraction space and silence were the principal elements. The whole area was very much like the old cemetery at its centre, where Landor's Rose Aylmer lies buried. . . .

The inhabitants of the locality prized the silence greatly, and they wrote angry letters to the newspapers against the tooting of horns by taxis prowling for fares at night.

For us Bengalis one street of the area came to acquire a dreaded notoriety. It was Elysium Row. This was an inviting name, to which the great Bengali barrister, Sir S.P. Sinha, the first Indian member of the Viceroy's Executive Council, and later to become Under-Secretary of State in India and the first Indian peer and Governor of an Indian province, who lived in the street, added greater lure. But the pleasantness of the name and the pride evoked by the association with Sinha were wholly smothered for us by the fear inspired by Number Fourteen, the headquarters of the Special Branch or the political police. There were few Bengali young men with any stuff in them who did not have dossiers in Number Fourteen, and many had to go there in person, to be questioned, or to be tortured, or to be sent off to a detention camp. After the passing of the Defence of India Act of 1915 we began to think of Elysium Row more in connexion with the police than with Sinha. To have been in Elysium Row came to be regarded as equivalent to being branded on the forehead or having a ribbon on the chest, according to the standpoint or courage of the dragooned visitor. My younger brother as a young man of eighteen was taken there, questioned by third-degree methods, and then photographed in full face and in profile for future identification. That did not, however, prevent his identity being mixed up in the mind of the police with quite a different person's, and this confusion caused no small amount of harassment to my brother. I did not have to go there at any time of my life, but at a late stage I had a dossier. In my school and college days I did not come in the way of the political police nor did they come in my way, and I never walked through Elysium Row. Therefore the spaciousness, the silence, and the flowers remained my only impressions of this part of Calcutta.

The rest of the Chowringhee façade was only skin-deep, and the hinterland was a strange world whose strangeness was not felt by us only because everybody took it for granted. Russa Road at the southern end of Chowringhee led into the old and respectable Bengali quarter of Bhowanipore, best known for its lawyers, and through Bhowanipore to the less wealthy but more religious quarter of Kalighat; Bentinck Street at the opposite end was famous for its Chinese shoemakers; Dhurrumtollah, which was at the same end, was itself a street of shops, bazaars and Eurasians, but it was also the ingress to the main Bengali parts of the city. An observer could stand at the Chowringhee ends of Dhurrumtollah and Russa Road and watch men coming out between nine and ten in the morning and going in between five and six in the afternoon like ants out of and into their holes. The Bengali parts of Calcutta, both north and south, sent them out in the morning for office work and sucked them back in the evening. These were the men to whom Calcutta belonged by birthright. They loved Calcutta as nobody else did. They lived in it like deep-sea fauna in the depths of the sea. Most of them would have preferred death to being removed from Calcutta.

Their Calcutta, which was also my Calcutta for thirty-two years, was an immense maze of brickwork cut up by streets and lanes. It was not labyrinthine like the Indian quarters of the cities of northern India, and it did not bring on that claustrophobia which impels new comers to those cities to rush out into open spaces in order to breathe easily. Nor did it have that putrid squalor which makes the inhabitants of the same upper-Indian cities feel like living in the intestines of the Leviathan. Also, there was not that accumulated dust, to try to remove which was equivalent to raising only more dust. All these unlovely features of urban life in upper India, our part of Calcutta did not possess, but there was no limit to its architectural meanness. Walking along the ever-lengthening streets and lanes of these quarters one expected at every turn and step to come upon some spot of handsomeness and repose, for instance, a fine building, a spacious square, a wide vista, or at least a colourful bazaar. These expectations were never fulfilled. The more one trudged, the more one felt like swallowing an endless tape of shabbiness.

On account of this all-pervasive inelegance even the wider streets gave no impression of being straight, although they were straight in layout. The awry fronts on either side, taken with the erratic skyline and the unfinished surfaces, checked the growth of any impression of symmetry and harmony. Three or four times every hundred yards the skyline would be falling down abruptly from sixty to ten feet and changing its outline from that of a straight parapet of a flat-roofed brick house to that of the sloping roof of a mud-walled and tiled *bustee*. For the same distance the street front would be presenting three or four incongruous patches: a gaping shed, a solidly built wall pierced by small windows, an unglazed shop window or, rather, a mere opening, and a house with venetian blinds. There was not a single inviting front-door anywhere. The Bengalis of Calcutta seemed to have a particular aversion to attractive entrances. One of the two entrances to a particular house I knew had a new door. But it had its attractiveness, which in truth was no more than that of newness, reduced if not wholly suppressed by an unfelicitous attempt on the part of the owner at being helpful to his visitor. What welcome the door offered was rendered unwelcome for persons with a sensitive verbal taste by a signboard bearing in English the inscription: 'Female Entrance.' Even where the interiors were luxurious the front door was made to disguise the fact as completely as possible. This particular aspect of the architectural dowdiness had its counterpart in the insensitiveness often displayed in Calcutta in the naming of persons. 'Demon', 'Goblin', 'Owl', 'Idiot', 'Tuppence', 'Snub-nosed', were quite common names for men and women there. In fact, through a whimsical affectation of Calcutta ways my eldest son came to acquire, to the great disgust and indignation of my father, the nickname of 'Imbecile'. Of course, these names never bore any relation to the appearance or abilities of the persons so named. When upon the announcement of such names you would expect the emergence of a corresponding physiognomy, a very handsome man indeed might step into your room. In regard to names the trick was meant to avert the Evil Eye or befool evil spirits, but I am unable to account for its extension to the design of front-doors, unless it happens to be a legacy from the days of Muslim rule when rich people did not care to give any outward expression to their affluence for fear of attracting the attentions of the tax-farmer.

To this morphological dinginess the Bengali parts of Calcutta added the ebbs and flows of a functional dinginess: the first daily, the second seasonal, and the third yearly. The Bengalis wash (*i.e.*, rinse in plain unsoaped water) their cotton *dhotis* and *saris* at home every day, and the Bengalis of Calcutta are even more fond of this daily washing than other Bengalis. Actually, the afternoon toilet of Calcutta women passes under the name of 'washing' in thoroughbred circles. Thus, at least twice a day, and sometimes more often, an immense amount of washing has to be hung up to dry. The front veranda, if there is any, or the roof is the place reserved for this purpose. In some houses there are a number of clothes-lines, in others the *dhotis* and *saris* are simply let down from the parapet or railing with the top ends tied to a pillar or rail. When wet they hang heavy and straight, dripping water on the footpath below, and when dry they flutter and twirl in the wind. As each piece is at least fifteen feet in length and forty-four inches in width, the houses when the washing is drying have the appearance of being draped in dirty linen. In addition, there always are subsidiary lines carrying the children's shirts, frocks, vests, and drawers, and the napkins and sheets of the very large number of babies that there always are in these houses, and on most occasions the exhibition of cotton garments is reinforced by bedclothes—mattresses and quilts, large and small, wetted by the children and the babies.

The gathering up of these articles in the afternoon is almost a ritual, like the hauling down of flags on warships in the evening. Except in the houses of the rich this is in the hands of the girls of the family. In the afternoon two or three comely persons appear on the veranda or roof, as the case may be, advance to the railing or parapet, and, leaning on the one or the other, carry out a composed survey of what is going on below. If anything particularly interests them they rest their chins on the rail or wall and contemplate it with wide open, round, solemn eyes. There never is any mobility or change in their expression, but suddenly a face is tossed up and an electric glance flashed towards the window across the street, where the presence of a lurking admirer is suspected. But this ripple passes away as soon as it makes its appearance. The face relapses into the usual immobile placidity, and the girls go on gathering up or pulling down the *dhotis* and *saris*, normally in a very unconcerned manner, by sometimes screwing a puckered mouth in undoing the knots. They move up and down, piling up the clothes on one of their shoulders or arms, and when at last they walk away they look like huge washerwomen.

Another source of untidiness in our parts of Calcutta was the inexplicable but at the same time the most complete non-co-operation between the domestic servants and the municipal sweepers. In Calcutta of olden days the municipal sanitary service was not haphazard as it has grown recently. The streets were regularly watered, swept, and even scrubbed. But while the street-cleaning ended by about six o'clock in the morning and three in the afternoon, the kitchen-maids would begin to deposit the offscourings exactly at quarter-past six and quarter-past three. Nothing seemed capable of making either party modify its hours. So little piles of waste food, ashes, and vegetable scraps and peelings lay in individualistic autonomy near the kerb from one sweeping-time to another sweeping-time. During this interval, however, the refuse deposit was respected like an archaeological deposit, and was never trampled on or kicked about. All Bengali Hindus are very particular about left-over food, which they consider to be very unclean; therefore they never go anywhere near it. A small boy I knew used to take the most intelligent conceivable advantage of this prejudice in order to escape punishment for his naughtiness. He would make straight for the garbage heap before his house and stand on it. Then there was nothing else to be done but for his elder sister to throw away all her clothing, go up to him, retrieve him, and, dragging him inside, give him a scrubbing under the tap and have an untimely bath herself. The prejudice did not, however, extend to fruit rinds. They were thrown indiscriminately on the footpaths to be trampled on by all and sundry. To slip on a mango or banana skin and have a sprained ankle was a very common mishap in Calcutta.

******

Life in Calcutta was the symbol and epitome of our national history, a true reflection of the creative effort in our modern existence as well as of its self-destructive duality. To live in Calcutta was to be reminded at every turn of the cultural history and achievements of modern India and to be aware of every significant activity of the present. The memories of the past were kept alive by the unending series of anniversary meetings which were a feature of the cultural life of Calcutta in my young days, and there was nothing that a student in Calcutta was more fond of than attending public meeetings and listening to speeches. ... There was something in Bengali Calcutta of the Athenian eagerness to say or hear something new. On account of the presence of this psychological necessity, life in Calcutta resembled the process of fermentation. It could mature into a rich, colourful, and full-blooded product when the persons living this life were capable of it.

On the other hand it could also turn into vinegar, and since the vinous analogy is being drawn a significant contrast should also be emphasized. The oddest thing about Calcutta was that the native human stock did not seem to be capable of taking the best advantage of the soil. With a small number of exceptions the men who made Calcutta the cradle of modern Indian culture were provincials brought up in the city. The supporters and adherents of this culture were even more decisively so. It was as if the red Pinot which makes the great wines of Burgundy had to be imported into the Cote-d'Or from Normandy.

The Pharisess: Native and Foreign

From this springs the paradox that the true natives of the city were extremely proud of it and also of themselves, and at the same time disposed to reject every reforming movement which originated in it. Let me deal with the pride first. Initially it was something worse than pride. In an old Bengali book from which I have learnt much about Calcutta society in the early nineteenth century occurs a passage which indicates that the gentry of Calcutta were given to the exhibition of a snobbery towards men from the country which bordered on the outrageous. The prevalence of this rudeness is referred to by the author in his preface, and he adduces it as his reason for writing the book. As he says: 'The citizens do not welcome the intervention of a villager on their conversation even when he makes a very proper and just remark. They exclaim, "you are only a rustic newly come to Calcutta and ignorant of its ways and therefore this discussion is none of your business," which abashes and aggrieves the villager. It is for this reason that I am embarking on the composition of this book, so that reading it, or having it read to themselves all newcomers might be able easily to understand the customs and manners of this city and quickly acquire skill in conversation.' The state of manners revealed by this explanation would have provoked class-war in these days, but in those it only evoked humble discipleship. Even a hundred years later the people of Calcutta had not wholly shed this arrogance. When I first came to the city I could still here the doggerel:

'He's no man—the Bengali of the East;
The Orissan's worse, for he is a beast;
None have tails, but it's wonderful to see
How these creatures swing from tree to tree.'

With the steady influx of ever greater numbers form East Bengal, this aggressive snobbery began to pass away, for it was not safe to sharpen one's wits on the humourless easterner without overwhelming numerical superiority. In private, however, the natives of Calcutta continued for a long time to use the contemptuous epithet 'Bengali' for us and sometimes prefixed the adjective 'bl—y' to it.

Even when not uncivil they were amazingly parochial. The world beyond the Hooghly River and the Mahratta Ditch was a wilderness to them. Whenever an outsider told the name of his district to a man of Calcutta the usual question put to him, as it was put to me also, was 'At which station do you get into train—Howrah or Sealdah?' If you said, 'Sealdah', you would be duly identified as a 'Bengal', if 'Howrah' as a 'Rehro' or as an 'Eater of bran'. The second adjective was the contemptuous epithet for the Bengali from the western most districts of Bengal and the third the even more contemptuous description of the Hindustani.

Yet, extraordinary to relate, this self-conceit was most assertive precisely among those who had never accepted the great movements of national revival and reformation which had originated in Calcutta. The natives of the city were as a rule extremely conservative. In the narrow lanes of Calcutta were to be found, surviving and spinning out an unnatural existence, rituals and beliefs, practices and superstitions, which by the beginning of the twentieth century had disappeared even in the backwaters of East Bengal. The people of Calcutta worshipped the 'Goddess of No Prosperity' together with the Goddess of Prosperity; they worshipped the Goddess of Skin Diseases and of Cholera; the Goddess of Smallpox was one of their major deities. Their womenfolk were extremely afraid of going into the water closet with their hair let down, and they always tied its ends in a knot before going in, because they believed the W.C.s to be the favourite haunts of evil spirits who would possess them unless their hair was up.

Moreover, that tiresome nuisance, purity mania, which marks most elderly women in Bengal, reached proportions in Calcutta which I have seen nowhere else. In Mymensingh the utmost length to which the women would go was to wash their quilts and other bedclothes every morning, or walk with a pot of cow-dung solution, sprinkling the ground before them with the solution in order to purify the path of their advance from one place to another. But in Calcutta the purity fiends went to the extreme of completely divesting themselves of clothes when doing any household work. They were mortally afraid of coming in contact with specks of cooked rice or other particles of waste food and spreading the resulting contamination through the *sari*. This garment, being made of cotton, was regarded like all cotton garments as the most dangerous conductor of impurity. If the end or even one-tenth of the end of a *sari* touched waste food the whole fifteen to eighteen feet of its length became polluted. The human body on the other hand was assumed to be a non-conductor, it was contaminated only in those parts which were actually smeared with waste food. Therefore the best prophylaxis against impurity was to confront all impure things with partial and even complete mudity. I have seen this spectacle without any effort on my part, for the elderly women do not really care who or how many bear witness to their devotion to purity. The demonstration is always more embarrassing to the beholder than to the beheld.

Given this general background of thought, it was not surprising that the natives of Calcutta should have been hostile to the reforming movements. The sternest denouncers of Rammohun Roy or Tagore, for instance, were the gentry of Calcutta. But while opposed to all kinds of reform, they were most opposed to religious reform and the emancipation of women. Thus it happened that the Brahmo Samaj, which had abolished the purdah, was their particular *bête noire*. Brahmo women were looked upon as legitimate prey, and the budding city rake would say with a jaunty and leering swagger, 'I've made love to Brahmo ladies,' which ordinarily amounted only to some eyeing and ogling from a safe distance, for in another aspect of their character the ladies in question had with these people the formidable reputation of being regular cats.

This insensibility, and in most cases also the hostility, of the people of Calcutta to the greatest glories of their city have always puzzled me. According to the Greek saying, the first requisite to happiness is that a man should be born in a famous city. The natives of Calcutta did not appear to stand in need of a second. This was extraordinary. But in one sense these men had their place in the scheme of things. Our great reformers made use of Calcutta as the fulcrum on which to shake and lift our society. They struck the flint that was Calcutta to produce the spark of new life. Would anything less hard or less solid have served their purpose? On this score the natives of Calcutta deserve the gratitude of all modern Indians.

I shall also say a few words about the other sect of the Pharisees of Calcutta, the so-called European, but, correctly speaking, the British part of the urban community. They normally ignored the new culture of modern India, but when brought into accidental contact with it, showed even greater hostility than did the native Bengali. To these men the Bengalis who were trying to understand and assimilate European civilization were Baboos. I never came in touch with English social life in Calcutta. The days after my first coming to Calcutta were the days of racial privileges in India, and certain parts of the Eden Gardens were roped off from us. Certain other amenities were also reserved, and even where there were no express reservations we were not politely treated. My invariable rule was never to go near any of these places to invite rebuffs. But there were many amongst us who tried to sneak into them with the help of a suit of English clothes and created a clamour when they were insulted. There were others who took a peculiarly wrong-headed pleasure in hanging about these places in order to freshen their sense of injury and replenish their self-pity. But I acted on the instincts and impulses of the healthy aborigine, and in this I was influenced by the example of my parents who never went into any kind of society in which they were not treated as equals. I entertained no ambition whatever of hobnobbing with the English in India. As long as I lived in Calcutta I wore no article of English clothing and had none. In general, I disliked and despised the local English. To my mind they alone justified the gibe that the English were a nation of shopkeepers.

Even now I see no reason to retract this poor opinion. If we Indians marked down the Englishman (as we saw him in rare mutual contacts), his own people ought to enter his name in their black books, for he has made a very substantial contribution to the downfall of the British Empire in India. From his land and nation the Englishman brought many fine qualities for his work and business in this country, but his residence among us seemed to engender in him certain very offensive attributes which were as pronounced as the overpowering smell of our wild red dog (*cyon cyon dukhunensis*), and which did untold harm to Britain's relations with India. These are matters of history. I refer to them only because my personal testimony would go a long way towards supporting the consensus of opinion among my countrymen about the Englishman in India in the days of his power. But I do not share the opinion of my countrymen regarding the Englishman who have remained in India after the disappearance of the Indian Empire of Great Britian. Their conduct today fills me with vicarious shame, for they are showing themselves as the same men now by their self-interested and ingratiating niceness towards us as they showed themselves in the past by their arrogant and power-intoxicated snobbery.

But at one time of my life I had an opportunity for seeing a side of English life in Calcutta which was not coloured by the prejudices of the local English against us and our prejudices against them. I saw it in the thirties in the concert hall of the Calcutta Symphony Orchestra. I went there in the Bengali dress, and though not stared at certainly looked conspicuous in that evening-dressed crowd. Of course, even there I had to maintain my aloofness. I do not remember to have been addressed or even greeted there by other persons except on two occasions, once by Mr. P.J. Griffiths, who at one time was the leader of the European Party in the Central Legislature, and on the second occasion by Dr. Bake, the Dutch musicologist, and his wife. But even that insulated contact helped me to form a juster conception of English life in Calcutta and I came to see that there was an amenity in it whose existence I had not suspected before, and indeed could not, by merely seeing Englishmen in the streets and shops and hearing about their doings and behaviour in their offices. In the concert hall foyer even their sipping of whisky did not look uncultured. Since I was theoretically quite familiar with the best type of English social life—memoirs and biographies were my favourite reading—I was not overwhelmed by what I saw. But my less sophisticated Indian friends whom I occasionally persuaded to accompany me to the concerts were generally disarmed in their nationalism by the spectacle of graciousness they saw, and at times even scandalized out of it by the charming *décolleté* of the ladies.

The British Empire in India has perished without my ever coming into intimate personal contact with Englishmen, with the exception of less than half a dozen whom I have known more or less well. I do not regret it, for with all the Anglicism of my spirit I should have felt a total stranger in the English society of Calcutta and would have been humiliated by the demonstration.

******

There was very little social life among the Bengalis of Calcutta, as understood even in the more frivolous connotation of the words 'society' and '*monde*'. No afternoon or evening parties, no dinners, no at-homes, and, of course, no dances, enlivened their existence. The heaviest social exertion in this sense that they could or would undergo was to pay formal calls. But there was something to offset this deficiency. What the native of the city lacked in sociability he made up in gregariousness. No better connoisseur of company was to be found anywhere in the world, and no one else was more dependent on the contiguity of his fellows with the same incomprehension of his obligations towards them. The man of Calcutta found the company he needed so badly and continuously readily assembled, without any effort on his part, in his office, or in his bar-library, or in his college, which were no less places for endless idle gossip than for work. In fact, an admixture of business and gossip furnished the connecting link between the activities which constituted the pursuit of money and those that constituted the pursuit of idleness. No one who has lived among Indians can have failed to have been struck by their infinite capacity to lengthen out the business of the day, at times from the early morning to midnight, and he may have been terrified by this *outré* devotion to self-interest. But all of it is not a boring excess of avarice. Quite and appreciable proportion of this assiduity in business is only a pretext for remaining in the company of fellow-men and chatting with them as long as possible. Thus, if an Indian's love of money or his conviction of the sanctity of self-interest converts all his conversation into shop-talk, it is his gregarious propensity which makes the shop-talk so interminable. What is applicable to Indian society as a whole, I found equally or more applicable to the Bengali society of Calcutta.

But the true expression of its gregariousness was disinterested. Perhaps gregariousness was the only disinterested thing in Calcutta society. Outside working hours the true native would always be roving in search of company, and his very striving for it often defeated its purpose. Every able-bodied person after his return from office and a hurried wash and tea rushed out of his house with the intention of meeting his friends, and these friends being on the same errand it occasionally happened that everybody missed everybody else. The more usual practice, however, was to avoid these misadventures by having fixed rendezvous or, as they were called in Bengali, *addas*. Each *adda* had its fixed adherents, who would begin to drop in one by one from about half-past five in the afternoon till in about an hour's time the attendance was full. These gathering-places were most often the outer parlour of one of the wealthier members of the group, but at times also an office after office hours, and, more rarely, a tea-shop. It was not obligatory for the host to be present, although he generally was, but invariably he was the least conspicuous individual in the company. The visitors had the freedom of the house, and ordered the host's servants about just as they pleased. No refreshments were served and none were expected, but a cup or two of tea was always to be had, and this collective tea was prepared by a servant at one end of the veranda or some other corner of the outer house. In a typical Calcutta household tea was no affair of the women of the family. Like the master's English clothes, it fell within the jurisdiction of the servants of the outer house. As a general rule, these meeting-places were located in the quarter in which the greater majority of the frequenters lived. But it was not at all unusual to find a man traveling five or six miles by tram in order to join his company. This happened when a family living in a rented house moved from one quarter to another. A man was far less ready to join a new *adda* than he was to shift to a new house in a new quarter. Sometimes many years passed before a man would think of changing his company in order to avoid the long daily journey.

The people of Calcutta being facile in speech, these congregations at times became garrulous and even voluble. But in their characteristic form they were unexpectedly quiet. In fact, the real art of gregariousness in Calcutta lay in being in company and at the same time making the fact outwardly immaterial. In sharp contrast to the demoniac energy shown in rushing to the rendezvous, the languor of the actual proceedings was startling. The briskness of his steps and the eagerness on his face would vanish as soon as a man passed the door of the assembly-room. He would hardly even nod recognition to his friends, and in his turn would not be nodded to by them. He would sit down quietly in his accustomed place and look extremely contented. If there was conversation it was so leisurely a verbal exchange that nobody could discover a thread in the half-drawled relay of words. Indeed, few cared for it, and most often even half-drawled words were not forthcoming but only hems and grunts. Besides, nobody took the trouble of looking into the eyes of anybody else, even if he spoke to him. The laconic remarks and exclamations resembled bubbles in still waters which indicate the presence of fish. For the greater part of the time the company remained silent, contemplating the ceiling or any section of the wall which presented itself conveniently to the eyes, and smiling beatifically. The winter evenings were even more luxurious. Then the company would cover themselves up from head to foot in their shawls and lie back on the pillows and bolsters, quivering their legs or waggling their toes. Even literary people, that talkative crowd, came to acquire these habits. After about two hours of this relaxation the company would rise one by one, and no trace of the previous leisureliness would be observable in their movements as they ran for the tram or bus and jumped into it.

I did not understand this behaviour until in 1922 I read for the first time McDougall's *Social Psychology*, in which I found the distinction between the social and the gregarious instinct clearly drawn and properly emphasized. Reinforcing my critical armoury from the book, I began to call the gregarious natives of Calcutta Galton's Oxen, that is to say, the oxen of Damaraland in Africa. Individually these animals hardly appear even to be conscious of one another, but if separated from the herd they display extreme signs of distress and do not rest until they have regained it and buried themselves in it. That is also how every native of Calcutta feels and acts. There is nothing he dreads more than isolation, and his complaint against every place other than Calcutta is that it has no 'society'. The abject dependence of these people on the company of their usual friends and acquaintances makes the more wealthy of them take at their own expense a whole party of cronies with them when they have their annual outing to the hills, the seaside, or some other holiday resort. Those who cannot afford the luxury entreat their friends to come to the same place and share expenses.

—extracted from Nirad C. Chaudhuri, *Autobiography of an Unknown Indian* (Berkeley: University of California Press, 1968), pp. 259–70, 360–4, 383–5.

Kenneth L. Gillion

Ahmedabad: A Study in Indian Urban History

Modern Indian historiography no longer confines its study to the activities of rulers. The Indian nationalist movement is receiving close attention from scholars in several countries, as are the effects of British law and land revenue settlements on the social structure of rural India. But those who wish to read about Indian cities are still more likely to look to the works of geographers and sociologists than to those of historians. This book is a preliminary excursion into Indian urban history. It is not intended to be a contribution to urban theory. It draws to some extent on work in the other social sciences, some general discussion and comparisons are included, and the pertinence of general theoretical concepts is kept in mind (if not always explicitly discussed). However, it is not primarily a book about Indian cities in general, but one about the unique experience of a particular city.

Ahmedabad, the capital of Gujarat, was chosen for study because it is both an old city—once the most splendid in India—and a modern industrial city—now India's sixth largest, with a population of more than one and a quarter millions, and per capita one of the richest. Unlike Bombay, Calcutta, Madras, and Kanpur, Ahmedabad was not a creation of the British, but a city which, while remaining true to itself, successfully adapted to the new industrial age, carrying over commercial and industrial skills and patterns of traditional social organization. In no great city of India can the continuity of past and present be seen as clearly as in Ahmedabad, and it is continuity, rather than change, which is emphasized in this book.

Ahmedabad is neither a well-known nor a much loved city. Since the seventeenth century it has been as much neglected by visitors as by writers. Its utilitarian and parochial spirit does not attract outsiders, while the Ahmedabadis are too modest and too busy to try to put the rest of the world right about their interesting city. The situation today is as it was in 1868 when the English social reformer, Mary Carpenter, wrote in praise of Ahmedabad: 'This extraordinary city is so little known on the other side of India, that when at Calcutta some months afterwards, I spoke to an educational inspector about schools in Ahmedabad, he remarked, "You may as well speak in England of what is done in the school of some remote village in Russia, as to us here of such a place as Ahmedabad."' The eulogies of Ahmedabad's architecture which appear in the standard guides do not attract tourists. Murray's Guide states: 'It is hard to account for the scant attention paid to Ahmedabad by modern travellers from Europe unless its reputation as an industrial centre and the fact that there has been prohibition there since 1938 has deterred them.' But the neglect is not new. Tourists fly over Ahmedabad, 'scrambling on to Agra and Delhi' as they did in 1890 when Caine wrote in his guide to India, 'Ahmedabad is one of the most beautiful and picturesque cities in India and no traveller should pass it by.' Scholars, too, have avoided this city, which has been an exception to many of the statements commonly made about India and Indian history.

This book reflects my conviction that in the study of Indian history not enough attention has been paid until recently to regional differences within India. Most of the generalizations made about Indian history are more applicable to Bengal or Hindustan than to Gujarat. The British came to Bengal earlier; many of the great issues of British policy in India were fought out there; several famous historians have written about Bengal; and a very high proportion of India's own historians are Bengalis. Indian historical studies have, in short, been dominated by Bengali themes and historians of Bengal. But Gujarat is not Bengal; if its experience in modern times has been different, this has been due not only to different external pressures, but also to differences in her traditional cultural pattern.

Situated between the Arabian Sea and the kingdoms of central and northern India, possessed of a long coastline and fertile soil, Gujarat for more than two thousand years has been a centre of trade and textile exports. Its traders and financiers, not its royal officials, nor its landholders and chieftains, nor even its Brahmins, set the tone of society in Gujarat long before modern times and made business valued and more than normally respectable for all. The Gujaratis are perhaps the least other-worldly of all the Indian peoples. In light-hearted vein, Yashodhar Mehta, writer and playwright of Ahmedabad, has written of his people:

> A poet has sometimes observed that wherever there is a Gujarati there is Gujarat. This may mean anything or nothing, but I may as well say that wherever there is money or even possibility of money, there always is a Gujarati. The lure of money takes him to all parts of the world and to all sorts of things. Wherever he scents money, all his faculties become immensely concentrated and like a yogi he applies all his wonderful powers of concentration to the extent of *samadhi*. God then reveals himself through money and the Gujarati is in ecstasy. He becomes a sort of Paramahamsa, all smiles, sweetness, good words, amiability, etc. He goes on buying and selling, investing and reinvesting, and creates, by his own concentration and perseverance, heaven on earth, if not for all, at least for his family; if not for his family at least for himself. This is not a mean achievement.

The Ahmedabadi is the Gujarati of the Gujaratis.

The traditional cities of India are most often viewed through the eyes of Bernier and other European travellers who visited the Mughal Empire, and in the light of Weberian and Marxist analysis. They are contrasted with the self-governing towns of medieval Europe with their charters, esprit-de-corps, united bourgeoisie, and independent military power. They appear to be disunited, often ephemeral conglomerations of subjects, dependent on the court and the military-official elite, and prevented from free association by caste rivalries and other religious restraints. But Ahmedabad was, to some extent, an exception. Here was a city with a corporate tradition and spirit, an hereditary bourgeois elite, and a history of indigenous financial, commercial, and industrial activity … Ahmedabad's wealth came from trade and industry, not from parasitic exploitation of the countryside; its handicrafts were independent of the patronage of a single court; its merchants and financiers were wealthy and constituted a superior social stratum in the city, a largely hereditary plutocracy; and, if it did not enjoy urban autonomy on the European model, still the financial power and social position of its wealthy Vanias and the survival there, but not in most other parts of India, of certain old institutions of Indian society—the Nagarseth, or city head, and the *mahajans*, or guilds—ensured that the government of the city was responsive to their wishes. Any explanation of this survival of the ancient urban mercantile values and institutions in Gujarat and Rajasthan must be very speculative. A few possible reasons were: the extensive trade which passed through these regions on the way to northern India, the interest of the rulers in taxing this trade, and hence their favouring of traders and financiers, and, by contrast with the Gangetic Plain, the restriction of the revenue available from agriculture, in Rajasthan by the infertility of the soil, and in Gujarat by the marked political fragmentation and independence of local chieftains.

Ahmedabad was distinctive in another way also. A British officer noted in 1830: 'It is a common reproach against our Government in this country, that towns always fall off under us, but Ahmedabad is a most gratifying exception.' More recently R. Palme Dutt has written: 'The old populous manufacturing towns, Dacca, Murshidabad (which Clive had described in 1757 to be as extensive, populous, and rich as the city of London), Surat and the like were in a few years rendered desolate under the 'pax Britannica' with a completeness which no ravages of the most destructive war or foreign conquest could have accomplished.' In Chapter II we shall first look at the reasons why Ahmedabad was able to survive the British industrial invasion and even recover some of the prosperity it had been losing under Maratha rule, when these other cities were declining, and then consider her response to British rule and the breakdown of her isolation in the second half of the nineteenth century.

This chapter will emphasize the limited British influence on Ahmedabad society in the nineteenth century.

Ahmedabad's history provides few illustrations of the familiar themes in general works on Indian history. The revolt of 1857 was a minor event in the history of Ahmedabad, and communalism a minor problem. This city did not succumb to England's laissez-faire. It had no great intellectual renaissance, no dramatic swing towards the West then away from it, but rather a slow and selective adaptation. Neither the Western-educated middle class nor the comprador class fills the centre of the stage here. Rather, Ahmedabad's story is of the survival and transformation of an important traditional centre of trade and industry into a modern industrial city, under the leadership of an indigenous financial and mercantile elite. Chapter III will deal with the steam powered textile industry, which has been responsible for Ahmedabad's modern growth and recovery of greatness and has earned it the title, 'The Manchester of India'. The distinctive character of Ahmedabad's industrialization and the carry-over of traditional patterns will be stressed. Modern Ahmedabad was built up by Ahmedabadis, not by Englishmen, Marwaris, or Parsis.

In Chapter IV, the changing urban environment and problems of Ahmedabad will be considered, and with it the history of municipal government and improvement in the city. In contrast to its rapid and successful adaptation to the new commercial and industrial order, Ahmedabad's social and political response to the West was delayed and not at first remarkable. Ahmedabad had one of the earliest municipal organizations in India, but this chapter does not tell a story which would differ significantly from that of other second-rank cities in nineteenth century India, except possibly in the civic-mindedness displayed by the old leading families (if not by the voters and elected commissioners, who opposed improvements and brought about the supersession of the Municipality for incompetence). Apart from any intrinsic interest there is in an account of urban problems and administration in an old Indian city in the mofussil, the point of the story is the limited correlation between economic progress and Western influence and social change in nineteenth century Ahmedabad. Until the First World War, Ahmedabad's economic progress was achieved within a society which remained socially conservative and politically backward.

*****

The influence of the financiers and merchants of Ahmedabad appeared in the survival there of certain old institutions of Hindu mercantile cities: the mahajans and the Nagarseth. Whereas in other parts of India the guilds, so powerful in the time of the Buddha and for centuries afterwards, had all but disappeared, squeezed between royal and caste power, they were still important in the nineteenth century in Gujarat, and to a lesser extent in Rajasthan, and traces of them were to be found as far east as Banaras and as far south as Poona. In Ahmedabad they are by no means unimportant even now. In pre-Mughal and Mughal days, they were as much rulers of the city as the royal governors and officials and for the individual of far more immediate significance.

The centre of the royal government of the city was its citadel, the Bhadra fort (named after a similar fort at Anhilvad Patan dedicated to Bhadra Kali, the goddess Kali in her auspicious form, and, incidentally, the patron goddess of Ahmedabad). In Mughal times the city was under the Subahdar (Governor) of Gujarat and was not self-governing in the sense that European cities were self-governing. The Subahdar was responsible for the defence of the city, criminal justice and the police, and the Diwan for finance. Among the important subordinate officials were the Faujdars or chiefs of police in the neighbourhood of Ahmedabad, the Kazis, who administered both civil and criminal law, and the Kotwal, who was head of the city's police. The Kotwal's duties included the watch and ward of the city, the regulation of the market (including the prevention of monopolies, overpricing, and short weights), the care and legitimate disposal of heirless property, the prevention of social abuses such as drinking, and the regulation of the cemeteries and slaughterhouses. The movements of strangers and any suspicious events were reported to him and he also acted as a criminal judge. The Karoris collected the market dues and tolls. However, much of this royal authority to which the Ahmedabadi was subject was filtered through the guilds and castes. It is important to remember, too, that the administrative functions of a traditional Indian city government were fewer than those of even a modern municipality. The provision of parks, hospitals, schools, road cleaning, and even water-supply to some extent, was usually left to private agencies. The giving of charitable donations for the service of society was considered a religious duty for those who could afford it. In Ahmedabad the mahajans performed many of the functions of the modern government and municipality.

The government was 'usually responsive if not responsible to' the opinion of the different communities in the city. Like the governments of other traditional societies, it worked within the framework of custom and did not seek to remake society as a modern totalitarian government would. The bankers and merchants were most influential, but every occupation, even the most lowly, was indispensable and its practitioners had customary rights and privileges as well as obligations. But what recourse did the people (I will not call them 'citizens,' for that word has a precise meaning in the European context) have against unjust measures on the part of the royal officers and infringements of customary rights? There was certainly no press to ventilate grievances and there were no popular political parties. Doubtless the occasional unpopular or uninfluential individual was treated unjustly or harshly. But the castes or mahajans could always threaten to migrate to another area—which indeed was a common practice in traditional India when people were fewer and states competed with one another for husbandmen and craftsmen. Through *hartals* (revived for political purposes by Mahatma Gandhi) the mahajans could bring business to a standstill. In 1816, four bankers went to the palace to remonstrate about the conduct of the Maratha officials and their informers in the city. When they received no satisfaction 'all the merchants' and 'men of every caste' sat down opposite the palace for a day and a night. This was not a non-violent hartal. Brickbats were thrown at the informers and one of them was paraded through the city on an ass and then stoned to death. The government confined the others as it had been asked to do, but it later sent armed men into the Manek Chowk (the principal business area of the city) on an errand of reprisal. This last however, was regarded as an instance of misgovernment and is the exception which proves the rule; generally the government acted in harmony with the mahajans and castes.

Then there was the Nagarseth to speak for the city. Maganlal Vakhatchand records that Shantidas Jawahari was given this title by one of the Mughal emperors for his services to the court. In 1725, when a Maratha army approached the city, Nagarseth Khushalchand Lakshmichand, a grandson of Shantidas, went out and begged them to spare the city from plunder, offering them his own money. In gratitude the mahajans of Ahmedabad conferred on his family in perpetuity the right to collect a percentage on the trade of the city. Successive Gaikwads conferred honours on the family, such as the rights to a state chair and canopy and to be preceded by torches. When necessary, the Nagarseth would call the heads of the mahajans together and preside over these meetings. When the fickle monsoon rains were late, he would circumambulate the city walls, pouring milk on the ground to

appease Indra. Doubtless there were many occasions when his prestige
and influence contributed to the settling of quarrels between mahajans
or individuals or in interceding with the royal officials. Similarly, there
were the Kazis to speak for the Muslim community. The office of chief
Kazi has been hereditary in one family for over 400 years. The Kazi was
not simply a servant of the Subahdar, but like the Nagarseth, a buffer
between the government and the communities within the city.

The Nagarseth family are Oswal Jains. This reflects the great
importance of the Jain community in Ahmedabad. At the census of
1872, they comprised 10.03% of the population and formed one of
its richest communities. The Vania castes of Rajasthan and Gujarat
remained strongholds of Jainism when it largely died out elsewhere
after the days of the great Jain communities of medieval India. The
prevailing vegetarianism in Ahmedabad, and its tenderness towards the
animal kingdom, are Jain legacies. Whether there is a causal relationship
between business success and Jainism is an even more controversial matter than the famous debate over the connection between Protestantism
and capitalism. But just as rapid economic growth has taken place in
many societies that are not Protestant, so the Jains are not the only
businessmen of Gujarat. It is just as likely that they were influenced by
the general environment favourable to business enterprise as the Parsis
were by the same environment. Similarly, the Jain Marwaris of Rajasthan
come from an infertile country crossed by trade routes, and their business
success in modern India derives more from this circumstance, and from
the contraction of local opportunities in trade and the financing of
princely wars, than from their religion. In the Karnatak, the Jains are
largely illiterate agriculturists. It is true, however, that the Ahmedabad
Jains were more prosperous as a community and better educated than
their Vaishnava fellow Vanias. Nor can it be denied that Jainism has
helped to mould the character of the Gujarati Vanias, but so too has
Vaishnavism.

There were about forty guilds in Ahmedabad. These were
predominandy Hindu or Jain bodies. The Muslim guilds were in 'weak
imitation of Hindu models' and not comparable with the guilds which
were so important in Islamic cities in the middle east. The guilds of
merchants and financiers were known as *mahajans* and their hereditary
heads as *seths*. Among them the most important were the sarafs' mahajan,
the cloth dealers' mahajan, and the raw silk dealers' mahajan. The
artisan guilds were known as *panch* and their heads as *patels*. A guild could
embrace members of several castes, and a caste members of several guilds;

in some cases they were coterminous. There was no strict separation of religious, social, and occupational problems. Admission to a guild was hereditary or by purchase. Expulsion was an occupational and often a social disaster. The guilds controlled admissions, restricted competition, maintained joint charities through levies on their members, kept up standards, determined wages, controlled prices (sometimes), set holidays, and safeguarded the interests of their members against the government, other guilds, and outsiders. The mahajans were able to exclude foreigners from the commerce of Ahmedabad and to tame social conflicts within the city. It is true that they could act as a brake upon innovation and improvement and Andrew Dunlop, the first Collector of Ahmedabad, deplored this, but in the traditional situation their advantages were more obvious.

The relationship between the institutions of sect, caste, guild, and Nagarseth, was complex. There was no clear differentiation among the various roles. For instance, the Nagarseth was head of the sarafs' guild and head of the Jain community, and he also spoke for the city as a whole, while he owed his position to the wealth, charities, and public spirit of his family over several generations. The head of the cloth-dealers' mahajan was sometimes called *chautano seth* (market chief) and he was also looked upon as the head of the Vaishnava sect. The two would consult together on important public matters. Yet both sarafs and cloth-dealers could be either Jains or Vaishnavas, and inevitably there was confusion of sectarian and commercial interests. The Jains, for example, collected funds from the cloth-dealers' mahajan for the support of their *panjarapol* (animal home). Similarly, penalties for breaches of caste rules could be enforced by a guild composed of several castes, even more so by those where caste and guild were coterminous; for instance, a Visa Shrimali Vania was expelled from the cloth dealers' mahajan, and thus compelled to leave Ahmedabad to make a living, because he married a widow.

As in other traditional cities, the social divisions of the population were reflected in the layout of the city. In old Ahmedabad there was less differentiation of working and living quarters than in the modern city. Most people worked at home, except when they went to market to sell their wares. The chief markets were the Friday fair (in the Maidan Shahi, the space between the Bhadra fort and the Tin Darwaza—three gates, as the people gathered for the Friday prayers in the Jama Masjid—great mosque), the Manek Chowk, and the market centres near the main gates. The size of most industrial or commercial undertakings did not warrant the employment of large groups of people outside the family. Exceptions were the paper factories and the silk industry, with its many complicated processes, each demanding specialized skills; and the offices of the government with their armies of clerks, for the ponderous bureaucracy of modern India predates even the British period. But most people lived and worked in a house-group known as a *pol*, normally (but not invariably) associated with one caste.

These pols, of which there were 356 in 1872, are still among the curiosities of India. They comprise a labyrinth of high wooden houses, streets too narrow for wheeled traffic, and cul-de-sacs. A pol would have only one, or at the most two entrances (apart from secret ones), one main street with crooked lanes branching on either side, and walls and gates (now removed) which were barred at night. There was often a quadrangle, with a temple and well, and there were common latrines at the entrance. To some extent the house property in the pol was held in common. This was the situation in 1879.

Formerly no man could sell or mortgage a house to an outsider without first offering it to the people of the pol. Though this rule is not now kept, inmates of a pol are careful to sell to men of their own class and never to people of low caste. When a house is mortgaged or sold, the people of the pol have a right to claim from one-half to two per cent of the money received. Again, on wedding and other great family occasions, each householder is expected to feast the whole pol, and in some cases all the men of the pol, though not of the same caste, are expected to attend any funeral that may take place. If the pol rules are slighted, the offender is fined, and, in former times, till he paid, he was not allowed to light a lamp in his house or to give a feast. The money gathered from gifts, fines, and the percentage on house property sales forms a common fund managed by the leaders, seths, of the pol. This is spent on repairs to the pol gate, the pol privies, or the pol well.

The lanes were shaded by multi-storied wooden houses, with carved, unpainted fronts, and eaves that almost met across the lanes. In 1903 Forrest wrote, 'Nowhere does one feel oneself more thoroughly in an eastern city of past times than in the narrow streets of Ahmedabad, thick with ancient houses, none so poor as not to have a doorway or a window or a wooden pillar carved finely.' The pols provided privacy to a group and warm or oppressive cosiness to an individual impossible in a modern city. There was, too, no differentiation of area of residence by wealth. The rich seths of Ahmedabad lived in the pols among their caste fellows, rich and poor alike, not as they do today, in surburban bungalows surrounded by spacious grounds.

In the days of Mughal rule, before the decline of Ahmedabad, there were many *puras* (suburbs) outside the walled city. Those on the other bank were connected with the city by ford in the dry weather or by boat. These puras were not dormitory suburbs for those who worked in the city, as are their modern equivalents on the same sites, but were the seats of Mughal officers. They were surrounded by gardens and were peopled by all those who served and followed the rich and powerful. They were miniature cities, owing their existence to the presence of the rulers; and when the rulers left, their puras died, leaving only isolated tombs and mosques and mounds of bricks, once fine walls or palaces. The palaces of the nobles used to extend from the present Ellis Bridge to Sarkhej. But some of the puras were founded by merchants and were extensions of the economic life of the main city of Ahmedabad. The suburb of Madhavpura, for instance, was founded by the Nagarseth's family in Maratha times. They built a square, surrounded by shops and warehouses, and were granted the right to levy dues on the cartmen who brought their goods to sell in this secure market place. Again, because the suburb of Raghunathpura 'was in a ruinous state and Vukhutchund Seth has been the means of causing the same Poora to be inhabited,' he was granted, again under the Marathas, the right to collect dues on the carts of grain and the cattle brought through the suburb.

It is said that Ahmedabad used to hang on three threads: gold, silk, and cotton. It was for her silk manufactures that she was chiefly famed, especially for the bright colours of the plain silks, and the durability and non-fading qualities of the brocades with patterns woven of gold and silver thread. Raw silk was imported from Bengal, China, and Central Asia. The manufacture was a complex process; from the imported raw silk to the final product there were eleven separate sets of workmen. The raw silk was imported by merchants called *tagias*, while other merchants would pay the workmen and export the finished product. Generally the workmen lived in their own houses, though there were workshops also, including, in Mughal times, state *karkhanas*. Cotton spinning and the weaving, dyeing, and printing of cotton cloth were also important industries. Ahmedabad's cotton cloth was not noted for its fineness but for its strength and fast bright colours. Other important manufactures were high-quality paper and woodwork. Of the goods which passed through the city and brought profits to its merchants, drugs and indigo were especially important.

Ahmedabad's fortunes were bound up with a wide area and the city provided a livelihood for many people outside it. There was its immediate hinterland which supplied raw cotton and food, and wood for houses, carts, and fuel. The Ahmedabad market in food grains was particularly important for the development of the fertile Kaira district and her tough and enterprising Lewa Patidar caste of peasant proprietors. The agricultural areas around Ahmedabad also provided tax revenues for the support of the government and new residents for the city. Like other pre-modern cities, Ahmedabad could not replenish its population without immigration from the rural areas. The excess of deaths over births was counteracted by the drift to the city of some of the more enterprising of the rural population, or deviants, misfits, and the curious. Many of these brought their families to the city or sent for them subsequently. In 1872 there were 58,477 males and 58,396 females in Ahmedabad, an equality of the sexes which one British authority thought remarkable for an Indian city. The population of Ahmedabad was essentially a rooted urban population, and was not made up of a large number of floating individuals. Few agriculturists lived in the city.

There was, however, a close connection between the city and the countryside. The Vanias of Ahmedabad played an important part in the process of converting the produce of the peasantry of the surrounding areas into tax revenues. Some of those entitled to receive a share in the produce of the soil—the proprietors of *taluqdari* villages—lived in the city. Many of the peasants were in debt to money-lenders and petty traders, who in 1825 were said to keep them in a state of 'interminable dependence,' and these borrowed, in their turn, from the larger firms in the city. Cloth woven in the villages by Muslims and Dheds was dyed in the city, and some of the preliminary stages of silk manufacture such as reeling and spinning were carried out in the adjacent villages, chiefly by Patidars in their spare time. There was no mass market in the villages for the city's manufactures as most of the people wore coarse homespun cloth. But some of the richer people in the countryside sought luxury articles made in the city, and other villagers did buy articles when they came to the Friday fair to sell their agricultural produce and cloth. Ahmedabad did not have the parasitic, exploitative relationship to the surrounding countryside so often assumed to have been true of Asian cities in general, but was more like traditional European commercial and industrial cities.

—excerpted from Kenneth L. Gillion, *Ahmedabad: A Study in Indian Urban History* (Berkeley: University of California Press, 1968), pp. 1–3, 4–17, 19–29.

The City Political: A Portfolio

A note on the artist by Vinay Lal

Among contemporary Indian artists, there are few whose work is as closely identified with the city as Sudhir Patwardhan. Over a period extending well beyond three decades, Patwardhan has wrestled and engaged with the city in a manner uniquely his own. Other Indian artists have had a long association with one or the other of the Indian cities—Bombay, Calcutta, Baroda, and more recently Delhi—that have helped shape the sensibility of modern Indian art, but there are few in whose work the city occupies, as it does in the work of Patwardhan, a presence that is at once magisterial, imposing, and yet familiar. 'Ambivalence' is perhaps the word that many would choose to describe Patwardhan's long and complex relationship to the city, but is there anyone, not entirely shorn of some sensitivity, who has not similarly had, at some juncture of his or her life, an ambivalent relationship to the city? Is the city not that which gives succor to life and fills one with the greatest ambitions and yet is insolently indifferent to the fate of individuals? Does the city, in the clichéd expression, wait for anyone? What is the territory of Patwardhan's ambivalence, and what are the streets, crossroads, over bridges, roundabouts, nooks, and crannies of Patwardhan's imagination of the city?

Patwardhan was born in 1949, less than two years after India attained independence from colonial rule, and spent his early childhood in Pune. We might say that he grew up alongside the nation-state, coming of age around the same time that India was beginning to emerge from the long shadows cast by an anti-colonial struggle that had left a considerable impress on many people in and outside India. To what extent the events of the 1960s and early 1970s can be tacitly felt if not experienced in his work is a matter of interpretation, but by 1973, when he graduated from the Armed Forces Medical College in Pune, India was moving towards a period of considerable turbulence. India had achieved a military triumph over Pakistan in the war of 1971, and shortly thereafter Indira Gandhi sought to seal her stamp over the political landscape by ushering India into the atomic age. Her admirers might well have been tempted to invoke, to use the slogan from our times, 'India Shining'; but the social, economic,

and political fissures in the Indian polity were not so easily disguised.
From an obscure part of India called Naxalbari, peasants in 1967 staged
a rebellion the reverberations of which are still experienced daily in many
parts of the country; in the Hindi-speaking heartland, meanwhile, the
Gandhian socialist Jayaprakash Narayan would, a few years later, give
the call for 'total revolution'. Strikes would rock the country, and the
lines of the educated unemployed grew longer every year. Satyajit Ray
underscored the bleakness of the period with a masterful line in his film
Jana Aranya ('The Middleman', 1976), where the protagonist Somnath
decides to give up his quest for a job when at yet another interview he is
asked, 'What is the weight of the moon?' Though the levels of everyday
violence to which Indians today are accustomed were certainly unknown
in the 1960s and 1970s, the rioters, hoodlums, and tough guys who
fill some of Patwardhan's capacious canvases were beginning to exert a
marked presence on Indian city streets.

The practice of medicine might have seemed to the young Patwardhan
a safe refuge from the economic uncertainties and political turmoil of
the 1970s. Patwardhan moved to Bombay shortly after completing his
medical education, and for thirty years, from 1975 to 2005, he worked
as a radiologist. We might well ponder over the relationship of his art
to his expertise in radiology. In those three decades, Patwardhan must
have interpreted the X-rays of thousands of patients, furnishing in each
instance as reliable a diagnosis as the evidence permitted with an eye to
assisting the attending physician to plot the most effective treatment for
the disease. We cannot say of his art that it is didactic, or even that he
furnishes a diagnosis of the difficulties that afflict Indian society; much
less is it the case that he aims at the reform of Indian society with his
candid representations of the violence on Indian streets. Nevertheless,
a viewing of his work leaves one with the unmistakable impression
that Patwardhan seeks to penetrate the core of urban Indian society,
going behind its façade to unearth the intensity, turmoil, frenetic pace,
and squalor of the city. Of course the city is much more than this: if
there are killings on the streets, and the smell of violence hangs in the
air, the city also has its quiet moments, chance encounters, curious
crowds, small pleasures—something like, as Bombaywallahs know only
too well, a visit to an Irani café, the subject of one of Patwardhan's
paintings.

In the accompanying portfolio of a small number of Patwardhan's city
paintings, the intent is not to trace the artistic genealogy of Patwardhan's
changing ideas of the city or to convey how his framing of the city has

undergone substantial changes over the last four decades. An analysis of Patwardhan's notion of the city, and his deeply ambivalent relationship to Bombay, is beyond the scope of this short note; but I would like to gesture briefly at some of the more prominent characteristics of his city paintings with a focus on just a couple of his recent works. 'Bylanes Saga', an acrylic painting on canvas that measures 6 feet by 8 feet, is representative of one of several styles that mark Patwardhan's oeuvre. Rendered as a diptych, the painting appears to divide into two halves, which can be viewed either from top to bottom or from left to right; and, yet, it also divides into four quarters, with each part revolving around one narrative. The top half of the painting is from Thane, where Patwardhan resides; the bottom half narrates scenes from Govandi, a neighborhood in the eastern part of Mumbai. How is the viewer to know that the painting fuses two parts of greater Mumbai into one whole—or is it one whole at all? Does the 'informed viewer', bringing a detailed knowledge of Mumbai and its surroundings, have a better insight into the painting and into Patwardhan's imagination?

If we begin at the bottom left-hand corner, people seem to be going about their business, the men in their mainly white shirts, a woman with a sleeveless red blouse in the foreground walking with purposeful strides, and a man dressed in a purple tee-shirt loitering about as is commonly seen on Indian city streets. Two shadowy figures set against a doorway, only just seen in the background, are, we surmise, engaged in conversation. But this street scene, rather than opening up to the sky, beckons to something more dramatic, certainly more ominous: a man who has collapsed on the street is being hoisted on his feet by three men, two of whom throw furtive glances around them. If they are helping the man to his feet, they should be focused resolutely on reviving him; but what if they are the perpetrators of the very violence the effects of which they seem to be ameliorating? Across from them, on the top right-hand side of the painting, a burqa-clad woman with a baby on her shoulder stands facing a man whose outstretched hands seem to implore her to place the baby in his care. Is he her father, and is he anxious about the safety of what appears to be his grandson? Are the two narratives intertwined? Is this, as the man's lungi and the woman's burqa amply suggest, a Muslim neighborhood, and are the three men helping, with evidently the anxiety that comes when violence can strike at an instance, the victim of a communal riot to his feet? Is the burqa-clad woman the wife of the man who is being helped to his feet, and is his wife taking her child to safety? The bottom right-hand corner of the frame echoes the scene at the other end, except that the men walking down the street do not have their backs against the viewer. Are these all discrete narratives, juxtaposing the normality of everyday life which sets the pace for the lower half of the painting with the tensions, often flaring up into explicit scenes of violence, of urban life represented in the painting's upper half? Is this deliberate juxtaposition in fact designed to reinforce the idea that urban violence has been normalized? Do we all as viewers partition our selves, such that even as we witness the violence around us we push ourselves into believing that life must go on and that violence must not obstruct us from carrying on with our lives? Is there even a witness? If indeed the man who has collapsed is the victim of a communal conflagration, or 'merely' a mugging, who is there to witness the crime? What is the voyeurism of spectatorship, and at what point does the spectator incline towards becoming a witness not only in the juridical but also spiritual sense?

'Bylanes Saga' thus lends itself to multiple readings, as is true of nearly all good works of art, but I mean something more by this proposition. The Japanese novelist, Junchiro Tanizaki, was to write in a small but extraordinarily rich essay, *In Praise of Shadows*, that what is distinctive about Japanese architecture is that buildings are judged not only on aesthetic grounds but also by the shadows they cast. Patwardhan galvanizes architecture in 'Bylanes Saga' to frame his narrative: the apartment blocks in the top half of the painting divide it neatly from the ramshackle structures and modest homes that fill the lower half. More to the point, Patwardhan's painting is also a song in canvas of the city in sunlight and shadows. Some parts of the city live in light, other parts in darkness. In India, this may be literally the case: darkness often envelopes the poorer parts of the city, those without electricity connections or with immense amounts of load-shedding, a term which is not part of the lexicon of the urban in the industrialized West. Some in the city swim in money, others have not a shirt on their back; some live in fortified palaces, others call the pavement their home. In 'Bylanes Saga', the play of light and shadows is all but critical, though every viewer may come to a different reading of just how this dialectic operates in the painting. Sunlight streams in besides the four men in the top left-hand side, but they are just in the shadows. Moments of liminality are accentuated by figures lurking in doorways, neither outside nor inside: perhaps this is one way to read the experience of most Indians in the city.

Not all of Patwardhan's paintings embody the idea of simultaneous narratives—or perhaps they do, invoking histories through absences. Among his most famous works, from three decades ago, is 'The Train'.

Nearly every resident of Mumbai would, at some point, have had the experience of the city's commuter train system, which is certainly unlike any in the world. Millions of people board these trains daily, the highest passenger density of any urban railway or metro system in the world, and sardines in a can could not have been packed any tighter in coaches where every inch is fought over with grim ferocity; a few people are lost to the screaming tracks every day, as they lose their grip over the iron rail that separates them from likely death. These are trains from which the doors have been removed, to make room for a few extra passengers; as men, and it is mainly men, hang on for dear life, partly in and partly outside, dodging the electricity poles, power cables, or branches of a tree that might come suddenly come upon them, a strange version of Russian roulette seems to be played out all so often. Yet, in Patwardhan's painting, the scene at the railway station is one of considerable serenity, as if to hint at the lull before the storm. A man stands casually by the train. The interior seems remarkably empty, though a ghostly figure can be seen seated through the window grill. Three men are seen by the doorway: one appears to be squeezing his way inside, as though he was making a surreptitious entry into the coach. A lone woman passenger is similarly standing at the doorway, though her feet are firmly planted on the inside of the door. The painting gives the appearance of being segmented into three parts, the seated figure and the man outside framing the middle half. The horizontal lines of the train are complemented by the upright human figures; the horizontal grid of the window has its counterpart in the vertical stairway railing. Here, as in much of his work, is to be seen Patwardhan's engagement with the idea of liminality, a notion rendered all the more poignant in a city such as Mumbai. The genius of the city is that it allows everyone into its portals, and yet no one is perhaps ever a complete insider. There is no intimation as such of the sheer density of the crowds that hover around Mumbai's train stations, at Churchgate, Victoria Terminus, Bandra, Andheri, and elsewhere; and, yet, it is only against the backdrop of the city's sheer crowds that Patwardhan can deliver an exercise in individuation. Decades later, when the bombs struck Bombay's trains and its train stations were terrorized, and faces and names were splashed on the front pages of newspapers, must it have dawned upon people that crowds are never only just crowds and a sea of faces, that amidst those masses are mothers and fathers, sisters and brothers, daughters and sons, and wives and husbands.

With his sketchpad and notebook, Patwardhan lingered around train stations, mills, chawls, and street corners. The mills, once so dominant

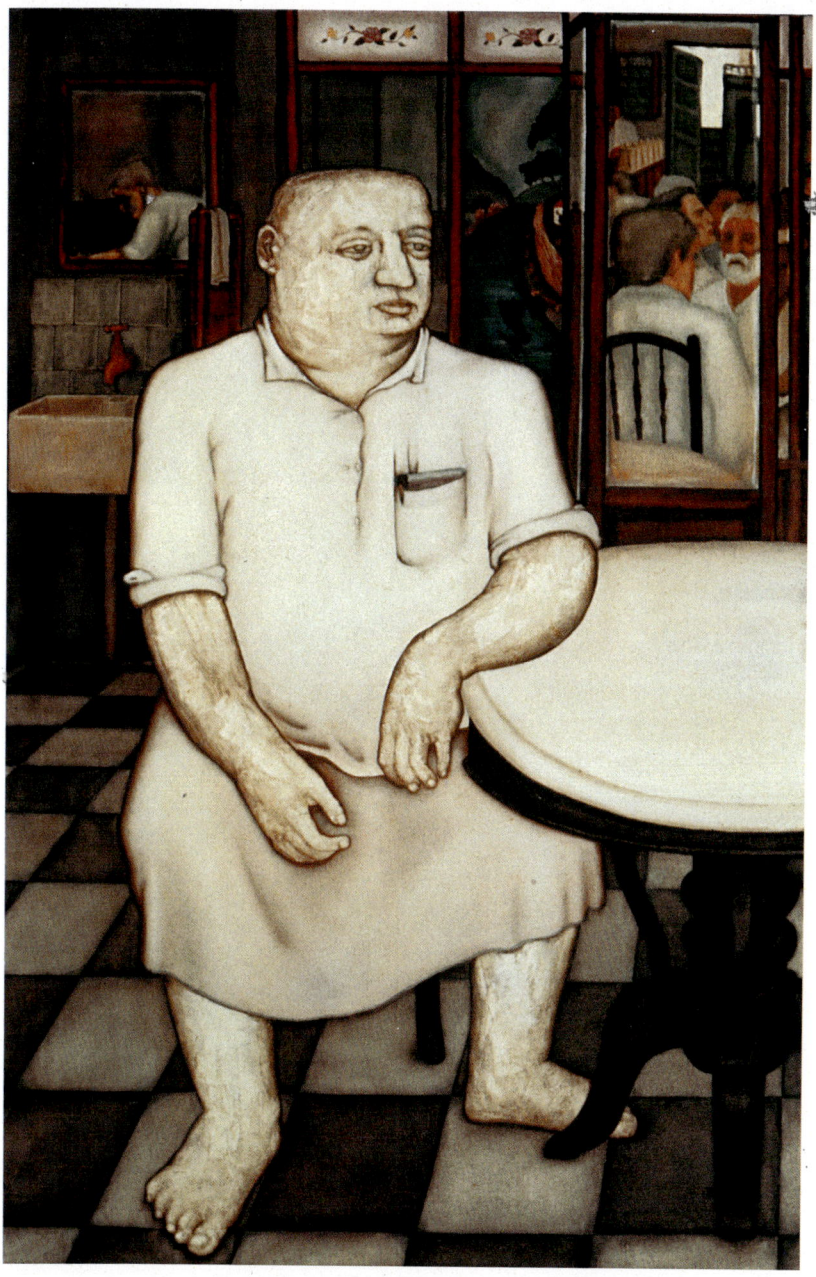

Iranian Restaurant; Painting credit and courtesy: Sudhir Patwardhan

Train; Painting credit and courtesy: Sudhir Patwardhan

Street Corner; Painting credit and courtesy: Sudhir Patwardhan

Overbridge; Painting credit and courtesy: Sudhir Patwardhan

Riot; Painting credit and courtesy: Sudhir Patwardhan

Bylanes Saga; Painting credit and courtesy: Sudhir Patwardhan

Lower Parel; Painting credit and courtesy: Sudhir Patwardhan

The Clearing; Painting credit and courtesy: Sudhir Patwardhan

a feature of Bombay's landscape, have largely disappeared; increasingly larger areas of what were once the city's remote outskirts have been absorbed into the metropolis. The 'clearing' of the land to pave the way for high-rises and industrial development has been accompanied by ethnic cleansing, as the Shiv Sena attempts to impose its own narrative of sons of the soil and enthrone the Marathi *manush* as the supposedly authentic inheritor of the land. Patwardhan has remained a careful observer of the urban scene through the decades: witness his painting of 'Lower Parel', which suggests with devastating effect the evisceration of a landscape once dotted with mills. He was always sympathetic to the working class and the labouring poor, and in the early years never disguised his political leanings; but he also became aware of the difficulties of advocating for the poor as a middle class artist. If his paintings are any guide in this matter, one should not be surprised if his political advocacy has become more nuanced, deeply reflective of a worldview in which the artist understands both the gravely moral implications of distancing and yet the artistic imperative of maintaining the tension between intimacy and distance. This small portfolio of Sudhir Patwardhan's paintings may yet move others to a greater exploration of one of India's most accomplished artists.

Further Reading

Hoksote, Ranjith. *Sudhir Patwardhan: The Complicit Observer*. Mumbai: Sakshi Gallery and Eminence Designs Pvt. Ltd., n.d.
Patwardhan, Sudhir. *Citing the City* [Exhibition Tour: November 2007 to March 2008]. Mumbai: Sakshi Gallery, 2007.

Film

Saacha ('The Loom', 49 mins., 2001), directed by Anjali Monteiro and K.P. Jayashankar: a film about a poet (Narayan Surve), a painter (Sudhir Patwardhan), and a city (Mumbai).

Spaces, Sights, Surroundings: Architecture of the City and Its Streets

Herbert Baker

The New Delhi

[What follows is the text of a paper first read by Herbert Baker at a meeting of the Royal Society of Arts, Indian Section, on 7 May 1926. The Right Hon Lord Hardinge of Penshurst described himself as greatly honoured to be in the chair, 'because, just as he was chiefly responsible for the transfer of the capital from Calcutta to Delhi, he was also in fact, as Viceroy, entirely responsible for the selection of Mr. Baker as one of the joint architects.']

New Delhi is in its 14th year. This autumn the Government of India will move from the temporary buildings which it has occupied since 1912, into the new Secretariat, and next January the members of the Assembly and Council of State will sit in the new Legislative Buildings. Some account, therefore, of the new Capital may now be of interest to the members of your Society, but I address you with great diffidence and reluctance, as the works of architects should speak for themselves, and these will very soon be able to do so. I am besides but one of other collaborators. So I propose to deal only with the more general intent and aspect of the subject.

The Commission appointed by the Government of India to report on the site of the new city consisted of Capt. Swinton, Mr., now Sir Edwin Lutyens, and Mr. Brodie. It went out in the summer of 1912, experiencing the worst heat of the Plains, and again in the cool weather of 1912–13. I followed in February, to find a controversy on two rival sites in full swing. The Commission reported in favour of a site to the south of the existing Delhi between its walled city founded by Shah Jehan and the many deserted cities of older Delhis. Its report urged against the northern site, the British Suburb which was naturally in every one's mind, on the unanswerable arguments of the experts that the ground ultimately required for the extension of a prosperous and growing city was fever-stricken, waterlogged and liable to occasional floods. This opinion was fully justified by the severe inundations of the whole area in 1924. But there existed a strong sentimental attachment to the old familiar Delhi on and around the northern Ridge, with its historical associations of the Mutiny and of the famous Delhi Durbars; and the Ridge with its fine views over the Jumna did seem to present architectural possibilities. The battle of science and of faith in the future of the new Capital against association and sentiment, and of a clean against a rather dirty architectural slate raged for some time, as in the longdrawn wars of the Mahabharata between Hastinapur and Indraprastha. But as in that Homeric contest Indraprastha won. For now the great central vista of New Delhi faces Indrapat, the reputed Indraprastha of the first legendary city of Delhi.

The new site consisted of arable land, much quarried outcrops of the quartzite ridge, the brickmakers' mounds of immemorial cities, and the foundations of the bazaars of Feroz-Shah's Delhi. Except for a small number of unknown and long since desecrated graves, the tombs and mosques of relative unimportance, there was no obstruction to the free planning of an ideal city. Of this opportunity Sir Edwin Lutyens and his two colleagues on the Commission took a masterful advantage. The centre point of the lay-out is an out-crop of the quartzite rock forming on the higher ground of the Raisina hamlet a spur at right angles to the Ridge which lies roughly parallel to the bed of the noble River Jumna, the great tributary of the sacred Ganges. I remember when the site had been settled, sitting on this rock with Mr. Herbert Fisher and Mr. Ramsay MacDonald and looking down over what was destined to be the great central avenue. We were engaged in speculating how a beautiful city could arise amidst what Lord Curzon had described, if I remember right, as 'the deserted cities of dreary and disconsolate tombs' when the sun setting beneath the rainclouds formed a perfect rainbow arch over the centre of the vista that was to be, just where the great arch of the Indian War Memorial is today rising. This good omen then acclaimed by us had been triumphantly fulfilled, as the building of the city has proceeded without a break throughout all the dark days of the war when there was more than the usual talk about the unluckiness of Delhi and evil prophecies that the war would last as long as the new city was a-building; and since the war ended it has weathered all the post war difficulties, delays, and, most dangerous of all, the Economy Commissions.

deserted cities of Delhi. London thrives happily enough on the ruins of
British, Roman, Saxon, Norman, Gothic and, alas to an increasing extent,
on Renaissance Londons. The truth may well be that in the climate of the
Plains the land surrounding a city soon became denuded and desiccated,
and its water contaminated. We know from the memoirs of European
sojourners in the Mughal Court, the horrors of the drinking water of
Delhi in the comparatively civilized 17th century. The Jumna too must
have changed its course as it has done in quite recent times. And so, with
an unlimited choice of site that could be defended on rock or by river, it
was more natural to build on new instead of upon the old ground. And
so again history has repeated itself. But surely Delhi may be counted
lucky rather than unlucky in being surrounded by such a wealth of well
preserved architectural relics reaching back into a memorable past.

But I confess that faith was required in those early days and one felt
the sting of Lord Curzon's gloomy criticism. The 'disconsolate tombs'
did seem endless and haunting. I used to ride most mornings for three
or four months during several years to a different building or group of
buildings, and even yet I have not seen them all. And nature in that
climate does little to heal the wounds of ruin; they seem for ever to
gape and stare. But the Archaeological Department is continuing within
its financial restrictions the good work initiated by Lord Curzon and is
transforming the ancient surroundings of Delhi. The Qutab, Haus Khas,
Feroz Shah's country palace, and the Lodi tombs are already refreshed
and shaded by lawns and trees. And the garden tomb of the Mughal
Governor Safdar Jang reposes, and now that sweet irrigation water has
replaced the old brackish wells, that of the Emperor Humayun with its
many attendant tombs and gateways will soon repose, amidst the beautiful
gardens designed by their pious founders. All these historical buildings of
Delhi in the mass may some day rival the world fame of Agra and its Taj
Mahal, the beauty of which depends so much on the skill with which its
designers set the architectural gem in the rich framework of its fairy water
garden. One thinks of the pleasure dome of Kubla Khan.

'bright with many a sinuous rill
Where blossomed many an incense breathing tree.'

The site of New Delhi has been called by its opponents an arid waste.
It lies in fact mostly on the deep alluvial soil of the Jumna, which with
the irrigation water now plentifully supplied can be extremely fertile.
The disturbance of the surface soil, due to the necessary leveling and

filling in of mosquito-breeding depressions dug out for the brick-earth of old Delhis, can be compensated quickly by manure and cultivation. It is true that around the central buildings which are founded upon the rock, much loosening and filling has to be done and special rock-loving trees, of which fortunately India possesses a good variety, will have to be planted.

The rock out-crop of the Raisina hamlet was chosen as the centre of a road system based on two great roads. The one leads from it to the old walled city of Indrapat, associated both with Hindu Vedic tradition and also with the Moslem Emperor Humayun, who died there. The other at an angle of 60 degrees centres on the dome and minarets of the Great Mosque, the Juma Musjid, of present Delhi. This angle of 60° gave the geometrical key to Lutyens' ingenious plan of the new city. It is a most original plan, except perhaps for the germ in L'Enfant's plan of Washington and Wren's rejected plan for London. This rock was about 50 feet high: 20 feet of it was blasted away, leaving a platform 32 feet high in front. By using the waste rock to fill the depressions, a great platform was made rising from the nearly level plain. On this platform are placed the central buildings, the Secretariat in two detached blocks, and Government House. At the time of its inception the analogy of the great base of Persepolis was pointed out. Perrot and Chipiez in their History of Art in Persia say that the object of Darius in erecting his stupendous platform was the same as that of the constructors of the great mounds in the plans of Chaldea and Assyria. It was to lift up a privileged royal enclosure in enjoyment of view and air above and city below.

The main walls of the two blocks of the Secretariat are 150 yards apart and are placed on the front of the great platform overlooking the Great Place with its great pierced stone railing, like those of the Buddhist shrines, and the 1½ mile long Maidan, avenues and water channels down to the War Memorial Arch, with the fortress walls of Indrapat and the river bed of the retreated Jumna beyond. Government House, Sir Edwin Lutyens' magnificent building, is placed on the centre line between the two Secretariats at a distance of 2,050 feet, or 683 yards from the dome of Government House to the centre of the Sectetariats. In the centre space between—called the Viceroy's Court—is the great column given by the late Maharajah of Jaipur. There will be fountains, trees, and as much green lawn as possible between the two blocks of the Secretariats to cool the air and relieve the eye against the red stone of the lower walls. The great steps and portico of the Viceroy's State Entrance face and command the view eastwards past the column and

through the coloumned pavilions and between their two domes of the
Secretariat. Wide Maidans and avenues lead away from the south and
north elevations. Behind to the west lie the private garden and the park
as far as the Ridge. Into the rock of the Ridge at this point it was
designed to quarry and build a semicircular amphitheatre half a mile
in diameter to take the place of the famous amphitheatres of the Delhi
Durbars, which were built of perishable earth on the remote plains on
the other side of the city, but no headway has been made with this
amphitheatre, which in its position on the Ridge and on the axis of
Government House, the Secretariats and the central vista, and in its
relation to the military cantonments on the one side and to the existing
city on the other, might in future royal Durbars have formed a stage for
pageants unrivalled in any ancient or modern city.

The position of the Secretariat Buildings on the same exalted
platform as Govrnment House above the level of the rest of the city,
has provoked criticism. It is said that the home of the Viceroy should
have been aloft and aloof from that of the officers of his Government
and thus more emphatically have expressed the supreme authority of
the great Lord Sahib. On that assumption Government House would
have stood in solitary grandeur on the rock platform in sole enjoyment
of the view over the trees of the surrounding battlements, domes,
minarets and towers. And it would have looked down on to the flat
roofs and chimneys of the Secretariats and not on the level past and
through the columns of its porticoes. From the Secretariats, moreover,
the Ministers and officers of the Government instead of sharing this
inspiring view, would when the trees grew up have seen nothing above
them. For the new city before very long will appear almost as a forest
city, the avenues of tall trees in every street hiding the one-storied
bungalows, and all but the greater buildings.

The criticism is natural enough and raises an interesting problem
in the architectural expression of the facts and ideals of governance. I
remember on my first voyage to India reading this eloquent statement of
what the Government of India stood for in an article in *The Round Table*
entitled 'the English in India.'

'So long as the consciousness of civilized man recognizes government
as the noblest task of the race, so long by administering India is our
pride of place unquestioned. No nation in modern times has done the
same or can aspire to do it.... Thothmes and Sennacherib, Alexander
and Napoleon never did the like. Only Rome in her greatest days did
what England has been doing. We Honour Rome, after two thousand

years, for her genius for law and order and administration; we kindle to her poet's boast,

"Haec est in gremium captos quae sola receipt,"

and yet with how much greater right can we make it ours? When the future annals of the world are written the achievement will rank higher than the broadest-minded decrees of the senate or the most generous edicts of the Caesars.'

Well, that was the idea which we architects within our limitations tried to express on the great red-stone platform, and I venture to assert that Lord Hardinge and his Government and advisers had a high and prophetic conception when they decided to give the architectural expression of a common dignity and distinction to the instrument of Government as a united whole. May not Governments, as individuals may do, rise to the distinction given to their office? The creation of that influence is one of the higher missions of architecture, and that it is possible must be the faith of architects. If in the future this faith is in the least justified the founders and designers of new Delhi, though they may not live to know it, will not by future generations be 'taxed with vain expense' or 'with ill matched aims,' albeit labouring, if not for 'a scanty,' yet for a modest band of Government officials only.

The Secretariat's three-storey building gives accommodation to all the administrative departments of the Government of India. On the first floor, the 'piano nobile,' are placed the offices of the Hon. members and the principal Secretaries. Each of the rooms allocated to Hon. members and committees has a distinctive colonnade and pavilion 52 feet above the level of the plain and through the white stone columns a wide and inspiring prospect beyond.

Otherwise, in addition to the innumerable offices the only special features in the building are a high domed entrance hall in the north block and in the south a general Conference Room surrounded by libraries and reception rooms, where the Government of India can entertain on its own behalf. Below the ground floor where the solid rock does not abut on the retaining wall of the great platform are record and storage rooms. In each block in the front of the platforms at the lower level under the Towers which face down the great avenue and water channels of the central vista, are vaulted chambers, in which are enshrined the foundation stones laid by their Majesties in 1917. The King's stone is in the South and the Queen's stone in the North Block. Over the stones are the Royal Insignia in bronze and above, cut into the stone vault, their

fountains which feed the larger fountains and the long water channels of
the Central Avenues.

The criticism that the Legislative Buildings are placed in a position
of inferiority to that of the Secretariats on the Acropolis may have some
justification. This building was the offspring of the new Constitution
created under the Act of 1919 and so it was conceived after the
foundations and basements of the Secretariat were born. The small
Legislative Assembly of the Morley-Minto Constitution, as it existed in
1913, was to have been placed in a wing of Government House. There
was no room on the raised Platform for the much larger building now
required. The best remaining site was chosen, as near as possible to the
Secretariat for the convenience of the Hon. Members and Secretaries, who
sit as members of the two Chambers. As the present Assembly Chamber
is actually located in the temporary Secretariat, there will at first be some
complaint of the separation of the two buildings, but I understand that
there are compensating advantages in a reasonable distance between
Ministers and officers and their files, and between legislators and the
offices of the Secretariat.

The legislative building consists of three chambers, the Legislative
Assembly, the Council of State and the Council of Princes. The building
is of a circular form suggested by my collaborator, Sir Edwin Lutyens, as
being best suited to its site, an equilateral triangle. The three chambers
are spaced at equal angles round a great central dome, 90 feet in diameter,
which will be generally used as a common library for Members of all three
Houses. On special occasions the Viceroy can here assemble any two or
all the three Chambers and so address or hold high Durbar with the
representatives of all India. The building will thus express the essential
unity of the three estates represented by the three Chambers. There are
also all the appurtenances of a Parliament House, public galleries—and
also Purdah galleries—the three Presidents' rooms and their officers' and
clerks, reading, writing, tiffin, committee rooms and a liberal number of
special rooms for the use of ministers, secretaries, and private members
and party leaders. The Princes' Chamber has its separate set of contingent
rooms. Three open courts with fountains separate the three chambers.

The acoustics of the Chambers present special difficulties on account
of their size, semi-circular form, and the great height thought necessary
for dignity and coolness and for effective clerestory lighting, skylights
being undesirable under a tropical sun. The Legislative Assembly now
consists of about 150 members, but the Chamber must be spacious

enough to seat ultimately 300 to 350 members. The floor space and the lower walls have therefore been contracted, so as to avoid empty benches and vacant floor space, which are both bad for acoustics and depressing to speakers. The wall will be set back when the House grows in numbers. The paneling up to the height of the gallery is sloped forward at an angle which will reflect back the sound down to the members, and all reflecting surfaces on the ceilings and higher walls are covered with a sound-absorbing plaster tile, invented, made and much used in America. But for one of the essentials of good acoustics—a full House and full galleries—the architects, as well as the well-wishers of Parliamentary institutions, require the co-operation of the people of India.

Besides these greater buildings there have been built, for the most part by the architects of the Public Works Department, the bungalows big and small, the streets and squares for the habitation of the different grades of Ministers, officers, clerks and menials who will work in the Government offices and Legislative Building and elsewhere in the city. These have mostly been built and occupied some years, the occupants traveling by car and omnibus to the present city some 7 or 8 miles distant. In addition, the Department has built post offices, police offices, schools, hospitals, hostels for members of the Assembly, bazaars and shopping centres. Then there is Sir Edwin Lutyens' Record office and his great War Memorial Arch and the temporary museum containing Sir Aurel Stein's frescoes from the deserts of Central Asia. The few living temples and shrines and the Junta[r] Manta[r], the huge brick and polished plaster astronomical instrument built by a Maharajah of Jaipur, have been enclosed with walls and gardens, and the famous Sikh shrine has an especially honoured enclosure close to Government House. The Sikh Guru, who lies buried here, was condemned to death by the Emperor Aurangzeb and died with a prophecy on his lips that a great white race would come from the west and destroy the Empire of his executioner.

Sites have been allotted to the Princes of India, but few of them have so far availed themselves of the exceptional facilities for building which now prevail, but which will cease when the industries, workshops and railway systems improvised for the new city are dismantled. The contemplated new Railway Station has unfortunately not been built, but the railway line which formerly ran through the site has been diverted and now runs round by the old river bed below Humayun's Tomb and Indrapat, and the new view of these two groups of ancient buildings adds greatly to the beauty and interest of the railway approach to the Capital. The roads are named, except for those of local significance, after great men and women

named roads come the names of the Viceroys more especially associated
with Delhi. Amongst famous Indians are Asoka and Prithvi Raj; Feroz
Shah and Akbar. One road is dedicated to Lady Hardinge, and open
spaces are named after Sultan Raziyah and Nur Jehan. Next to the names
of Clive and Hastings come those of two famous Empire builders who
strove so valiantly for their country only to meet on their home coming
with its ingratitude—Dupleix and Albuquerque.

Much more should be said on the building and engineering
achievements, but we are lucky in having amongst us Sir Hugh Keeling,
the engineering and organizing father of the building of New Delhi, and
I hope he will speak on this subject which is his own.

The raison d'être of the sites of all the former cities of Delhi has been
the Jumna, and it is a misfortune for the new site that the flight from the
mosquito placed the city where the river that once washed the walls of
Shah Jehan's Fort and Palace, Feroz Shah's Fort, Indrapat and Humayun's
Tomb, has now retreated from its well-known bands. But a future and
wealthier India, proud of its Capital, may complete the plan which shows
a great lake fed by a canal from the Jumna, as one termination of the
central vista as well as the projected Durbar Amphitheatre at the other.

Speaking for the buildings only for which I am responsible, and more
especially for the Secretariat, the principle which has prompted the design,
as far as any principle in building is conscious or can be put into words,
has been to weave into the fabric of the more elemental and universal
forms of architecture the thread of such Indian traditional shapes and
features as may be compatible with the nature and use of the buildings.
The most pleasing characteristics, I think, in the old buildings of India
are the wide, flat spaces of bare, sunlit walls, contrasted and enriched at
rare intervals with the more elaborate features of doors, windows and
balconies, which the Indian craftsmen love to adorn. Indeed, there is no
more radical fact than the solid front to the public thoroughfare and
the open court life within. The architecture of the south of Spain is
distinguished by the same characteristics. I venture to suggest that the
failure of so many attempts to adapt old Indian architecture to modern
usage and conditions of life is due to the mistaken attempt to overload
the close fenestration necessary for modern utilitarian buildings with too
many 'purple patches' of elaborate detail.

The Indian features which have been specially adopted are the Chajja,
the familiar cornice of stone slabs which, supported on brackets or cove,
over-hangs the wall to a width of sometimes 8 or 9 feet. Its function is in

stone that of the great eaves of Italian and Spanish buildings in wood and tiles, casting deep shadows down the sun-scorched walls and protecting the windows from tropical rains. The Jaali, or pierced stone or marble slabs of intricate patterns, have been largely used in windows, screens and railings. It would be interesting to trace the historical origin of the Jaali; how far it may be derived from the cancelli or chancel screens, and the pierced masonry windows of Rome—and the connection of both with the Byzantine examples such as those in the mosque of Damascus and those taken, no doubt, in spoil from the East, in St. Mark's at Venice. Under Muhammadan influences they developed into an infinite intricacy of geometrical pattern. The Chattri, or open canopied turret, the umbrella or symbol of royalty, has been used very sparingly, and the Exedra, the high arched and domed portal that distinguishes the Mughal buildings.

A bold departure from Indian architecture has been taken in the planning and designing of the Secretariat by the omission of continuous verandahs to protect the walls from the sun. It was reasoned that verandahs on east and west walls are of little protection against the slanting rays of the sun, unless their height is so reduced as objectionably to darken the rooms behind in dull weather and in evening light, and that the heat clings in verandahs long after the sun has departed from the walls. On the other hand, experiments were made to prove that a very thick or hollow wall does not get heated right through even in the most torrid season. The heat, too, as the sun goes off it, radiates more quickly from the open than the covered wall. In the Secretariat the glass has been set on the inside of these thick walls and jalousie shutters on the outside, so that no sun need shine on and heat the glass. Moreover, by the use of shutters the lighting of the room can be regulated, the full direct light being enjoyed up to the twilight, a real boon to the late worker. The experience of the offices which have been occupied for the last few years seems to justify the departure; in fact, complaints so far have been directed rather to the coolness of the offices due to some extent, I think, to the slow drying out of the thick walls.

It has been a disappointment that it has been impossible to call in the aid of the traditional skill of India in the arts and crafts. At the beginning in 1912, a petition, it may be remembered, was presented to the Secretary of State for India, signed by a good many distinguished people known for their interest in and knowledge of the arts, in favour of employing as designers of the new buildings the native master builders of India instead of alien and unsympathetic architects! There was no difficulty, however, in convincing the Viceroy of the fallacy of this petition as far as the architecture was concerned, but it was agreed that there was some truth underlying it in respect of the arts and crafts. The Government of India consequently inserted a clause in the Architects' agreements to the effect that it proposed to found a school of Craftsmen at Delhi to collaborate with the architects in the building. But the war came; then the post-war fever of economy, from the shivering fits of which we have hardly yet recovered.

But in the more essential and humbler crafts of masonry and joinery a wonderful work has been done. The stone yard is perhaps unrivalled. Between 2,000 and 3,000 masons have worked through these years continuously and the murmur of the saws has ceased neither by night nor by day. One wonders what these masons will do when the work stops! But India will be richer by many thousands of good masons and mistri who will return more highly skilled in their craft to their different stone-working districts. In joinery, as distinct from carpentry and wood-carving, Indians have been traditionally less skilled than in masonry—perhaps because wood furniture is little used. But in the Delhi joinery shops, started with the encouragement of Lord Chelmsford, the Sikhs have now reached the level of, and even overtaken, their skilled Chinese rivals. In the carving in stone and wood that the limited funds have permitted the skilled craftsmen have learned a less superficial and more virile touch and found a broader scope in harmony with the scale and restraint of the buildings.

In case it may not be generally known, it may be as well to state that the contractors, all the workmen and craftsmen, the mistri, foremen and inspectors, are Indians, and that the only British employed under the rank of Executive Engineer and the Resident architects, are some dozen super-foremen. These have been the salt of the job and speak with just pride of the good work done by their Indian fellow-workers.

Little, however, has been attempted to revive to give an opportunity to the many traditional Indian arts and crafts, some merely inactive from want of a market, some quite dormant. Through the medium of these much might have been done to enhance New Delhi in the eyes of India by giving expression to Indian ideas, to her symbolism, heraldry, history and philosophy, so far as these can be embodied in art. At the same time an outlet might have been given to the artistic and intellectual activities and self-expression of Indians. The Indian people are good sightseers; the old buildings gain much in live interest and beauty by the gaily dressed troops of visitors. They will surely come to see the New as well as the Old Delhi, and will, I believe, even now, and increasingly as knowledge grows, grasp the meaning to be read in the stone and marble of the buildings of their capital. But the sands are running out, and as the scaffolding is being removed, the opportunities for the craftsmen are vanishing. For the painters and sculptors, however, there is yet time to take advantage of this unique opportunity of the continuity of patronage and certainty of market which is necessary for any artistic revival.

*****

Delhi has 6 or 7 months of tolerable climate, or more if the rains are included, and 4 or 5 of these months have a perfect climate. It is, of course, a misfortune that its climate is not tolerable all the year round, but there is no such place with a climate to be so described in the plains of Northern India. If there had been the history of India might have been different, and it might not have been necessary for a race which recruited its vigour overseas to hold sway there for so long. But the test has yet to be made of the capacity of the new buildings, with their thick walls and roofs and the vast space they enclose from the sun, to lengthen the more tolerable period of coolness in the plains. Science, in addition to motor transport and electric fans and the discovery of the malaria germ, may yet do more for the tropics by the invention of some cheap system of cooling the air—cheaper and safer manipulation of liquid air, as a hint to the inventor!—to mitigate the period in the Indian summer during which neither European nor Indian can work with comfort.

The success of Delhi as a pleasant and beautiful city will largely depend on the Government and votes of the Legislature for the full and clean maintenance of its avenues, lawns, gardens and fountains, both in the new city and in the surrounding circle or older Delhis, and for the afforestation of the Ridge necessary to temper the prevailing summer winds. If this duty is liberally accepted and performed, the capital of India, with its Delhis new and old, may become all one garden city and the pride of India, affording in the future full justification for the faith, courage and foresight of its founders.

It was the wise Sir Christopher Wren who said: 'Architecture has its political uses: it establishes a nation.' And when we consider the glorious part India took in the Great War, and in the Peace Conference at Paris, and her great stride forward in political development under the New Constitution, the founders of New Delhi would seem to have been prophetic in foreseeing her need of a new capital as an essential in the establishment of her ideal of national unity.

The Chairman (Lord Hardinge) said that the Society was greatly indebted to Mr. Baker for his very interesting paper. To the speaker personally it had been of absorbing interest, for he had always regarded New Delhi as his special child. No mother had ever been through a more difficult and anxious time in nurturing her offspring than he had been, from 1911 to 1916, in nursing that frail and delicate infant. There were many people who treated it very unkindly; some of them tried to strangle it, and some to mangle it, and others sought to starve it, but the new Delhi infant had a very strong constitution and happily survived all efforts made to put an end to it, and perhaps, owing to the very vicissitudes through which it had passed, this delicate child was growing up to a very strong and robust manhood. He had no fear that this new capital of Delhi would not some day be the crowning edifice of national unity, embodying Indian aspirations and the traditional imperial policy of Great Britain.

He hoped that Mr. Baker would pardon him if he corrected him in this statement that the Commission appointed by the Government of India, consisting of Captain Campbell Swinton (whom he was very pleased to see present that evening), Sir Edwin Lutyens, and Mr. Brodie, took, as he said, a masterful advantage of the absence of any obstruction in the surroundings of Delhi to the free planning of an ideal city. He did not wish to belittle in any way the efforts and work of that Commission, which he had always appreciated as being of great value; but he was afraid that the description given by Mr. Baker was not quite accurate. It was perfectly true, as Mr. Baker had said, that this Commission worked very hard, and spent the summer in 1912 at Delhi, in great heat, riding on an elephant round and round Delhi looking for a site. It was in September that he was overjoyed on receiving a message to the effect that a site had been chosen by the Commission, and as soon as the site selected had been mapped out and the positions assigned to the principal Government buildings and to the roads, he went down to Delhi to inspect it, taking with him some members of his Council and also some engineers. They rode out to the proposed site, and he remembered so well his feeling of dismay on being brought to its central point. He had a feeling of oppression; there was no view, the site was shut in, and was close to a rocky hill, part of the prolonged ridge from which it was evident that great heat would radiate in the summer. Even on that October day it was, he remembered, very hot. He sat there on a stone and listened for nearly three hours to all that the commission had to say in favour of the site, and he weighed very carefully their replies to his objections. But he was profoundly depressed, so much so that he remembered saying to one of his staff that he would sooner not build a New Delhi at all than build it on that site. He then mounted his horse and asked Mr. Hailey, the commissioner of Delhi, to accompany him. He rode to the top of a hill some distance away, in order if possible to see if he could not himself find a site that would appeal to him more than the one which had been selected. When he reached the top of the hill he saw before him a most wonderful panorama of old Delhi, the domes and dimarets of the Jumma Masjid, Indrapat, Humayun's Tomb, Safdar Jang and the Qutub with the river Jumma, like a streak of silver, in the foreground, winding its sluggish way between its ever changing banks. It was to him a wonderful vision, and he turned at once to the Commissioner and said, 'This is the site of the Government House.' When the rest of the party arrived he told them what he thought, but he remarked that the top of the hill would not provide much space for a really fine Government House with all the surrounding ground which was requisite. An engineer officer, however, who happened to be present, said at once that there would be no difficulty in cutting off the top of the hill. That surprised him very much, though one ought never to be surprised at anything in India. And he was right. He (the speaker) accordingly gave directions for this new site to be investigated on the lines of the removal of the top of the hill, and about twenty feet of height was removed, thereby making a large plateau upon which there was ample room for both Government House and the Secretariat Buildings. This, with due deference to Mr. Baker, was the true story of the choice of the site of New Delhi.

He had at first intended that Government House should stand alone on the hill, but the architects convinced him that for many reasons it would be a finer scheme if the Secretariat were at the entrance of the plateau on the main approach to government House, and he thought they were right. It was unfortunate that the war intervened to arrest the building of the new city, owing to the impossibility of getting the necessary steel girders and also for other reasons; but he was delighted to hear from Mr. Baker that the Secretariat Buildings would be completed and in occupation during the next winter, and that the Legislative Buildings would also be in use, and he hoped it would not be long before the very beautiful and imposing structure which Sir Edwin Lutyens had designed for Government House would be completed and in occupation by the Viceroy. He was quite convinced in his own mind that the city of new Delhi, so happily inaugurated as it was by the King and Queen, would in a few years' time be one of the finest and most beautiful capitals

in the world. (Applause). Before concluding his remarks he wished to
pay a tribute not only to the architects, but to all officers and servants of
the Government of India, for the energy and enthusiasm which they had
put into their work, and in particular Sir Malcolm Hailey and Sir Hugh
Keeling during the years that he (the speaker) supervised the planning
and building of the new city. He was glad to see the latter gentleman
present, and hoped he would contribute to the discussion.

*****

Capt. G.S.C. Swinton (Chairman of the Town-Planning Committee of
the new Imperial city of Delhi) said that he was quite sure that in the
history of the world no city had had such an opportunity as Delhi from
the architectural point of view. The Chairman on that occasion, then the
Viceroy, showed great wisdom in selecting the architects who carried it
out, and from the photographs which had been exhibited its scale and
magnificence could be appreciated. He did not believe that any city had
had the opportunity of achieving such spaciousness and fine architecture,
and he hoped the city would be worthy of it for all time. After the
Chairman's allusion to the choice of the site, he wanted to say one thing
which he felt he must say in justice to his colleagues, Sir Edwin Lutyens
and Mr. Brodie. The Chairman was perfectly correct in what he said
about the siting of the great buildings, but he thought the audience might
mix this up with the choice of the site for the whole new city. When
his Committee was appointed to go out to Delhi a site on the northern
side had been chosen. He remembered going to see Lord Roberts on
the subject, and Lord Roberts only laid down one injunction. He said:
'Do not build on the ridge,' by which he meant the Mating Ridge. His
Majesty the King said the same thing, 'You must not build on the Ridge.'
It was holy ground. If they were warned off the Ridge, where then, on the
north, could they build? Much of the land was liable to flooding. They
were told that sixty-five donkeys had been drowned in one hollow not
long before! Eventually they decided, with Lord Hardinge's agreement,
on the southern site. Lord Hardinge, however, who was a very sick man
a little later, might not be aware what tremendous pressure was exerted
then to move them back to the northern. It was a very strong movement,
and Lord Hardinge was a very sick man. (Lord Hardinge: I was well
enough to resist it.) The speaker knew that Lord Hardinge resisted it, but
the pressure from all sides, and a good deal from home, was very strong,
and he thought that his Committee, especially Mr. Brodie, who spoke

from the engineering point of view, deserved a certain amount of credit for standing firm. (Lord Hardinge: Oh, I agree.)

—slightly abridged from original publication in *Journal of the Royal Society of Arts*, vol. LXXIV, no. 3841 (2 July 1926), pp. 772–93.

Charles Correa

Space as a Resource

Visiting a city like Bombay or Calcutta, the first thing that strikes one is the poverty all around. This urban poverty is perhaps the worst pollution of all. Way before you see smoke in the sky or smell sulphur in the air, you see people all around, living and dying on the pavements. Is it inevitable that poverty should degrade life in this manner?

The same poverty, in rural India, has a far different expression. The people are as poor, in fact perhaps even poorer, but they are not so dehumanized. In the village environment, there is always space to meet and talk, to cook, to wash clothes. There is always a place for the children to play. Need we take a look at how these same activities occur in our cities? Obviously, there is no relation between the way our cities have been built and the way people have to use them.

Urban living involves much more than just the use of a small room of, say, 10m². The room, the cell, is only one element in a whole system of spaces that people need. This system is generally hierarchial. For us, under Indian conditions, it appears to have four major elements:

Firstly, the space needed by the family for exclusively private use, such as cooking, sleeping, storage and so forth;

Secondly, the areas of intimate contact, i.e. the front doorstep where children play, you chat with your neighbour;

Thirdly, the neighbourhood meeting places (e.g. the city water tap or the village well) where you become part of your community;

Finally, the principal urban area—e.g. the 'maidan'—used by the whole city.

In different societies, the number of elements and their inter-relation might vary, but all human settlements throughout the globe (from the little hill towns of Italy to the sprawling metropolii of London or Tokyo) have some analogue of such a system; an analogue which modulates with climate, income levels, cultural patterns, etc., of the society concerned.

Now there are two important facts about the workings of these systems. The first is that each of the elements consist of both covered spaces as well as open-to-sky spaces. This is of fundamental significance to developing countries, since almost all of them are located in warm tropical climates where a number of essential activities can—and indeed do—take place outdoors. For example: cooking, sleeping, entertaining friends, children's play, etc. need not be exclusively indoor, but can function effectively in an open courtyard (provided of course, that privacy is reasonably assured). In Bombay, for instance, we estimate that at least 75% of essential functions of living (sleeping, cooking, entertaining friends, etc.) can occur in an open-to-sky space; and, since the monsoons are limited to 3 months, this holds true for about 70% of the year. Thus open-to-sky space has a usability coefficient of about half (i.e. .75 × .70) that of a built-up room. Similarly, we can estimate the usability coefficient of the other built-form conditions (verandahs, pergola-covered terraces, and so forth—even that of a tree-shaded courtyard!) that lie in the spectrum between the enclosed room and open-to-sky space.

Now, just as they have *usability* coefficients, each of these spaces also has a *production cost:* brick and cement in the case of the room, more urban land (and hence longer service infrastructure lines) in the case of the courtyard. The point of trade-off between these two variables determines the *optimal* pattern—and density—of housing at a particular location. And if you look around the Third World today, you will find countless examples of marvellously innovative habitat, from the Casbah in Algiers to the paper houses of Tokyo. Each one being an adroit trade off between the usability coefficient of these various kinds of spaces on the one hand, and their production cost on the other.

The second important fact about this hierarchy is that all the elements are mutually inter-dependent. That is to say, less space in one can be adjusted by providing more in one of the others. For example, smaller dwelling units may be compensated by larger community spaces, or vice versa. Sometimes there are glaring imbalances: public open spaces in Delhi, for instance, follow the usual norm of 1.5 hectare per 1000 persons— which works out to about 75 m^2 of public open space per family. But what a staggering difference it would have made to the families living in the packed hovels of Old Delhi, if even just a *fraction* of this public space (now mostly squandered in the monumental vistas and parks of New Delhi) had been traded off as a small courtyard for each family. The pattern of their lives would undergo a sensational improvement.

To identify this hierarchical system, and to understand the nature of these trade-offs, is of course the first essential step towards providing viable housing. Without this, one is in grave danger of formulating the wrong questions. This misunderstanding is the reason why so many attempts at low-cost housing perceive it only as a simplistic issue of trying to pile up as many dwelling units, (as many cells) as possible on a given site, without any concern for the other spaces involved in the hierarchy. The result: environments which are inhuman, uneconomical—and quite unusable. Environments that ignore the fundamental principle, namely, that in a warm climate—like cement, like steel—space itself is a *resource*.

In using open-to-sky spaces, the territorial privacy of the families is of decisive importance. For as the surrounding buildings get taller, these spaces get more and more restricted in function. A ground floor courtyard can be used by a family for many purposes, including sleeping at night. Two storeys, and you can still cook in it. Five storeys, and it's only for children to play in. Ten storeys, and it's a parking lot. The old indicators of so many square metres of open space per 1000 persons are too simplistic and crude; we have got to *disaggregate* these numbers, both qualitatively and quantitatively, in order to anticipate their real usefulness.

Estimating accurately the production cost of these various spaces (rooms, courtyards, verandahs, etc.) of course involves examining the relation between building heights and overall densities, since the latter is a key determinant of infrastructure costs at the *city scale*. This relationship depends on a number of factors, including the size of the housing units and the community space per family. For Indian urban conditions, (i.e. an average housing unit of 25 m^2 and a community area of about 30 m^2 per family for tot-lots, health centres, etc.), we find that ground floor housing can accommodate per hectare about 125 families, each on a plot of 44 m^2· 5-storey walk-up apartments double this figure to about 250 families; 20-storey buildings will double it again to about 500 families. Thus as the building heights increase twenty-fold, gross neighbourhood densities increase only about four-fold.

And if we step back to see a larger context—the overall city—then the variations in density become even less pronounced. For, contrary to popular belief, doubling building heights doesn't save drastically on the overall area of a city. Only about a third of a city is used for housing (the rest is for industry, transport, green areas, educational institutions, etc.). Furthermore, if we calculate the housing sital area itself (i.e. the area of the housing sites, *without the neighbourhood roads*, etc.) then we find that the percentage of land-use devoted to housing sites is usually about 20%, the variation being dependent on the floor area ratio (i.e., FAR) permissible on each site.

Studies undertaken three decades ago for Hook New Town in the U.K. demonstrated that for a circular town, reducing residential densities from 250 persons per hectare to 100 persons per hectare would increase the area of the circle by 42%, and the radius (i.e. distance from periphery to city centre) by only 19%. This is an important principle even in cold climates, but what I seek to emphasize here is that, in the context of the warm climates prevailing in the Third World, these variations in residential densities will cause crucial mutations in the living patterns—really the *lifestyles*—of the people! In exchange for only marginal decreases in overall city size, they drastically reduce the open-to-sky space (and hence, in our climates, the *usability*) of the housing.

Furthermore, these variations will make decisive differences to the *cost* of the construction. For in a warm climate, shelter can be made from a wide variety of simple materials—ranging from mud and bamboo to sun-dried brick. These constructions are of necessity low-rise. As they go taller (to four storey walk-ups and higher) the construction has to change to RCC—not because the *climate* demands it, but for *structural* strength. This of course brings an enormous escalation in cost. In contrast, in the cold climates of Europe and North America variations in construction costs (as a function of building height) have a much narrower range, since even a ground-floor house must be constructed of relatively expensive thermally-insulated materials.

By low-rise, one means not only self-help housing, but traditional vernacular architecture in general—those wonderfully rich languages created by people all over the world, without benefit of professional architects! Not only are these indigenous building systems more successful in economic, aesthetic and human terms (as any reasonably honest architect will cheerfully admit) but far more appropriate socio-economic processes are involved in their production. For, as we have seen earlier, money invested in vernacular housing is pumped into the economy at the *bazaar* level, right where it generates the greatest amount of tertiary employment—namely, for those migrants pouring in from the rural areas.

How then does one explain the staggeringly high densities prevailing in Third World cities around the globe? Sadly enough, these are generally achieved not through high-rise buildings, but firstly, from an extraordinarily high occupancy rate per room, and secondly by the criminal omission of play spaces, hospitals, schools and other social infrastructure in the neighbourhood. London, for instance, has approximately 3 hectares of green area per thousand population, Delhi has 1.5 hectares; in Bombay island the figure is 0.1 hectare—and this includes the 'grass' on the traffic islands! Even roads, usually at least 25% of land-use (higher in Los Angeles!), are only 8% in Bombay island. So naturally the gross residential densities become astronomical, reaching figures which make living conditions quite impossible.

Yet merely increasing the *maidans* (open spaces) is not necessarily the solution; for they are not used by the entire populace, but only by certain age groups for cricket, football and other such games. No little toddler of two or three years would dare to play here; nor does one see middle-aged couples using them for evening strolls. On the other hand, the pavements along the seafront in Bombay—which incidentally do not show up in the statistics!—are the great community spaces of our city. Obviously we should generate many more such promenades. They are the heart of the social life of the tropical temperate zones. The Latin cities—Paris, Rome, Rio de Janeiro—have always understood this; hence the boulevards with their broad pavements and cafes. Land used for such boulevards is far more cost-effective than conventional "green areas". (Perhaps one tree on the Boulevard San Michel is worth an acre of green in the Bois de Bologne?)

In conclusion, it must be emphasized that any investigation of optimal densities is largely determined by the *scale of the context* we establish. For instance, to a developer looking at an individual urban site, the trade-off between cost of construction (which rises with building height) and the land component (which varies inversely with the floor space generated), will lead to a certain density.

To an authority responsible for a larger context—say the whole neighbourhood—this trade-off will certainly give another answer, since they must take into account the area needed for the schools, roads, and other infrastructure necessitated by his decision.

To anyone looking at the overall city, in fact at the whole nation and its resources, the answer will change again. Given the awesome scale of urban growth facing the Third World, there can be little doubt that it is within the larger parameters that we should view this issue.

For too long have we allowed the densities of our cities to be determined in the narrowest context by the random (and self-interested) decisions of individual commercial developers—higher densities triggering off higher land values, and vice versa, in an increasingly vicious spiral, like a serpent that feeds off its own tail. Today, almost the entire building industry in all our major cities is turning out a product that only the middle and upper classes can afford, forcing half of our society out on to the pavements. In their confusion and desperation, architects and engineers start searching for new 'miracle' technologies (rather like the medieval alchemist's fevered hunt for the elusive touchstone which would convert dross into gold). Too long have we struggled for these answers, when all along the land-use planners have stated the question wrongly to begin with. The problem of housing the vast majority of our urban people is not one of finding miracle building materials of construction technologies; it is primarily a matter of density, of *re-establishing land-use allocations.*

—originally published as Chapter 3 of Charles Correa, *The New Landscape*
(Bombay: The Book Society of India, 1985), pp. 31–44.

Arjun Appadurai

Street Culture

In our concern for the preservation of India's cultural and natural heritage, we have tended to concentrate excessively on her arts and her crafts, her traditions of thought and performance, her monuments and mausolea, her birds and her beasts. But we have tended to ignore some of India's more obvious cultural resources, resources found in settings which do not fit our preconceived notions of high culture or unspoilt nature. The Indian street is one such setting, whose cultural ambience is changing in troubling ways today. Street culture is about to become an endangered resource.

Streets, and their culture, lie at the heart of public life in contemporary India. Especially in those many cities where urban housing is crowded and uncomfortable, and where the weather is never too cold, streets are where much of life is lived. Streets are many things: thoroughfares, bazaars, theatres, exhibitions, restaurants. They encompass a huge range of activities from worship and business, to political protests and funeral and marriage processions.

Streets intensify the culture experience of urban life at the same time as they facilitate its logistics. With the possible exception of the railroad, streets capture more about India than any other setting. On its streets, India eats, works, sleeps, moves, celebrates and worships. The street is a stage that rarely sleeps.

Genuine street culture occurs neither on the great highways of India nor in the narrow lanes that characterize neighbourhoods in villages or in very small towns. When a thoroughfare is too dominated by vehicles, especially modern vehicles, it is no longer hospitable to the complexities of street culture. Such thoroughfares are just instruments of travel and transport. They do not have sufficient human traffic, and sufficient concentrations of spectators and hangers-around to meet the key requirement of street culture: a sheer density of human interactions. The great tarred highways and their rural counterparts are not the sites of street culture.

Nor can one expect to see the culture of the street in the lanes and gullies of restricted neighbourhoods in villages and towns. Here the problem is a different one: when a street is insufficiently open to the noise of commerce, the drama of seeing strange persons, sights and sounds, when it is too much an extension of the intimacy of families, castes or other small groups, then too street culture is not likely to be found in full bloom.

Yet the seeds of contemporary street cultures do lie in great thoroughfares and the tiny gullies of pre-modern India. Historically, it is in such streets and thoroughfares that Indians have learnt to traffic with the world, unprotected by the certainties of the family, unrestrained by the proprieties of caste. The great highways of colonial India, such as the Grand Trunk Road, have always symbolized the romance of travel, adventure, even danger. In Kipling's *Kim* or in the romances associated with the thugee phenomenon of central India, the great thoroughfares and highways that linked cities, villages and regions, were the seedbeds of cosmopolitanism. They brought together travelers, officials of the state, brigands, itinerant priests and pilgrims, men and women, and groups that would otherwise never encounter each other.

Pilgrimage, of course, was one of the principal historical contexts for the emergence of these regional and national thoroughfares. Scholars have paid considerable attention to the end-points of these journeys: the *tirthas*, the sacred places that enticed the pilgrim to travel far from home. But have we paid enough attention to the journey itself, to the logistics and cultural challenges that travel must have implied in pre-modern India? It was in these lengthy road journeys that urbane travelers had to negotiate with local villagers for their sustenance, where roadside shrines must have emerged to satisfy the needs of itinerants, where codes of conduct must have emerged for dealing with strangers.

How did roads and highways in pre-modern India function? What was the culture of provisioning and of worship along them? Did the *dharamsalas* and early eating operations along these roads contain the seeds of contemporary restaurant culture, along with the royal courts? Did the needs of travelers provide a significant stimulus to inter-urban commerce? To what extent did travelers seek self sufficiency and to what extent did they see travel as an occasion for exploring the foods, clothing, and shelter of new regions and groups?

Whatever the answers to these questions, they are likely to confirm the intuition that in the great thoroughfares of traditional India, especially those that provided the arteries for religious travel, we have the beginnings of contemporary cosmopolitanism in India. It is in these settings that Indians, both wealthy and poor, are likely to have developed a taste for the sights, sounds, smells and tastes of those different from them. Contemporary Indian street culture, in all its aspects, must owe a good deal of its élan to these early public thoroughfares.

Equally, however, the tiny lanes and streets that characterize the *mohullas* of the north, the *agraharams* of the Tamil south, the *wadas* of Maharashtra, and the other semi-insulated zones of rural and small town India, have provided the historical beginnings of street culture. In these small lanes and byways, often too narrow for vehicles of any sort, domestic life simply spills outside and encounters the larger world. It was in these small lanes that the commercial impulses of the wider world penetrated small markets, largely in the form of itinerant vendors and merchants, carrying fruits, vegetables, textiles, combs, bangles and prepared foods to householders in small urban neighbourhoods and to villages.

Here too, in these small lanes and streets, public festivities, both religious and secular, would take place, and occasionally street performers would come through, entertaining, soothsaying, importuning the householder at his doorstep. This humble end of street life still exists in the villages and in the mofussil, a mild echo of the hurly-burly of mainstream street culture, reflecting one of the historical streams that have fed contemporary street cultures. The domestic end of R K

Narayan's Malgudi captures this backwater street culture as well as any other representation.

In these diametrically opposed settings, Indians developed a taste for the dramas of life in public. Today, these two types of thoroughfares continue to play an important role in supporting public life, but they are no longer the key arenas in which to observe street culture. The great thoroughfares, often replaced by modern highways, now are instruments for the rapid movement of goods and people and thus constitute part of the infrastructure of cosmopolitanism, not its front stage. The small lanes and gullies are the backwaters of cosmopolitanism, pale reflections of what goes on elsewhere. Where street culture really exists today is in the crowded urban and urbanizing settings of contemporary India, in the roads and streets that, throughout India, constitute the core of the cities and towns. Their models are Anna Salai in Madras, Pherozeshah Mehta Road in Bombay, M G Road in Pune, Town Hall Road in Madurai, Chowringhee in Calcutta, and their many counterparts in these and other cities. It is the culture of these streets that lies at the heart of public culture today.

It is worth emphasizing that street culture is not a homogeneous thing throughout contemporary India. The street cultures of the great colonial cities of Bombay, Madras, and Calcutta are different from those of the railway cities like Nasik, Renigunta or Bilaspur, or those of the industrial cities like Jamshedpur, Pimpri or Dhanbad. These in turn are different from the street cultures of the old royal centres like Madurai, Varanasi or Pandharpur. Even within each of these types of city, the great main streets can differ from the specialized ones, some of which might be dominated by entertainment, others by commerce, yet others by the ambience of religion.

But for all this variation—which makes it essential to think of street cultures in the plural—there is something shared, which justifies the use of the singular. The two most important features of what is shared are the great range of activities that occur on Indian streets and give them their ambience and the way in which street culture blurs the line between private and public life.

Although Indian streets are essential to public life, they have not, till recently, been antagonistic to what we would think of as private activities. Roadside shrines and trees are often the scene of intensely personal acts of worship or meditation. Barbers, ear-cleaners and fortune tellers conduct intimate transactions with their clientele on the street. Clothes are washed, baths are taken, meals are cooked in the full view of passersby. This is sometimes the product of sheer exigency. But Indian streets are a reminder that the sharp demarcation of public from private spheres is a recent addition to the Indian consciousness. Though important changes are afoot in this regard, Indian street culture is an example of those classical Indian designs for living that did not rely on sharp breaks between 'inside' and 'outside', private and public, personal and collective activities.

The street is above all a commercial space. The world of goods is a central part of the experience of street life in urban India today. The eye is everywhere assaulted by billboards that hawk movies, political parties, fancy goods and services. The billboard is the central device of capitalist realism in urban India, the place where the icons and messages of cosmopolitanism are etched into the public imagination. Under the gaze of these billboards and posters are the many settings for buying and selling.

Hawkers and vendors are the base of street life, selling everything from food and ballpoint pens to aphrodisiacs and calendars. Shops and their store fronts, especially in commercialized streets, dominate the texture of street culture, with their displays often spilling on to the pavements, pushing their way into the space of the street vendor and the roadside stroller. In the traditional shopping areas of urban India, these streets are indeed bazaars in the classical sense: settings where goods and specialists are enclaved, and stretches of brassware shops are followed by stretches of clothing, further stretches of leather goods and so forth.

The Indian street shopper typically operates in an economy of small differences, where nuances of display, personal style or supply can make a good day for one shop rather than another. Shopping in these bazaar streets is a noisy, social activity, where the cold forces of supply and demand are still encased in the human drama of bargaining, seducing, cheating and cajoling. The commercial dimension of street culture is thus enormously complex, stratified and multi-layered. The products and images of the billboards may be directed to the affluent, Amul Butter, Nirula's Fast Food, Khaitan Fans, while the store fronts are targeted to the middle class, and the hawkers and vendors target the working classes and the truly disenfranchised.

Yet, all these kinds of products and images occupy a single aesthetic and auditory space. In this space, while a range of goods and services do change hands, the key cultural fact is that the street is an emporium of commercial images and temptations, in which the casual stroller is exposed to the seductions of consumption. The street is the guerilla theatre of commerce in contemporary India.

But this should not suggest that Indian urban streets are simply marketplaces in disguise. For shoppers, and for the many persons who simply hang around, live or work in the streets, streets are also places for organized idleness. Hanging around is a highly cultivated aspect of street culture, and here certain settings, such as the *paan* and cigarette shops, are key backdrops. While one stream of human traffic is purposive, going from one place to another, and another stream of vehicles is equally purposive, there is always a steady audience of those who are in no hurry to go anywhere.

They are there just to watch, perhaps to talk, perhaps to sell, but mainly just to pass the time. This audience includes the occasionally employed, the under employed and the unemployed of India's cities, as well as those wealthy or idle enough to afford not to be in a hurry. For this audience, who provide the counterpoint to those in motion, there is a series of things to watch, for Indian streets are natural stages for spectacle.

Such spectacles fall into many categories. Streets are the favoured haunt of itinerant entertainers, some of whom feature trained animals, particularly bears and monkeys, some of whom perform various forms of gymnastics, others are magicians. These street entertainers are always surrounded by a circle of spectators, who frequently melt away when the routine is over and the hat is passed around. During Ganesh Chaturthi in Pune and Bombay, Durga Puja in Calcutta, and Makar Sankranti in Ahmedabad, streets become the settings for elaborate processions and pageantry, displays of floats and mock ups, religious sermons and performances in temporary structures of every sort.

During these religious processionals, streets are still public space but they become marked by the claims of various communities and interest groups. In these latter contexts, as we have seen frequently in recent times, the street becomes a potentially contested space, where the tiniest affront can set the tinder of community divisions ablaze.

These spectacles can also be explicitly political. Often groups of workers take out their protest marches through streets. Politicians often, especially when they are only local figures, give speeches to local constituencies on street corners, and political rallies and processions are a frequent part of street action. Such processions and rallies are matched by displays of state power and pageantry, which occur often on public thoroughfares. The grand example of the latter type of spectacle is the Republic Day parade in Delhi, but there are many humbler replicas of these spectacles, which involve the police and military forces of cities, states and localities.

Street cultures bring together spectacle and entertainment with state power and community identity. This is the dimension of street culture which is peculiarly volatile. Beneath the traffic of commerce, and the relaxed aesthetics of hanging around, lie the potential for highly ritualized displays of power, potent challenges to the power of others, and the recklessness that can turn crowds into mobs.

Streets provide not only circuses but bread. The provision of food on Indian streets is a topic worthy of a monograph in its own right. Street food is increasingly essential to the feeding of India's urban workforces. Cities are famous for their distinctive street foods: Delhi for its Punjabi *dhabas* serving *chola bhathura* and for its *chaat* shops; Bombay for its *bhelpuri* vendors and sugarcane juice; Lucknow for its *kababs* and *parathas*. These foods threaten the sanitary sensibilities of the upper middle classes, but they constitute the key to the aroma and graphics of street culture.

Some aspects of street food are rapidly spreading throughout India: most notably the juice-bar, where the modern technology of electric blenders and the large scale marketing of fruits enable a national consumption trend. Also, it is often street vendors who are the vanguard of inter-regional culinary adventures: the *masala dosa* of the south now competes with traditional Punjabi foods in many streets in Delhi, just as the *puris* and vegetables of the north have hit the streets of Madras and Madurai. City street vendors are always looking for new culinary ideas in their own hinterlands: the phenomenal rise in popularity of the Goan *pao bhaji* in the streets of Bombay in the last decades is an excellent example.

Streets also cater to special culinary interests in restaurants, ranging from small and dingy tea stalls to fancy 'Grade A' restaurants. The clientele for the humbler restaurant is essentially the same clientele that patronizes street vendors. Providing food for the human traffic on Indian streets is a challenging business. These guerilla entrepreneurs have to deal with the uncertainties of police harassment, the problems of water supply, the challenges of storage in the open, and the always present threat of excess rain or sun. But the incentive is also great: without the encumbrances of a large staff, fancy equipment, or a fussy clientele, street vendors can concentrate on high turnover, low overhead transactions. All they have to assure is that they provide something that is cheap, tasty, seductive.

Streets, of course, are also residential settings. Many of India's urban poor live on its streets. Living on the street is the fate of a very wide range of people. These street dwellers include vendors and shopkeepers who in effect live with their businesses; securely employed persons who cannot afford any other type of dwelling; itinerant traders, performers, and holymen, who would not think of spending money on a space to sleep in; the young men and boys who work as mechanics, busboys, cleaners and low paid helpers in a host of street establishments; and the truly indigent, refugees, beggars and the destitute, who live entirely in public spaces, such as streets, stations, *maidans* and the like.

This population, for whom the street is not a thoroughfare, nor even a spectacle, but shelter, is the most complex part of the ecology of street culture. These individuals are least visible during the day and the evening when the street is dominated by traffic, by commerce, by work and by the presence of those who go indoors to sleep. But at the very late hours of the night, and in the very early hours of the morning, these are the bodies that lie shrouded on the street, making the street a human space even when it is least active. These street dwellers, often looked upon with irritation and contempt by civic authorities and by the affluent urban classes, constitute the infrastructure of much that these dominant groups take for granted: the sweeping of public spaces, the provision of human services for the working class, and the dirty work of those restaurants, stores and workshops whose existence is taken for granted by the affluent. For these groups who survive in the interstices of street culture, the street is both their prison and their salvation.

Street cultures are not just visual cultures, where people, goods and performances are on display for each other. Streets are also supremely auditory settings, in which the radio and loudspeaker compete with the sounds of car engines and horns. Film music and political speeches, the songs of street performers and the shouts of hawkers form the auditory high points against a steady backdrop of human and vehicular noise. Yet for those who routinely navigate Indian streets, whether as consumers, as passersby or as businessmen, the noise of the street is not disturbing: these are the sounds of vitality, of spectacle, of life. They constitute the auditory counterpart to the sights, colours and visual drama of the Indian street.

The sort of street culture I have described is not likely to last forever in India. As shopping becomes more interiorized, as entertainment moves from the street to auditoria and permanent structures, as political pageants and speeches increasingly come through radio and TV, and as the middle class finds its pleasures increasingly 'at home', or away in less crowded suburban settings, street culture is likely to become steadily impoverished and less pluralistic. This process is part and parcel of the deepest social and cultural changes occurring in contemporary India.

Over the last century in urban India, there has been a steady increase in the separation of work place and residence. This applies both to shopkeepers, who prefer to live away from their places of business if that is economically viable, as well as to the urban middle classes, who aspire to ownership of flats in colonies and suburbs rather than to stay in the crowded 'old' sections of many cities. Thus, the pluralistic, rather complex, class composition of many such 'old' cities, is giving way to a more fragmented and polarized population, where businessmen, regular residents, and casual hangers-around, no longer have multiple social ties.

This segregation of work from residence is exacerbated by the new ecology of shops and shopping, where even the lower middle class is increasingly seduced into large indoor or underground complexes, in which commerce is insulated from the rest of the action of the street. Of course, the growth of glass and steel storefronts, the steady sharpening of the boundary between store front and pavement, the eclipse of casual soliciting by shopkeepers of customers, the emergence of the airconditioned shopping space, all reduce the commercial vitality of the public space of the street.

Finally, the steady privatization and interiorization of entertainment is doing a good deal to impoverish the street as a setting for leisure. More urban households and buildings own or share television sets, more spectacles are available on the television or cinema screen and more auditoria, stadia and other permanent structures are emerging to rope off spectacles, and the income generated by them, from everyday life. The street is thus in danger of becoming one of two things: just a thoroughfare for getting people and goods from one place to another, or a staging area for lumpen violence.

It is this latter process that we need to guard against. It may seem unduly alarmist to suggest that the great cultural and aesthetic plurality of India's streets is gradually being reduced, and surely public violence in urban India has many causes. But the interiorization of key aspects of commerce, entertainment and family life in urban Indian surely is a part of the picture. The cultural ecology of streets in places like Meerut, Ahmedabad and old Delhi has many dimensions. But one of the messages of street violence may be that we need to be cautious about putting our cultural life behind closed doors and moving ourselves into the sanitized settings of new suburbs and colonies, for the streets may then become settings for public confrontation alone.

This is not just a cultural issue, but a social and political one. To resolve it, we do need to notice that we are impoverishing an important aspect of our cultural lives, but we also need to ask who we are abandoning to the dramas of public violence in our urban cores, why we are commoditizing and merchandising entertainment in an increasingly privatized manner, and how we are defining property and space so that the dramas of the Indian street are increasingly violent ones.

—*The India Magazine*, Vol. 8 (December 1987).

P. Thankappan Nair

A History of Calcutta's Streets

The evolution of streets is an interesting chapter in the urban growth of Calcutta.[1] The nomenclature used in Calcutta for designating a street[2] is indeed bewildering. No less than thirty one terms are in vogue to designate a street, i.e., 1. Approach, 2. Avenue, 3. Bithi, 4. Circle, 5. Corner, 6. Court, 7. Dahar, 8. Garden, 9. Gulle, 10. Lane, 11. Bye Lane, 12. 1st Bye Lane, 13. Cross Lane, 14. 1st Lane, 15. 2nd Lane, 16. 3rd Lane, 17. 4th Lane, 18. Park, 19. Path, 20. Place, 21. Range, 22. Road, 23. Row, 24. Sarani, 25. Siding, 26. Scheme, 27. Spur, 28. Street, 29. Terrace, 30. Village,[3] 31. Way.[4] The most common designations applied are Avenue, Lane, Road, Sarani, and Street.

Half a dozen designations are used to denote an enclosed place where the public have the right of recreation such as 1. Bag, 2. Garden, 3. Kanan, 4. Maidan, 5. Park and 6. Square. We are, therefore, called upon to banish from our mind any preconceived notion about a street or park as the designations in Calcutta have little relevance to their accepted

[1] Calcutta means Municipal Calcutta, as defined in the Calcutta Municipal Corporation Act of 1980.

[2] The word 'Street' in this study means any road, street, square, court, alley, or passage, whether a thoroughfare or not, over which the public have a right of way, falling within one of the 31 designations applied to it.

[3] There are 12 villages included in Calcutta which are located in wards 57 & 58.

[4] The following abbreviations are used: 1. Ave. (Avenue), 2. Le. (Lane), 3. RD. (Road), 4. Si. (Sarani) and 5. St. (Street).

connotations. For instance, no Calcuttan will now think of Mandeville Gardens as a place of recreation. There is no park in Ballygunge Park and there is no square at Chowringhee. These misnomer have their own tales to tell and a study of the evolution of the street names is, therefore, an imperative need to understand the urban growth. Unfortunately, it is difficult, if not impossible, to trace the history of the names of streets in Calcutta as there are few records and much more myths. The streets, as the city itself, grew according to the demands of the users.

Calcutta by the end of 1983[5] had no less than 2027 streets (which include all places where the public have a right of way) and 176 parks (all enclosed places where the public have the right of recreation). Their number would swell considerably if we count the ones recognized by the Postal Authorities and the guides brought out by enterprising publisher. Our figures relate to those streets and parks only which have the official stamp of the Corporation of Calcutta. The orthography of the street names is taken from the Corporation's latest *List of streets*. We ignore in this study the streets like Chowk, Katra, and other designations given to, or recognized by, the Calcutta Postal Authorities for expeditious delivery of the mail. The spellings given by the Postal Authorities and guides published by un-official agencies are also not accepted. After these preliminary remarks, we shall define Calcutta for our purpose.

Calcutta for the purpose of our study means only the town as defined in the Calcutta Municipal Corporation Act, 1980. The municipal Calcutta does not include (1) Fort William, (2) that part of the Hastings north of the south edge of Clyde Row and Strand Road to the river bank, (3) the port area, and the (4) Canals. The area under the jurisdiction of the Municipal Corporation of Calcutta is 23,629 acres or 36.92 sq. miles as on 31st December, 1983. The area of the City of Calcutta (which includes the Canals—278 acres, and Fort William—551 acres) is 24,458 acres or 38.23 sq. miles. The Census Authorities give the area of the City as 39.75 sq. miles. 'The town Directory and Primary Census Abstract of the Calcutta District' and the 'District Census Handbook' published by the Census of 1971, give the area of municipal Calcutta as 98.79kms , and that of the City of Calcutta as 104 sq. kms.

The total number of streets in Calcutta was 4 in 1706, 154 in 1756, 91 in 1794, 156 in 1850, 600 in 1876, 1616 in 1924, 1996 in 1948 and

---

[5] 1983 has been taken as the cut-off year for this study as from January 1, 1984 Calcutta, for municipal purposes, includes the South Suburban, Garden Reach and Jadavpur municipalities.

2027 in 1983. The authenticity of the number given by A.K. Ray (*Short History of Calcutta*, 1902) for 1756 is doubted. The numbers for other years are, more or less, correct as they are based on maps, directories and official lists issued by the Municipal Corporation or its predecessors. A.K. Ray's figures for 1726 (Streets 4 and Lanes 8), 1742 (Streets 16 and Lanes 517) are exaggerated, for they are not named so in contemporary maps. A public walk, as long as it has not been given a name, is not called a street in this study.

The total length of all streets given by A.K. Ray for 1901 is 328 miles. There were, as on December 31, 1983, 512.18 miles of streets in the municipal area of Calcutta and 3.47 miles in the Dock area, making the total of the City at 516.34 miles (Calcutta Corporation Yearbook, 1979-81, p. 435). The streets with bituminous pavement varying from half and inch to three inch thickness totaled 272.73 miles in 1982. The longest street in Calcutta bearing one and the same name is Acharya Jagadish Bose Road (4 miles). The widest street in Calcutta is Southern Avenue (renamed Dr. Meghnath Saha Si.) which has a uniform width of 150ft.

✳✳✳✳✳

Anomalies

Majority of the streets are named after celebrities, old and new. Of the 2027 streets, there are only 21 named after ladies. [In contrast, 130 Englishmen and 100 Muslims, at least, are commemorated through streets named after them in Calcutta.] Ladies, unlike in other cities, have played a decisive role in the freedom movement, philanthropy and education in Calcutta which included plebians and princesses. Their names are: Bibi Rozio (Le.), Bindu Basini (St.), Ghore Bibi (Le.), Leela Roy (Si.), Ma Sarada Moni (Si.), Maharani Hemanta Kumari (St.), Maharani Swarnamoyee (Rd.), Panchi Dhobani (Gullee), Rani Rashmoni (Ave., Rd., Garden Le., Bazar Rd.), Rani Sankari (Le.), Rokeya (Park), Sarojini Naidu and Suhasini Ganguly. Of the three foreign ladies whom the City Fathers have chosen for honouring with street names, Nellie Sengupta (Si.) was the wife of Deshapriya Jatindra Mohan Sen-Gupta, five times Mayor of Calcutta. She was also an Alder (wo)man of the Corporation. Sister Nivedita belonged to the R.K. Mission and adopted India as her field of work. Helen Keller (Si.) visited Calcutta sometime ago and is an inspiration to the physically handicapped.

There are complaints against the raison d'etre of the renaming of the streets in Calcutta. Some of the Calcutta streets have been, it is asserted in knowledgeable quarters, renamed by the City Fathers without any regard to history, evolution, and canon of convenience of the users. Simplicity, brevity, utility etc. have gone to the winds in the process of renaming. Passion and political considerations have played, it is said, their role in renaming, bringing chaos, confusion and cost to the business community. The renaming of Neemuch Mahal (Rd.) and Koilaghat (St.) was nothing short of thoughtlessness, historians assert, for these two streets were connected with the early history of Calcutta. The absence of the name of the Founding Father of Calcutta is a shame to Calcutta. Charnock Place had a life of 50 years or so and its renaming was the greatest disservice to the Englishman, who was no better than an Indian in life and dress. Calcutta is proud of his mausoleum, for it is the oldest piece of masonry in the city founded by him. It is not understood why Wajid Ali Shah the deposed king of Oudh who was settled in, and died, the Garden Reach, is neglected.

Confusion is worst confounded when different streets in different localities bear the name of one and the same person. Two Netaji Subhas Roads are rather a source of confusion than an honour to Netaji himself. Rani Rashmoni has an Avenue, a Road, a Bazar Road and a Garden Lane. Deshapriya J.M. Sen-Gupta has at least 5 streets or parks named after him, but fortunately they are not bearing the same name. Shaheed Khudiram Bose Road and Khudiram Sarani do little honour to that boy revolutionary as these create an impression in the minds of the common man that they are two different persons. Principal Khudiram Bose (Rd.) has turned him in his grave. Rustomjee has taken offence as he finds himself Rustomjee in one place and at another as Rustomjee Parsee. Sib Krishna Daw and Sib Kristo Daw cannot be two different individuals. Anomalies of this and similar kind are not wanting in the nomenclature of Calcutta streets.

Calcutta, unlike Bombay, is a city where the name of a street matters much as people refer to the premises' numbers. Buildings and names of housing colonies have displaced the street names in Bombay.

New street names in Calcutta are tongue-twisting. Biplabi Trailokya Maharaj turns in his grave when his admirers in Calcutta cannot pronounce his hallowed name with ease and felicity and the man in the street takes him to be a Maharaja. People seldom care for such unfamiliar, uneasy and lengthy street names and start shortening or abbreviating it for official purpose. APC (Acharya Prafulla Chandra) Road is a headache to the common-man and the Postal Authorities. Who knows Netaji when his road is abbreviated into N.S. Road? Distorted versions of lengthy street names are indeed delightful. The abbreviated listing of lengthy street names in telephone directories and other official publications defeats the very purpose of honouring individuals. The need of the hour is simplification of the street names in order to save time, money and stationery. The business community bears the brunt of this burden without any return. Sido-Kanho-Dahar and other such primitive names will remain as heathenish to Calcutta as the Santal heroes were.

There is no dearth of materials in Calcutta street names to write a full length history of India from Asoka (Rd.) to Ambedkar (Si.). But for the craze for renaming Calcutta streets, the history of Calcutta streets themselves would have provided materials for writing the history of the city. Antiquarians will find the study of the evolution of Calcutta streets amply rewarding. Calcutta can certainly feel proud of the nomenclature of its streets, as every facet of the growth of the city and the Nation itself is reflected in it.

A History of Calcuttta's Streets, Part II

Chowringhee Road

—30, Jawaharlal Nehru Road

Corporation Wards:	Nos. 31 & 44 to 54—Park Street
Nos. 31 to 58 and 94	P.O. (16)
to 96—Ward 63	Nos. 32 to 43 & 55 to 58—
Nos. 59A to 82—Ward 70	Middleton Row P.O. (71)
Nos. 83 to 93—Ward 71	Nos. 59 to 96—Lala Lajpat Rai Sarani
	P.O. (20)

Chowringhee Road from its beginning up to Park street crossing has been renamed Jawaharlal Nehru Road and the original premises Nos. 1 to 30 have been transferred to that road. Chowringhee Road, after the renaming, extends from Park Street-Outram Road-Jawaharlal Nehru Rd. Junction to the junction of Lala Lajpat Rai Sarani—Sambhu Nath Pandit Street—Asutosh Mukherjee Road.

Cheringhy, Cheringy, Chauringy, etc. are some of the forms used in early English documents for the road now known as Chowringhee Road. The road originally began at what is now the junction of three roads, viz., Dharamtala, Esplanade and Chittaranjan Avenue and ran in a straight line southwards, crossing Lower Circular Road, until it merged with Asutosh Mukherjee Road. It is in fact only a portion of a long road which, tradition says, ran from Halisahar, about 30 miles north of Calcutta, up to the famed shrine of Kali known as Kalighat, and so on to Barisha, 6 miles to the south of the city. It is said that this long road was constructed to connect the two branches of the Savarna Raichaudhuries, one branch residing at Halisahar and the other at Barisha. The Road was also known as the Pilgrim Road and Road to Kalighat in the 18th century. Old documents refer it as the 'road to Collegot'.

The etymology of Chowringhee has baffled historians. The name comes from the village, Cherangi, which means '*Chera anga*', i.e. (cut-up body), referring to the legendary origin of the Kalighat shrine that was situated there. The dismemberment of the Sati's body by the discus of Vishnu is well known to every student of Hindu mythology. Jangal Giri Chowringhee was not a mythological personage (see this author's *Calcuta in the 17th Century*, pp. 50–1). Bengali poets have waxed eloquent upon Chowringhee and here we quote Bishnu De:

The evening star beckons back to the dark and quiet
All those who are scattered by the sun's rule—
Cows from pastoral Chowringhee—the lost selves
The industrious clerks, and the perambulators—
And infants to their mother's breasts. ...

(*Bengali Poems on Calcutta*, translated by Subhoranjan
Dasgupta & Sudeshna Chakravarty, Calcutta, 1972, p. 32)

'Chowringhee road, the eastern boundary of the great plain' is said to have received its name from the Hindustani word *Chowringhee*, which means many-coloured, the houses in that locality commanding views of various sorts and colours (Sarat Chandra Mitra, *National Magazine*, December 1889, p. 459). The name Chowringhee existed long before the Palaces of the Sahibs reared their heads there. It is not a corruption of *char* (four) + *Dighi* (tank) (which existed there, though only two remain now), as the tanks were dug in the 18th century.

✸✸✸✸✸

Lenin Sarani

—1, Jawaharlal Nehru Road

Corporation Wards:	Dharamtala P.O. (13)
Nos. 1 to 34B and 168 to End	— Ward 46
Nos. 149A to 167/7	— Ward 47

The Oxford Anthology of the Modern Indian City

The Corporation at its weekly meeting held on Friday, July 18, 1969, renamed Dharamtala Street as Lenin Sarani. The notification in this connection was issued on August 21, 1969 (*C.M. Gaz.*, August 23, 1969, p. 13). It was Councillor Haroprasad Chatterjee who moved the proposal that 'Dharamtala Street be named as Lenin Sarani, waiving all formalities' as a tribute to the great Communist leader, on the occasion of his birth centenary. Councillor Nil Ratan Sinha who seconded the proposal felt that the birth of a 'prophet and leader' like Lenin on earth was 'a rare occasion'. The objections of Dr. Birendra Chandra Basu to the renaming of Dharamtala Street after V.I. Lenin were overruled (*C.M. Gaz.*, July 26, 1969, p. 562).

'Dharamtala Street became Lenin Sarani following a ceremonial inauguration by the Mayor, Mr. Prasanta Sur on Saturday' (i.e., February 28, 1970), says the Staff Reporter of the *Amrita Bazar Patrika* on March 1, 1970, under a single column news captioned, 'Ceremonal Opening of Lenin Sarani'. The paper adds: 'Mr. Sur said, the public thoroughfare, described once as the abode of righteousness, was renamed after the great leader Lenin so that the memory of the great revolutionary might shine as a beacon light for ever in the life of the masses in this city ... Deputy Mayor, Mr. Mani Sanyal said the Calcutta Corporation did a right thing by renaming the street after Lenin the friend of the 'oppressed humanity' ... West Bengal Ministers, Mr. Md. Amin and Mr. Abdul Rezzak Khan also ... spoke on the occasion'.

The etymology of Dharamtala (Dhurrumtolla/Dharamamtallah) Street is derived by some from *Darma* (mats) stored in the area for the construction of the present Fort William. These mats came in boats by the creek, now dried up, and were stored in Chandney.

The late Binoy Ghosh was inclined to trace the origin of Dharamtala from the Gajan festival of Dharma Thakur held in the locality. The temple of Dharma Thakur nearby is still in existence. Doms, outcastes, were the priests of Dharma Thakur. Dharma Thakur was later on elevated as Lord Siva in the Hindu pantheon. This is true in the case of the Siva temple at the junction of Lansdowne and Hazra Road. In short, Dhaarmatala was the *talla* of Dharma (Thakur).

Rev. James Long says: 'Dharamtala was formerly called the *avenue* as it led from town to the Salt-water Lake and the adjacent country. Last century it was a 'well-raised causeway, raised by deepening the ditch on either side' with wretched huts on the south side; while on the north a creek ran through a street, still called Creek-Row, through the Wellington Square Tank, down to Chandpal Ghat. Large boats could come up it—if it had been kept clear and had been widened, it might have been very useful for the drainage, as Colonel Forbes, in his memoranda to the Municipal Commissioners in 1835, recommended the digging of a similar creek in that direction. The road was, according to an old useful Hindu practice, shaded with trees on both sides, as we find was the practice in other parts at that period. *Dharmatala* is so called from a great mosque, since pulled down, which was on the site of Cook's stables; the ground belonged, with all the neighbouring land, to Jafir, the jamadar of Warren Hastings, a zealous Mussalman. The *Karbela*, a famous Mussalman assemblage of tens of thousands of people, which now meets in the Circular-road, used then to congregate there, and by its local sanctity, gave the name to the street of the *Dharmatala* or Holy *street.*' (*Calcutta Review*, December, 1852, p. 289).

Cotton (p. 304) quotes Dr. Hoernle, who 'discerns in the name a reference to Dharma, one of the units in the Buddhist Trinity, and points to the Buddhist Temple in Jaun Bazar hard by, in confirmation of his theory'.

The Corporation, vide notification dated March 4 and May 9, 1957 (*C.M. Gaz.*, March 9 & May 11, 1957, p. 476 and p. 62), proposed to rename Dharamtala Street from the junction of Wellington Street up to Lower Circular Road as Dr. Ramandas Mukherjee Street. This proposal was objected to by Councilor S.K. Gupta, Chairman of the Calcutta improvement Trust at the Corporation's meeting held on Friday, November 15, 1957, as the 'History of Old Calcutta' by the late Harihar Sett was not very authoritative and was full of contradictions. He reiterated his objections to this 'half-hazard' (haphazard?) manner of changing names of streets (*C.M. Gaz.*, November 23, 1957, p. 107). The proposal was, therefore, shelved.

Vladimir Ilyitch (Ulyanov) Lenin (1870–1924), leader of the Russian Bolshevik Revolution was born at Simbirsk (renamed Ulyanovsk in 1924) on the Central Volga, some three hundred miles east of Moscow. Alexander Ulayanov, his elder brother, was hanged on May 20, 1887 for plotting against the Tsar. He studied law and took final examination in the subject in 1890. He left Russia in July 1900 and remained abroad until 1917 except for the winter of 1905–06. Lenin was in London from April 1902 to May 1903, as well as in the Spring of 1907. At other times he lived in Brussels, Paris, and Cracow, but his principal home in exile was on the outskirts of Geneva. By 1903 he was accepted as the leader of the revolutionary Social Democrats ('Bolsheviks'); his authority stemmed from the combination of a powerful intellect with a trenchant pen, and was expressed in numerous pamphlets and revolutionary journalism. Lenin made three major contributions to Marxist theory.

The overthrow of Tsar Nicholas II in March 1917 induced Lenin to return to Russia in the following April, but he had again to seek refuge in Finland from July 24 to October 23. Lenin returned to Petrograd to lead a Bolshevik revolt against Kerensky's Government (November 6–8, 1917). Lenin shifted his capital to Moscow on March 10, 1918. Lenin was shot on August 30, 1918 and seriously wounded by Fanya Kaplan. He had three strokes between May 1922 and March 1923. He died on January 21, 1924. Nadeshda Krupskaya, whom Lenin married in July 1898 while in Siberia, was hardly separated from him for more than a few days throughout their 25 years of marriage (Alan Palmer, *Who's Who in Modern History*, 1860–1980, London, 1980, pp. 200–01).

'Erasing Dharmatala Street in favour of Lenin Sarani will certainly not be questioned. Dharamtala, in post-mortem view, had deeply native associations. But many, like poet Iswar Gupta, did not like it. *Dharamtala dharmaheen gohatyar dham*, wrote the indignant bard. The new name, therefore, not only associated our city with an illustrious crusader against injustice and exploitation but obliterates the irony of the last name. The renaming has been popular. Only the tattered beggar who is wont to sleep away his hungry hours opposite the site of inauguration remained blissfully unaware that one who had given the most of his life to the redemption of the poor has come spiritually so near' (Khagen Roy, 'Re-Christening Streets', *Amrita Bazar Patrika*, March 5, 1970).

✳✳✳✳✳✳

Mahatma Gandhi Road

—24, Acharya Prafulla Chandra Road

The proposal to rename Harrison Road as Mahatma Gandhi Road was notified by the Corporation on January 5, 1956 (*C.M. Gaz.*, January 21, 1956, p. 255) and the name was sanctioned by the municipal body at its weekly meeting held on August 31, 1956. Mahatma Gandhi Road, as every child knows in Calcutta, is named after the father of the Nation, whose love for Calcutta is well known.

Originally called Harrison Road or Central Road at the time of
its construction, the road has a length of 8,900ft. (or 1.685 miles)
with a uniform breadth of 70ft., including 50ft. of carriage-way and
two footpaths, each 10ft. wide. Starting directly opposite the original
Howrah Floating Bridge and connecting Sealdah Railway Station, this
road cost the Corporation Rs. 47,09,667 (Rs. 281/4 lakhs according to
C.M. Gaz., November 29, 1924, p. 100). The construction of the road
was begun on April 11, 1889 and the work was completed in 1892–93.
The first section of the road from Clive Street (=Netaji Subhas Road) to
Strand Road was opened to traffic on June 28, 1890, absorbing the lane
leading direct from Clive Street to the old Neemy Churn Mullick Ghat,
constructed by the illustrious Singbahini Mullicks of Barabazar, which
was a gift of Ram Mohan Mullick, son of Neemy. The Mullicks of
Barabazar made a free gift of 4 bighas, 3 cottahs and 6 chittacks of land
to the Corporation, of which 1 bigha, 10 cottahs, 12 chittacks and 4 sq.
ft. was Debuttar property valued at Rs. 63,000/- for the construction of
this road.

Originally called Central Road, Harrison Road was named after
Sir Henry Leland Harrison, the popular Chairman of the Calcutta
Corporation. Cally Churn Ghosh was the first Bengali Land Acquisition
Deputy Collector who in the early eighties of the last century acquired the
land for Harrison Road. Cally Churn Ghosh was one of the executors of
the last will and testament of Pandit Iswar Chandra Vidyasagar. A road
is named after him in Cossipore (S.V. Kali Charan Ghose Road, Ward
2) at the suggestion of Nagendra Chandra Mozumdar, Hitabadi office
(*C.M. Gaz.*, March 30, 1940, p. 662).

The name of Harrison Road was given to this road at the Special
Meeting of the Corporation held on May 17, 1892. The construction
of this road was his greatest achievement. On December 11, 1924, the
portion of Nur Muhammad Lane, between Baitakkhana and Harrison
Road was renamed and amalgamated with Harrison Road.

Sir Henry Leland Harrison was Chairman of the Corporation from
April 18, 1881 to April 15, 1890. He was the Collector & District
Magistrate of Midnapore for 6 years before he was appointed Chairman
of the Corporation. Son of the Rev. James Harwood Harrison, Henry
was born in 1837 and was educated at Westminster and Christ Church.
He joined the Bengal Civil Service in 1860. Harrison is remembered
for reclaiming the *bustees* of Calcutta and providing the city with open
spaces. The old Bysack Dighi was filled up and the Marcus Square was
constructed in its place. Sir Henry could carry out the improvements of

Calcutta as he was a member of the Bengal Legislative Council from 1886 to 1892. The amalgamation of the areas in the east and south of Circular Road to Calcutta was effected by him in 1888. He was knighted in 1887 and was promoted a Member of the Board of Revenue on August 24, 1890. His sudden death at Chittagong on 5th May, 1892, at the age of 55, from an attack of cholera, was mourned in Calcutta.

Apart from renaming the busiest road that carries the highest number of vehicles during the day time, connecting Howrah Railway Station in a straight way with the Sealdah Railway Station, the city has honoured itself with a statue of Mahatma Gandhi in its heart at the junction of Park Street-Jawaharlal Nehru-Outram Road-Guru Nanak Sarani. Sculptured by Debi Prasad Roychowdhury in his *Dandi-Yatra* pose, Gandhiji's statue, which replaced the equestrian statue of Outram, has been removed from its site on September 16, 1977 and installed at the crossing of Mayo (= Guru Nanak Sarani) Road and Dufferin Road. The operation of removal began at 10p.m. and was over in about 20 minutes. The statue, weighing 8 tons, was lifted by a crane and installed at its new habitation in the presence of West Bengal P.W.D. Minister Jatin Chakravarty and Metro Railway's General Manager and others. The statue is expected to come back to its original site as the construction of the Metro Railway is over on that stretch of the Maidan (*C.M. Gaz.*, October 29, 1977, p. 170).

Gandhiji's first visit to Calcutta was on March 12, 1915 and the *Statesman's* report on the event is reproduced here: 'Some six thousand Indians, mostly Marwaris, Guzeratis and up-country Hindus, were present yesterday morning at Howrah Station to receive Mr. Gandhi who came down to Calcutta accompanied by Mrs. Gandhi on his way to Rangoon. Mr. Gandhi on his arrival was presented by Mr. Bhupendra Nath Basu to several prominent Indians who led him to a carriage. Several young men unyoked the horses and dragged the carriage in the midst of a procession to the residence of Mr. Bhupendra Nath Basu at Shambazar, where Mr. Gandhi will reside during his short stay in the town'. Gandhiji's last visit to Calcutta was during the great Hindu-Muslim riot and killing (1946–1947). He stayed in Bellliaghata for quite some time to restore peace. Sodepur Ashram was his headquarters in Calcutta during the latter years, but he stayed with Deshbandhu Chittaranjan Das and Netaji Subhas Bose during his earlier visits to the city.

*****

—11, HARE STREET

The Corporation, at its meeting held on Wednesday, the 13th August, 1947, took a unanimous decision to 'rename the entire length of the road-way of Dalhousie Square West, Charnock Place and Clive Street up to Harrison Road as Netaji Subhas Road' (*C.M. Gaz.*, 2nd–30th August, 1947, p. 88). The then Mayor, Sudhir Chandra Roy Chowdhury, himself took the initiative in renaming the street.

The Corporation, at its meeting held on August 9, 1957, renamed that part of Clive Street from the junction of Harrison (Mahatma Gandhi) Road to the junction of Mirbahar Ghat Street as Netaji Subhas Road. (*C.M. Gaz.*, August 17, 1957, p. 412).

… Here, in a hundred snake-like veins,
Streams of people come and go.
Through these shrunken veins the blood
Of the country must flow…
O mighty city's beating heart,
O Clive Street of Bengal,
A thousand dumb veins freeze to make
The cornerstone of your high hall.

—Dinesh Das, 'Clive Street' (translated Subhoranjan Dasgupta and Sudeshna Chakravarty, *Bengali Poems on Calcutta*, Calcutta, 1972, p. 35).

Clive Street, which has been renamed as Netaji Subhas Road, was earlier called the Road to the Great Bazar. The western portion of the B.B.D. Bag, i.e., Netaji Subhas Road from the corner of Hare Street to Reserve Bank of India's new building, was originally called the Old Fort Street and subsequently Dalhousie Square West. The Calcutta G.P.O. (No. 4), Collectorate (No. 3), and the Custom House (presently site occupied by the Reserve Bank of India's building—Nos 1 & 2) were the four premises that were included in Charnock Place from the beginning of the present century till Independence. This is why No. 1 is now at the junction of Netaji Subhas Road—Council House St.—Hare St. whereas No. 2 is just after the Writers' Buildings, separated by Lyons Range.

The western side of Dalhousie Square has within the last five or six years been named *Charnock Place* in honour of the Father of Calcutta. It is almost entirely taken up with public offices, but until the closing years of the eighteenth century it was disfigured by the derelict remains of the old fort and adjoining warehouses. A portion of the ruins was pulled down in 1819, to make way for the Custom House, and the remainder was removed in 1856 to make way for the new General Post Office. (Cotton, pp. 328–9).

'Clive Street commences from the north-western corner of Dalhousie Square and extends in a northerly direction until it meets Durmahatt, the 'Street of the makers of reed-mats'. The origin of its name is self-evident. It has always been the great commercial thoroughfare in Calcutta. In the early days we find it described as 'the grand theatre of business, and there stood the Council house and every public mart in it', the reference being to the first Council House, which was discarded in 1764. Much of the street is on ground reclaimed from the river, and with Chitpore Road and the 'avenue leading to the eastward', it takes rank among the oldest streets in the city. The building now known as the Royal Exchange was once the residence of Clive. (Cotton pp. 339–40).

Described as a 'patriot of patriots' by Mahatma Gandhi, Subhas Chandra Bose fought for Indian independence with courage and conviction. But his role in the Indian struggle was different from that of Gandhiji himself, for Bose's most spectacular gestures were military ones.

Born on January 23, 1897 at Cuttack, as the son of Janaki Nath Bose, a prominent lawyer, Netaji was reportedly dead in a Japanese hospital on August 19, 1945, after his plane had crashed in Taiwan. Subhas Bose, called Netaji, was Chief Executive Officer of the Calcutta Corporation (17.5.1924 to 14.12.1924), alderman, and Mayor (22.8.1930 to 14.4.1931). Till his escape from his Elgin Road residence in 1940, his political activities were conducted from Calcutta to a great extent. He gave the British intelligence a slip in 1940 from his residence in disguise and reached Germany. . . .

******

Old China Bazar Street

—63J, Radha Bazar Street

Corporation Ward No. 45   G.P.O. (1)

'Old China bazaar, *pooranah cheenabazar*, in a line north with radah bazar', says *Bengal and Agra Directory* of 1850, p. 492. China Bazar got its name from the sale of Chinese goods there, brought by ships that plied between Calcutta and Canton in the good old days. China may be an item in it. Since Carey (*Good old Days of John Company*, vol. II, Calcutta, 1907, pp. 104–11) has given us a good description of China Bazar and the goods sold there, it is

note from the *Statesman* of November 14, 1876, will be of interest.

'THROUGH CHINA BAZAAR—There are few people who have been long in Calcutta, who have left it without a visit to the China Bazaar. There is certainly nothing very fascinating about a bazaar, in which dirt and disorder reign paramount. It is fatal indeed to betray any knowledge of its existence, if you desire to be considered one of the "Upper Ten" of society, and yet if you are not over susceptible, there is no small amount of amusement to be got out of the bazaar, while the economy and advantages it offers are patent.'

'To reach the ultima Thule we leave our carriage at home, and engage the unassuming ticca gharry, both to avoid injury to our property, and for strategical purposes, if we have purchases to make. Leaving St. Andrew's Church on the left, and driving due north, we find ourselves approaching a very unfashionable quarter. We are in a very narrow street, on either side of which are little dens of native shops of all shapes and sizes, except those which right lines would give them. In the windows, eau de Cologne, Burmese cigars, and tenpenny nails lie fraternally side by side in repose; whilst spiders, flies, and mosquitos, disport among them, fearless of the avenging chowrie. Turning a sharp corner, we find ourselves at once in this Indian Babel. A roar of many voices, increasing every moment as we advance, is sufficiently suggestive to the hardy explorer, of the vultures that are awaiting him at no great distance. Suddenly we come to a dead stop. On looking out to ascertain the cause, we find a line of heavily laden wagons blocked across the road. One of the leading bullocks is half inside a barber's shop, but it is of no consequence and the intrusion is not resented. There seems no likelihood of moving for a couple of hours. We are deafened by the excited jabbering of the touts, who in pithy but unparliamentary language contradict each other's vigourous recommendations of their respective employers. Above the din, a highly pitched insinuating voice shrieks on our right, 'Mine very good shop, Sir! Hats, bonnets, and stationery got! Not want? Then Sahib say 'what will have my shop all got!' A fortissimo bass on the left drowns every other sound, by his energetic denial of number one's statements, 'You not believe him Sar, I know him long time; him very big scoundrel; my shop here close got, all things very cheap'.

China Bazaar came into existence after the recovery of Calcutta in 1757, as it is mentioned in Wood's map of Calcutta (1784). There were 235 premises in Old China Bazaar in 912 and 90 percent of them were owned by Bengali merchants. Today the street is the centre of retail glass, stationery, and paper merchants. There are no Chinese in the bazaar, nor is *chini* (sugar) sold there.

—excerpted from *A History of Calcutta's Streets*, 'A Tercentenary History of Calcutta', Vol. II (Calcutta: Firma KLM Private Ltd., 1987), pp. 3–4, 49–50, 259–60, 518–20, 543–5, 626–7, 642–4.

Gautam Bhatia

Baroque Architecture in the City

As a member of the new moneyed class, the Punjabi is part of that unlikely and silent minority that sets the architectural example for the rest to follow. India's own architecture, he feels, is but a modest parochial rendition of some more significant style. And in looking for too long at the havelis and pols and bungalows he has lost some of his enthusiasm for these Indian types. Outside the country there was a much wider range to turn to, a range full of inner life and hidden meaning and an infinite adaptability. Moreover the idea of a well tested imitation was far less expensive than any untried originality. So he grasped it wholeheartedly.

As wealth and power—unaccounted and political—grew amongst people of lesser means, more of the new populace turned to the new-found sources of high art, and since the sources of high art were themselves so diffuse—spread over eighteenth century France and twelfth century England—it was highly unlikely that references to it would be true to the original. But the Punjabi had never been satisfied with his Indian origins anyway. Fate had been unfair to him; if he had had his wish he would have been a count or an earl on some English estate, or a medieval monarch in a chateau in France. He set about rectifying this grave injustice by making his Panchsheel Park house in his own image of a country manor, its servants' quarter in a plaster replica of Chombord. A Buddhist pagoda roof, when set on a structure of Roman Corinthian columns, was seen by the Punjabi as a structure fit to provide shade to his red Maruti.

In a traditional house, the shortest distance between two floors was up or down a steep staircase; in the havelis of Baroda, the pol houses of

Ahmedabad, the courtyard plans of Lucknow and Delhi, the stair was intrinsically linked to the courtyard. Its confinement within darkened walls, and almost ladder-like steepness of risers made it an element of circulation, of quick passage between floors without the spatial characteristics of ease and grace exhibited in the wider, more generous treads of palaces. The stair was merely an expedient device connecting different floors and supporting the body in short-term movement.

Yet the sculptural quality of the staircase in the Punjabi Baroque home, and its ability to impede or facilitate motion, makes it a feature of fascination for anyone inclined towards theatre. While moving along it or gazing at it from above or below, the structure appeals for its connotations of celebration and choreography. The invariable question of whether to make an exhibition of this movement up and down, or to integrate it into the plan in an unobstrusive way, always poses a dilemma for an architect seeking to balance the client's budget and the Punjabi's wish for fantasy. The stair is a magical hallucination. So naturally the Punjabi's desire to make a ceremonial event out of the most mundane of architectural episodes can turn its ordinary stepping function into a setting for domestic ritual and ceremony. The staircase, central to a Punjabi home, looms into view from every corner of the house, twisting, contorting, turning into precarious curves. Its movement from one floor to the next can no longer be easily restrained by walls or thoughts of a convenient device to change floors. In the theatricality of the Punjabi's architecture, the rising treads become a potent medium for the expression of his own increasing power. It is a theatricality modulated by size and height, by the continually shifting movement of design, and by the expensive textures of material that envelop the treads. No Punjabi housewife would practice her descent into the servant-riddled domain of the living-room on a rickety wooden structure; she is more likely to make her entrance on marble, protected by a plexiglass parapet, hand gliding balefully over a polished brass rail.

Bania Gothic

The Oxford Dictionary defines 'banian' as a white vest-like apparel, two sizes too short and worn by the male members of the Bania tribe of North India. Nobel laureate George Vesterton, an anthropologist, has, in his most recent book, *Annals of Bania Culture—An Anthropological View of a New People*, traced the origins of the banian to ancient Greece, the very cradle of western civilisation.

Whatever its origins, historians tell us that the banian did not appear on the Indian scene till after the Mutiny of 1857. The early Banias were a rootless, restless and ruthless people. Being rootless made them restless, and being restless made them ruthless. In the end they were all these things, and also very confused. They looted to live and they lived to loot. The Bania was a Robin Hood; he robbed from the poor and gave to the rich, which very conveniently happened to be himself.

The modern Bania carries on the traditions of his forefathers. But his is a subtle kind of looting. Not one of stick-ups and violence but one of gentle manoeuvring and controlled exploitation. Every morning, for instance, two Bania families sit down to morning tea somewhere in different parts of the same city, and pick up the same newspaper. One is anxious and apprehensive; as parents of a dark-complexioned girl with a nervous squint, who failed her B.A. exam, they have reason to be. The other, a set of in-laws, is more confident and hopeful; as parents of a dark-complexioned boy with a dangerous squint in his right eye who has also failed his B.A. exam, they too should be anxious and apprehensive. But the boy's father has a family business that ensures permanent employment to the most hopeless of progeny, and so they need not be troubled. Their visions and ambitions need not be clouded by their son's academic failure, his physical deformities or cosmetic inappropriateness. They too have placed an ad in the Sunday paper and are now ready to taste the pickings.

In a country where day-to-day situations make it virtually impossible for the sexes to meet, the matrimonial column becomes an absolute necessity for the Bania. Ration card holding 149 cm females, however homely, pretty, or hunched, need to issue a public call to invite inquiries from 149 cm green card holding Bania males, hunched or otherwise, for a successful alliance. It may even happen that the slight wheatish-complexioned maiden with the dangerous squint will live happily ever after with the barley-complexioned knock-kneed wrestler with the awkward hunch. Or the newly divorced but issueless Bania linguistics teacher with a limp will discover life's satisfaction in the company of an insurance salesman who has no handicap other than his job.

Pious Bania families, marrying off their incompetent sons, think of dowry as a God-given right and practise it privately as vigorously as they deny it in public. On the other hand, pious Bania families marrying off their wheatish-complexioned, slightly hunched daughters, abhor the practice. Dowry for them is a sin. But without the essential protection of adequate dowry they know that their dark newly-wed daughter is in trouble. She will be the subject of continual harassment in not bringing to her new family a range of scooters and fridges, she will be reminded of her selfish nature, she may even appear as a charred statistic on the third page of the daily newspaper shortly after the holy event.

But death is no laughing matter. Facing death may have been difficult enough but the processes that follow are even more so, and the body of a sinning Bania must pass through complicated religious rituals, the rites of passage, before it is readied for final departure. Here the newspaper comes to the rescue and allows the departing soul to make one final bid for immortality. Religion may be one thing, but for the Bania there is no greater immortality than that achieved in print, in obituary columns, and in the personal appeals for godly recognition and forgiveness.

Most of them begin with a pensive twenty-year-old black and white portrait of the departed with a line stating his lifelong professional affiliation, like Founding Father of Indian Ghee and Natural Cheese Association (IGNCA) and then go on to fill the expensive eight-by-four-inch space with a range of important personal plaudits. *May his soul leave for heavenly abode so we may fill his unfillable void and rest in peace* ... then explain in graphic detail—for those unable to witness the passing—the nature of his short, industrious but pious life.

> Our beloved father Shri Sita Ram Bania, wholesale merchant, a hoarder and racketeer (1920–84) choked on a bit of adulterated sugar last night. Frantic friends and neighbouring black marketers made desperate attempts to dislodge the alleged piece from his throat, but to no avail. Sitaji gasped his last breath at 3 a.m. this morning and died almost immediately after that. He left for his heavenly abode early in the morning by the 142 Down Heavenly Passenger. Cremation will be held at Nigambodh Ghat and the ashes sprinkled over the still unadulterated food items in the family godown. Kirya and Bhog will be combined into a joint ceremony in the East Lawn of the Gymkhana Club. Mourners are requested to refrain from obscene gestures and uncontrollable laughter while filing past the body. A word of advice to the latecomers. Please note: Wailing will begin at 8 p.m. sharp. Kindly take your seats on time. No one will be admitted once the wailing has begun. Bar-be-cue to follow.

And the final epithet: *May his soul adulterate in peace.*

Such a man created his own architecture. Inspired perhaps by 'Lootyens' whom he claimed as one of his own, Bania architecture was a 'Loot-Mar' style of building. His houses, like treasure chests of building spare-parts, borrowed elements from some of the more architecturally enlightened periods in history, and transformed them completely. The Bania was an inspired radical. A Gothic arch under his influence, could even become something wholly original. It could even become a cone-shaped door.

Such transformations were only signs—architectural fragments—that heralded the golden age of Bania Gothic architecture. In the expensive looking window made cheaply was the myth of the good life, of excessive wealth and unreasonable desire. The great mushroom columns and grand red brick arches that supported three storeys of a multi-spaced mansion cast an ignoble shadow on the mud shanty next door. But the Bania learned to read this as ironic juxtaposition. He laughed heartily through the curtained window of his Contessa at so much irony juxtaposed so closely. But he knew that all across the land, in virtually every seething metropolis and megalopolis, a great band of involuntary labour writhed in their makeshift hutments at night, only to rise the next morning to work tirelessly on facsimiles of haciendas and Greek temples. To the Bania, this was the ultimate ironic juxtaposition. But it was also obviously a labour of love. At thirty rupees a day—crushing stone for a building that was eventually going to cost ten thousand times his entire wage—it could be nothing else.

Drive-in

Mahatma Gandhi was an image, sacred to Ahmedabad, as sacrosanct as Ram or Allah, protected and cocooned by history. He was a lone historic individual in a city now seeking an association with other, more worldly goals. As a result the more promising aspect of the new city was not the ashram on the banks of the Sabarmati, but the drive-ins, the fast food restaurants, the ice-cream parlours and other symbols of affluent consumption that had begun to proliferate on its outskirts.

Fast food centres, drive-ins, and revolving restaurants. To me their glittery effervescence, the chrome and hype of their external glossiness seemed strangely incongruous in a setting of piety and historical abstinence. Moreover, as foreign ideas, they had been appropriated only in a half-baked way. I had always thought that convenience was the single most important fact of fast food, that the use of a car an essential prerequisite to a drive-in, and that the slowly unfolding panorama of the city or country made the revolving restaurants worth eating in. Not food. But India has successively ruptured these hallowed visions of twentieth century culture. It was more important to eat at fast food restaurants than to worry about the menu; the pleasure of seeing a movie at a drive-in far exceeded the content of the movie.

A five-storey high concrete wall concealing a windowless sliver of a building behind, the drive-in was set appropriately away from the centre of town, away from the Gandhi Ashram, in the town's southern outskirts. Beyond it lay a dry field, as dry as the Sabarmati in mid-summer. Still, it attracted a populace that had grown used to the Gandhian presence, a presence they had now come to take for granted, a presence from which they could not move away. The five-storey-high wall sitting in agricultural land held just that kind of promise—a promise that no mahatma could fulfill. The drive-in was, in fact, a symbol of progress; it had nothing to do with the backward ways of the Mahatma; it was linked to the industrial future of the city.

But as a building, the drive-in had a marked and ungainly presence. Its unusual height and odd function made it something of a monument to the residents of the area. If you lived anywhere within a two-mile vicinity of the drive-in, the rickshaw driver merely followed the most direct route to the new movie palace, before calling for the specifics of a personal address. It was not unusual to find letters marked—Behind Drive-In, Near Drive-In, or Opposite Drive-in—for the building's visible bigness indicated the approximate postal position from a far distance; even from the height of the plane carrying the postal bag.

Of course, it was difficult to have a sixty-feet-high hoarding up, and not have it buckle under the slightest lateral wind. The six storeys of the wall needed the necessary structural support of a building; so the concrete frame that supported the screen of the drive-in had acquired thin slabs, and narrow windowless floor space behind—floor space that to my eyes seemed trapped in its own skeleton. I wondered what it might be like to work in the place, closeted in a windowless room, not knowing if it was raining outside, or if the rest of the city had been reduced to rubble by a nuclear bomb or some minor communal conflagration between Hindus and Muslims. I could see a company typist sitting at his desk behind the wall, deeply preoccupied in the six columns of figures of the annual report, while a few feet away, Rekha or Mandakini in her wet clothes was raising the crowd to a new level of sexual frenzy. Unaware of the rare proximity and missed opportunity, he would diligently complete the typing, cover up the typewriter with a plastic sheet, pick up the empty tiffin box and return home. Home to a quiet night of Doordarshan, wife beating and fantasies of life with Rekha and Mandakini in wet clothes.

The building, I learnt, had been inaugurated by Maganbhai Patel, Gujarat's Minister for Agriculture. The chief minister had been away. *The Times of India* had featured the event on the front page, reducing the headline,

'Floods in Bangladesh' to sixteen-point Times Roman, to accommodate the photograph. The picture was a blur, but it was not difficult to make out the heavy pot-bellied frame of the Minister reaching out to cut a ribbon being held in place by two of his many smiling supporters. Why the Minister for Agriculture should be asked to officiate at the opening of a structure for the exhibition of the performing arts was difficult to understand. Perhaps the opening feature was to be a film on some newly developed rice varieties, I thought; or maybe Maganbhai was an avid film buff. Who after all doesn't like Rekha even in a dry sari. Or perhaps it had something to do with the location being an open agricultural field.

But the drive-in was not for serious movie goers. It was an attraction in itself, and it reminded me of the opening of the new wing of the National Gallery in Washington, which I had attended some years earlier. The severity and boldness of its modernist design appeared to be in striking contrast to the neo-classical facade of the original building, to which it was meant to be a mere addition. At its inaugural celebration, the radical nature of the new architecture had so overwhelmed the exhibits that the art reviewers reviewed the building instead of the paintings that it displayed. Here too it mattered little which movie was playing at the drive-in; the idea was to go with the crowd, to experience a new method of cinematic projection.

The day I went, or rather the night I went, was only a few days after the inauguration. But the inaugural dust had still not settled, and I sensed— like the Minister before me—that I was going to be part of some future historic moment. We were a group of four office colleagues without a car, going to a drive-in cinema. It seemed there were several other such groups; there were many groups of families, office colleagues, classmates, all going to a drive-in cinema without a car. But the absence of a vehicle, something to drive into a drive-in, did not hinder our entry into the place. We were happily accommodated in a hall resembling and smelling much like an overused cowshed, built at the far end of the field. But fortunately for us the architect of the hall had very conveniently forgotten to build its enclosing fourth wall, which appeared to have moved half a mile upfield and become the actual drive-in screen.

We sat there like a pack of laboratory rats, gibbering, waiting to be subjected to the first dose of the new medium. We watched as the parking-lot ahead of us filled up. Cream-coloured Ambassador cars drove in, swirling up the dust once again, then cream-coloured Fiats, and cream-coloured two-wheel scooters. These were not young couples in love, here to take collective advantage of the darkness and to entangle themselves in a physical situation that was forbidden at home. (The Ambassador car or the Vespa scooter is not designed for an easy roll in the back seat in any case.) These were whole families, nuclear and joint, with extensive broods of pre-adolescent youngsters sitting cheek by jowl, lap upon lap, grandsons and grandparents—three generations within the steel frame of a discarded model and all eager witnesses in a new, unexplored movie arena.

The film, when it began, remained from title to finish in soft focus. For us in the wall-less hall, it was additionally blurred both by distance and by the enveloping dust of the foreground. It could have been a slushy Hollywood romance; it could have been a Russian melodrama; it could have been a science fiction thriller; we would not have known the difference. There were apocalyptic scenes of fires enveloping whole palaces, there was heroism and villainy on the scale of Sicilian mafia life; but mainly it was the touching story of romance between a guileless rich boy and a spunky poor girl. The obvious and unfortunate liaison eventually dragged the relationship into deep and unrelenting poverty, but not before the hero had—despite his affluent overweight frame—chased the slight woman up steep Himachal hillsides shrouded in snow, not before he had sung to her in a familiar playback voice on the surprisingly picturesque beaches of the Bombay shore line. Not before he had had the chance to discover that she was the long lost daughter of an eminent politician, and a close family friend. It was a rare and finely developed story, full of pathos, some ethos and a dose of bathos. Certainly there was a great deal of chance encounter and lucky coincidence, both essential ingredients to the situation of bizarre irony that the director wanted so desperately to create. But we, in the detached hall, felt oddly cheated; we kept waiting for the story to develop, we kept waiting for the screen to focus, and kept waiting for the dust to die down. I kept waiting for the popcorn man.

After a while, when one of the cars ahead of us decided to turn on the engine and spew the dust in our direction, the focus became unbearably soft; so soft that we could barely make out the players from the stage set; we could easily have been watching a pornographic film. The rising dust had an additionally blurring effect on the plot. It was difficult to tell whether Rekha had been jilted or Dimple Kapadia. It was moreover difficult to tell who was doing the jilting—Rajesh Khanna or Harish Mehboob. There was a great deal of sobbing and coughing going on in the hall, far in excess of what the story-line warranted. And I imagine it had something to do with the heat and dust and melodrama, all of which is generally palpable in any large public gathering in Ahmedabad in June.

But the standard formula story-line of a Hindi film allows each of the viewers to conceive the tragic-adventure-comedy-thriller from his or her own fresh vantage point. My office colleague next to me had decided that Rekha had perished several frames earlier in a train accident. For me, Rekha was still alive, and I associated the brown blob dressed in white sari with her. I didn't know that the train had met with an accident. In fact I couldn't remember when a train had appeared on the screen. We were all watching the same movie, but in our minds there were several personal subplots in progress.

—from Gautam Bhatia, *Punjabi Baroque and Other Memories of Architecture* (Delhi: Penguin Books, 1994), pp. 55–61, 88–92.

Suketu Mehta

A Lover's Embrace

The manager of Bombay's suburban railway system was recently asked when the system would improve to a point where it could carry its five million daily passengers in comfort. 'Not in my lifetime,' he answered. Certainly, if you commute into Bombay, you are made aware of the precise temperature of the human body as it curls around you on all sides, adjusting itself to every curve of your own. A lover's embrace was never so close.

One morning I took the rush hour train to Jogeshwari. There was a crush of passengers, and I could only get halfway into the carriage. As the train gathered speed, I hung on to the top of the open door. I feared I would be pushed out, but someone reassured me: 'Don't worry, if they push you out they also pull you in.'

Asad Bin Saif is a scholar of the slums, moving tirelessly among the sewers, cataloguing numberless communal flare-ups and riots, seeing first-hand the slow destruction of the social fabric of the city. He is from Bhagalpur, in Bihar, site not only of some of the worst rioting in the nation, but also of a famous incident in 1980, in which the police blinded a group of criminals with knitting needles and acid. Asad, of all people, has seen humanity at its worst. I asked him if he felt pessimistic about the human race.

'Not at all,' he replied. 'Look at the hands from the trains.'

If you are late for work in Bombay, and reach the station just as the train is leaving the platform, you can run up to the packed compartments and you will find many hands stretching out to grab you on board, unfolding outward from the train like petals. As you run alongside you will be picked up, and some tiny space will be made for your feet on the edge of the open doorway. The rest is up to you; you will probably have to hang on to the door frame with your fingertips, being careful not to lean out too far lest you get decapitated by a pole placed close to the tracks. But consider what has happened: your fellow passengers, already packed tighter than cattle are legally allowed to be, their shirts drenched with sweat in the badly ventilated compartment, having stood like this for hours, retain an empathy for you, know that your boss might yell at you or cut your pay if you miss this train and will make space where none exists to take one more person with them. And at the moment of contact, they do not know if the hand that is reaching for theirs belongs to a Hindu or Muslim or Christian or Brahmin or untouchable or whether you were born in this city or arrived only this morning or whether you live in Malabar Hill or Jogeshwari; whether you're from Bombay or Mumbai or New York. All they know is that you're trying to get to the city of gold, and that's enough. Come on board, they say. We'll adjust.

—excerpted from 'Mumbai', *Granta* no. 57, *India: The Golden Jubilee* (1997), pp. 125–6.

Vinay Lal

The Urban Landscapes of Deewaar

Deewaar, by common consent one of the most iconic works of popular Hindi cinema, is eminently a city film. To say this is not to suggest that it is a city film before it is anything else, and much less should one think of *Deewaar*, which pits two brothers—the older one, Vijay (Amitabh

Bachchan), a smuggler and mafia don, the younger (Ravi, played by Shashi Kapoor) a police officer—against each other, as the first significant city film in the commercial Hindi film oeuvre. The space of the urban had been carved out in Hindi cinema long before *Deewaar*, sometimes to signify the distinction between the country and the city,[1] often to gesture at the city as the site of a great experiment in nation-making, and nearly always to signal the relationship of the urban to the irresistible dream of modernization. In Bimal Roy's greatly acclaimed *Do Bigha Zameen* ('Two Acres of Land', 1953), the action shifts from the village in the first half of the film to the great metropolis of Calcutta, where the peasant Shambu, leaving behind his wife and aged father, has arrived harboring the desperate hope that some quick earnings will enable him to retain his ancestral farmland which the unscrupulous moneylender, to whom Shambu's land (and effectively his life) are mortgaged, proposes to sell to an urban developer. In the late colonial period, we have been told, the museum appeared to many Indians as a *jaadu ghar*, a house of magic[2]; but seldom has not only the awe, magic, and mystery of the city, but its sheer presence as a force of intimidation, been so palpably felt as when Shambu and his son Kanhaiya find themselves dwarfed by the immense Howrah Bridge.[3] A montage of shots—pedestrians darting in and out of streets, tram cars, automobiles with blaring horns, the density of city crowds—helps to establish a contrast between the leisurely pace of village life and the frenetic activity which marks the urban. This classic opposition of the

[1] One classic exposition of this theme is Raymond Williams, *The Country and the City* (London: Chatto & Windus, 1973), though it may be argued that, for Williams as for many English writers, the English countryside has as much to do with Englishness as it has to do with the country. The twentieth century outpouring in England of anti-urbanism, as encountered in the work of George Stuart [*Change in the Village*, 1911], can be read mainly as a lamentation on a disappearing England; if Indian nationalist views construed the village as the repository of everything that is enduring and foundational in Indian life, though Ambedkar would have disagreed with such an assessment, the experience of the city had not yet entered into the calculus of nationalism. I still recall the words of the environmentalist Sunderlal Bahuguna on a visit to his ashram-home in 1987: 'The soul of India', he told me gently but unequivocally, 'lives in its villages'.

[2] Gyan Prakash, *Another Reason: Science and the Imagination of Modern India* (Princeton, New Jersey: Princeton University Press, 1999), 64.

[3] Ritwik Ghatak, in *Bari Theke Paliye* ('The Runaway', 1958), likewise suggests how the Howrah Bridge might have appeared to a boy from the village at first sight. The bustling metropolis is at once intimidating and intoxicating.

village and the city would find analogous treatment in another landmark
film marking the advent of India into modernization, *Naya Daur* ('New
Era', 1957). The political economy and moral economy of the village
are alike disrupted when the city-returned entrepreneur, a captive to the
ideology of fast-track development that would be embraced by newly
decolonizing countries, sacrifices his father's trusted employees at the
altar of machinery.

Naya Daur did not disguise the contrast of the village and the city,
rather highlighting it in a ditty, '*Main Bambai ka babu*', sung by a journalist
who has made his way to the village from Bombay, where the '*daulat
wallahs*' or men of wealth are pitted against the '*himmat wallahs*' or men of
courage and character. Whatever the representations of the village as the
embodiment of goodness, innocence, simplicity, restraint and, most of all,
community, *Do Bigha Zameen* was by no means naïve in its understanding
of the exploitative social structures of village life; but the city, in
contrast, unambiguously stood for self-aggrandizement, sophistication,
unsuppressed greed, and utter lack of moral restraints. Perhaps nowhere
in the cinema of the 1950s and 1960s were the contrasts more acutely
present as in the films of Raj Kapoor. According to one informal school
of thought, which has many adherents among those Indians who can
claim some popularity with popular Western culture, the Hindi film
is almost always a 'copy' of some American (and less often European)
film—an argument often advanced apropos the films of Raj Kapoor. The
vagabond figure who makes his way through the city and the travails of
life in *Awara*, to summon one instance of such imitation, was modeled on
Chaplin's tramp who confronts modernity as best as he can. Whatever the
merits of this observation,[4] it is not accidental that *Awara*, four decades
before *Dilwale Dulhaniya Le Jayenge* (1995) and other films cognizant of the
diasporic sensibility are thought to have inserted the Hindi film onto the

---

[4] The idea that the popular Hindi film is very often a copy can be disputed on
numerous grounds, but this is not the place for such a discussion. We ought to
recognize, at least, that no easy distinctions are possible between the original
and the copy, nor is the conception of the 'real' without ambiguity. Many have
questioned the fetish of the original, and there is also the pressing consideration
that the copy may, in aesthetic or critical terms, be superior to the original.
There is, equally, a spectrum between the original and the copy. The film *Sholay*
('Embers', 1975), as an instance, is not easily described as a copy of the spaghetti
Western, even if it has adopted liberally from the classical Western and the
spaghetti Western.

world stage, would become the vehicle for the globalization of popular Hindi cinema. It is, I think, inconceivable that a commercial film centered on the Indian village would have gathered for itself the accolades or the markets that *Awara* did when it took Iran, much of Africa, the Arab world, China, the Soviet Union, and Eastern Europe by storm.[5] The authors of one of the earliest scholarly studies of Indian cinema had this to say about *Awara's* reputation in some parts of the world:

> The Soviet Union is said to have made a massive distribution of *Awara*, dubbed into a number of its languages. Prints were even flown in to the Soviet Expeditions near the North Pole. The Soviet distribution began in 1954, after Raj Kapoor, Nargis, Abbas and the others had visited Moscow as members of a film delegation. On a return visit to the USSR two years later, Raj Kapoor and Nargis were astonished to find themselves well-known film personalities. Bands played *Awara Hun* at airports. *Awara* is reported to have become a favourite film of Mao Tse Tong.[6]

The Indian city, then, would straddle the village and the world. Raj Kapoor populated the village, as in the opening scene of *Shri 420* (1955), with elephants, belles, maharajas, cobras and other icons of what is imagined as traditional India, but as the vagabond Raju enters the great metropolis of Bombay he does so under a huge billboard advertising Coca-Cola. The city, he is told by a beggar, is a heartless place, and before a few hours have elapsed since his arrival he is stripped clean of the money that he had obtained by pawning his 'honesty medal'. The hard grit of city life, one is tempted into thinking, allows no room for

---

[5] *Mother India*, notably, did well in Indian and overseas markets; it was also showered with awards at home and abroad, losing out to Fellini's *Nights of Cabiria* by a single vote for the Oscar for Best Foreign Film. But, it is well to remember, the way to overseas markets had been paved by *Awara* (1951), released six years before *Mother India*.

[6] Erik Barnouw and S. Krishnaswamy, *Indian Film* (New York: Oxford University Press), cited by Mihir Bose, *Bollywood: A History* (New Delhi: Roli Books, 2006), 184. Ravi Shankar was to state in an interview, 'The creations of Shankar-Jaikishan in *Awara* and *Shree 420*—"*Awara hoon*" and "*Mera joota hai japani*" were on the lips of every Russian and Chinese. "*Awara hoon*" was a favorite number of even comrade Mao Tse Tung.' In conversation with Rana Dasgupta: see (accessed 15 October 2011) <http://windsfromtheeast.blogspot.com/2009/03/pt-ravi-shankar-and-cinema.html>. A more recent scholarly treatment of the popular Hindi film's reach in at least one country is to be found in Sudha Rajagopalan, *Indian Films in Soviet Cinemas: The Culture of Movie-going after Stalin* (Bloomington, Indiana: Indiana University Press, 2009).

sentimentality, and even the pavement dwellers attempt to extract rent
from Raju before an elderly woman intercedes and, in a scene uniquely
characteristic of the Hindi film, adopts him as her own.[7] That the moral
economy of the village nevertheless persists amidst the cacophony,
callousness, and corruption of the city is also worthy of note, since it is
the same community of pavement dwellers who, towards the film's end,
remind Raju that love and fellow feeling alone can triumph can over crass
materialism and unadulterated greed. A man may leave his village, but
the village is his inner dwelling; as one commentator put it with much
insight, the city in India is also 'the unintended city'.[8] If in the West the
rural countryside was taking on features of the industrial landscape in
a renewed thrust towards modernization, in India there was a different
continuum between the rural and the urban as the village came into the
city and installed itself to create a new conception of the urban.

It is against this backdrop, then, that we can profitably turn our
attention to a consideration of *Deewaar* as another foray into the physical
and mental landscape of the city. The location of *Deewaar* in the city
anchors the film, I have already suggested, in crucial ways in mainstream
Hindi-language cinema as much as in the narratives of the nation-state
under conditions of modernity. Tremendous as was the scale of the
movement of people across borders during India's partition, there has
been a much greater influx, albeit over a longer period of time, of people
into the cities from the countryside. While this phenomenon, termed
by one recent interpreter of the urban as 'The Great Migration',[9] is by
no means unique to India, perhaps nowhere else did it have as much
poignancy as it did in a civilization that was widely believed to have
acquired most of its principal characteristics from its essentially rural
outlook. Such migrations commenced in the last half century of colonial
rule, greatly accelerated in the aftermath of independence, and have not
fundamentally abated since then—and they are perhaps best captured,
not in the mass as much as in scattered stories of individuals, most vividly
in Hindi films. Vijay, Ravi, and their mother depart for the city, leaving
behind a social order that is simultaneously more intimate and more

The Urban Landscapes of Deewaar

---

[7] This elderly woman, played by Lalita Pawar, takes the name of Gangamai,
'Mother Ganges'; not surprisingly, she is the kindly matriarch whose word is
akin to the law.
[8] Jai Sen, 'The Unintended City', *Seminar* (1975), and reprinted in this volume.
[9] Jeb Brugmann, *Welcome to the Urban Revolution: How Cities are Changing the World*
(New Delhi: HarperCollins, 2010).

unforgiving: one cannot escape one's social markers so readily in the village or the small town. As the treatment meted out to Anand Babu and members of his family amply shows,[10] the social order of the village is in some respects less tolerant of transgressions than the city.

Though the opprobrium of their village brethren drives them out, there is also a tacit assumption that as the breadwinner of her family Sumitra Devi's prospects are better in the metropolis. When the social history of India in the second half of the twentieth century is written, with more than a mere gesture to the fullness of the sociological, cultural and political phenomena encapsulated under city life, the familiar story, today rehearsed in most middle- and upper-class homes where domestic help is widely used,[11] of the migrant who is the lifeline to the family in the village will find a treasured place. *Deewaar* echoes this phenomenon with unusual anticipation, and unexpectedly so in the story of a worker, Satyendra Dubey, at the docks where Vijay is employed. Samant, the local crime boss, has a stranglehold over the lives of the dockworkers, extorting protection money from them through his henchmen. Satyendra objects to parting with his hard-earned money—*kis baat ke paise lete hain* ('On what account do they take money?'), he asks—but is advised by Rahim Chacha, an elderly Muslim worker whose hair has gone white working at the docks over the years, to comply with the practice and avoid confrontation. Satyendra describes his family in the village awaiting the money order, and the sister whose dowry he must collect: thus his refusal to place a percentage of his earnings in the loot box. He is pushed in the path of a speeding truck, the money flies out of his hands; as he

---

[10] At the commencement of the film, Anand Babu is shown as an upright labor union leader commanding immense respect from the workers; in a successful attempt to coerce him to bargain away the rights of the workers, the owner of the mill abducts Anand Babu's wife, Sumitra Devi, and their two sons, Vijay and Ravi. Anand Babu's betrayal of the workers leads to his ostracism, and he becomes the absconding father; his wife and their two sons gravitate towards the city. Vijay's earnings as a shoeshine boy help to send Ravi to school; in time, however, the dockworker Vijay joins a smuggling ring led by Davar, while Ravi is recruited into the police services.

[11] Call it political correctness or, what seems doubtful, a new-found sensitivity to the humanity of the under-class, but in many homes servants have been replaced with 'domestic help', a category that encompasses maids, cooks, drivers, sweepers, nurses, nursing assistants, and what at one time were called ayahs. However, even those inclined to the new phraseology have found no adequate substitute for 'servants' quarters'.

desperately scrambles to collect the notes blowing in the wind, crying out aloud, *'Ma ke paise'* ('My mother's money'), he is run over by the truck. It is at this moment, as the started workers gather around Satyendra's body, that the gaunt expression on Vijay's face suggests the emergence of the 'angry young man'.

As Vijay determines to take on the dock mafia, the viewer also senses the explosion of urban India; the 'angry young man', a new hero emerging from the bowels of the city, represents the anger of a generation whose dreams lie in tatters. 'Twenty-five years I have been here', says Rahim Chacha to his fellow dockworkers as they sip tea at the canteen, 'and I have never seen anyone decline to give protection money.' Rahim and Vijay are sitting with their back to the wall; behind them, but facing the viewer, is a poster of Mohandas Gandhi in what is unquestionably his most iconic posture, firmly wielding a walking stick. 'What has not transpired in twenty-five years is about to happen now', says Vijay: 'Next week, one more coolie will refuse to pay those ruffians protection money.' The camera has zoomed in on him and the picture of Gandhi on the wall is now occluded from the viewer's gaze. Vijay has been twirling the bidi in his mouth; now he stands up, tosses the bidi aside, and walks away. The framed picture of Gandhi, a staple of the police station and the politician's office, under which bribes are freely handed out and the politician's goons hatch plots to murder opponents or righteous men, has come alive as the wellspring of resistance. It has been summoned to express the rage of young and urban India; but it is also, as Gandhi himself would have said, an urgent call to walk alone when no one walks by one's side. The bidi thrown away, Vijay will soon move to cigarettes—another sign of his being cast into the urban world.

As Vijay wrestles control of the docks away from Samant's men, we are tempted into thinking that he is increasingly embracing the urban world as his own, refusing to be beaten into submission by the unruliness and hurly-burly ways of the city. The *docks* are among the many signs of the urban, and even the global: as Vijay secures his entry into the underworld, he begins to take charge of the smuggled goods coming from Dubai. The city is everywhere in *Deewaar* and the film skillfully signposts urban spaces. Newly arrived from the city, Vijay's mother finds works at a large *construction site.* The stone that Vijay hurls at his mother's tormentor as she hauls bricks on her head is not about to launch an intifada, but it is equally a weapon of the weak, a missile fired at those who are heartless and stone cold. Sumitra and her two sons make their home under the *bridge*: it is not the overhead traffic over the bridge that makes the city, but the tens of thousands indeed millions sheltered under it who, yet again, give birth to 'the unintended city'. The great migrations into the city gave rise to the *slums*, with their population of labourers, tradesmen, prostitutes, and petty criminals, and it is from the *housing tenements*, some under the bridge, that one gets what has been described as the 'slum's eye view of Indian politics'.[12] From their modest home under the bridge, the young Ravi arrives at the gate of the nearby *school*; and to ease his younger brother's way into respectable society, Vijay takes up a job on the *footpath* to send Ravi to school.

Slowly but surely, the plot of *Deewaar* drifts into other ineluctable spaces of the urban landscape. It is from a *high-rise* building that Vijay looks down upon Marine Drive, which puts the land in conversation with the sea, and accepts a place within Davar's organization. Vijay moves through the ranks and, as a measure of winning Davar's trust, he also begins to inhabit the more exclusive spaces of urban modernity. It is at the *swimming pool* of the *five-star hotel* that men of leisure convene for casual business talk, and it is in the *board room* of such a hotel that the organization takes decisions. Meanwhile, in a chance encounter at the hotel's *night-club* Vijay encounters Anita; however, unlike the women at the bar or at the card tables encountered by Raj Kapoor's Raju, Anita is not merely an embodiment of womanhood gone hideously astray. A chase through *city streets* seems inescapably a part of every cop-and-robber narrative, and so it appears with *Deewaar* as it winds its way towards a conclusion with Ravi in furious pursuit of his older brother, a fugitive from the law. Yet, the chase is less significant than the notion of the urban marked out by city streets. Earlier in the film, Ravi chased down a poor boy through the streets and over the railway tracks—as they run, the underside of the city comes into full view. There is life below the tracks and besides them, just as there is life underneath the bridge. Now, as Vijay appears to be cornered, his mastery of the maze of streets is called into question as he is pursued with relentless intensity by his brother, who has not only sworn to uphold the law but also surely hears the constant din of that stinging reprimand thrown at him by the boy's mother: 'You, the righteous upholders of the law! What is this justice of yours? Does this justice of yours consist only of pumping bullets into the naked and the hungry? What has my son done? He stole some bread

---

[12] Ashis Nandy, 'Indian Popular Cinema as a Slum's Eye View of Politics', introduction to idem, *The Secret Politics of Our Desires: Innocence, Culpability and Indian Popular Cinema* (Delhi: Oxford University Press, 1998).

for his hungry mother and mother, isn't that it? If you are such a mighty advocate of the law, go shoot those whose *warehouses* are full of grain.'

Moving as he does between the extremes, from the village to a global trade in smuggled goods, from the uniform of a mere coolie at Bombay's docks to tailored suits, we should not be surprised that Vijay teeters between the *footpath* and the *skyscraper. Deewaar* has justly been described as a film that gives vent to the explosive anger of discontented young urban India, as well as a film that, while exploring, partly through tacit invocations to the rich mythic material found in the Mahabharata, the inexhaustible theme of fraternal conflict,[13] provides an allegorical treatment of the eternal struggle between good and evil within oneself. Compelling as are such readings, I would nevertheless suggest that *Deewaar* also sets up a dialectic between the footpath and the skyscraper, the two preeminent signs of the urban landscape in the film. The footpath or pavement, I have hinted in my discussion of *Shri 420*, has ever been present in the Hindi film, to be numbered indeed among the dramatis personae. The ubiquity of the footpath as home to the homeless, migrant labourers, and myriad others living at the margins of society is too self-evident to require comment. One can think of it more imaginatively as a school where life's lessons are imbibed: while Ravi goes to school, where under the umbrella of the textbook, the national anthem, and the discipline of the rod he will learn to become the dutiful subject of the state, Vijay takes up shining shoes on the footpath.[14] It is on this footpath that some of the dialogues inescapably associated with *Deewaar* take place: issuing a retort to Jaichand, Davar's right-hand man, for throwing money at him after his shoes have been polished, the young Vijay says, 'I polish shoes and do not beg for money. Pick up the money and place it in my hands.' Vijay, Davar later cautions Jaichand, is the steed that runs long races (*'lambi race ka ghoda'*): *'Yeh umar bhar boot polish nahi karega. Jis din zindagi ki race*

Ashis Nandy, 'An Intelligent Critic's Guide to Indian Cinema', in *The Savage Freud and Other Essays on Possible and Retrievable Selves* (Delhi: Oxford University Press, 1995).

So does Kanhaiya, Shambu's son, when it appears that Shambu may not be able to put together the money required to free his land from the moneylender's firm grip. *Do Bigha Zameen* appeared in 1953, the same year as Zia Sarhadi's *Footpath*. Sarhadi's film appears to have more than a visceral presence in *Deewaar*. Noshu (Dilip Kumar) takes to black marketeering, in an attempt to escape from the humdrum of bourgeois life, but in so doing he puts his brother's life in grave jeopardy and succeeds in alienating himself from his family and wider community.

 The Urban Landscapes of *Deewaar*

mein isne speed pakdi, yeh sab ko peeche chorh jayega. Meri baat ka khayal rakhna. Ek din yeh ladka kuch banega' ('He is not going to be shining shoes the rest of his life. The day he catches life by the neck, he will leave everyone behind. Mark my words: One day this boy will make something of himself').

Sure enough, Vijay gravitates from the footpath to the skyscraper. Vijay's first thought is to gift his mother a skyscraper—built with nothing less than her blood, sweat and tears. All the insults and humiliations heaped upon her, he deludes himself into believing, are thereby avenged. It is the impossible gift, but for many more reasons than he can imagine. No sooner has he gained possession of the skyscraper than his fall commences, as if the footpath were beckoning him to return to his roots and plant his feet on the ground. *'Meri ma ne yahan eente uthai thi'* ('my mother carried bricks on her head here'), Vijay informs the businessman from whom he purchases the skyscraper, but the fact that his claim on this skyscraper is ephemeral, and ultimately undeserving, is underscored by the fact that the viewer's sight of the building is barred throughout their negotiations. Even more significantly, the footpath takes ontological precedence over the skyscraper: the skyscraper holds no intrinsic interest for Vijay, indeed its very existence is refracted through the footpath. It is because Vijay has spent a portion of his life on the footpath that the skyscraper acquires meaning. The footpath is literally that: the path where the foot trod, where every footfall becomes a trace of memory. At every turn of his confrontation with Ravi, Vijay seeks, unsuccessfully, to remind him of their shared histories on the footpath: *'Ravi, tume yaad hain bachpan mein kitni raaten footpath pe khaali pet guzarin?'* ('Ravi, do you recall how many nights we spent on the footpath on empty stomachs?')

Ostensibly a film shaped around fraternal conflict, *Deewaar* belongs overwhelmingly to Vijay. The footpath and the skyscraper are alike spaces that he inhabits; Ravi, by contrast, belongs to the middle and genteel world of the bungalow. The bucolic space of the bungalow garden, where one might sip tea or swirl around a tree with a romantic song on one's lips, sits easily with Ravi. Whatever one's disinclination to accept such a reading, considering how far Ravi will become the embodiment of the law of the Father, Ravi appears to be equally distant from the footpath and the skyscraper alike. He refuses to surrender to the power of memory, and appears to have made a resolute decision to leave behind the past; and if one is left relatively clueless about how Ravi imagines the city, it is a sign of his remoteness from the urban landscape. Ravi may be consigned to the world of those about whom can neither say whether they like or dislike the city. Vijay, in contradistinction, has a relationship to the city that is, if not in equal parts, antagonistic and life-enhancing. Intimacy in the city is not easily achieved, and it is not accidental that the only close bond he forges is with Anita who, plying a profession that is considered disreputable by bourgeois society, herself lives at the margins. When, in the closing scene of the long flashback that is the film, Vijay describes himself as fulfilled by the sleep of the just as he dies in his mother's lap, we seem to be returning to Gandhi's imagination of the village as the site of authentic if harried innocence. But the city, by the same token, has bestowed upon Vijay a new lease of life, and permitted him the luxury of an existence shorn of the village's debilitating markers of identity. In the last analysis, however, it is not the exile from the village that is most decisive in shaping the contours of his life. Vijay is a stranger to himself and, to this extent, exile is the enduring condition of his being.

—slightly modified from Vinay Lal, *Deewaar: The Footpath, the City and the Angry Young Man* (New Delhi: HarperCollins, 2011), pp. 55–72.

Vinay Lal

Further Reading:
A Select Bibliography

The literature on Indian cities, as my introduction to this anthology
points out, is not only growing rapidly but no longer dwells exclusively or
largely, as was the case until quite recently, on urbanization, demographic
changes, or the sociological features of the city. Much of the earlier
literature can be safely located within a rather narrow conception of the
social sciences, and very little of the trajectories that are quite amply
on display in the best of Indian history, from postcolonial theory and
poststructuralism to feminism, were to be witnessed in the scholarly and
popular literature on Indian cities until a few years ago. Even today, there
is scant treatment in the literature on the modern Indian city as metaphor,
and on the city as a site of art, music, theatre, public performance,
literature, popular culture, and street culture. Much of the best work in
this vein, such as Arjun Appadurai's elegant even prescient little essay,
'Street Culture', which appeared in the now-defunct *India Magazine*, has
been included in this anthology. Surprisingly, notwithstanding the
increased proliferation of scholarly studies informed by feminist insights,
no book-length study of 'the gendered city' in the Indian context has yet
been attempted, and indeed one would be hard-pressed to find more than
a handful of scholarly articles.

A few other observations are in order. Though several studies—
among them, Ravi Kalia's three books on Gandhinagar, Chandigarh, and
Bhubaneswar—have been published in recent years of cities that serve
more as provincial capitals than as cosmopolitan centres, the scholarly
lens continues to be focused on the three metropolises of Calcutta,
Bombay, and Delhi. To be sure, a city such as Lucknow has been

relatively well-served by both popular memory and scholarly scrutiny, but the sheer paucity of scholarly literature, at least in English, on Kanpur, Allahabad, Mysore, Pune, and even Jaipur (a major tourist destination) and Ahmedabad (a city, as is evident to all students of Indian history, of immense political and economic calculations) should be sufficient indication of the fact that Lucknow, for reasons having to do with the course of its history—as the site of a distinct culture, its reputation for syncreticism, or its pivotal place in the rebellion of 1857—remains something of an exception among the second and third tiers of Indian cities. Notwithstanding the persistent hullabaloo over Bangalore and Hyderabad, each with a population of over five million, as modernist icons of resurgent India, these cities have generally been poorly served by scholarship.

This reasonably comprehensive but still select bibliography is intended, then, as an aid to those readers who are rather more intrigued by historical and cultural studies, or who are interested in understanding what have been the fruits of 'the urban turn' in the study of Indian history and society. Many of the better-known historical narratives of the principal cities have been included in the bibliography. Works of fiction, among them some of the novels of Salman Rushdie, Rohinton Mistry, Amitav Ghosh, Aravind Adiga, Vikram Chandra, and others have been excluded; I have likewise generally omitted poetry, plays, and other literary works. This bibliography would have become unmanageable had I included novels set in the Indian metropolis. Indian literature in English is displaying a rather new sensibility—an attachment to the idea of the urban and equally a tenuous relationship to the idea of 'home', unless it be the city itself that is imagined as home. The city makes possible relationships that were inconceivable in the village, and the plots in recent novels by Shashi Deshpande, K.R. Usha, Manu Joseph, Anjum Hasan, and Adiga do not revolve around the family. In Kavery Nambisan's novel, *The Story That Must not Be Told* (2010), the urban slum—rather uniquely, in Chennai rather than Mumbai or Delhi—makes more than just an appearance; the story is set in it. Moreover, once one moves beyond Indian writing in English, the canvas is impossibly large. David Gregory Roberts's *Shantaram* (2005), wildly popular in India, is as much as anything else a novel about Bombay; but the city's distinctive landmarks are encountered in a wide array of other works from non-Indian writers, from the Inspector Ghote novels of H.R.F. Keating (1926–2011) to the little-known *Stones of Bombay* (1950), a novel by the Hungarian-Australian writer David Martin.

There is another important respect in which this bibliography (and, though to a lesser extent, the anthology itself) is constrained. I have drawn almost exclusively upon works in English, even though, to take one prominent example, there is a considerable and distinct literature in Bengali on Calcutta. An occasional work in Hindi or Bengali appears in the bibliography, but it would have been impossible to do justice to the material in any language other than English. Translations from Indian languages into English do not have the storied history one associates with translations from one major European language into another, and I suspect it will require another at least another two generations or more of sustained translation work before most translations into English from Hindi, Oriya, Bengali, Assamese, Kannada, and so on can be deemed as literary works in their own right. Still, there is an attempt being made to bring to readers in English literature that has long been inaccessible to them, and on the city there are works such as Gangadhar Gadgil's gargantuan *Prarambh* ('The Beginning', translated by Arvind Dixit and published by the National Book Trust, 2006), which furnishes considerable insight into the growth of Bombay from 1818 to 1869, that readily come to mind. On the other hand, the work of the gifted and pioneering novelist of the urban, Gitanjali Shree—for example, *Hamara Shahar Us Baras* (Rajkamal Prakashan, 2007)—remains largely untranslated. In any case, since I have omitted fiction in English from this bibliography, barring a few exceptions, I need not justify a similar exclusion of fiction in Indian languages, even when it is available in English.

The bibliography is divided into three parts: a very short list of general works on the city, extending beyond India, is followed by a general bibliography on the city in India. The first part is very much a personal list, and other scholars and readers, drawing upon a vast body of work, are likely to have their own list of favourites or list of books that they have found particularly insightful; moreover, here I have taken the liberty of drawing upon allied fields of inquiry, such as the scholarship on the production and politics of space. The third and by far the longest part of the bibliography is focused on particular Indian cities and the scholarship woven around them. Scholarly articles, with but a few exceptions, have been excluded. There is enough in the bibliography of interest to scholars, researchers, and more serious readers, but those interested in some of the periodical literature can turn with profit to the research bibliography that I have made available on my pedagogic website on India, MANAS: http://www.sscnet.ucla.edu/southasia/History/biblio_city.html

A. The City: General Works

Abu-Lughod, Janet L. *New York, Chicago, Los Angeles: America's Global Cities*. Minneapolis: University of Minneosta Press, 1999.

Appadurai, Arjun. *Modernity at Large*. Minneapolis: University of Minnesota Press, 1986.

Auge, Marc. *Non-Places: Introduction to an Anthropology of Supermodernity*. Trans. John Howe. London: Verso, 1995.

Bachelard, Gaston. *The Poetics of Space*. Boston: Beacon Press, 1969.

Banham, Reyner. *Los Angeles: The Architecture of Four Ecologies*. Harmondsworth: Penguin Books, 1971.

Basu, D.K., ed. *The Rise of the Colonial Port City in Asia*. Santa Cruz and Berkeley: Center for South and Southeast Asian Studies, University of California, 1979.

Benjamin, Walter. *One Way Street and Other Writings*. London: Verso, 1985.

———. *The Arcades Project*, ed. Rolf Tiedemann. Trans. Howard Eiland and Kevin McLaughlin. Cambridge, Mass.: Belknap Press of Harvard University Press, 2002.

Blum, Alan. *The Imaginative Structure of the City*. Montreal: McGill-Queen's University Press, 2003.

Bridge, Gary and Sophie Watson, eds. *The Blackwell City Reader*. 2nd edn., Chichester, West Sussex, UK: Wiley-Blackwell, 2010.

Burgin, Victor. *In/Different Spaces: Place and Memory in Visual Culture*. Berkeley: University of California Press, 1996.

———. *Some Cities*. Berkeley: University of California Press, 1996.

Calvino, Italo. *Invisible Cities*. London: Pan Books, 1979.

Davis, Mike. *City of Quartz: Excavating the Future in Los Angeles*. London: Verso, 1990.

———. 'Planet of Slums: Urban Involution and the Informal Proletariat.' *New Left Review*, 26 (March–April 2004), 5–34.

Feldman, David and Gareth Stedman Jones, eds. *Metropolis London: Histories and Representations since 1800*. London: Routledge, 1989.

Ghurye, G.S. *Cities and Civilization*. Bombay: Popular Prakashan, 1962.

Girouard, Mark. *Cities and People: A Social and Architectural History*. New Haven: Yale University Press, 1985.

Harvey, David. *The Urban Experience*. Baltimore: The Johns Hopkins University Press, 1989.

Hibbert, Christopher. *Cities and Civilizations*. New York: Weidenfeld and Nicholson, 1986.

Kunstler, James Howard. *The Geography of Nowhere: The Rise and Decline of America's Man-Made Landscape*. New York: Simon & Schuster/Touchstone, 1994.

Lefebvre, Henri. *The Production of Space*. Oxford: Blackwell Publishers, 1991.

———. *The Urban Revolution*. Trans. Robert Bononno. Minneapolis: University of Minnesota Press, 2003.

Marcuse, Peter and Ronald van Kempen, eds. *Globalizing Cities: A New Spatial Order?* Oxford: Blackwell Publishers, 2000.

Mazower, Mark. *Salonica, City of Ghosts: Christians, Muslims and Jews, 1430-1950.* London: HarperCollins, 2004.

Mumford, Lewis. *The City in History: Its Origins, Its Transformations, and Its Prospects.* New York: Harcourt, Brace & World, 1961.

———. *The Highway and the City.* New York: Harcourt Brace Jovanovich, 1953.

Murphey, Rhoads. 'City and Countryside as Ideological Issues: India and China'. *Comparative Studies in Society and History,* 14, no. 3 (June 1972), 250–67.

Pamuk, Orhan. *Istanbul: Memories of a City.* Trans. Maureen Freely. London: Faber, 2005.

Pile, Steve and Nigel Thrift, eds. *City A-Z.* London: Routledge, 2000.

Rodwin, Lloyd and Robert Hollister, eds. *Cities of the Mind: Images and Themes of the City in Social Sciences.* New York: Plenum Press, 1984.

Royle, Trevor. *Precipitous City: The Story of Literary Edinburgh.* New York: Taplinger Publishing, 1980.

Sassen, Saskia. *The Global City: New York, London, Tokyo.* 2nd edn. Princeton: Princeton University Press, 2001.

———. *Cities in a World Economy.* 4th edn. Thousand Oaks, California: Sage, 2012.

———, ed. *Global Cities, Linked Networks.* New York: Routledge, 2002.

Schlor, Joachim. *Nights in the Big City: Paris, Berlin, London 1840-1930.* Trans. Pierre Gottfried Imhof and Dafydd Rees Roberts. London: Reaktion Books, 1998.

Sennett, Richard. *The Conscience of the Eye: The Design and Social Life of Cities.* New York: Alfred A. Knopf, 1991.

Spate, O.H.K. 'Factors in the Development of Capital Cities'. *Geographical Review,* 32, no. 4 (October 1942), 622–631.

Tinker, Hugh. 'The City in Asia'. in his *Reorientations: Studies on Asia in Transition,* 29-48. Singapore: Donald Moore Books, 1965.

Wallis, Brian. *If You Lived Here: The City in Art, Theory and Social Activism.* Seattle: Dia Art Foundation and Bay Press, 1991.

Watson, Sophie and Katherine Gibson, eds. *Postmodern Cities and Spaces.* Oxford: Basil Blackwell, 1995.

Watson, Sophie and Gary Bridge, eds. *The New Blackwell Companion to the City.* Oxford: Blackwell, 2000.

Weber, Max. *The City.* Trans. Don Martindale and Gertrud Neuwrith. New York: The Free Press, 1958.

Weimar, D.R. *The City as Metaphor.* New York: Random House, 1966.

Zardini, Mirko, ed. *Sense of the City: An Alternate Approach to Urbanism.* Montreal: Canadian Centre for Architecture, 2005.

Ameen, Farooq, ed. *Contemporary Architecture and City Form: The South Asian Paradigm.* Mumbai: Marg Publications, 1997.

Ashokamitran. *The Eighteenth Parallel.* Trans. Gomathi Narayanan. Hyderabad: Disha Books/Orient Longman, 1993.

Ballhatchet, Kenneth and John Harrison, eds. *The City in South Asia: Pre-Modern and Modern.* London: Curzon Press; Atlantic Highlands, New Jersey: Humanities Press, 1980.

Banga, Indu, ed. *The City in Indian History: Urban Demography, Society, and Politics.* Delhi: Manohar for Urban History Association of India, 1991.

Bhatia, Gautam. *Punjabi Baroque and Other Memories of Architecture.* New Delhi: Penguin, 1994.

Bose, Ashish. *India's Urbanization, 1901-2001.* 2nd edn. New Delhi: McGraw-Hill, 1978 [1973].

Caine, W.S. *Picturesque India, a Handbook for European Travellers.* London: George Routledge & Sons, 1890.

Chandavarkar, Rajnarayan. *History, Culture and the Indian City.* Cambridge: Cambridge University Press, 2009.

Chaudhuri, K.N. 'Some Reflections on the Town and Country in Mughal India'. *Modern Asian Studies,* 12, no. 1 (Feb. 1978), 77–96.

Chaudhuri, Nirad. *Thy Hand, Great Anarch! India: 1921–1952.* London: Chatto & Windus, 1987; Reading, Mass.: Addison-Wesley, 1988.

Crooke, William. *Things Indian: Being Discursive Notes on Various Subjects Connected with India.* New York: C. Scribner's Sons, 1906.

Forrest, G.W. *Cities of India.* Westminster: Archibald Constable & Co., 1903; reprint edn., Bombay: Publishers & Distributors, 2002.

Fox, Richard, ed. *Urban India: Society, Space and Image.* Durham, North Carolina: Duke University, Program in Comparative Studies on Southern Asia, 1970. [Monograph and Occasional Paper Series, no. 10.]

Frater, Alexander. *Chasing the Monsoon.* New Delhi: Viking, 1990; Penguin Books, 1991.

Geddes, Patrick. 'The Temple Cities', *Modern Review,* 25 (1919).

———. *Patrick Geddes in India,* ed. Jaqueline Tyrwhitt. With an intro. by Lewis Mumford. London: L. Humphries, 1947.

Ghurye, G.S. 'Cities in India'. *Sociological Bulletin,* 2 (1953).

Gillion, Kenneth L. *Ahmedabad: A Study in Indian Urban History.* Berkeley: University of California Press, 1968.

Goodfriend, Douglas E. 'Nagar Yoga: The Culturally Informed Town Planning of Patrick Geddes in India, 1914–1924'. *Human Organization,* 38, no. 4 (1979), 343–355.

Goody, Jack. *The East in the West.* Cambridge: Cambridge University Press, 1996.

Grewal, J.S. and Indu Banga, eds. *Studies in Urban History.* Amritsar: Guru Nanak Dev University, Department of History, 1981.

Grewal, J.S. *In the By-Lanes of History: Some Persian Documents from a Punjab Town.* Shimla: Indian Institute of Advanced Study, 1975.

Gupta, I.P. *Urban Glimpses of Mughal India: Agra, the Imperial Capital (16th & 17th Centuries).* Delhi: Discovery Publishing House, 1986.

Heber, Reginald. *Narrative of a Journey Through the Upper Provinces of India from Calcuta to Bombay, 1824-1825.* London: John Murray, 1829.

Hindu Folio: Cities, special supplement to the *Hindu Sunday Magazine* (12 August 2001).

Kaarsholm, Preben, ed. *City Flicks: Indian Cinema and the Urban Experience.* Kolkata: Seagull, 2004.

Keyserling, Count Hermann. *Travel Diary of a Philosopher.* Trans. J. Holroyd-Reece. New York: Harcourt, Brace & Co., 1925; reprint edn., Bombay: Bharatiya Vidya Bhavan, 1969.

King, Anthony D. *Colonial Urban Development: Culture, Social Power, and Environment.* London: Routledge & Paul, 1976.

Kumar, Ravindra. 'Changing structure of urban society in colonial India'. *Indian Historical Review,* 5, nos. 1–2 (1978–1979), 200–15.

Laquian, Aprodicio A., Vinod Tewari, and Lisa M. Hanley, eds. *The Inclusive City: Infrastructure and Public Services for the Urban Poor in Asia.* Washington, DC: Woodrow Wilson Press; Baltimore: Johns Hopkins University Press, 2007.

Latif, Syed Muhammad. *Lahore: Its History, Architectural Remains, and Antiquities, with an Account of Its Modern Institutions, Inhabitants, Their Trade, Customs, & Co.* Lahore: New Imperial Press, 1892; reprint edn., Lahore: Ahmad Ali Shiekh, Oriental Publishers & Booksellers, 1981.

Levy, Robert. 'The Power of Space in a Traditional Hindu City'. *International Journal of Hindu Studies,* 1 (January–April 1977), 55–71.

Low, Sydney. *A Vision of India.* 2nd edn. London: Smith, Elder, & Co., 1910.

Macleod, Norman. *Days in North India.* Philadelphia: J.B. Lippincott & Co., 1870.

Menon, A.G.K. 'Imagining the Indian City'. *Economic and Political Weekly* (Mumbai), 32, no. 46 (15 November 1997).

Metcalf, Thomas R. *An Imperial Vision: Indian Architecture and Britain's Raj.* Berkeley: University of California Press, 1989.

Mishra, Pankaj. *Butter Chicken in Ludhiana: Travels in Small Town India.* New Delhi: Penguin, 1995.

Misra, R.P., ed. *Million Cities of India.* New Delhi: Vikas, 1978.

Naipaul, V.S. *India: A Million Mutinies Now.* New York: Penguin Books, 1990.

Nandy, Ashis. *An Ambiguous Journey to the City: The Village and Other Odd Ruins of the Self in the Indian Imagination.* New Delhi: Oxford University Press, 2001.

Nilsson, Sten. *The New Capitals of India, Pakistan and Bangladesh,* trans. Elisabeth Andreasson. Lund, Sweden: Studentlitteratur, 1973.

Pinto, Jerry and Rahul Srivastava. *Talk of the Town: Stories of Twelve Indian Cities.* New Delhi: Puffin Books, 2008.

Rai, Vibhuti Narain. *Curfew in the City.* Trans. C.M. Naim. New Delhi: Roli Books, 1998.

Ramanujan, A.K. 'Towards an Anthology of City Images', in *Urban India: Society, Space and Image*, ed. Richard G. Fox. Durham, North Carolina: Duke University Program in Comparative Studies on Southern Asia, 1971, and reprinted with corrections in *The Collected Essays of A. K. Ramanujan*, ed., Vinay Dharwadker, 57–72. New Delhi: Oxford University Press, 1999.

Redfield, Robert and Milton Singer. 'The Cultural Role of Cities'. *Economic Development and Cultural Change*, 3, no. 1 (October, 1954), 53–73.

Roberts, Emma. *Scenes and Characteristics of Hindostan, with Sketches of Anglo-Indian Society*. 3 vols. London: W.H. Allen & Co., 1835.

Rosenthal, Donald B., ed. *The City in Indian Politics*. Faridabad: Thomson Press, 1976.

Russell, Ralph, ed. *The Oxford India Ghalib: Life, Letters and Ghazals*. New Delhi: Oxford University Press, 2003.

Sarai. *The Cities of Everyday Life*. Sarai Reader, 02. New Delhi: The New Media Initiative, CSDS, 2002.

Schwartzberg, Joseph E., ed. *A Historical Atlas of South Asia*. Chicago: The University of Chicago Press, 1978.

Seabrook, Jeremy. *In the Cities of the South: Scenes from a Developing World*. London: Verso, 1996.

Sen, Jai. *The Unintended City: An Essay on the City of the Poor*. Calcutta: Cathedral Relief and Social Services, 1975 [pamphlet].

Singer, Milton B. *Semiotics of cities, selves, and cultures: explorations in semiotic anthropology*. Berlin & New York: Mouton de Gruyter, 1991.

Singh, Khushwant and Shobha De. *Uncertain Liaisons: Sex, Strife and Togetherness in Urban India*. New Delhi: Viking, 1993.

Spodek, Howard. 'From 'Parasitic' to 'Generative': The Transformation of Post-Colonial Cities in India'. *Journal of Interdisciplinary History*, 5 (1975), 413–43.

———. 'Studying the History of Urbanization in India'. *Journal of Urban History*, 6 (May 1980), 251–95.

———. 'The Urban History of India: An Update', *Journal of Urban History*, 12 (May, 1986), 293–308.

Subramanian, Lakshmi. *Ports, towns, cities: a historical tour of the Indian littoral*. Mumbai: Marg Publications, on behalf of the National Centre for the Performing Arts, 2008.

Tagore, Rabindranath. 'City and Village' [lectures delivered at Santiniketan, 1928]. *Towards Universal Man*, 302–322. London: Asia Publishing House, 1961.

Tavernier, Jean Baptiste. *Travels in India*. Trans. V. Ball. 2 vols. London: Macmillan & Co., 1889.

Tewari, V.K., Jay Weinstein, and V.L.S. Prakasha Rao, eds. *Indian Cities: Ecological Perspectives*. New Delhi: Concept Publishing Company, 1986.

Trojanow, Ilija. *Along the Ganga*. New Delhi: Penguin Books, 2005.

C: Indian Cities

I BANARAS

'Homage to Varanasi' [various authors, in two parts]. *Illustrated Weekly of India* 85, nos. 6 and 7 (9 and 16 February 1964).

Altekar, A.S. *Benares and Sarnath: Past and Present.* 2nd edn., Varanasi: Banaras Hindu University, 1947.

Anon. [Sherring, M. A.] 'Benares Past and Present'. *Calcutta Review* 80, no. 40 (1864), 253–94.

Bharati, M. 'Banarasi Jiwan men Kajri ka Sthan'. *Jaydesh* (31 August 1982).

———. 'Kashi ki Sangeet Sadhana aur Vidyadhari'. *Aj* (13 June 1971), 1–13.

Cape, C. Phillips. *Benares: The Stronghold of Hinduism.* London: Charles H. Kelley, 1909.

Chaturvedi, Sitaram and Vishwanath Mukherjee, eds. *Yaha Banaras Hai.* Varanasi: Thalua Club, 1962.

Dalmia, Vasudha. *The Nationalization of Hindu Traditions: Bharatendu Harischandra and Nineteenth-century Banaras.* New Delhi: Oxford University Press, 1997.

Dwivedi, Thakur Prasad. *Sri Ramlila: Ek Samajik Mahayajna.* Varanasi: Royal Printing Works, n.d.

Eck, Diana L. *Banaras: City of Light.* Princeton: Princeton University Press, 1983.

———. 'Kashi: City and Symbol'. *Purana* 20, no. 2 (1978).

Freitag, Sandria B. *Culture and Power in Benares: Community, Performance, and Environment, 1800-1980.* Berkeley: University of California Press, 1989.

Gaenszle, Martin and Jorg Gengnagel, eds. *Visualizing Space in Banaras: Images, Maps, and the Practice of Representation.* Wiesbaden: Otto Harrassowitz GmbH & Co., 2006; reprint edn., New Delhi: Oxford University Press, 2008.

Greaves, Edwin. *Kashi the City Illustrious or Benares.* Allahabad: The Indian Press, 1909.

Gujarati, Ganeshdas. 'Banarasi Jiwan ki Ek Saras Jhanki: Nadia Kinare'. *Aj* (12 April 1959).

Gutschow, Niels. *Benares: The Sacred Landscape of Varanasi.* Fellbach: Axel Menges, 2006.

Harishankar. *Kashi Ke Ghat: Kalatmak Evam Sanskritik Adhyayan.* Varanasi: Vishwavidyalaya Prakashan, 1996.

Havell, E.B. *Benares, the Sacred City: Sketches of Hindu Life and Religion.* London: Blackie & Son, 1905; reprint edn., Varanasi: Vishwavidyalaya Prakashan, 1990.

Heber, Reginald. *Narrative of a journey through the upper provinces of India.* 2 vols. London: John Murray, 1861.

Hertel, Bradley R. and Cynthia Ann Humes, eds. *Living Banaras: Hindu Religion in Cultural Context.* Albany: State University of New York Press; reprint edn., New Delhi: Manohar, 1998.

Jayakar, Pupul. 'Naksha Bandhas of Banaras'. *Journal of Indian Textile History,* 22, no. 7 (1967).

Kapera, Constance. *The Worship of Kali in Banaras: An Inquiry.* Delhi: Motilal Banarsidass, 1966.

Kapur, Anuradha. 'Actors, Pilgrims, Kings and Gods: The Ramlila at Ramnagar'. *Contributions to Indian Sociology* (New Series) 19, no. 1 (1985), 57–74.

Kennedy, James. *Life and Work in Benares and Kumaon.* New York: Cassell & Co., 1895.

Kumar, Nita. 'Mud, Water and Gamchcha: The Dying World of Benaras Akharas.' *India Magazine* (1985).

——. 'Open Space and Free Time: Pleasure for the People of Benaras'. *Contributions to Indian Sociology,* 20, no. 1 (1986), 41–60.

——. 'The Mazars of Benaras: A New Perspective on the City's Sacred Geography'. *National Geographical Journal of India,* 33, no. 3 (1987), 263–267.

——. *The Artisans of Banaras: Popular Culture and Identity, 1880-1986.* Princeton: Princeton University Press, 1988.

Lannoy, Richard. *Benaras Seen from Within.* Seattle: University of Washington Press, 1999.

——. *Benares, A World Within A World: The Microcosm of Kashi Yesterday and Today.* Varanasi: Indica Books, 2002.

Marg. [Special issue, in part, on Banaras.] Vol. 57, no. 2 (December 2005).

Mcleod, Norman. *Days in North India.* Philadelphia: J.B. Lippincott & Co., 1895.

Michel, George and Rana P.B. Singh, eds. *Banaras: The City Revealed.* Photographs by Clare Arni. Mumbai: Marg Publications, 2005.

Misra, Baldevprasad. 'Kashi ke Kuchh Prasidha Mele'. *Hans* (1933): 74.

Mukherjee, Viswanath. 'Banarasi Picnic'. *Aj* (2 February 1956).

Narain, A.K. and Lallanji Gopal, eds. *Introducing Varanasi.* Varanasi: Banaras Hindu University, 1969.

Nevill, H.R. *Benares: A Gazetteer.* [*District Gazetteers of the United Provinces of Agra and Oudh,* Vol. XXVI.] Allahabad: Government Press, 1909.

Pandey, Raj Bali. *Varanasi: The Heart of Hinduism.* Varanasi: Orient Publishers, 1969.

Parry, Jonathan P. *Death in Banaras.* Cambridge: Cambridge University Press, 1994.

Prinsep, James. *Benaras, Illustrated in a Series of Drawings.* 3 vols. London, 1831; new edn., with 'James Prinsep and Benares', by O.P. Kejariwal. Benares: Pilgrims Publishers, 2009.

Saraswati, Baidyanath. *Kashi: Myth and Reality of a Classical Cultural Tradition.* Shimla: Indian Institute of Advanced Study, 1975.

Schechner, Richard and Linda Hess. 'The Ramlila of Ramnagar'. *Drama Review,* 21 (September 1977), 51–82.

Sharma, Kedar. 'Banaras aur Banarasi'. *Aj* (6 April 1958).

Sherring, M.A. *The Sacred City of the Hindus: An Account of Benares in Ancient and Modern Times.* London: Trubner & Co., 1868. Reprinted as *Benares: The Sacred City of the Hindus in Ancient and Modern Times.* Delhi: B.R. Publishing Corporation, 1975.

Sherring, M.A. *Hindu Tribes and Castes as represented in Benaras.* Calcutta: Thacker, Spink & Co., 1872.

Singh, R.L. and Rana P.B. Singh. 'Cognizing Urban Landscape of Varanasi: A Note on Cultural Synthesis'. *The National Geographic Journal of India,* 26, nos. 3 & 4 (1980), 113–123.

Singh, Rana P.B. *Cultural Landscapes and the Lifeworld: Literary Images of Benares.* New Delhi: Indica, 2004.

————. *Banaras: Making of India's Heritage City.* Newcastle upon Tyne: Cambridge Scholars Publishing, 2009.

————, ed. *Banaras: Cosmic Order, Sacred City, Hindu Traditions.* Varanasi: Tara Book Agency on behalf of Varanasi Studies Foundation, 1993.

Sinha, Surajit and Baidyanth Saraswati. *Ascetics of Kashi, an Anthropological Explanation.* Varanasi: N.K. Bose Memorial Foundation, 1978.

Sukul, Kuber Nath. *Varanasi Down the Ages.* Patna: Kameshwar Nath Sukul, 1974.

Upadhyay, Baikuntha Nath. *Ramnagar ki Ramlila aur Uske Patra. Aj* (2 October 1976).

Vidyarthi, L.P., B.N. Saraswati, and Makan Jha. *The Sacred Complex of Kashi.* Delhi: Concept Publishing Co., 1979.

II BANGALORE

De, Aditi, ed. *Multiple City: Writings on Bangalore.* New Delhi: Penguin Books, 2008.

Hasan, M. Fazlul. *Bangalore Through the Centuries.* Bangalore: Historical Publishers, 1970.

Heitzman, James. 'Corporate Strategy and Planning in the Science City: Bangalore as 'Silicon Valley'?'. *Economic and Political Weekly,* 34, no. 5 (30 January–5 February 1999), PE2-PE11.

————. 'Becoming Silicon Valley'. *Seminar,* no. 503 (July 2001), 40–48.

————. *Network City: Planning the Information City in Bangalore.* New Delhi: Oxford University Press, 2004.

Issar, T.P. *The City Beautiful: A Celebration of the Architectural Heritage and City Aesthetics of Bangalore.* Bangalore: Bangalore Urban Arts Commission, 1988.

Kodkani, Jayanth and R. Edwin Sudhir, eds. *Beantown Boomtown: Bangalore in the World of Words.* New Delhi: Rupa, 2007.

Manor, James. *Power, Poverty and Poison: Disaster and Response in an Indian City.* New Delhi: Sage Publications, 1993.

Nair, Janaki. *The Promise of the Metropolis: Bangalore's Twentieth Century.* New Delhi: Oxford University Press, 2005.

Pani, Narendar, Sindhu Radhakrishna, and Kishor G. Bhat, eds. *Bengaluru, Bangalore, Bengaluru: Imaginations and Their Times*. New Delhi: Sage Publications, 2010.

Pott, Janet, Elizabeth Stanley, and Romola Chatterjee. *Old Bungalows in Bangalore, South India*. London: Pott, 1977.

Prakasha Rao, V.L.S. and V.K. Tewari. *The Structure of an Indian Metropolis: A Study of Bangalore*. New Delhi: Allied, 1979.

Srinivas, Smriti. 'On the religious imagination of the city'. *Seminar*, no. 445 (September 1996), 43–47.

———. *Landscapes of Urban Memory: The Sacred and the Civic in India's High-Tech City*. Minneapolis: University of Minnesota Press, 2001.

Vyasulu, Vinod and Amulya Kumar N. Reddy, eds. *Essays on Bangalore*. Bangalore: Karnataka State Council for Science and Technology, 1985.

III BOMBAY/MUMBAI

Albuquerque, Teresa. *Bombay: A History*. New Delhi & Bombay: Rashna & Co., 1992.

Anon. *Life in Bombay, and the Neighbouring Out-Stations*. London: Richard Bently, 1852.

Appadurai, Arjun. 'Spectral Housing and Urban Cleaning: Notes on Millennial Mumbai'. *Public Culture*, 12, no. 3 (2000), 627–651.

Attwood, D.W., M. Israel, and N.K. Wagle, eds. *City, Countryside and Society in Maharashtra*. Toronto: Center for South Asian Studies, University of Toronto, 1988.

Bhojani, Namas and Arun Katiyar. *Bombay: A Contemporary Account of Mumbai*. New Delhi: HarperCollins, 1996.

Boo, Katharine. *Behind the Beautiful Forevers: Life, Death, and Hope in a Mumbai Undercity*. New York: Random House, 2012.

Burnell, John, fl. 1712. *Bombay in the days of Queen Anne, being an account of the settlement written by John Burnell, with an introd. and notes by Samuel T. Sheppard*. London: Hakluyt Society, 1933.

Boman-Behram, B.K. and A.N. Confectioner. *The Decline of Bombay*. Bombay: [no publisher], 1969.

Chopra, Preeti. *A Joint Enterprise: Indian Elites and the Making of British Bombay*. Minneapolis: University of Minnesota Press, 2011.

Clutterbuck, George W. [Rev.]. *In India: the land of famine and of plague: or, Bombay the beautiful, the first city of India: with incidents and experiences of pioneer mission work in western India; illustrative of the country, customs and creeds*. 3rd edn. London: Ideal Publishing Union, 1897.

Correa, Charles. *The New Landscape*. Bombay: The Book Society of India, 1985.

Cunha, J. Gerson da. *Origin of Bombay*. Bombay: Society's Library, 1900.

David, M.D. *History of Bombay, 1661-1708*. Bombay: University of Bombay, 1973.

David, M.D. *Bombay, the City of Dreams: A History of the First City in India*. Bombay: Himalaya Publishing House, 1995.

Dhasal, Namdeo. *Poet of the Underworld: Poems 1972–2006*. Selected, introduced and trans. from Marathi by Dilip Chitre. With photographs by Henning Stegmuller. Chennai: Navayana, 2007.

D'Monte, Darryl. *Ripping the Fabric: The Decline of Mumbai and Its Mills*. New Delhi: Oxford University Press, 2002.

Dossal, Mariam. *Imperial Designs and Indian Realities: The Planning of Bombay City, 1845–1875*. Bombay: Oxford University Press, 1991.

Douglas, James. *Bombay and Western India*. London: Sampson Low, Morston & Co., 1893.

Dwivedi, Sharada and Rahul Mehrotra. *Bombay: The Cities Within*. Bombay: India Book House, 1995.

Edwardes, S.M. *The Gazetteer of Bombay City and Island*, 3 vols. Bombay: Times of India Press, 1909–1910.

———. *The Rise of Bombay: A Retrospect*. Bombay: Times of India Press, 1902. [Reprinted from Vol. X of the Census of India Series 1901.]

———. *By-Ways of Bombay*. Illustrations by M.V. Dhurandhar. Bombay: D.B. Taraporevala Sons & Co., 1912.

Faleiro, Sonia. *Beautiful Thing: Inside the Secret World of Bombay's Dance Bars*. New Delhi: Penguin Books, 2010.

Farooqui, Amar. *Opium City: The Making of Early Victorian Bombay*. New Delhi: Three Essays Collective, 2006.

Gadgil, Gangadhar. *Crazy Bombay*. Illustrated by R.K. Laxman. Bombay: Popular Prakashan, 1991.

Ganesh, Kamala, Usha Thakkar, and Gita Chadha, eds. *Zero Point Bombay: In and Around Horniman Circle*. New Delhi: Roli Books, 2008.

Hansen, Thomas Blom. *Wages of Violence: Naming and Identity in Postcolonial Bombay*. Princeton: Princeton University Press, 2001.

Ingram, Alexander Robertson. *The Gateway to India; the story of Methwold and Bombay*. London: Oxford University Press, 1938.

Karkaria, R.P., ed. *Charm of Bombay: An Anthology of writings in praise of the First City in India*. Foreword by H.E. Lord Willingdon, Governor of Bombay. Bombay: D.B. Taraporevala, 1915.

Kosambi, Meera. *Bombay in Transition: The Growth and Social Ecology of a Colonial City*. Stockholm: Almqvist & Wiksell International, 1986.

Mark, Mary Ellen. *Falkland Road*. New York: Knopf, 1981; reprinted as *Falkland Road: Prostitutes of Bombay* (London: Steidl, 2008).

Masselos, Jim. *The City in Action: Bombay Struggles for Power*. New Delhi: Oxford University Press, 2007.

Mazumdar, Ranjani. *Bombay Cinema: An Archive of the City*. Minneapolis: University of Minnesota Press, 2007; New Delhi: Permanent Black, 2009.

Mehta, Suketu. *Maximum City: Bombay Lost and Found*. New York: Vintage, 2005.

Menon, Meena and Neera Adarkar. *One Hundred Years, One Hundred Voices: The Millworkers of Girangaon, An Oral History*. Introduction by Rajnarayan Chandavarkar. Kolkata: Seagull Books, 2004.

Padgaonkar, Dileep. *When Bombay Burned*. New Delhi: UBSPD, 1993.

Patwardhan, Sudhir. *Citing the City*. Mumbai: Sakshi Gallery, 2007.

Patel, Sujata and Alice Thorner, eds. *Bombay: Metaphor for Modern India*. Bombay: Oxford University Press, 1996.

————, eds. *Bombay: Mosaic of Modern Culture*. Bombay: Oxford University Press, 1997.

Patel, Sujata and Jim Masselos, eds. *Bombay and Mumbai: The City in Transition*. New Delhi: Oxford University Press, 2003.

Pinto, Jerry and Naresh Fernandes, eds. *Bombay, meri jaan: Writings on Mumbai*. New Delhi: Penguin, 2003.

Prakash, Gyan. *Mumbai Fables: A History of an Enchanted City*. Princeton: Princeton University Press, 2011; New Delhi: HarperCollins, 2011.

Proeschel, Diana C. and Saroj Merani. *Flavours: A Select Guide to Eateries in Bombay*. Cartoons by Mario Miranda. Bombay: Perennial Press, 1988.

Ramana, M.V. *Bombing Bombay: Effects of Nuclear Weapons and a Case Study of a Hypothetical Explosion*. IPPNW Global Health Watch Report Number 3. Cambridge, Mass: International Physicians for the Prevention of Nuclear War, 1999.

Rohatgi, Pauline, Pheroza Godrej, and Rahul Mehrotra. *Bombay to Mumbai: Changing Perspectives*. Mumbai: Marg Publications, 1997.

Seabrook, Jeremy. *Life and Labour in a Bombay Slum*. London: Quartet Books, 1987.

Sharma, Kalpana. *Rediscovering Dharavi: Stories from Asia's Largest Slum*. New Delhi: Penguin Books, 2000.

Shaw, Annapurna. *The Making of Navi Mumbai*. Hyderabad: Orient Longman, 2004.

Sheppard, Samuel. *Bombay*. Bombay: Times of India Press, 1932.

Stamp, Gavin. 'Victorian Bombay: Urbs Prima in Indis'. *Art and Archaeology Papers*, no. 11 (June 1977).

Tambe, Ashwini. *Codes of Misconduct: Regulating Prostitution in Late Colonial Bombay*. Minneapolis: University of Minnesota Press, 2009.

Tindall, Gillian. *City of Gold: The Biography of Bombay*. London: Temple Smith, 1982.

Tyrewala, Altaf. *Mumbai Noir*. New York: Akashic Books, 2012.

Wacha, D.E. *Shells from the Sands of Bombay, 1860–1875*. Bombay: Bombay Chronicle Press, 1920.

IV CALCUTTA/KOLKATA

Banerjee, Sumanta. *The Parlour and the Street: Elite and Popular Culture in Nineteenth Century Calcutta*. Calcutta: Seagull Books, 1989.

————. *Crime and Urbanization: Calcutta in the Nineteenth Century*. New Delhi: Tulika Books, 2006.

Basak, G.D. 'Kalighat and Calcutta'. *Calcutta Review*, 92 (1891), 309–322.

Banerjea, Dhrubajyoti. *European Calcutta: Images and Recollections of a Bygone Era*. New Delhi: UBSPD, 2005.

Banerjee, Samik. *Calcutta 200 years: A Tollygunge Club Perspective*, ed. Narendra Kumar Nayak. Calcutta: The Club, 1981.

Bialobrzeski, Peter, ed. *Calcutta: Chitpur Road neighborhoods—Kolkata Heritage Photo Project*. Translations by Melissa Hause & Barbara Holle. Ostfildern, Germany: H. Cantz, 2008.

Biswas, Anil Ranjan. *Calcutta and Calcuttans: From Dihi to Megalopolis*. Calcutta: Firma KLM, 1992.

Blechynden, Kathleen. *Calcutta, Past and Present*. London: Thacker, 1905; reprint edn., New Delhi: Sundeep Prakashan, 2003; also new edn., ed. N.R. Ray, Calcutta: General Printers and Publishers, 1978.

Bose, Nirmal Kumar. 'Modern Bengal'. *Man in India* (December 1958), 229–295.

———. 'Social and Cultural Life in Calcutta'. *Geographical Review of India* (December 1958), 1–46.

———. 'Calcutta: Premature Metropolis'. *Scientific American* (Sept. 1965), 91–102.

———. *Calcutta 1964: A Social Survey*. Bombay: Lalvani Publishing House, 1968.

Busteed, H.E. *Echoes from Old Calcutta, Being Chiefly Reminiscences of the Days of Warren Hastings, Francis, and Impey*. 4th edn., London: W. Thacker & Co., 1908 [1897].

The Calcutta Psyche, special issue of *India International Centre Quarterly* 17, nos. 3–4 (Winter 1990–91).

Chakrabarti, Hiren, ed. *Bengal Past and Present* 109, nos. 208–209 [Calcutta Tercentenary Special 1990]. Calcutta: Calcutta Historical Society, 1990.

Chaudhuri, Nirad. *Autobiography of an Unknown Indian*. London: Macmillan, 1951; reprint edn., Berkeley: University of California Press, 1968.

Chaudhuri, Pradip and Abhijit Mukherjee. *Calcutta: People and Empire: Gleanings from Old Journals*. Introduction by Nemai Sadhan Bose. Calcutta: India Book Exchange, 1975.

Chaudhuri, Sukanta, ed. *Calcutta: The Living City*. 2 vols. Calcutta: Oxford University Press, 1990.

Choudhury, Ranabira Ray. *Calcutta: A Hundred Years Ago*. Bombay: Nachiketa Publications, 1988.

Cotton, H. E. A. *Calcutta, Old and New: A Historical and Descriptive Handbook to the City*. Calcutta: W. Newman, 1907; 2nd edn., ed. N.R. Ray (Calcutta: General Printers and Publishers, 1980).

Das, Soumitra and Christopher Taylor. *White and Black: Journey to the Centre of Imperial Calcutta*. With foreword by Olaf van Cleef. New Delhi: Niyogi Books, 2009.

Das, Suranjan and Jayanta K. Ray. *The Goondas: Towards a Reconstruction of the Calcutta Underworld*. Calcutta: Firma KLM, 1996.

Dasgupta, Minakshie, Bunny Gupta, and Jaya Chaliha. *The Calcutta Cookbook: a treasury of over 200 recipes from pavement to palace*. Illustrations by Utpal Basu. New Delhi: Penguin Books, 2005.

Datta, Partho. 'Celebrating Calcutta', *Urban History*, 19 (April, 1992), 84–98.

Dasgupta, Subhoranjan and Sudeshna Chakravarty, eds. and trans. *Bengali Poems on Calcutta*. Calcutta: Writers Workshop, 1972. With work by 62 poets & sketches by Paritosh Sen & Desmond Doig.

Deb, Binaya Krishna. *The Early History and Growth of Calcutta*. Calcutta: Romesh Chandra Ghose, 1905; reprint edn., Calcutta: Riddhi, 1977.

Doig, Desmond. *Calcutta, An Artist's Impression*. Calcutta: *Statesman*, 1968.

Douglas, Mick. *Tramjatra: Imagining Melbourne and Kolkata by Tramways*. New Delhi: Yoda Press; Melbourne: RMIT Press, 2005.

Dutta, Krishna. *Caclutta: A Cultural and Literary History*. Foreword by Anita Desai. New Delhi: Roli Books/Lotus Collections, 2003.

Emanuel, Louis. *Jottings and Recollections of a Bengal "Qui Hye!"* London: James Blackwood & Co., n.d.

Fruzzetti, Lina and Ákos Östör, eds. *Calcutta Conversations*. New Delhi: DC Publishers, Chronicle Books, 2003.

Gangopadhyay, Sunil. *City of Memories: Selected Poems*. Trans. Kalyan Ray and Bonnie MacDougall. Foreword by Allen Ginsberg. New Delhi: Viking, 1991.

Ganguly, Narendranath. *The Calcutta Cricket Club, Its Origin and Development*. Calcutta: N. Ganguly, 1871.

Grass, Gunter. *Show Your Tongue*. Trans. John E. Woods. London: Secker & Warburg, 1989.

Hardgrove, Anne. *Community and Public Culture: The Marwaris in Calcutta, 1897–1997*. New York: Columbia University Press, 2004.

Hutnyk, John. *The Rumour of Calcutta: Tourism, Charity, and the Poverty of Representation*. London: Zed Books, 1996.

———. 'Calcutta'. In Vinay Lal and Ashis Nandy, eds., *The Future of Knowledge and Culture: A Dictionary for the Twenty-first Century*. Delhi: Viking/Penguin, 2005.

Jetwings [the magazine of Jet Airways]. Special issue on Kolkata 5, no. 12 (December 2005).

Kaviraj, Sudipta. 'Filth and the Public Sphere: Concepts and Practices about Space in Calcutta'. *Public Culture*, 24, no. 1 (1997), 83–114.

———. 'The Art of Despair: The Sense of the City in Modern Bengali Poetry'. *Evam: Forum on Indian Representation*, 2, nos. 1–2 (2003), 228–47.

Kiernan, Thomas Patrick. *Calcutta Full Frame: Photographs in Black and White*. Kolkata: Earthcare Books, 2009.

Lapierre, Dominique. *The City of Joy*. New York: Warner Books, 1991 [1985].

Long, (Rev.) James. *Calcutta and Its Neighbourhood: History of people and localities from 1670 to 1837*. Reprint edn., Calcutta: Indian Publications, 1974.

Long, (Rev.) James. *Calcutta in Olden Times: Its Localities and Its People.* 1864. Reprint edn., Calcutta: Granthan, 1974 [1864].

Losty, J.P. *Calcutta, City of Palaces: A Survey of the City in the Days of the East India Company, 1690-1858.* London: The British Library; New Delhi: Arnold Publishers, 1990.

Martin, David William. *The Changing Face of Calcutta.* Delhi: Vikas Publishing House, 1997.

Massey, Montague. *Recollections of Calcutta for over half a century.* Calcutta, 1916; reprint edn., Calcutta: Bibhash Gupta, Microform Publication Division, 1986.

Mitra, Asok. *Calcutta, India's City.* Calcutta: New Age Publishers, 1963.

Moorhouse, Geoffrey. *Calcutta.* New York: Holt, Rinehart and Winston, 1985 [1971].

Mukherjee, S.N. *Calcutta: Myths and Histories.* Calcutta: Subarnarekha, 1977.

Mukherjee, Samir. *Calcutta: A City Lived In and Remembered.* Illustrations by Debashish Deb. Calcutta: Sampark Publishing Company, 2011.

Nair, Thankappan P. *A History of Calcutta's Streets.* Tercentenary History of Calcutta, vol. 2. Calcutta: Firma KLM, 1987.

———., ed. *Calcutta Bevy: a collection of rare poems.* Calcutta: Punthi Pustak, 1989.

———. *Calcutta in the 17th century.* Tercentenary History of Calcutta, vol. 1. Calcutta: Firma KLM, 1986.

———., ed. *Calcutta in the 18th century: Impressions of Travellers.* Calcutta: Firma KLM, 1984.

———., ed. *Calcutta in the 19th century: Company's Days.* Calcutta: Firma KLM, 1989.

Pal, Pratapaditya, ed. *Changing Visions, Lasting Images: Calcutta Through 300 Years.* Bombay: Marg Publications, 1990.

Pearson, Roger. *Eastern Interlude: A Social History of the European Community in Calcutta.* Washington, D.C.: Scott-Townsend Publishers, 1977 [1954].

Ray, Nishit R. *Calcutta: The Profile of a City.* Calcutta: K.P. Bagchi & Co., 1986.

Ray, Satyajit. *Jakhan Chhoto Chilam* [When I was a Child]. Calcutta: Ananda Publishers, 1981.

Roy, Ananya. *City requiem, Calcutta: Gender and the Politics of Poverty.* Minneapolis: University of Minnesota Press, 2003.

Roy, B.V. *Old Calcutta Cameos.* Foreword by Amal Home. Calcutta: S.K. Chatterjee, 1946.

Seth, Mesrovb Jacob. *Armenians in India, from the Earliest Times to the Present Day.* Calcutta: The author, 1937; reprint edn., New Delhi: Asian Educational Services, 1992.

Siddiqui, M.K.A., ed. *Aspects of Society and Culture in Calcutta.* Calcutta: Anthropological Survey of India, 1982.

Singh, Khushwant. *Kalighat to Calcutta, 1690-1990.* New Delhi: Lustre Press, 1990.

Singh, Raghubir. *Calcutta: The Home and the Street.* Intro. by R.P. Gupta. New York: Thames & Hudson, 1988.

Sinha, Kaliprasanna. *The Observant Owl: Hootum's Vigenettes of Nineteenth-century Calcutta.* Trans. Swarup Roy. Foreword by Partha Chatterjee. New Delhi: Black Kite/Permanent Black, 2008.

Sinha, Pradip. *Calcutta in Urban History.* Calcutta: Firma KLM, 1978.

———. ed. *The Urban Experience, Calcutta: essays in honour of Professor Nisith R. Ray.* Calcutta: Riddhi-India, [1987].

Solomon, Sally. *Hooghly Tales: Stories of Growing Up in Calcutta under the Raj.* Illustrations by Alexandra Solomon Angel. London: David Ashley Publishing, 1998.

Suraiya, Jug. *Rickshaw Ragtime: Calcutta Remembered.* Illustrations by Gopi Gajwani. New Delhi: Penguin, 1993.

Sykes, Laura, ed. and comp. *Calcutta Through British Eyes, 1690-1990.* New York: Oxford University Press, 1992.

The Statesman. Calcutta Tercentenary Issue (February 1990).

Taylor, Joanne. *The Forgotten Palaces of Calcutta.* New Delhi: Niyogi Books, 2006; rev. edn., 2011.

V CHANDIGARH

Barbel, Hogner. *Chandigarh living with Le Corbusier.* With contributions by Clemens Kroll, Arthur Rüegg, Arno Lederer and a conversation with M.N. Sharma. Berlin: Jovis Verlag, 2010.

Crane, David. 'Chandigarh Reconsidered'. *American Institute of Architects Journal,* 33 (May 1960), 32–39.

D'Souza, Victor Salvadore. *Social Structure of a Planned City, Chandigarh.* Bombay: Orient Longmans, 1968.

Evenson, Norman. *Chandigarh.* Berkeley: University of California Press, 1966.

———. 'Chandigarh: Monumental Sculpture' in H. Wentworth Eldredge, ed., *World Capitals: Toward Guided Urbanization,* 391–429. New York: Anchor Press/Doubleday, 1975.

Kalia, Ravi. *Chandigarh: The Making of an Indian City.* New Delhi: Oxford University Press, 1999; previous edition published as *Chandigarh: In Search of an Identity* (Carbondale: Southern Illinois University Press, 1987).

Prakash, Vikramaditya. *Chandigarh's Le Corbusier: The Struggle for Modernity in Postcolonial India.* Seattle & London: University of Washington Press, 2002.

Panjabi, R.M. 'Chandigarh: India's Newest City'. *The Geographical Magazine,* 31, no. 8 (1958), 401–414.

Sarin, Madhu. *Urban Planning in the Third World: The Chandigarh Experience.* London: Mansell Publishing, 1982.

Ahmad, Nazir. *The Bride's Mirror: A Tale of Life in Delhi a Hundred Years Ago.* Trans. G.E. Ward. Afterword by Frances W. Pritchett. Delhi: Permanent Black, 2001 [1903].

Andrews, C.F. *Zaka Ullah of Delhi.* With Introductions by Mushirul Hasan & Margit Pernau. New Delhi: Oxford University Press, 2003 [1929].

Baker, Herbert. 'The New Delhi'. *Journal of the Royal Society of Arts,* 74, no. 3841 (July 1926), 772–93.

Banerjee, Sarnath. *Corridor: A Graphic Novel.* Delhi: Penguin Books, 2004.

Barr, Frederick. *Imperial City: The Story of Delhi and Her Royal Rulers.* Shimla: Times Press, 1902.

Barton, G. and L. Malone. *Old Delhi: Ten Easy Walks.* Delhi: Rupa, 1988.

Blake, Stephen P. *Shahjahanabad: The Sovereign City in Mughal India, 1639-1739.* Cambridge: Cambridge University Press, 1991.

Chaudhuri, D.N. *Delhi: Light, Shades, Shadows.* New Delhi: Niyogi Offset Books, 2005.

Dalrymple, William. *City of Djinns: A Year in Delhi.* Delhi: Penguin, 1993.

Dayal, Maya, ed. *Celebrating Delhi.* New Delhi: Penguin Viking & Ravi Dayal, 2010.

The Delhi Omnibus, with an Introduction by Narayani Gupta. Delhi: Oxford University Press, 2002. [Comprises: Percival Spear, *Delhi: A Historical Sketch*; Percival Spear, *Twilight of the Mughals: Studies in Late Mughal Delhi*; Narayani Gupta: *Delhi Between Two Empires 1803-1931: Society, Government and Urban Growth*; and R.E. Frykenberg, ed., *Delhi Through the Ages: Selected Essays in Urban History, Culture and Society.*]

Dupont, Veronique, Emma Tarlo, and Denis Vidal, eds. *Delhi: Urban Space and Human Destinies.* Delhi: Manohar; Paris: Institut de Recherche pour le Development, 2000.

Ehlers, Eckart and Thomas Krafft, eds. *Shahjahanabad/Old Delhi: Tradition and Colonial Change.* Stuttgart: Franz Steiner Verlag, 1993; 2nd edn., New Delhi: Manohar Publishers, 2003.

Fanshawe, H.C. *Delhi: Past and Present.* London: John Murray, 1902.

Farooqui, Mahmood, compiler and trans. *Beseiged: Voices from Delhi, 1857.* New Delhi: Viking/Penguin, 2010.

Frykenberg, F.E., ed. *Delhi Through the Ages: Selected Essays in Urban History, Culture and Society.* Delhi: Oxford University Press, 1981. [Included in the *Delhi Omnibus,* Delhi: Oxford University Press, 1992.]

Ghosh, B. 'Successive Delhis: From the Sensuous architecture of the past to the insignificance and inappropriateness of the present'. *Design* 24, no 3 (1980), 25–36.

Ghosh, Vishwajyoti. *Delhi Calm.* New Delhi: HarperCollins, 2010.

Gupta, Narayani. *Delhi Between Two Empires 1803-1931: Society, Government and Urban Growth*. Delhi: Oxford University Press, 1981.

————. 'From Kingsway to Rajpath—the Democratization of Lutyens' New Delhi', in C. Asher and T.R. Metcalf, eds. *Perceptions of South Asia's Visual Past*. New Delhi: Oxford and IBH, 1994.

————. *Delhi Between Two Empires 1803-1931: Society, Government and Urban Growth*. New Delhi: Oxford University Press, 1981.

Havell, E.B. 'The Building of the New Delhi'. *Journal of the East India Association*, 4 (1913), 1–30.

Hearn, G.R. *Seven Cities of Delhi: A Description and History*. Calcutta: Thacker and Spink, 1909.

Irving, Robert Grant. *Indian Summer: Lutyens, Baker and Imperial Delhi*. New Haven: Yale University Press, 1981.

Jhabvala, C.S.H. *Delhi: Stones and Streets*. Delhi: Ravi Dayal, 1990.

Kaul, H.K., compiler and ed. *Historic Delhi: An Anthology*. New Delhi: Oxford University Press, 1985.

Kumar, Sunil. *The Present in Delhi's Pasts*. New Delhi: Three Essays Press, 2002.

Lal, Ranjit. *Birds of Delhi*. Delhi: Oxford University Press, 2003.

Lewis, Karoki and Charles Lewis. *Delhi's Historic Villages*. Delhi: Ravi Dayal, 1997.

————. *Mehrauli: A View from the Qutb*. Delhi: HarperCollins, 2002.

Marg. [Special issue on Delhi.] Vol. 56, no. 3 (March 2005).

Masselos, Jim and Narayani Gupta. *Beato's Delhi 1858, 1997*. New Delhi: Ravi Dayal Publisher, 2000; republished as *Beato's Delhi: 1857 and Beyond*, New Delhi: Viking/Penguin, 2011.

Miller, Sam. *Delhi: Adventures in a Megacity*. New York: St. Martin's Press, 2009.

Mitchell, Maurice. *Learning from Delhi: Dispersed Initiatives in Changing Urban Landscapes*. Trans. Shamoon Patwari and Bo Tang. Surrey: Ashgate Publishing, 2010.

Naim, C.M. 'Ghalib's Delhi: A Shamelessly Revisionist Look at Two Popular Metaphors (for Ralph Russell)'. *Annual of Urdu Studies*, 18 (2003), 3–24.

Sarda, Shveta et al. *Trickster City: Writings from the Belly of the Metropolis*. New Delhi: Viking/Penguin, 2010.

Sawhney, Hirsh, ed. *Delhi Noir*. New York: Akashic Books, 2009; reprint edn., New Delhi: HarperCollins, 2010.

Seminar, no. 515: *First City: A Symposium on Remembering Delhi*. July 2002.

Sharp, Henry Sir. *Delhi: Its Story and Buildings*. Oxford: Humphrey Milford, Oxford University Press, 1921; 2nd edn., 1928.

Singh, Balmiki Prasad and Pavan K. Varma. *The Millennium Book on Delhi*. Delhi: Oxford University Press, 2001.

Singh, Patwant. *Of Dream and Demons: An Indian Memoir*. Delhi, 1994.

Spear, Percival. *Delhi: A Historical Sketch*. Bombay: Oxford University Press, 1945. [Included in the *Delhi Omnibus*, Delhi: Oxford University Press, 1992.]

————. *Twilight of the Mughals: Studies in Late Mughal India*. Cambridge: Cambridge University Press, 1951. [Included in the *Delhi Omnibus*, Delhi: Oxford University Press, 1992.]

Spear, Percival and Margaret. *India Remembered*. 2nd rev. edn., New Delhi: Orient Blackswan, 2010 [1981].

Upadhyaya, R.D. 'Delhi As It was 100 Years Ago'. *Modern Review*, 1 (March 1965).

Varma, Pavan K. and Sondeep Shanker. *Mansions at Dusk: The Havelis of Old Delhi*. Delhi: Spantech, 1992.

VII HYDERABAD

Banagiri, Vanaja, ed. *Hyderabad Hazir Hai: Writings from the City of Nizams*. New Delhi: Rupa, 2009.

Imam, Syeda, ed. *The Untold Charminar: Writings on Hyderabad*. New Delhi: Penguin Books, 2008.

Jaisi, Sidq. *The Nocturnal Court: The Life of a Prince of Hyderabad*. Trans. Narendra Luther. New Delhi: Oxford University Press, 2004.

Khalidi, Omar, ed. *Hyderabad, After the Fall*. Wichita, Kansas: Hyderabad Historical Society, 1988.

———, ed. *Memoirs of Cyril Jones: People, Society and Railways in Hyderabad*. New Delhi: Manohar, 1991.

Luther, Narendra. *Hyderabad: A Biography*. New Delhi: Oxford University Press, 2006.

Lynton, Harriet Ronken and Mohini Rajan. *The Days of the Beloved*. Berkeley: University of California Press, 1974.

Naidu, Ratna. *Old Cities, New Predicaments: A Study of Hyderabad*. New Delhi: Sage, 1991.

VIII LUCKNOW

Ali, Mrs. Meera Hasan. *Observations on the Mussalmans of India*. Edited with notes and an Introduction by W. Crooke. Reprint edn., Karachi: Oxford University Press, 1974 [1917].

Alli, Darogha Ubbas. *The Lucknow Album: Containing a Series of Fifty Photographic Views of Lucknow and Its Environs . . .* Calcutta: G.H. Rouse, Baptist Mission Press, 1874.

Dodgson, D.S. *General Views and Special Points of Interest of the City of Lucknow*. London: Day and Son, 1860.

Frayer, Joseph. *Recollections of my Life*. Edinburgh and London: William Blackwood and Sons, 1900.

Graff, Violette, ed. *Lucknow: Memories of a City*. New Delhi: Oxford University Press, 1997.

Hay, Sidney. *Historic Lucknow*. Illustrated by Enver Ahmed, and with an Introduction by Lord Hailey. Lucknow: Pioneer Press, 1939; reprint edn., New Delhi: Asian Educational Services, 1994.

Hilton, Edward Henry. *Hilton's Guide to Lucknow and the Residency*. Lucknow: Lucknow Publishing House, [1934].

Inglis, Julia Selina. *The Siege of Lucknow: A Diary*. London: A.D. Innes & Company, 1895.

Llewellyn-Jones, Rosie. *A Fatal Friendship: The Nawabs, the British, and the City of Lucknow*. New Delhi: Oxford University Press, 1985.

————, ed. *Lucknow: City of Illusion—The Alkazi Collection of Photography*. With essays by Peter Chelkowski and Neeta Das. New York: Prestel, 2006.

Llewellyn-Jones, Rosie and Ravi Kapoor. *Lucknow, Then and Now*. Mumbai: Marg Foundation, 2006.

The Lucknow Omnibus. New Delhi: Oxford University Press, 2001. [Comprises: Abdul Halim Sharar, *Lucknow: The Last Phase of an Oriental Culture*; Rosie Llewellyn-Jones, *A Fatal Friendship: The Nawab, the British, and the City of Lucknow*; and Veena Talwar Oldenburg, *The Making of Colonial Lucknow, 1856-1877*.]

Marg. [Special issue, in part, on Lucknow.] Vol. 55, no. 1 (September 2003).

Markel, Stephen, with Tushara Bindu Gude. *India's Fabled City: The Art of Courtly Lucknow*. Los Angeles: Los Angeles County Museum of Art; New York: DelMonico Books/Prestel, 2010.

Misra, Amaresh. *Lucknow, Fire of Grace: The Story of its Renaissance, Revolution and the Aftermath*. New Delhi: HarperCollins, 1998.

Mukherji, P.C. *Pictorial Lucknow*. Lucknow, 1883; reprint edn., New Delhi: Asian Educational Services, 2003.

Oldenburg, Veena Talwar. *The Making of Colonial Lucknow, 1856-1877*. Princeton: Princeton University Press, 1984.

————, ed. *Shaam-e-Awadh: Writings on Lucknow*. New Delhi: Penguin Books, 2007.

Parthasarathi, Vibodh and Pooja Kaul. 'The "missing" city'. *Seminar*, no. 445 (September 1996), 60–62.

Petievich, Carla. *Assembly of Rivals: Delhi, Lucknow and the Urdu Ghazal*. New Delhi: Manohar, 1992.

Rudra, Sudhir Kumar. *Our food: Lucknow City*. Allahabad: Government Central Press, 1944.

Ruswa, Muhammed Hadi. *Umrao Jan Ada: The Courtesan of Lucknow*. Trans. Khushwant Singh and M.A. Husaini. Calcutta: Orient Longman, 1961.

Sharar, Abdul Halim. *Lucknow: The Last Phase of an Oriental Culture*. Trans. E.S. Harcourt and Fakhir Hussain. Boulder, Colorado: Westview Press, 1976. [Also included in the *Lucknow Omnibus*.]

Siddiqi, W.H. *Lucknow: The Historic City*. New Delhi: Sandeep Prakashan, 2000.

Ståhlberg, Per. *Lucknow Daily: How a Hindi Newspaper Constructs Society*. Stockholm: Department of Social Anthropology, Stockholm University, 2001.

Tandon, Banmali. 'The Architecture of the Nawabs of Awadh Between 1722 and 1856'. Unpublished Ph.D. Dissertation, Cambridge University, 1978.

Barlow, Glyn. *The Story of Madras.* Madras: Oxford University Press, 1921.

Barnett, Steve. 'Urban is As Urban Does: Two Incidents on One Street in Madras City, South India'. *Urban Anthropologist,* 2, no. 2 (Fall 1973), 129–60.

Buchanan, Hamilton Francis. *A Journey from Madras through the Countries of Mysore, Canara and Malabar.* London, 1807; reprint edn., London: British Library, Historical Print Editions, 2011.

Dodwell, Henry. *Nabobs of Madras.* London: Williams & Norgate Ltd., 1926.

Kalpana, K. and Frank Schiffer. *Madras: The Architectural Heritage.* New Delhi: INTACH, 2003.

Lakshmi, C.S. *The Unhurried City: Writings on Chennai.* New Delhi: Penguin, 2003.

Lawson, Sir Charles. *Memories of Madras.* London: Swan Sonnenschein & Co., 1905.

Leighton, David. *Vicissitudes of Fort St. George.* Madras: Addison Press, 1902.

Lewandowski, Susan J. 'Changing Form and Function in the Colonial Port City in India: An Historical Analysis of Madurai and Madras'. *Modern Asian Studies,* 2, no. 2 (April 1977), 183–213.

————. 'The built environment and cultural symbolism in post-colonial Madras'. In *The City in Cultural Context,* eds. John A. Agnew, John Mercer, and David E. Sopher, 237–254. Boston: Allen & Unwin, 1984.

Love, Henry D. *Vestiges of Old Madras, 1640-1800.* 4 vols. London: Published for the Government of India, 1913; reprint edn., New Delhi: Asian Educational Services, 1997.

Madras Tercentenary Celebration Committee. *The Madras Tercentenary Commemoration Volume.* London: Oxford University Press, 1939; reprint edn., New Delhi: Asian Educational Services, 1994.

Marg. [Special issue, in part, on Chennai.] Vol. 57, no. 4 (June 2006).

Maitland, Julia. *Letters from Madras during the years 1836-1839.* Introduction, notes, and appendices by Alyson Price. Otley, West Yorkshire: Woodstock Books, 2003.

Muthiah, S. *Madras Discovered: A historical guide to looking around, supplemented with tales of 'Once upon a city'.* New Delhi: East-West Press, 1987.

————. *Tales of Old and New Madras: The Dalliance of Miss Mansell and 34 other stories of 350 years.* New Delhi: Affiliated East-West Press, 1989.

————. *Madras, its past and its present.* New Delhi: Affiliated East-West Press, 1995.

Nayudu, Krishnaswami W.S. *Old Madras.* Madras: Solden, 1965.

Seminar, no. 535: 'Changing Chennai: A symposium on the queen of the Coromandel' (March 2004).

Singer, M. 'The Great Tradition in a Metropolitan Center-Madras'. *Journal of American Folklore* (July–September 1958), 347–388.

Solomon, Sally. *Where Rivers Meet: Memories of Madras, 1948-1972.* Illustrations by Alexandra Solomon Angel. London: David Ashley Publishing, 2011.

Srinivasachari, C.S. *History of the City of Madras.* Madras: P. Varadachary & Co., 1939.

Venkatachalapathy, A.R. 'Street Smart in Chennai: The City in Popular Imagination', in his *In Those Days There Was No Coffee: Writings in Cultural History*, 59–72. New Delhi: Yoda Press, 2006.

Wheeler, J. Talboys. *Madras in the Olden Time, Being a History of the Presidency from the First Foundation.* 3 vols. Madras: Graves & Co. for J. Higginbotham, 1861–1862; reprint edn., New Delhi: B.R. Publishers, 1985.

X POONA/PUNE

Bapat, Meera. *Shanty Town and City: The Case of Poona.* Oxford: Pergamon, 1981.

Diddee, Jaymala. *Pune: Queen of the Deccan.* Pune: Elephant Design Pvt Ltd, 2000.

Elwin, Edward Fenton. *Thirty-four years in Poona City: being the history of the Panch Howds, Poona City Mission.* Oxford and London: A.R. Mowbray, 1911.

————. *Indian jottings, from ten year's experience in and around Poona city.* London: J. Murray, 1907.

Gokhale, Balkrishna Govind. *Poona in the Eighteenth Century: An Urban History.* Bombay: Oxford University Press, 1988.

Kosambi, Meera. *Bombay and Poona: A Socio-Ecological Study of Two Indian Cities, 1650-1900.* Stockholm: University of Stockholm, 1980.

Moledina, Muhammed Hashim and M.H. Merchant. *History of Poona Cantonment, 1818-1953.* Poona: Poona and Kirkee Cantonments' Citizens' Association, 1953.

Parasanisa, Dattatraya Balavanta. *Poona in Bygone Days.* Bombay: Times Press, 1921.

XI OTHER CITIES

Briggs, Henry G. *The Cities of Gujarashtra: Their Topography and History Illustrated.* Bombay: Times Press, 1849.

Chandrakanta. *A Street in Srinagar.* Trans. Manisha Chaudhary. New Delhi: Zubaan Books, 2010.

Datta, V.N. *Amritsar: Past and Present.* Amritsar: Municipal Committee, 1967.

Glover, William J. *Making Lahore Modern: Constructing and Imagining a Colonial City.* Minneapolis: University of Minnesota Press, 2008.

Harrison, J.B. 'Allahabad: A Sanitary History', in *The City in South Asia: Pre-Modern and Modern*, eds. Kenneth Ballhatchet and John Harrison, 167–95. London: Curzon Press; Atlantic Highlands, New Jersey: Humanities Press, 1980.

Haynes, Douglas E. *Rhetoric and Ritual in Colonial India: The Shaping of a Public Culture in Surat City, 1852-1928.* Berkeley: University of California Press, 1991.

Kalia, Ravi. *Bhubaneswar: From a Temple Town to a Capital City*. Carbondale: Southern Illinois University Press, 1994.

—. *Gandhinagar: Building National Identity in Postcolonial India*. Columbia, South Carolina: University of South Carolina Press, 2004.

Kanwar, Pamela. *Imperial Simla: The Political Culture of the Raj*. 2nd edn., New Delhi: Oxford University Press, 2003.

Mehrotra, Arvind Krishna, ed. *The Last Bungalow: Writings on Allahabad*. New Delhi: Penguin Books, 2006.

Roy, Ashim Kumar. *History of the Jaipur City*. Columbus, Missouri: South Asia Books, 1978.

Singh, Fauja, ed. *The City of Amritsar: An Introduction*. Patalia: Punjabi University, Publication Bureau, 1990.

Spodek, Howard. *Ahmedabad: Shock City of Twentieth-Century India*. Bloomington: Indiana University Press, 2011.

Tillotson, Giles. *Jaipur Nama: Tales from the Pink City*. New Delhi: Penguin, 2006.

Tillotson, Vibhuti and Giles Sachdev. *Building Jaipur: The Making of an Indian City*. London: Reaktion Books, 2004.

Yagnik, Achyut and Suchitra Sheth. *Ahmedabad: From Royal City to Megacity*. New Delhi: Penguin Books, 2010.

Notes on Contributors

U.R. Ananthamurthy is recognized as one of the leading writers of India and as one of the principal representatives of the 'Navya' [new] movement in Kannada literature. He was educated in a traditional Sanskrit school and grew up as a 'Gandhian socialist'; he went on to acquire a Ph.D. in English from Birmingham. He has published five novels, among them *Samskara*, ten volumes of essays, several plays, and translations of Rilke and Yeats. He has been honoured with numerous awards and accolades, including the Jnanpith Award, and he has served as President of the Sahitya Akademi, the National Academy of Literature.

Arjun Appadurai is one of the world's leading social theorists and anthropologists. He earned his Ph.D. at the University of Chicago and then taught at the University of Pennsylvania. He held chaired professorships at the University of Chicago, Yale University, and the New School, where he also served as Provost, before assuming his present position as Goddard Professor of Media, Culture, and Communication at New York University. He is a co-founder of the distinct and influential journal, *Public Culture*, author of *Modernity at Large* (1996), and editor of the path-breaking *The Social Life of Things* (Cambridge University Press, 1988).

Sir Edwin Arnold (1832–1904) was an English poet and journalist, as well as Principal of the Government Sanskrit College in Poona from 1856–63. *The Light of Asia*, published in 1879, played a significant role in introducing the life of the Buddha to Western readers, and in India itself it won Arnold considerable renown, even being translated into Hindi by the critic Ram Chandra Shukla.

Herbert Baker (1862–1946) was a prominent British architect and, with Edwin Lutyens, instrumental in giving shape to imperial New

Delhi. However, it is his work in South Africa, where he arrived at the age of thirty, which first earned him his reputation. He established an architectural practice in Cape Town and early in the twentieth century was invited to design the Government Buildings at Pretoria for the new Union of South Africa. Baker's buildings are also to be found in the United Kingdom, Kenya, and France (where he designed many cemeteries in the aftermath of World War I).

Bageshree S. writes frequently for the literary pages of the *Hindu* and has translated over 30 books for Tulika, a progressive independent publisher based in Delhi, from Kannada into English. She is also a contributor to *Gulabi Talkies and Other Stories* (Penguin, 2006).

D.K. Banerjee is a poet, critic, and translator who earned a Ph.D. in Comparative Literature from Harvard University with a dissertation on the influence of Dante on T.S. Eliot. He served as the contributing editor to *Metamorphoses* (Smith College) for many years. His translations from the Bengali were published in UNESCO's World Poetry Library Series as *The Delta Rising: An Anthology of Modern Bengali Poetry* (1990). His publications include *L'Antica Fiamma* (1995).

Sumanta Banerjee is a cultural historian with a particular research interest in popular culture, particularly of the colonial period. He is the author of many books, including *In the Wake of Naxalbari: A History of the Naxalite Movement in India* (1980), *The Parlour and the Streets: Elite and Popular Culture in Nineteenth Century Calcutta* (1990), and *Dangerous Outcast: The Prostitute in Nineteenth Century Bengal* (1998). He has written the foreword to Mahasweta Devi's *Bait: Four Stories* (Seagull Books, 2010).

Sarnath Banerjee is an Indian graphic novelist and artist who lives in Delhi. He was born in Calcutta in 1972 and studied at Goldsmiths College, London. He has published three graphic novels: *Corridor* (2004), *The Barn Owl's Wondrous Capers* (2007), and *The Harappa Files* (2011).

Ashok Banker is a Mumbai-based writer whose oeuvre extends to crime thrillers, fiction, and retellings of the Indian epics. A trilogy of crime novels—*The Iron Bra, Murder & Champagne*, and *Ten Dead Admen*, all published in 1993—was succeeded by his eight-volume retelling of the Ramayana, which has done phenomenally well in India and abroad. Banker is often credited with having revived interest in Indian epics among middle-class readers and is now at work on an eighteen-volume retelling of the Mahabharata.

Gautam Bhatia graduated in Fine Arts and went on to get a Masters degree in Architecture. A Delhi-based architect, he has received several awards for his drawings and buildings and has also written extensively on architecture. Besides a biography on *Laurie Baker*, he is the author of *Punjabi Baroque, Silent Spaces*, and *Malaria Dreams*—a trilogy that focuses on the cultural and social aspects of architecture. *Whitewash: A Tabloid that is about the India that isn't* appeared in 2008. *Lie: A Traditional Tale of Modern India* was published in 2010. Bhatia is currently working on *Below the Horizon—City Underground*, a project of drawing and ideas.

Amitabha Bhattacharya is based in Calcutta and writes on Bengali literature and cinema.

Buddhadev Bose is one of the major Bengali writers of the twentieth century, often mentioned as the greatest literary figure in Bengali literature since Tagore. He founded *Kavita*, the leading journal of Bengali poetry, in 1935 and remained its editor for 25 years. His prolific outcome of something like 200 volumes includes novels, short stories, collections of verse, plays, essays, literary criticism, and translations—of Kalidasa, Rilke, Hoelderlin, and Baudelaire. His residence at 202, Rashbehari Avenue, 'Kavita Bhavan', in Ballygunge, became a legendary hangout for Calcutta's literati and embodied the spirit of the 'adda'.

Nirendranath Chakravarty writes in Bengali and has published over two dozen collections of poems. He received the country's highest distinction in literature, the Sahitya Akademi award, in 1974 for *Ulanga Raja* ('The Naked King'). He is also known for writing crime thrillers and children's literature, and for many years he edited *Anandamela*, a well known children's magazine in Bengali.

Nirad C. Chaudhuri lived to the ripe old age of nearly 102, passing away in 1999 in Oxford, thus fulfilling many a Bengali intellectual's cherished hope to be close to what used to be imagined as the home of civilization. A master of English prose, Chaudhuri acquired fame for such books as the *Autobiography of an Unknown Indian* (1951), *The Continent of Circe* (1965), and *Thy Hand, Great Anarch!* (1987), the second leg of his autobiography. He was made Commander of the Order of the British Empire (CBE) in 1982.

Dilip Chitre (1938–2009) was an internationally recognized writer, critic, and translator. He first gained prominence as one of the leaders of the 'Little Magazine Movement' of the sixties in Marathi. The three volumes of *Ekoon Kavita* (*Collected Poems*, 1990s) cemented his reputation, but Chitre also had the distinction of being celebrated for his translations from the entire span of Marathi literature, from Jnandev in the twelfth century to the 17th century bhakta Tukaram (*Says Tuka*, 1991), and the contemporary Dalit poet Namdeo Dhasal. Chitre was also a filmmaker and painter of considerable distinction.

Charles Correa is one of India's leading architects, indeed a major figure in contemporary world architecture. His most famous buildings include the Jawahar Kala Kendra (Jaipur), Delhi's Crafts Museum, LIC Building, and the British Council, Bharat Bhawan (Bhopal), and the Brain and Cognitive Sciences Center at MIT. He was the chief planner of Navi Mumbai and was honoured by the Royal Institute of British Architects with its Gold Medal in 1984.

Ravi Dayal was educated at St. Stephen's College and University College, Oxford, where he studied with the philosopher H.L.A. Hart. He joined Oxford University Press in Bombay in 1962, and eventually, after serving as Chief Editor, became head of its operations in India. He saw to press such landmark works as *Subaltern Studies* and the 10-volume *Handbook of the Birds of India and Pakistan*. He set up his own publishing firm, Ravi Dayal Publishers, in 1989, and introduced the world to Amitav Ghosh among other writers.

Vinay Dharwadker is a scholar of literature, translator, critic, and poet, and presently Professor in the Department of Languages and Cultures of Asia at the University of Wisconsin, Madison. He earned his Ph.D. in 1989 from the University of Chicago, where he studied with A.K. Ramanujan. He is editor of the *Collected Essays of A.K. Ramanujan* (Oxford, 1999), and author of many books, among them *Cosmopolitan Geographies* (2001) and *Kabir: The Weaver's Songs* (2003). His own verse includes *Sunday at the Lodi Gardens* (2004).

Dhoomil, or Sudama Panday 'Dhoomil' (1936–1975), published only one volume of Hindi poetry, *Sansad se Sarak Tak* ('From Parliament to the Street'), in his lifetime. A posthumous work, *Kal Sunana Mujhe* ('Listen To Me Tomorrow'), appeared in 1979 and was awarded the Sahitya Akademi award in Hindi. Dhoomil's poetry has radical political

Nirupama Dutt was born in 1955 and has had a lengthy career as a journalist. She is also one of the leading writers in Punjabi and her first poetry collection appeared in 2000. She is an independent writer and has endeavoured to make better known, through two volumes of translations, the work of Pakistani women and resistance writers.

Diana L. Eck is Professor of Comparative Religion and Indian Studies at Harvard Divinity School, as well as Professor of Law and Psychiatry at Harvard University. Her work has a dual focus, on religion in India and the US. She is the author of *Banaras: City of Light, Darsan: Seeing the Divine Image in India*, and *India: A Sacred Geography* (2012). She has also been the Director of the Pluralism Project at Harvard since 1991, and is the author of *A New Religious America* (2001), which explores religious pluralism in the US. She delivered the Gifford Lectures in 2009 and was honoured with the National Humanities Medal by President Clinton.

Nissim Ezekiel was born in Mumbai in 1924 and passed away in the same city in 2004, having lived nearly his entire life there. His first collection of verse was published in 1952 and a steady stream of poems appeared for the next three decades. Oxford University Press published his *Collected Poems 1952–88*. Ezekiel, who belonged to the Bene Israel community of Jews, is numbered among the most influential and loved Indian poets who wrote in English. He was conferred the Sahitya Akademi award in 1983 for *Latter-Day Psalms*.

Amar Farooqui is Professor in the Department of History, University of Delhi. His publications include *Smuggling as Subversion: Colonialism, Indian Merchants and the Politics of Opium, 1790-1843* (new edition, 2005); *Opium City: The Making of Early Victorian Bombay* (2006); and *Sindias and the Raj* (2011). He is currently working on a history of nineteenth century Delhi.

Lina M. Fruzzetti is Professor of Anthropology at Brown University. Her research work is primarily based on India (West Bengal) and North and East Africa. The focus of her work is on social anthropology, kinship, politics, and study of ritual and the construction of gender. Her books include *Concepts of Person: Kinship, Marriage and Caste in India* (1992) and *The Gift of a Virgin: Analysis of Women, Marriage, Ritual and Kinship in Bengali Society* (3rd reprint, 1993). She also has an abiding interest in visual anthropology and she has directed several documentaries, including *Kalfan and Zanzibar* and *Fishers of Dar.*

Sunil Gangopadhyay (1934–2012), who was born in what is now Bangladesh and was settled in Calcutta for decades, was one of India's most acclaimed and prolific writers. His work includes nearly twenty volumes of poetry, as many novels, and over thirty volumes of essays, short stories, and children's stories, all in Bengali. He has served as President of the Sahitya Akademi (National Academy of Literature) and as editor of *Desh*, the most well known magazine in Bengali. *Pratidwandi* ('The Adversary') and *Aranyer Din Ratri* ('Days and Nights in the Forest') are two of his stories that Satyajit Ray turned into films.

Kenneth L. Gillion (1929–1992) was born in New Zealand and had a brief career as a diplomat before turning to scholarship. His *Fiji's Indian Migrants: A History to the End of Indenture in 1920*, published by Oxford University Press in 1962, was one of the first works of its kind, and he followed it up with *The Fiji Indians: Challenge to European Dominance, 1920-46* (ANU Press, 1977). His history of Ahmedabad was published by the University of California Press in 1968.

Sunita Jain was born in Ambala and went on to earn a Ph.D. in English from the University of Nebraska. She writes in English and Hindi and has published over sixty books. She was awarded the Padma Shri in 2004.

Kulwinder Kaur lives in Sangam Vihar, Delhi. Apart from her schooling, she has taken courses in sewing, painting, and martial arts. She works as a teacher in a learning centre for young children.

Amitava Kumar is the author of several works of literary non-fiction. His latest book, *A Foreigner Carrying in the Crook of His Arm a Tiny Bomb*, was described by the *New York Times* as a 'perceptive and soulful' meditation on 'the cultural and human repercussions' of the global war on terror. He is also the author of a novel, *Home Products*, which was a finalist for the Vodafone Crossword Prize. Kumar is Professor of English at Vassar College.

Ranjit Lal has written 25 books, including fiction and non-fiction for both adults and children. His works include *The Crow Chronicles, The Life* and *Times of Altu Faltu, The Battle for No. 19, Faces in the Water* (for which he won the Vodafone-Crossword award for Children's Writing for 2010), *Smitten, Birds from my Window*, and *The Birds of Delhi*. He lives in Delhi.

Vinay Lal teaches history at University of California Los Angeles (UCLA) and also writes widely on politics, cinema, and knowledge systems. His dozen books include *Empire of Knowledge: Culture and Plurality in the Global Economy* (2002), *The History of History: Politics and Scholarship in Modern India* (2003), *Of Cricket, Guinness and Gandhi: Essays on Indian History and Culture* (2003), and (edited) *Political Hinduism* (2009). He has co-edited with Ashis Nandy *Fingerprinting Popular Culture: The Mythic and the Iconic in Indian Cinema* (2006) and *The Future of Knowledge and Culture: A Dictionary for the Twenty-first Century* (2006).

Sidney James Mark Low (1857–1932) was a British journalist, essayist, and historian. He was educated at Oxford University, at Pembroke and later Balliol, before being called to the Bar at the Inner Temple in 1892. He served as the *Standard*'s Special Correspondent and covered such events as the visit of the Prince of Wales to India in 1905. He wrote widely on English politics and history and was knighted in 1918.

Narendra Luther lives in Hyderabad, of which he has been an indefatigable chronicler for several decades. He has written in English and Urdu on Hyderabad in something like a dozen books. He has also had careers as a civil servant and columnist.

Bonnie MacDougall earned her Ph.D. from Columbia University in English literature and is at present Professor and Interim Academic Vice President at Bergen Community College in the Greater New York area.

Mala Marwah is a free-lance translator whose work is represented in such volumes as the *Vintage Book of Modern Indian Literature*, edited by Amit Chaudhuri (2004).

Suketu Mehta was born in Calcutta and raised in Bombay. He moved to New York in 1977 with his family. He is the co-author of the screenplay of the Vidhu Vinod Chopra film, *Mission Kashmir*. He published *Maximum City: Bombay Lost and Found* in 2004; the rest, as the cliché goes, is history. The book was shortlisted for the Pulitzer Prize, selected by the *Economist* as one of the year's best books, and won the author innumerable accolades. He lives in Manhattan and is on the journalism faculty at New York University.

P. Thankappan Nair is one of the leading chroniclers of the history and culture of Calcutta. He has written books on the origins of Calcutta, on the city's police, and on the presence of other Indian communities; and he is also the author of a multi-volume history of Calcutta in the colonial period.

Ashis Nandy is a cultural psychologist, scholar and critic based in Delhi. He is often included in the list of the world's most influential thinkers. His twenty books, most of them published by Oxford University Press in India, include *The Intimate Enemy: Loss and Recovery of Self under Colonialism* (1983); *Traditions, Tyranny and Utopias: Essays in the Politics of Awareness* (1987); and the *Romance of the State and the Fate of Dissent in the Tropics* (2003). Oxford University Press in India has honoured him with three volumes of the *Ashis Nandy Omnibus*.

Pritish Nandy is a poet, journalist, painter, former Editor of the *Illustrated Weekly of India*, Publishing Director of The Times of India Group, former Member of Parliament, and producer of over 25 films. He writes one of the most popular blogs in India, which also appears as a weekly column in *The Times*. He is most easily found at @PritishNandy on twitter.

Kunwar Narain was born in Faizabad district, Uttar Pradesh, in 1927 and educated at Lucknow University. In 1956, he published *Chakravyuh*, a collection of poems now considered a landmark in Hindi literature, and over the next four decades he published a series of highly influential works in poetry and literary criticism. Narain has received nearly all of the country's highest literary honours, as well as many international accolades, and is perhaps the country's best living poet in Hindi.

K.S. Narasimha Swamy (1917–2003) was a prominent poet in Kannada and he published over twenty volumes of poetry. Among Kannada readers, he is also known for his translations of Robert Burns. His popularity may be gauged by the fact that his collection, *Mysooru Mallige*, has gone through over thirty reprints. He received the Sahitya Akdemi award in 1978.

Aditya Nigam is Senior Fellow at the Centre for the Study of Developing Societies, Delhi. He is interested in contemporary politics and has published on questions of modernity, nationalism, identity, and radical

politics. Nigam is author of *The Insurrection of Little Selves: Crisis of Secular-* 375
nationalism in India (Oxford University Press, 2006); *Power and Contestation:*
India Since 1989 (with Nivedita Menon, Zed Books, London), *After Utopia:*
Modernity and Socialism in the Postcolony (Viva Books, Delhi, 2010), and *A*
Desire Named Development (Penguin, 2011).

Gieve Patel is a painter and writer who lives in Mumbai. He has published
three books of verse, the last being *Mirrored, Mirroring* (Oxford University
Press, 1991). *Mister Behram and Other Plays* was published by Seagull Books
in 2007. For the last 18 years, he has conducted a poetry workshop for
students at Rishi Valley School, Andhra Pradesh, and *Poetry with Young*
People (Sahitya Akademi, New Delhi, 2007) is an anthology of poems
written by his students. His paintings are in public and private collections
in India and abroad. Gieve has also worked as a medical practitioner in
rural and urban India.

Sudhir Patwardhan is one of India's leading painters, though he has
also led another life as a radiologist. His first solo exhibition was held
in 1979. Apart from exhibitions in most of India's major cities, his
work has been shown in London, New York, Houston, and in Australia,
Switzerland, Italy, Spain and the Middle East. His paintings are housed
in the permanent collections of the National Gallery of Modern Art,
New Delhi and Mumbai; Prince of Wales Museum, Mumbai; and the
Peabody Essex Museum, USA.

Saleem Peeradina is Associate Professor of English at Siena Heights
College, Michigan. He has published three volumes of poetry, *First Offence*
(1980), *Group Portrait* (Oxford, 1992), and *Meditations on Desire* (2003), as
well as a prose memoir, *The Ocean in My Yard* (2005). Many in India
still remember his discriminating and pioneering anthology, *Contemporary*
Indian Poetry in English (1972).

William Radice is well known for his translations of the poems and
stories of Tagore for Penguin. He has been a lecturer in Bengali at the
School of Oriental and African Studies (SOAS), University of London
since 1988. His many books include nine collections of his own poems,
Myths and Legends of India, Teach Yourself Bengali, and *The Poem of the Killing*
of Meghnad—an annotated translation of an epic poem by Michael
Madhusudan Dutt (1824–1873). In recent years he has written opera
libretti. More information can be found at www.williamradice.com

Notes on Contributors

Ram Rahman is a Delhi-based photographer, designer, curator, and activist. He held his first one-man show at MIT in 1977 and has since had solo shows in New York, Bombay, New Delhi, Amsterdam, and Cleveland, besides taking part in group shows in Berlin, London, Chandigarh, and elsewhere. He is also the principal designer for the posters and publications of SAHMAT, the Safdar Hashmi Memorial Trust, which has a distinct place in the artistic and intellectual life of the nation's capital. He is known for his artistic contributions to struggles for social justice.

A.K. Ramanujan (1929–1993) held multiple appointments at the University of Chicago, among them William Colvin Professor of South Asian Languages and Civilizations, before his untimely death in 1993. A celebrated critic, scholar, translator, poet, and folklorist, and winner of the MacArthur 'Genius' Grant, Ramanujan is remembered for such works as *Speaking of Siva* (1973), *Hymns for the Drowning* (1981), *Poems of Love and War* (1985), and *Folktales from India* (1991).

Kalyan Ray is an educator, novelist, translator, literary critic, and social activist. His Ph.D. is from the University of Rochester and he is at present Program Director (India) for the International Partnership for Service-Learning and Leadership.

Swarup Roy is Associate Professor of English at Ramakrishna Misssion College, Belur Math. His areas of interest include translation studies and postcolonial studies, and most particularly the Bengal-Britain interface in the nineteenth century. He is presently at work on two translation anthologies: one on nineteenth-century Bengali travel writings and the other on sports literature in Bengali.

Vicky Roy was born in 1987 in West Bengal and graduated from the Salaam Baalak Trust (SBT). He studied photography at Triveni Kala Sangam, New Delhi and the International Center of Photography, New York. In 2007, he held his first solo exhibition titled 'Street Dream' at India Habitat Centre, and a year later he travelled to the US with support from the Ramchander Nath Foundation (RNF) and the US-based Maybach Foundation to photo-document the reconstruction of the World Trade Center in New York. *Time Out* magazine recognized him among 25 achievers under 30 in July 2009.

Salman Rushdie is one of the better-known novelists writing in English. He was born in Bombay, two months before Independence in 1947, but earned his college degree from Cambridge. His second novel, *Midnight's Children*, was awarded the Booker Prize and put him on the world literary map. Since then he has has published *Shame* (1983), *Fury* (2001), *Shalimar the Clown* (2005), and several other novels, besides several volumes of essays and criticism. *The Satanic Verses* (1988) provoked the Iranian clergy to issue a fatwa calling for his death.

Shveta Sarda was born in 1979 and since 2001 she has been working at Sarai, the media project at the Centre for the Study of Developing Societies (Delhi). Her translations of Neelofer, Kulwinder Kaur, and Sunita Narshad in this anthology are excerpted from *Trickster City*, which she translated from the Hindi. She is conducting research into the question of auto-didacticism.

Ghulam M. Sheikh is one of Indian's most renowned artists. He was born in Gujarat in 1937 and has ever since been associated with that state, and in particular with Baroda. He had his first solo exhibition at the Jehangir Art Gallery in Bombay over five decades ago, and has since had solo exhibitions in Delhi, Paris, London, Tokyo, Brussels, and elsewhere; his paintings are in the permanent collections of the Victoria & Albert Musuem, the National Gallery of Modern Art (Delhi), and the Peabody Essex Museum, Salem. He has also published several volumes of poetry and essays in his native Gujarati.

H.S. Shivaprakash is a major Kannada poet, playwright, scholar, and translator. He has translated Yeats, Pound, Neruda, Cavafy, and Paz into Kannada, and Kannada writers into English; and some of his own work, comprising seven collections of poems, a dozen plays, and several books of essays and scholarly criticism, has been translated into major Indian languages. He is also Professor in the School of Arts & Aesthetics at Jawaharlal Nehru University, and presently Director of the Tagore Centre in Berlin. His scholary and creative work encompasses Shaivite mysticism, bhakti literature, Mahayana Buddhism, and Marxism.

Kedarnath Singh is an eminent Hindi poet, critic, and essayist. He received the Sahitya Akademi award for his poetry collection, *Akaal Mein Saras* ('Cranes in Drought'), in 1989. His long poem, *Bagh*, is considered a classic of modern Hindi poetry and is taught widely. He was Professor of Hindi at Jawaharlal Nehru University (JNU) from where he took retirment, though he still lives in Delhi.

Kaliprasanna Sinha was born in 1840 in Jorasanko, Calcutta, and attended Hindu College. He was a playwright and translator into Bengali of the Mahabharata, an undertaking in which he employed numerous pandits. He died, apparently of excessive drinking, at the age of 30, but not before completing *Hootum Pyanchar Naksha*, which Bankimcandra described as 'a collection of sketches of city-life' in 'racy, vigorous language', somewhat in the manner of Dickens' *Sketches by Boz*.

Majrooh Sultanpuri (1919–2000) is one of the most important figures both in 20th century Urdu literature and mainstream Indian cinema where he earned his reputation as a lyricist. He worked with the best known music directors, among them O.P. Nayyar, Laxmikant Pyarelal, Shankar Jaikishan, Anand-Milind, and, most recently, A.R. Rahman. He wrote the lyrics for such immensely successful films as *Teesri Manzil* (1966), *Yaadon ki Baarat* (1973), and *Qayamat se Qayamat Tak* (1988).

Rabindranath Tagore is by universal acclaim one of the titans of Indian literature and clearly the most influential figure in Bengali literature. The 18 gigantic volumes of *Rabindra Racnabali* bring together the vast output of his writing, consisting of novels, short stories, plays, and essays. An entire genre of music, 'Rabindra Sangeet', revolves around the 2200 songs that he is said to have composed. The 150th anniversary of his birth (1861) has been celebrated with dozens of seminars, festivals of art and literature, and other festivities.

Mark Twain, born Samuel Langhorne Clemens (1835–1910), was one of the leading American writers of the 19th century. Among his most well known novels are *The Adentures of Tom Sawyer* (1876) and *Adventures of Huckleberry Finn* (1884). Though as late as the mid-1890s Twain described himself as a 'red-hot imperialist', in later years he became closely associated with the American Anti-Imperialist League.

Copyright Statement

380   Buddhadev Bose, 'Calcutta', translated by Sumanta Banerjee, in *India International Centre Quarterly*, 17, nos. 3–4 (Winter), 1990–1. Reprinted with permission from India International Centre.

Pritish Nandy, 'calcutta if you must exile me', in *Masks to be Interpreted in Terms of Messages*, Calcutta: Dialogue Publications, 1971. Reprinted with permission from the author.

Nirendranath Chakravarthy, 'Calcutta's Jesus', translated by D.K. Banerjee, in K. Satchidanandan (ed.), *Signatures: One Hundred Indian Poets*, New Delhi: National Book Trust, 2004. Reprinted with permission from the translator and National Book Trust.

Sunil Gangopadhyay, 'City of Memories', translated by Kalyan Ray and Bonnie MacDougall, Calcutta: Indiana, 2006. Reprinted with permission from the author, translators, and Indiana.

Lina Fruzzetti, *Calcutta Conversations*, in Lina Fruzzetti and Ákos Östör (eds), with notes by Tarun Mitra, New Delhi: Chronicle Books/ DC Publishers, 2003. Reprinted with permission from the editors and DC Publishers.

Kedarnath Singh, 'Banaras', translated by Sunita Jain, in K. Satchidanandan (ed.), *Signatures: OneHundred Indian Poets*, New Delhi: National Book Trust, 2004. Reprinted with permission from the editor and National Book Trust.

Ravi Dayal, 'A Kayastha's View', *Seminar*, no. 515 (July), 2002. Reprinted with permission from Mala Dayal, Penguin Books, and *Seminar*.

Ghulam M. Sheikh, 'Delhi', translated by the poet and Mala Marwah, in K. Satchidanandan (ed.), *Signatures: One Hundred Indian Poets*, New Delhi: National Book Trust 2004. Reprinted with permission from the editor and National Book Trust.

Sarnath Banerjee, 'Corridor: A Graphic Novel', New Delhi: Penguin Books, 2004. Reprinted with permission from Penguin Books.

Kulwinder Kaur, 'Daily Hurts', in *Trickster City: Writings from the Belly of the Metropolis*, translated by Shveta Sarda, New Delhi: Penguin/Viking, 2010. Reprinted with permission from the author and Penguin.

Ranjit Lal, 'Wild City: Nature Wonders Next Door', Delhi: Penguin Books, 2008. Reprinted with permission from the author and Penguin Books.

Kunwar Narain, 'Lucknow', translated by Deepak Sharma, *The Little Magazine*, July–August 2000. Reprinted with permission from *The Little Magazine*.

K.S. Narasimha Swamy, 'From House to House', in 'Maneyinda Manege', translated by H.S. Shivaprakash from the book *Malligeya Maale:*

Collected Poems of K.S. Narasimha Swamy, Bangalore: Lipi Prakashana, 1986. Reprinted with permission from the translator.

Dhoomil, 'The City, Evening, and an Old Man: Me', translated by Vinay Dharwadker, in Vinay Dharwadker and A.K. Ramanujan (eds), *The Oxford Anthology of Modern Indian Poetry*, Delhi: Oxford University Press 1994. Reprinted with permission from Vinay Dharwadkar and Oxford University Press.

Nirupama Dutt, 'Cityscape', translated by the author, in *The Little Magazine*, May–June 2001. Reprinted with permission from *The Little Magazine*.

Folktale from West Bengal, 'Oh! Calcutta', in Brenda E.F. Beck, Peter J. Claus, Praphulladatta Goswami, and Jawaharlal Handoo (eds), *Folktales of India*, Chicago: The University of Chicago Press, 1987. Reprinted with permission from The University of Chicago Press.

Salman Rushdie, 'Bombay was Central', in *The Moor's Last Sigh*, New York: Vintage Books, 1997. Reprinted with permission from Pantheon Books, a division of Random House, Inc.

Amitabha Bhattacharya, 'Satyajit Ray's Calcutta: Friend or Adversary?', in *India International Centre Quarterly*, 17, nos 3–4 (Winter), 1990–1. Reprinted with permission from India International Centre.

Diana L. Eck, 'Banaras: City of Death', in *Banaras: City of Light*, New York: Random House, 1982. Reprinted with permission from the author and Alfred A. Knopf, a division of Random House, Inc.

Amitava Kumar, 'In the Light of Small Towns', in *Bombay London New York*, New York: Routledge, 2002. Reprinted with permission from the author.

Aditya Nigam, 'Theatre of the Urban: The Strange Case of the Monkeyman', in *Sarai Reader*, no. 2: 'The Cities of Everyday Life', New Delhi, 2002. Reprinted with permission from the author.

U.R. Ananthamurthy, 'Ooru and the World', translated by Bageshree S., in Aditi De (ed.), *Multiple City: Writings on Bangalore*, Delhi: Penguin Books, 2008. Reprinted with permission from the author and Penguin Books.

Ashis Nandy, 'Time Travel to a Possible Self: Searching for the Alternative Cosmopolitanism of Cochin', in *Time Warps: Silent and Evasive Pasts in Indian Politics and Religion*, Ranikhet and Delhi: Permanent Black, 2002. Reprinted with permission from the author and Permanent Black.

Kaliprasanna Sinha, 'The Observant Owl: Hootum's Vignettes of Nineteenth-century Calcutta', translated by Swarup Roy, Ranikhet and Delhi: Black Kite/Permanent Black, 2008. Reprinted with permission from the translator and Permanent Black.

Amar Farooqui, 'Opium City: The Making of Early Victorian Bombay', Gurgaon: Three Essays Collective, 2006. Reprinted with permission from the author and Three Essays Collective.

Narendra Luther, 'Parade of Diwans', in *Hyderabad: A Biography*, New Delhi: Oxford University Press, 2006. Reprinted with permission from the author.

Nirad C. Chaudhuri, 'Man and Life in Calcutta', in *Autobiography of an Unknown Indian*, Berkeley: University of California Press, 1968. Reprinted with permission from the author's son, Prithvi N. Chaudhuri.

Charles Correa, 'Space as a Resource', in *The New Landscape*, Bombay: The Book Society of India, 1985. Reprinted with permission from Hatje Cantz Publishers.

Arjun Appadurai, 'Street Culture', in *The India Magazine*, vol. 8 (December 1987). Reprinted with permission from the author.

P. Thankappan Nair, 'A History of Calcutta's Streets', in *A History of Calcutta's Streets*, 'A Tercentenary History of Calcutta', vol. II, Calcutta: Firma KLM Private Ltd., 1987. Reprinted with permission from Frima KLM.

Gautam Bhatia, 'Baroque Architecture in the City', in *Punjabi Baroque and Other Memories of Architecture*, Delhi: Penguin Books, 1994. Reprinted with permission from the author.

Suketu Mehta, 'A Lover's Embrace', in 'Mumbai', *Granta* no. 57, *India: The Golden Jubilee*, 1997. Reprinted with permission from the author.

Gieve Patel, 'Off-Lamington Road, 1983–86', collection of Mick Yates. Included with permission from the Artist.

Ram Rahman, 'Sikh Riots Survivors, Kalyanpuri Sector 13, Delhi 1984'; 'Bhagirath Place, Delhi, 1993'; 'Peanut seller, Red Fort, Delhi, 1995'; 'Market in Old Delhi, around Id, 2007'. Included with permission from the Photographer.

Vicky Roy, 'Playing with Pages'; 'Boys Dreaming'; 'Pappu and Nandu at Jorbagh', New Delhi; 'Untitled'. Included with permission from Vicky Roy and Ojas Art.